The Anthropology of Evil

Edited by
DAVID PARKIN

Basil Blackwell

Copyright © Basil Blackwell Ltd 1985

First published 1985
Reprinted and first published in paperback 1986

Basil Blackwell Ltd
108 Cowley Road, Oxford OX4 1JF, UK

Basil Blackwell Inc.
432 Park Avenue South, Suite 1503,
New York, NY 10016, USA

British Library Cataloguing in Publication Data

The Anthropology of evil.
  1. Social interaction
  2. Good and evil
  I. Parkin, David, *1940–*
  302   HM299

  ISBN 0-631-13717-3
  ISBN 0-631-15432-9 Pbk

Library of Congress Cataloging in Publication Data

Main entry under title:

The Anthropology of evil.

  Includes index.
  1. Good and evil—Addresses, essays, lectures.
  2. Man—Addresses, essays, lectures. I. Parkin, David.
  BJ1401.A67 1985   291.5   84—20344
  ISBN 0-631-13717-3
  ISBN 0-631-15432-9 (pbk.)

Typeset by Pioneer, East Sussex
Printed in Great Britain by
The Camelot Press Ltd, Southampton

Contents

Preface

Much has been written on evil in other disciplines but, curiously, in spite of Max Weber's early sociological interest, little in anthropology, which through detailed ethnography can make a distinctive comparative contribution, as O'Flaherty suggests in her own monumental work on evil in Hindu mythology (1976: 10). This book results from a series of seminars held at the School of Oriental and African Studies of the University of London and at two subsequent symposia in 1983, after each of which the chapters were revised as we identified some common interests. The Introduction suggests a framework for these concerns. We have accepted as a challenge rather than an obstacle the many perspectives on the phenomenon of evil. It is the very irreducibility of the varying concepts of evil that has attracted us. The variations are intelligible in the light of each other and can be regarded as part of the broad discourse on human destructiveness and suffering.

Following the Introduction, chapters 2 and 3 of the book provide some general theological and philosophical perspectives, often from a Judaeo-Christian viewpoint. Chapters 4 and 5 continue the European focus, with analyses of pre-industrial England and modern Macedonia, both of which complement nicely Favret-Saada's recent study of malevolence in rural France (1980). Thereafter the chapters provide ethnographic examples from the world religions as well as localized ones. Such distinctions are not without significance and yet are also cross-cut by such separate themes as personal as against divine fallibility and responsibility, the definition of human as either morally distinct from or an aspect of other creatures, and absolute versus relative judgements of evil.

David Parkin

1

Introduction

David Parkin

In describing the Azande of Central Africa, Evans-Pritchard refers to witchcraft as their prototype of all evil. More humorously, the Azande also liken certain animals to witches; it is the apparent cunning and strangeness of such nocturnal creatures as the owl that fosters the identification. The intelligence of these animals may be admired as well as feared. The most feared is a species of wild cat, which can have sexual relations with women and produce kittens by them. But a man who sees such a cat will die. The Azande further associate cats with lesbianism: both involve female activities which kill men who witness them. Yet another witch-like agency is a person who had cut his upper teeth first. He brings bad luck and is clumsily destructive. He is aware of his evil influence but does not intend to cause harm. Fortunately, he does not kill and is not regarded seriously or as a menace (Evans-Pritchard, 1976: 236—9).

From this short paraphrase we can see at a glance why the English word 'evil' has been so useful to social anthropologists. It can refer to extreme fear, death and destruction, but also to lesser misfortunes. It may denote an agent's firm intention to harm, or instead may be seen as originating in an unintended human or non-human condition. Evil agents may be abhorrent, but they may also be admired for their cleverness. While people may be terrified of the deadly effects of the worst kinds of evil, they can at other times joke about it and make humorous parallels. Talk about evil thus ranges over the terrible and serious as well as the playful and creative.

It might at first be tempting to blame the anthropologists' elastic use of the term for this wide span of meaning and association. But it is clear from the account that the Azande themselves see a gradation of witchcraft-like acts and effects, a view found elsewhere in the world, whether or not a distinctive term for evil exists. It is only the beginning of our enquiry to regard the term as an odd-job word. The language games that it or its equivalent inspire among both anthropologists and the peoples they study point to different areas of understanding between which linkages are not always apparent. It is precisely because the term has been so loose analytically that it has been able to reveal so much empirically.

There are two main, and related, objections that some anthropologists might have to defining an area of interest through the use of a concept of doubtful analytical value. The first is that we should use an already anthropologically established analytical framework, such as that of witchcraft, because it more narrowly specifies the kinds of behaviour being referred to and so makes the task of comparison more manageable. Indisputably, the many studies of witchcraft in the discipline have been at its core and, frequently recast and re-interpreted, will continue to sustain it. However, as a result of this recasting of analytical concepts, it has become clear that the anthropologists' notion of witchcraft is itself part of a more general cross-cultural understanding of the manner in which persons are morally evaluated (see Crick 1976: 115—20), and so has lost its former specificity. Witchcraft is one of many perspectives on good and evil and deserves no privileged place in analysis. None of the chapters in this volume feels a need to focus only on beliefs in and practices of witches.

An extension of the first objection might be that, while it may be conceded that witchcraft can no longer be studied separately from other modes of personal evaluation, it is still analytically more fruitful to approach the problem from the viewpoint of a particular 'concrete' activity. We could, for instance, focus study on the issues of homicide, of preferred marriage alliances, of explanations of disease, and so on. I have sympathy with this approach, inasmuch as it draws on the anthropologists's field experience and observations of what people may call good and evil rather than on unobserved reports of it. Even so, it has first to satisfy itself that the notion of, say, homicide evokes some common, basic understandings between cultures. Among the Ilongot of the Philippines, headhunting is part of the process by which the killer builds up his selfhood (Rosaldo 1980: 137—76); among the Giriama of Kenya, killing even an enemy *detracts* from one's selfhood, which must thereafter be repaired; among yet other peoples, killing may, as military duty, have little or no effect on the killer's sense of self. What people regard as being good or bad about these different kinds of homicide may depend less on the relation between killer and victim than on other fundamental ideas, each specific to the culture, such as those concerning the nature of death and its relationship to life. In other words, so-called 'concrete' activities are variously premised in different cultures on what each people regards as first principles of cause, effect, process and transformation. Put simply, we must know the philosophy or ontology of a people before we can know what they understand by what we call homicide, or marriage, even though our entrée into their society is through participating in such apparently obvious social events as weddings, and funerals involving 'bad deaths'.

The second objection might then make two points. First, we should study not evil but morality. After all, it might be claimed, evil is a negative aspect of any moral system. The bad cannot be studied without also knowing the boundaries of the good. Second, in view of the immense contribution to social anthropology of Durkheim's assertion that society is a moral system, we should study comparative ethics.

There are, however, broadly two different ways in which we can compare moral systems, though neither is prevalent in social anthropology. The first would be to work from the Durkheimian assumption that moral rules are created by and for society. By this assumption a typology of societies would reveal a commensurate typology of ethical systems. Apart from the well-known correlational difficulties of such typology-making, this task seems unlikely to provide much more than the grossest generalizations, such as that tyrannies (however these are defined) normally admonish through fixed, absolute and undebatable distinctions of right and wrong, while elective regimes (variously defined) rule through more rapidly shifting moral categories. Going much beyond such generalizations produces the never-ending list of exceptions, thence classified as variables, with which we are familiar. Moreover, the finer metaphysical distinctions of good and evil are thereby lost.

A second main method of comparative ethics in fact proceeds from such differences of metaphysics and ontology. It asks how peoples distinguish human from non-human and evaluate states, acts, conditions and consequences in the light of this distinction. As early as 1955 K.E. Read, following suggestions made by Bidney (1953: 156—82), made a plea for this aproach in an article on moral concepts of the person among the Gahuku-Gama of New Guinea. He makes quite clear that among this people moral norms, as he calls them, are not based on a universal and abstract principle of reverence for humanity. Humanity devoid of specific social ties is irrelevant: it is the particular social links obtaining at a particular moment between two people that constitute their personhood and morality. By contrast, Western and Christian ethics (broadly speaking) insist on a notion of all humans being moral equals, regardless of our relationships with them and whether we are linked to them at all: their humanity supersedes in significance their social position. However, whereas the New Guinea people match their ontology to the ways they behave towards one another, it can hardly be said that the Christian primacy of the human over the social is much reflected in practice in the West.

One of Read's main points is that, among the people he studied, the moral and the social are embedded in each other. This much would satisfy Durkheim. But Read does not outline the composition and interrelationship of the groups, statuses and roles making up Gahuku-Gama society and then see moral norms as supporting this structure. Rather, he starts the other way round. He takes their moral concepts of the person — that is, what counts as appropriate behaviour by and towards someone under different conditions — and regards this as informing what we call social relationships. Differences in the moral concept of person across cultures would presuppose contrasting views of society.

There has in the last decade been an outpouring of works in social anthropology on the concept of person, some of them inspired by Mauss's early work (and see Mauss 1979) and a few dealing, like Read, with the idea that to outline indigenous theories of the person is *ipso facto* to define the society's moral categories (for two recent collections see Heelas and Lock 1981; and Jacobson-Widding 1983). That said, social anthropologists have not focused much attention on morality as a field of cultural presuppositions informing and creating, rather than supporting, social relations between groups and persons. While moral philosophy is big industry, an anthropology of moral systems in the above sense is very recent (see parts of Fürer-Haimendorf 1967; and some of the contributions to Mayer 1981). Just as some philosophers would argue that moral philosophy is implicit in other philosophical work and so has no legitimacy to stand alone, so many anthropologists would contend that the best ethnographies necessarily include descriptions of peoples' ethical systems. In part and sometimes more fully, this may be so. But there is surely a vast area that has hardly been entered. A comparative ethics freed of *a priori* Western assumptions and extracted from indigenous practical philosophies has barely begun. As recently as 1981 T. N. Madan, speaking of South Asian societies, could still argue 'that the anthropological study of moral choices . . . would be greatly enriched if it is carried out in the light of native categories of thought' (1981: 149).

Why should anthropologists have been so reluctant? Even Evans-Pritchard, while noting that the key to understanding first Zande and then Nuer philosophy lay in such religious concepts as *mangu* (witchcraft) and *kwoth* (spirit), did not think that he need consider Nuer moral judgements in general but only those that concerned their religious thought and practice (1956: vi—viii). Wolfram (1982) attributes this reluctance among anthropologists to study other peoples' ethical systems to a number of possible factors. Is it that the subject simply never recovered from its long period of unfashionability? Or that anthropologists did not know how to begin to agree on the definition of, say, an odious moral character? Or may we say that Durkheim so conflated the moral with the social that ethnographers could not isolate for analysis those contemplative moments of moral reflexivity that, rather than strict and unambiguous rules, most typify human activity and predicaments?

A central problem in all this has been anthropologists' shyness to say what they understand by morality beyond that it is a form of socially sanctioned behaviour. A few recent attempts have, however, tackled the issue, though to different ends. Kiernan (1982) urges us to escape what he regards as the deadlock of a moral dichotomy of good and evil. In a study of ancestral intervention among the living, he shows that ancestors have been characterized by ethnographers as noxious when they punish affines but as firm and caring when they punish lineal descendants. We should, he says, see these not as contrasting facets of good and evil but as the complementary ways in which ancestors act on behalf of society, each legitimate in its own manner. This is an ingenious recasting, but it does not resolve for us the more general problem of how and to what extent a people evaluates the good and the bad. The harmful actions of ancestors may well be rooted in benign concern. But how far might this view extend to other acknowledged agents and conditions of maleficence? The moral dichotomy of good and evil may sometimes be overdrawn and imposed too readily on other peoples' ideas, but in perceiving the shadow in human behaviour it still raises many as yet unanswered questions.

Evens (1982) warns against the tendency in the discipline to oscillate between what he calls the weak and the strong senses of morality. The first is the functionalist sense with which Durkheim is mainly associated, and sees moral rules as serving to perpetuate society. The second is taken from a semantic or interpretive understanding of morality as concerned with choice and conflict between choices, and as resulting in the very creation of moral alternatives. Evens's proposed resolution of this theoretical oscillation of moral holism and individualism is to posit an intermediary zone of indeterminate ambiguity, though the idea is only hinted at.

Evens does at least raise the question of moral choice rather than choice between alternative expediences. The pragmatic approach of some so-called transactionalists has resulted in a tendency to oppose morality to expediency, as in the title of a recent book (Bailey 1977). But, if we take the stronger sense of morality as to do with the conflicts thrown up by the very fact of choice presupposing happiness for some but unhappiness for others, then alternative expediences are themselves alternative moralities. The point here, as Wolfram emphasizes (1982), is that a classical utilitarian version of morality as concerning the greater happiness of most members of a society admirably fits the empirical data available to anthropologists, even though few have collected them systematically. The Durkheimian view of morality as being socially sanctioned rules covers only one dimension. There are acts thought morally wrong which are neither breaches of rules nor socially punished. Conversely, many social rules, often codified as laws in modern society, may not always be regarded as part of society's morality. Let us assume instead that throughout society acts are judged to be morally good, bad or indifferent according to the happiness or misery of those involved.

This presupposes a rather broad definition of happiness/misery and, moreover, assumes that such a concept is seen as a measure of morality in all societies. As a working assumption, however, it does oblige us to understand what it is of a people's culture that they see as conducive to their well-being. The only problem with starting with a search for a people's ideas of what makes them happy is that, normally, such notions are unmarked. The existences of most people (let us further assume) are of contentment recognized as happiness, if at all, after the event. It is the periods of suffering that are culturally marked and are experienced immediately as such. Personal and collective crises can be observed and experienced by the ethnographer as they occur and as they are identified and, hopefully, resolved by the participants. Such suffering is further marked by being linked either to ideas of evil or, say, to just retribution. The approach to the study of evil is therefore signposted more directly than that simply to morality. This is not only a matter of empirical convenience. In the association of evil with human suffering and the negation of happiness, our attempt to understand other peoples' ideas of evil draws us into their theories of human nature: its internal constitution and external boundaries; how much it is part of and how much separable from surrounding forces and influences; and how self-determining it is.

EVIL AS IMPERFECTION

The villagers of Skopska Crna Gora in Macedonia say that evil is already in abundance and is increasing; that there is a powerful climate of distrust, suspicion and secrecy. The vivid picture provided by Rheubottom in chapter 5 below makes it unsurprising that beliefs in the evil eye should persist. By contrast, the people of a village in Essex in the few centuries preceding the Industrial Revolution appeared to use the term 'evil' only rarely, and hardly ever in reference to the strong sense of a mysterious black force destructive of human happiness. Macfarlane, in chapter 4, remarks that, today also, we no longer think of evil in this sense, and that such a concept is virtually obsolete. Against this is Pocock's suggestion (chapter 3) that it is precisely because the term does have such strong connotations in modern Britain that it is sparingly used.

We touch here on two sets of distinctions: descriptive as against moral evil, and, within the moral sphere, the strong or radical versus the weak sense. We shall see how shaky these appear when applied to other cultures, but for the moment they serve an initial Western, Judaeo-Christian viewpoint.

Descriptive evil is discussed by Taylor (chapter 2) in his analysis of the etymology of Hebrew terms. These are not discussed by Weber in his study of Judaism (1952), but they provide important insights of a general nature as well as into the early development of the religion. *Ra* meant worthless, unclean, and thence bad, ugly and even sad. Other terms were used later to refer to the breaking of the covenant with God and variously denoted disorder through such root notions as 'falling short of a target', 'breaking of a relationship, or rebelliousness', and 'twisting, making crooked or wrong'. In a number of languages, such as those of Bantu Africa described by Willis and Parkin (chapters 12 and 13), or Balinese by Hobart (chapter 10), some terms translatable as bad or evil also have a sense of physically rotten, misshapen, and ugly. Among the Piaroa Indians of Venezuela discussed by Overing in chapter 14, the evil powers of madness are semantically linked to ugliness and dirt, which, being further associated with the immoderate heat of the sun, must be cleansed by the pure and unrestrained light of the moon. *Tamas*, in the Hindu texts analysed by Inden in chapter 9, refers at root to inert and benighted lethargy, that is, to something not properly alive and yet capable of being activated as evil. This and many other terms in other societies, rendered by us as evil or bad, denote blackness, obscurity and unfulfilment.

Dirt, blackness and ugliness all have the sense of physical incompleteness or unwholesomeness, an aspect made more explicit in the Hebrew terms ('worthless', 'falling short', etc.) and the Bantu ones ('rotten', as of fruit as well as people). Ricoeur's view of evil, as primordially that of defilement or staining what was clean or pure (1967: 25—46), does not quite capture this more profound notion of physical imperfection. It is mildly evident in the various collective representations of the 'weak' left hand as inauspicious (Needham 1973). We may also speculate that, in the 'concrete' language of early man, it would be failed harvests and depleted forests and jungles, ravaged by flood or burnt by sun and drought, or the decaying corpses of animals and people that might strike him as 'bad'. The very concept of 'bad death', such as through accidents and homicide, many cases of which have been gathered by anthropologists from all over the world, refers to a human exit that was ill-timed and so failed to satisfy the normal expectations associated with natural death (Metcalf 1982: 254—7). It passes from human control and cannot therefore be reactivated as new life (Bloch and Parry 1982: 15—18). More paradigmatically, it leaves the living with an incomplete picture of the deceased (chapter 13). The best death in our own society is regarded as one in which, after having lived life to the full, one comes to a peaceful end in a bed surrounded by a family which is comforted by the sight of a seemingly tranquil transition. The worst thing about 'bad deaths' is that they mar or detract from that possible completeness. 'Missing presumed dead' obscures the final image; the abruptness of an accident distorts it, and so cuts it short in a different way.

Can we go further and say that the various cultural expressions of a human quest for completeness or perfection, of living life to the full, as we say, are a response to fears of such loss? Ideas of human perfection tend to have an abstract moral cast. But it may be better to think of them as first being based on an attempt to reverse the possibilities of a depredation, or privation in Augustine's sense (Copleston 1955: 143—6), that was originally thought of in material terms. Thereafter, through metaphorical extension, we express it as spiritual and emotional loss. If this is so, then 'morality' (the means to human perfection and happiness) is the attempt to avert a kind of cosmic theft, the untimely taking away of life, while evil is that theft. Morality is then produced by reflections more on 'bad death' than on 'natural' or 'good death'. The latter is fitted into the main stream, in that those who die 'natural' deaths become either souls or ancestral spirits. By contrast, the victims of bad deaths have an indeterminate destiny: they may become evil spirits or simply 'lost', in either case less than whole.

This would then seem to be the barest level of descriptive evil, at which, as in early Hebrew discussion (chapter 2), a term 'evil' was not distinct from that for 'bad', and was opposed simply as 'rotten', 'failed' or 'incomplete' bad to 'wholesome' good.

It is thereafter a question of how theodicies are built upon this sense of privation as bad. Let me offer another speculation. Hinduism and Buddhism accommodate imperfection, for example ignorance, as evil within a theory of unified existence. Thus, for a being to 'fall short' in this life entails he/she/it becoming a lesser creature in the next, but one that is nevertheless integral to the whole and never separately opposed to it.

By contrast, Manichean and Iranian dualism makes of the imperfection an evil force and, paradoxically, gives it a power that it previously lacked and that may be almost equivalent to that of good itself. While different in other respects, neo-Confucianism, including its modern expression in Japan, provides a clear case in which imperfection has been converted into a powerful force. It comprises the 'goodness' of abstract principle (man's essential nature derived from *ri* — or *li* in Chinese) and the 'badness' of material imperfection (man's physical nature and his selfish desires derived from *ki* — *ch'i* in Chinese). Moeran shows how this balanced duality, itself dependent on that of quiescent *yin* and mobile *yang*, undergoes successive transformations in Japanese ideas, culminating in two views of Japanese society: that of a 'bad' individualistic and selfish inclination (*ninjo* replicating that of physically imperfect *ki*), and that of a group-directed altruism (*giri* premised on *ri*). These are not metaphysical ideas remote from the lives of ordinary, modern Japanese. Rather, they inform the vocabulary of their talk and debates concerning Japan's future relations with the rest of the world.

Somewhere between these monist and dualist theodicies are Judaism, and thence Christianity and Islam, which have retained the opposition of the less-than-whole (fallen Satan) to the whole (omnipotent God), but have generally not converted it into a sustained contest of equal or near-equal forces.

If this reconstruction is valid, it suggests that a primordial sense of incompleteness, imperfection or privation can be stretched in two main directions: as a necessary or inevitable weakness of a cosmic totality; or as threateningly opposed to the whole of which it was once part. For ordinary people in a society, whatever its formal theodicy, these reflect the kinds of conflicting judgements to which they are subject but which, to a greater or lesser degree, are contestable. They must answer to the question of whether their evil is a tolerable weakness or a power to be curbed.

THE CONTESTABILITY OF EVIL

Both Manicheism and Confucianism, then, are full dualisms in Caplan's terms (chapter 7), each made up of the two co-eternal cosmic principles of good and evil which are separate and opposed to one another. At the other end of a continuum are those theodicies that are monist, that is to say, that regard everything including evil as an aspect of God, examples of which are the Hindu pantheon of gods and spirits in Madras (chapter 7) and a similar structure in Bali (chapter 10), and the three strands of existence (*guna*) of the Pancaratra Vaisnava order of Hinduism (chapter 9). Equally monist are the Malay Sufi Muslims described by Bousfield in chapter 11. Buddhism lacks a belief in a God and so, exposing the problems of any typology, does not fit well into this continuum. But its theory of *karma*, as in Hinduism, argues that what a man *does* causes him to become what he *is*, and so defines him as 'naturally' embodying both good and evil acts and states.

This at least suggests a non-dualistic view. In between are Christianity, orthodox Islam and Judaism. Pre-prophetic Judaism had, as Taylor shows in chapter 2, a near-monist theodicy in which there was no idea of evil as a force or principle opposed to God, even though there was a belief in bad spirits (*ruach*) which only later came under God's control. Otherwise, the three Semitic religions are semi-dualist, each with beliefs in Satan, who appears to act independently of God at times, but whom God has in the past already vanquished, and whom ordinary mortals should now conquer with God's help (chapters 5 and 13).

These are necessarily broad outlines, and best should be taken not as accurate descriptions of particular religious theodicies, within which there are of course remarkable variations, but as theological tendencies which sometimes conform to practice but often do not.

Indeed, they can be taken as a field of possible directions open to peoples in their attempts to describe evil and its place in the cosmos. Outside the world religions, with no scriptures to constrain local interpretations, the variations are enormous. The Piaroa Amerindians combine both ends of Ricoeur's evolutionary continuum: they have the ritual symbols of defilement and fault and express their sins communally; yet they also suffer the interiorization of guilt as individuals. Overing goes on to argue, in chapter 14, that Ricoeur's typology is best seen not as evolutionary but as the various possible ways in which people within a single ethical system may experience, symbolize and judge evil. The examples of African animistic religion given by Parkin and Willis, and that of Beidelman's analysis of the Nuer concept of *thek* and sin (1981), give support to this view.

Ricoeur's insights are ingenious, but his limitation is in assuming that his evolutionary continuum can be applied generally to other cultures, or at least in not making it clear that it is confined to his own tradition. In chapter 2 Taylor shows that it does indeed fit well the development of Hebrew religion, and out of it Christianity and Islam. As Judaism became more and more institutionalized, there was a shift from the idea of man being collectively burdened by fault and defilement, that is of communal sin, to that of the individual man suffering guilt as the author of his own sinful deeds. The increased institutionalization of the religion brought about personal interiorization of guilt. It converted descriptive into moral evil, the wrongful acts of man himself rather than of the cosmos surrounding him.

But what does institutionalization here mean? It is the emergence of a hierarchy of priestly office and power and the definition by this elite of what constitutes evil and who the sinners are. This is to give, as Hobart puts it, an essentialist definition of evil; that is to say, to make of it something fixed, firm, basic and unquestionable. It is what the Balinese priestly and aristocratic elite does. By presenting evil and evil agents as uncontestably so, the elite tries to block dissident interpretations as to whether an act is or is not immoral. The commoners, by contrast, have many different perspectives on the same act and are governed in their judgements by situational and personal interests more than by the uncontrovertability of their collective position. What one commoner says is good another regards as bad, and even then they present variations on each. As heirs to a Judaeo-Christian tradition, like Ricoeur, we run the same danger of imposing on other peoples our idea of what evil is. Evil *is* not any*thing*: it denotes rather an area of discourse concerning human suffering, human existential predicaments and the attempted resolution of these through other humans and through non-human agencies, including a God or gods. In asking whether evil can be eliminated, people are also led into considering the possibility that good may in fact sometimes come out of evil; that it may even be necessary, and that it can be personified, perhaps among people known to them.

Dualistic and semi-dualistic theodicies entail a notion of separable and therefore absolute evil. But it is when we talk of moral rather than descriptive evil, of human rather than cosmic wrongdoing, that the discourse reveals a vocabulary of dichotomous absolutes: is the heinous act explicable or inexplicable, intended or unintended, remediable or irremediable, forgiveable or unforgiveable, and so on? Or is evil, as in the minds of some people, always only one or the other? Or, as in the case of the Giriama mother (chapter 13), can the act be described at all in these absolute ways; and, if not, then how can the acknowledged suffering be discussed?

Paradoxically, such lexical distinctions give people generally the means to discuss and so evaluate human suffering and destruction, but it may also divide them into powerful judges and powerless judged. The ontology of moral absolutism tries to 'make' people more than simply to define them, but it does not always succeed. The theological distinction discussed by Inden (chapter 9) between India's higher and lower selves as 'good' and 'bad' underwrites the caste hierarchy and the associated rules concerning personal purity and pollution, and even different parts of the sub-continent itself. Yet, when interacting with each other, people may counter the theology and dissolve the dichotomy by evaluating each other's actions in a gradable rather than fixed manner. Seeing something of the same opposition among Sinhalese Buddhists, Southwold (chapter 8) distinguishes austere Meditation from the less demanding Ministry Buddhism, the first being located mainly in the scriptures and favoured only by scholars, and the second preferred by most people, including villagers, in their everyday lives.

For Macfarlane (chapter 4), the use of money in emergent capitalist society relativized the absolute distinctions of good and evil that existed earlier. Money gave everything a price, thereby enabling evil to be converted into good and so blurring all moral dichotomies except that pertaining to free enterprise itself, which was valued above all else.

In moving into either orthodox Islam or fundamentalist Pentecostal Christianity, the Mijikenda people of Kenya appear to be engaging in a reverse exchange of views. Traditionally, they saw as intrinsically evil certain human acts, but not the perpetrators themselves, a view shared by the Piaroa Amerindians. Indeed, the evil acts are an understandable aspect of being human. But, as more Mijikenda enter the new religions, they are taught to believe that it is the person himself who is good or evil, sometimes irredeemably so. They are undergoing change from a relativized to more absolute version of moral evil.

The point here, as Inden stresses, following Gallie (1968), is that evil is an 'essentially contested concept'. As academics we may contest the view that there is an essence to evil, but so can the peoples we study. At least they may shift from absolutist to relativist judgements, so generating perspective upon perspective. But in defining and explaining the moral evil of others, persons also make statements about themselves, their view of humanity and their own capacity to cope with suffering.

Evil that means no more than (very) bad, is, by definition, removable through existing procedures available to a group, such as rites of purification or confession (chapters 2, 12 and 13), through appeasement (chapter 7) or by denouncing the evil person and stripping him of his powers (chapter 14). Inexplicable evil, as Pocock calls it in chapter 3, responds to no such ready-made therapy available to the group. 'Hanging's too good for them' is a cry of exasperation at the failure to understand, to explain, and to punish satisfactorily. It introduces a conundrum in our understanding of humanity. Humans often kill, maim and ill-treat each other, but sometimes they engage in such wanton destructiveness and cruelty that they appear to observers to have exceeded definable bounds of humanity. They are thus monsters, 'worse than animals' and, like the *wakindi* of the Kaguru (Beidelman 1963: 61—3) or the *ifituumbu* of the Fipa (chapter 12 bleow), are wholly malicious and yet thinking creatures of no determinate category. If we use 'evil' to refer to these, we are giving the word an ontological weight that is not captured by their being described as 'extra-group phenomena' or the like. Rather, just as the term 'human' or its translated equivalent in a society refers to a field of possibilities, so the term 'evil' when applied to monsters denotes a field of human impossibilities.

Nevertheless, the humanly impossible may happen. Pocock records the horror felt throughout Britain during 1983 at the random abduction and raping of a six-year-old boy by three men. Yet people's perspectives change: the men were, some like to believe, foreigners, and so it was not after all an act committed by 'us'; the men did, at least, leave the child alive when they abandoned him; and so on. What this suggests is that the definitional line between the possible bad and the impossible evil is always liable to shift. Puritanism pushes it so as to extend the possibilities of evil, while liberalism aims to reduce them.

Pocock's survey in chapter 3 of British uses of the term 'evil' gives a revealing breakdown into two kinds of view. A majority is prepared to use the word in the radical sense of inhumanly monstrous, and so to engage in an absolute distinction between acceptable and unacceptable kinds of human being. A minority is reluctant to use the word at all, because, Pocock suggests, it is too strong and reveals a reluctance to so totally convert fellow humans into monsters.

We can see this as yet another aspect of the human conundrum. If the majority, absolutist, view held full sway, then there would be a commensurate loss of human charity, which is otherwise valued in the country. But if the minority view were dominant, apparent human malice might be excused but not always explained. A balanced tension between the two might produce charitable explanation. But the extent to which such a balance can be achieved depends on the dominant forms of discourse: the treatment in Britain of the Falklands war by the mass media may well have increased the number of recruits to the majority view.

EVIL AS AMBIVALENT POWER

The essential contestability of notions of evil and the many perspectives on human maleficence and suffering point metaphysically in two main directions: imperfection and over-perfection, between which mankind tries to strike a balance. On the one hand, as the second section of this chapter indicated, a descriptive sense of evil includes an idea of physical incompleteness, of falling short. On the other hand, evil is often thought of as a surfeit of human or godly desires, whose harmful effects are denounced by a system of moral rules and prohibitions where these exist. The rules and prohibitions recognize that moral evil here exerts a power that ought to be controlled and might, if redirected, actually be of benefit. We even get a hint of this latter feature in our English term, 'evil'.

The English triad of terms, 'good', 'bad' and 'evil', is sometimes understood as favourable, unfavourable and extremely unfavourable. Equivalents are found in a number of European languages, including Macedonian and other Slavic tongues (chapter 5). This proportional rendering is not the only one. The examples given in the section above of actions that exceed the acceptable bounds of humanity suggest another, which is particularly marked and comes under Southwold's sense of strong or radical evil (chapter 8). Etymologically, Pocock notes, the term derives from an idea of gross excess, of having gone too far beyond prescribed limits, and it seems to be part of an archetypal notion of entanglement, as discussed by Taylor and Parkin (chapters 2 and 13), and apparent also as Augustine's image of evil (Evans 1982: 4). It fits the ontological description of inexplicably human, inhuman monsters, and so is not simply a term opposed to 'good'. Indeed, archetypically situations of confused excess can create conditions that are regarded as aiding mankind. Prophets 'go out' into the wilderness and engage in behaviour that is beyond the bounds of human understanding, but return and convert their madness into human hopes. We can so easily be trapped by an apparently similar triad of concepts in another culture, or by only two such terms, and think that they are European equivalents. The primordial sense of ambivalent power arising from excess is a safer common focus, whether or not, and however, it is expressed in words.

Nietzsche points to the political context of this ambivalence and its rendering as evil. The opposition of 'good' and 'bad' reflects the morality of masters who see themselves as noble and therefore good and their slaves as contemptible and therefore bad. Their noble goodness is in being able to inspire the fear that subjugates. By contrast, slaves depict themselves as morally good but dominated by masters who are evil because they rule by fear. But, while contemptibility is a neutral and passive designation wanted by no one for themselves, evil denotes a source of dangerous power sought by slave and master alike. To be called evil here is preferable to being called bad: better to be feared than to be contemptible (Nietzsche 1966: 204–7). For Nietzsche the opposition of good and evil originates in this contrast between slave and master moralities. Reversing this, Southall (1979) notes from many ethnographies that what is regarded as evil in ordinary men's hearts (such as witchcraft) becomes the legitimate, if terrifying, power of supreme rulers, just as among the Lugbara *ole* is a restorative force in the hands of elders but is maleficent when used by juniors (Middleton 1960). Piaroa wizards similarly can tap cosmic power for the good of humanity but can easily take too much, an excess that may not be intended to harm but which, through bad judgement, may kill and create havoc (chapter 14). The supreme *Vaya* elders of the Giriama (Mijikenda) similarly have powers that can benefit or destroy humanity. In their case, their destructiveness is intended, for they are seen to possess the 'normal' human emotions of jealousy, envy, greed and anger which they occasionally express (chapter 13). More abstractly, the followers of Malay Sufi Islam regard the mystical power that sustains them as dangerous if unrestrained by the law (*shariah*) (chapter 11).

The archetype of evil as ambivalent power, and not simply as the opposite of good, has echoes in people's uncertainty about how to explain misfortune and maleficence. There are cultures in which misfortune is seen primarily as resulting from human malice, such as those in Africa in which sorcery and witchcraft predominate. There are others that blame non-human spiritual agencies, and even non-human, non-spiritual ones, sometimes to the point of elaborating the complex theodicies described above in which God relates in a number of ways to an abstract, independent evil force. Most cultures in fact recognize all aspects to some degree. Witchcraft and sorcery in the African societies described by Parkin (chapter 13) and Willis (chapter 12) are indeed seen by the people as the prototype of all evil, but lesser spirits and forces are also inauspicious, sometimes seriously so. Among the south Indian Christians discussed by Caplan in chapter 7, the *peey* spirits are especially vicious, while witchcraft and sorcery, which may include human use of the *peey*, are correspondingly less significant.

A breakdown of our own uses of the word 'evil' reveals at least three senses: the moral, referring to human culpability; the physical, by which is understood destructive elemental forces of nature, for example earthquakes, storms or the plague; and the metaphysical, by which disorder in the cosmos or in relations with divinity results from a conflict of principles or wills. Pocock, following Aquinas, suggests in chapter 3 that all are in fact aspects of the metaphysical, since what is regarded as moral, social, physical or natural depends on the particular culture's understanding of these distinctions. The Piaroa concept of culture itself refers to the correct amounts of knowledge needed both to benefit and be safe from the earth's resources. The potential for wildness in culture thus has to be tamed and controlled, while nature consists simply of passive elements. Overing notes in chapter 14 that this distinction is a reversal of anthropologists' normal ethnocentric view that culture is the rational means by which we domesticate wild nature, and helps us understand the Piaroa predicament: it is necessary to have cultural knowledge in order to survive and become distinguished from animals, yet this knowledge, like that of the biblical tree of the knowledge of good and evil, can lead to madness and the destruction of fellow humans. Noting Willis's concern at what he calls the non-human rationality of modern technology and bureaucracy (chapter 12), that of Southwold on contradictory views of the Bomb held by dangerously unaware churchmen (chapter 8) and of Inden (chapter 9) on the widespread acceptance of President Reagan's denunciation of the Soviet Union as 'that evil empire', we might feel that the cautious Piaroa view of knowledge is actually one that befits ourselves as much as them.

However, because different metaphysical schemes refer not to demonstrable, universal truths, but to cultural presuppositions, the variations will always continue. Inden's analysis of the texts of one of the major orders of Hinduism, the Pancaratra Vaisnavas, shows them to conform not at all to the conventional Western view of quietist, passivist Indian religion, of which there are certainly examples in other Hindu orders. The history of the evil king, Vena, forcefully explains the division of India into its 'higher' and 'lower' halves. The Brahmans in the story triumph over the king but reveal in their discourse the independent operation of the three cosmic strands that make up the chain of being. The king is certainly credited with an independent will to make right or wrong decisions, but he does so against a background of metaphysical possibilities which obscure any such distinction.

The interrelationship to each other of these three strands bears some similarity with that of the colour triad described for the Fipa of Central Africa by Willis (chapter 12). The three strands of *sattva, rajas* and *tamas* refer respectively to quiescent goodness, passionate energy and inert badness. The first and third compete, so to speak, for mastery of the intermediary energy, *rajas*. If *sattva* succeeds, then enlightened intellect triumphs, but if *tamas* appropriates passionate energy, then its inherent badness is unleashed. The three are also characterized as white, red and black, which, among a number of African peoples and more widely throughout the world, also designate good, either-good-or-bad, and bad. Among the Fipa, however, both black and red are ambivalent, each having positive as well as negative attributes. But, unlike the linking of *rajas* and *tamas*, red and black among the Fipa are never paired. White alone brings together all that is auspicious. Whether paired with red or with black, it extracts from each of them its benignly creative features, such as energy and sexual reproduction, and, as in the case of black, the more obscure and mysterious forces of creation.

Following the view given above of evil as ambivalent power, it is clear from both these examples of the Pancaratra Hindus and the African Fipa that no unambiguous concept of badness exists. *Tamas* is, by itself, inactive and therefore harmless. Black among the Fipa is good as well as malign in its association with death and physical violence.

Some peoples make the ambivalence explicit and then resolve it in their theodicy. The most remarkable case is that of Malaysian Sufi Islam described by Bousfield in chapter 11. For the Sufi, all that exists and is experienced comes from God and from no other source. It would be an insult to God to argue that any other creator existed. While among Hindus man is part of a chain of being, among Sufi Muslims man is part of the unity of being. Man *is* God, and man's apparently evil actions are also those of God. Such a view is heresy in more orthodox versions of Islam. Among the Swahili Sunni Muslims of East Africa described in chapter 13, a worshipper knows what alternatives God has offered him and what rewards and penalties await his moral strengths or frailties. He alone is responsible for any evils he perpetrates, for they are not of God's creation, any more than God ordained the fall of Satan and malevolent angels.

For the Malay Sufis, then, the evildoer *is* God. The Sufis are well aware that good and evil emotions and actions contradict each other. They resolve these contradictions by seeing them as part of the necessary experience by which a person comes to know himself and thereby his God. Thus, to commit evil or be its victim is to suffer. But to suffer in this way is to know the power to resist sin or to transgress. To know this power, which is that of creation itself, is to know as God does, to experience, and therefore to be, as God. The sixteenth-century teachings of the great Malay Sufi, Hamzah Fansuri, are much more complex than this short summary can indicate, and they are not without their logical flaws, as Bousfield notes. But they stand in marked contrast to those Christians and orthodox Muslims who see the clash of good and evil as likely to result in religious collapse if unresolved.

Bousfield raises the interesting question of whether, in its spread across South-East Asia, Sufism succeeded in drawing upon pre-existing ideas which bear some similarity with that of the unity of being. He suggests that the Sufi notion of 'extinction', by which knowledge of the self leads to its transcension, appealed to the Buddhist concept of *nirvana*; and that the God of Sufism, being both the general and the particular, or the one and the many, might have made sense to Hindu ideas of a 'pantheistic' Brahma. This seems plausible in the light of what Caplan (chapter 7) and Inden (chapter 9) say of the hierarchy of Hindu gods and demons, some of the lowest of which are the ghosts of people who have died 'bad deaths', and of Southwold's description (chapter 8) of *nirvana* as a long-term or ultimate goal for ordinary, village Buddhists whose patience, we may speculate, may have been strengthened by the possibility of some modification of their basic ideas through Sufism.

Certainly, Hobart in chapter 10 found his informants incredulous that he, a Westerner, should imagine that God could be any other than both good and evil. How could He ever know good if He had not also experienced bad, they ask. While the Balinese do not go so far as to claim that man is God, as do the Malay Sufis, they see parallels between human and divine characteristics: Rangda, the queen of the witches, comes across not as unqualified evil but as a familiar if extreme human-like mixture of emotions and characteristics.

We might at first ascribe the ambiguously sinister and yet occasionally laughable antics of Rangda to the admixture of Hindu, Buddhist and Tantric ideas in Bali, the diversity of metaphysical presuppositions being expressed in the inconsistent image of Rangda. No doubt the two reinforce one another.

That there is something inherently ambiguous in people's understanding of evil is suggested by comparison with the Piaroa characterization of their god, Kuemoi. He, too, is both feared and mocked. His madness drives him to evil acts but also gets him into hilariously absurd predicaments. But this inconsistency of behaviour, which humans can easily recognize in themselves, does not stem from any wider cultural diversity. The Piaroa are relatively isolated from other Amerindian jungle peoples. As Overing notes in chapter 14, evil stands on the threshold of humour, as we willingly seek reasons to convert our terror of evil into laughter at its impotence, at its human-like frailties. Evil may, then, be regarded as ambivalent power, but, through its 'personification', it becomes more accessible to people's management, even to the point of being temporarily dissolved: to 'know' evil as one might know a person is at least to communicate with it, directly, indirectly through a god, or even as part of a god.

THE PERSONIFICATION OF EVIL

It is clear that the ontologies of many cultures do not make a clean-cut, once-for-all separation of human and non-human. There is the Hindu theory of reincarnation and chain of being; the unity of being in Malay Sufism; the conversion of victims of 'bad deaths' into *peey* evil spirits in Madras; and the affinity of men and animals among the Piaroa of Venezuela. These are but some of the examples that warn us against assuming the sharp separation typical of Judaeo-Christian and orthodox Islamic thinking. Buddhism differs from Hinduism in stressing the supremacy of the human over and above gods as well as other life-forms, since there are no gods in Buddhism and Buddha himself was human. Similarly, though to a lesser extent, some forms of African animism view humans and their ancestors as discretely superior if also self-accountable, though existing alongside non-human spirits and a weak idea of a High God. The broadest distinction we can make, then, is between those indigenous theories that only ever see a gradation of being, or in some cases a number of possible transformations of being, and those that see humanity as quite distinct from other life forms and from nature itself.

In the light of such variation, it would be nonsense to talk generally of the personification of evil, for the very concept of human person must also vary considerably. By personification, therefore, I refer to the attribution to creatures of qualities that appear to resemble at least in part those of the people themselves in interaction with each other.

The resemblance can only be partial, of course. The European idea of an Anti-Christ presents a serene and beatific face masking hideous malevolence (Nugent 1983). It is a notion that, as modern horror movies have discovered, can send a chill through the stoutest of hearts. In the Japanese television 'noodle westerns' described by Moeran in chapter 6, exaggerated characters portray evil: the unkempt *samurai*, the bald priest and the merchant or lord, his face half-illuminated by a flickering candle. Sometimes 'real' persons are used. Women in Macedonian Skopska Crna Gora are held to cause evil through their weak, indolent nature. It is the mother who, lacking firmness, fails properly to wean a suckling child by allowing it to resume breastfeeding when it cries. Such a child develops the evil eye. Through their quarrels women also divide households. More generally, it is the trusted dependant who can create evil by betraying confidences to outsiders. This fits the remarkably self-contained and inward-looking cosmology of the people whose boundaries of acceptable humanity are drawn very tightly around each individual household, and who even then may also suspect those closest to them.

More often, spirits, demons and gods personify evil: the *peey* in Madras; the Piaroa creator god of knowledge; the Balinese *buta/kala* spirits or goddess Rangda, otherwise called queen of the witches; and the fallen gods of Christianity and Islam, and of Hinduism, such as Satan and forms of Parvati (chapter 7). Just as the Hindu pantheon of gods contains a middle tier who are partly good and partly malevolent, so more generally other personifications of evil often reflect an ambivalence of intent and motive not unlike that experienced by human beings themselves. Forms such as Satan and the *peey* are wholly evil, but others like Wahari of the Piaroa, the Sinhalese Buddhist mythological figure Mara (chapter 8) and some African spirits reflect the moral indecisiveness and uncertainty that may lead to acts judged as evil in the culture but are also regarded as normal human qualities.

Personifying evil in these various ways does provide a means of placing it cosmically, often with a view to containing it, sometimes to the extent of negotiating with it, as is often the case with possessionary spirits. But while the personification of evil may indeed facilitate its management, it also points to other possibilities. Marlowe's Dr Faustus bargained with Mephistopheles because he was disillusioned with his, or anyone's, prospects of obtaining salvation. He substituted his own rationality for faith and calculated that a period of ecstasy with the beautiful Helen of Troy was worth more than his chances with God and Heaven. The significant point here is that Mephistopheles represented to Faustus not just evil, but an experience that could not be obtained by either divine or secular means. The devil for, let us say, the reckless, brave and foolish here offers a third world.

Quite independently, we see this vision of alternative existences in, say, the cases of shamanism, much documented throughout the world. The spirits possessing shamans may at times do no more than demand appeasement, or proffer cures and restorative medicine; but on other occasions they may offer good luck and a new life. They are in this latter respect the personification of those Cargo cults of New Guinea which, much more dramatically, promise immediate Utopia. The step from Faustus's devil to capriciously benevolent spirits might seem too wide; but it is not if we consider that both operate in a cosmic area which, while it may ultimately be under a superior divinity's control, is for that moment unpatrolled. It constitutes an area of potential amorality which invites experimentation.

Pleasure and happiness may be the prize, but the risks of a grim future are also high. Faustus came to know this by translating the symbols of evil into costs and benefits. Sometimes the calculator himself comes to be regarded as the greater evil agent. National glory is good but war is bad, people may say. But they may also distinguish between justified and unjustified wars, such that the political leader who initiates the latter apparently to further his or her ends at great cost of human life may come to be regarded as the 'real' evil. This was an accusation levelled at both the British prime minister and the Argentinian president over the Falkland war. More complicated still, a prominent member of the British opposition, who made this accusation against his own prime minister some time after the end of the war, was himself accused of being evil for having dishonoured British soldiers who had died.

Switching blame from one person to another in this way is reminiscent of anthropological accounts of witchcraft. But shifting blame from an impersonal to personal agent, from war to one who is held to initiate it, or the reverse, is a quite different phenomenon. It presupposes a separation of the act from the person, and has raised over the years a number of severe moral problems and questions. Thus, to stay with the example of war, if dropping bombs on civilian cities becomes regarded as a 'necessary evil' intended to end the prolonged suffering of an otherwise long war, does this exonerate whoever gave the order to do so? In Western politics it is commonplace for this separation to be made, often to the credit of the agent who is said to have taken a 'courageous decision', a view that history has a curious way of reversing.

At first we might be tempted to see this as a distinctive feature of a Western epistemology which argues that it is a person's motive and intention that should be judged over and above the consequences of his judgement. We might contrast this with the view of some of the peoples discussed in this book who see the evil of an act as also a constituent part of the agent, as in the South Asian theories of *karma* and *dukha*, or as being evil regardless of whether it was intended, as among the Piaroa. Yet, not dissimilarly, the English Poor Law was premised on the idea that the lot of the 'undeserving poor' was due to their own moral misdoing, and that their wretchedness was evidence of their immorality. Among the Macedonian villagers described by Rheubottom in chapter 5, exactly the same idea obtains, so much so that they feel entitled to steal from and inflict even more harm upon the poverty-stricken, for do they not deserve it? Such double-edged argumentation fits societies in which personal worthwhileness is judged in terms of property and secular power, and in this respect appears to differ from the Asian theories, which stress an innate ontological link between what a person does and what he is or becomes.

Nor need the separation of the evildoer from the harm done his victim have the significance it has in Western law and morality, where retribution is emphasized. The Sinhalese Buddhists do not dwell on the distinction but rather stress the harm that will come to the wrongdoer from his own destructive act. Nor will he be punished by a god, since there is none. The evil agent is his own victim, for his suffering follows the act naturally, 'as smoke follows fire'. For Southwold (chapter 8) this is why Buddhism lacks a concept of radical evil, for people are reluctant to attribute serious maleficence to their own actions. Much the same can be said of Malay Sufism, in which the personal suffering of the evildoer even becomes the means of self-redemption and thence a path to oneness with God. In such ontologies the evil that is admitted is unlikely to be vicious. Elsewhere, blaming other persons allows for a much fuller expression of evil destructiveness, punishable by other humans and/or by divinities, but also sometimes allowing for redemption.

This suggests a further broad distinction: between cultures that seek some kind of first cause to explain wanton destructiveness, and those that tend to merge agent, intention and consequence as being inseparably part of the order of things, but within which no first cause is discernible, nor even sought. The contrast is most vividly illustrated by the difference between Judaeo-Christian biblical linearity ('In the beginning . . .') and the Hindu cycle of *yugas* (Ages) which succeed each other indefinitely (O'Flaherty 1976: 17—19).

The concern with First Cause, or Creator, has been especially associated, therefore, with Christian theology. If God is benevolent, omniscient and omnipotent, then why does he permit the existence of evil? The question has been asked and answered in numerous ways, a consideration of which would take us beyond the concerns of this volume. Throughout, however, it raises the problem of how much a god or gods can be held to personify not merely benevolence but also evil. In this volume, Parvati, Rangda, Mara, Wahari (the counterpart to Kuemoi), the Sufi God and ancestral spirits have all been mentioned as combining, to a greater or less degree, good and evil characteristics.

Depending on the cultural viewpoint, such cases of ambivalent divinity may be regarded either as a collective representation of human frailties or as an ontological extension of them. But can they ever be dissociated from the changing existential dilemmas that confront people? The Christian devil became for the Bolivian tin-miners a god-like symbol of their own integrity, in opposition to the white conquerors who feared and denounced him (Taussig 1980). Similarly, following the rapid political, economic and social changes in the Asian sub-continent, will there develop a sharper separation than exists at present between the various metaphysical components that make up the cosmos? At present they are each, including *tamas* or evil, integral to the whole — indeed, necessary for it. But as local and regional interests, and international ones, become framed by each other, and as new social divisions emerge, will they become the new means of explaining misfortune, disadvantage and oppression? The Hindu *peey* spirits described by Caplan in chapter 7 have an explanatory significance for lower-class Christians in Madras that is greater than that for other groups. Overall, however, the continuities are strong. Weber's view of Hinduism as 'characterized by a dread of the magical evil of innovation' (1958: 122) seems mistaken to us nowadays, but his prediction that the doctrine of *karma* (which he called 'the most consistent theodicy ever produced by history' (1958: 121)) and the caste system in some form would continue to reinforce each other has been vindicated, for there are no reports of significant change in this relationship.

Such change, should it occur, is unlikely to be in one direction only, however. The growth of so-called religious transcendentalism in certain parts of the West may be viewed as a protest against individualistic self-seeking. But it appears also to be an attempt to bring together within a single system of explanation what are seen by adherents as ever-increasing, contradictory human aims and ethoses in the wider society.

It typifies all ideological construction and seems to be a part of a more general cycle: of totalitarian reasoning, placing the collective above the individual; and of argument through particular cases emphasizing primacy of self. The cycle has wide-scale political as well as religious and moral significance. In it the place of evil seems assured but changing, from gradable and relativist to collectively held absolute judgements. Augustine expressed relief in concluding that evil was not, after all, created by or part of God, nor was it existing as an autonomous force external to man, but it was of man's own doing and therefore not to be regarded as an insurmountable problem (Evans 1982: 114, 149). Nominally at least, bourgeois liberal values are the heir to this formulation. These Christian views are as different from those of the Christian Cathars, who were influenced by Manichean dualism, as are the theodicies of other quite distinct religions.

The many perspectives that peoples place on what we translate as evil may, as Hobart points out, reflect linguistic as much as philosophical differences. The metaphors created out of the concept of evil may seem to refer to widely disparate phenomena, from the deeply sinister malevolence of indeterminate agency described by Macfarlane in chapter 4 to the seemingly much milder human neglect in Japan of the Confucian Five Fundamental Relationships discussed by Moeran (chapter 6), with much variation between these on the extent to which destructiveness is personified.

The variations turn on a range of human predicaments that, because they have language, people may talk about, even if they lack terms which do not quite translate as the English evil. Suffering may be culturally defined, but is never lacking. The predicaments are therefore many. How is the boundary to be drawn between human and non-human victim and perpetrator? Given the view of some cultures that man is not intrinsically evil, how are death, disease and other kinds of depradation to be explained? What is to be made of benign intentions that somehow lead to harmful excesses? How, given the expectation in some religions of piety and total submission towards a God, are men to realize inspirations and ambitions that cannot be accommodated by such a belief? What is to be made of those existential puzzles concerning right and wrong which are surely found in any culture but for which there is no apparent solution? How does a theodicy cope with the questions of God's omnipotence and benevolence that have already been raised, and with the apparent heresy that, since he is fashioned in the image of God, mankind should be equally able to create good and evil?

Questions of these kinds may hover around what we define as the problem of evil. In asking them, people reveal their cultural assumptions about being, fallibility and culpability. But the answers given, whether by prophets or others, are sometimes unexpected and so carry special weight and conceivably alter the way in which power and discourse are related. More generally, the main suggestions of this Introduction are that evil refers to various ideas of imperfection and excess seen as destructive; but that these are contestable concepts which, when personified, allow mankind to engage them in dialogue and reflect on the boundaries of humanity.

As regards the term 'evil' itself in English, its loose analytical value has enabled the contributors in this volume to go beyond such conventional categories as ghost or witch in their studies, and to pick out what they see as distinctive in the cultures they look at. Their attempts to translate equivalent concepts can never be more than partially successful. But even this has its advantages. The polysemy of the concept and its rendering in other cultures increases our perspectives, which nevertheless remain intelligible in relation to each other. This growing semantic shape is of course made up of many discourses, including those of the investigators. Perhaps there may now be value in re-casting it in new terms, such as imperfection or privation, excess and entanglement, and contestability, as a prelude to further deconstruction. As an approach this might suggest that such odd-job words as 'evil' are in fact good for anthropologists to think.

REFERENCES

Bailey, F. G. (1977). *Morality and Expediency.* Oxford: Blackwell

Beidelman, T. O. (1963). 'Witchcraft in Ukaguru' in J. Middleton and E. H. Winter (eds), *Witchcraft and Sorcery in East Africa.* London: Routledge and Kegan Paul

Beidelman, T. O. (1981). 'The Nuer concept of *thek* and the meaning of sin'. *History of Religion* Special Issue: Defining a Humanistic Approach to Religion. Berkeley: University of California Press

Bidney, D. (1953). *Theoretical Anthropology.* New York: Schocken

Bloch, M. and Parry, J. (eds) (1982). *Death and the Regeneration of Life.* Cambridge University Press

Copleston, F. C. (1955). *Aquinas.* Middlesex: Penguin

Crick, M. (1976). *Explorations in Language and Meaning.* London: Malaby Press

Evans, G. R. (1982). *Augustine on Evil.* Cambridge University Press

Evans-Pritchard, E. E. (1956). *Nuer Religion.* Oxford University Press

Evans-Pritchard, E. E. (1976). *Witchcraft, Oracles and Magic among the Azande.* Oxford University Press (an abridged version, with an introduction by Eva Gillies, of the 1937 original)

Evens, T. M. S. (1982). 'Two concepts of "society as a moral system": Evans-Pritchard's heterodoxy'. *Man 17,* 205–18

Favret-Saada, J. 1980 (1977). *Deadly Words: Witchcraft in Bocage.* Cambridge University Press

Fürer-Haimendorf von, C. (1967). *Morals and Merit: A Study of Values and Social Control in South Asian Societies.* London: Weidenfeld and Nicolson

Gallie, W. B. (1968). 'Essentially Contested Concepts'. In his *Philosophy and the Historical Understanding.* New York: Schocken

Heelas, P. and Lock, A. (eds) (1981). *Indigenous Psychologies.* London: Academic Press

Jacobson-Widding, A. (ed.) (1983). *Identity: Personal and Socio-Cultural.* Uppsala: Almqvist and Wiksell; New York: Humanities Press

Kiernan, J. P. (1982). 'The "problem of evil" in the context of ancestral intervention in the affairs of the living in Africa'. *Man 17,* 287–301

Madan, T. N. (1981). 'Moral Choices: An Essay on the Unity of Asceticism and Eroticism'. In A. C. Mayer (ed), *Culture and Morality.* Delhi: Oxford University Press

Mauss, M. (1979). 'A category of the human mind: the notion of person; the notion of "self" ' (trans Ben Brewster). In *Sociology and Psychology.* London: Routledge and Kegan Paul

Mayer, A. C. (ed.) (1981). *Culture and Morality.* Delhi: Oxford University Press

Metcalf, P. (1982). *A Borneo Journey into Death.* Philadelphia: University of Pennsylvania Press

Middleton, J. (1960). *Lugbara Religion.* Oxford University Press (for International African Institute)

Needham, R. (ed.) (1973). *Right and Left: Essays on Dual Symbolic Classification.* Chicago: University of Chicago Press

Nietzsche, F. (1966). *Beyond Good and Evil* (trans Walter Kaufmann). New York: Vintage Books

Nugent, C. (1983). *Masks of Satan: The Demonic in History.* London: Sheed and Ward

O'Flaherty, W. D. (1976). *The Origins of Evil in Hindu Mythology.* Berkeley: University of California Press

Read, K. E. (1955). 'Morality and the concept of the person among the Gahuku-Gama'. *Oceania 25*, 233—82. Reprinted in J. Middleton (ed.) *Myth and Cosmos* (1967). New York: The Natural History Press

Ricoeur, P. (1967). *The Symbolism of Evil* (trans. E. Buchanan). Boston: Beacon Press

Rosaldo, M. Z. (1980). *Knowledge and Passion.* Cambridge: Cambridge University Press

Taussig, M. (1980). *The Devil and Commodity Fetishism in South America.* Chapel Hill: University of North Carolina Press

Weber, M. (1952). *Ancient Judaism.* (trans. and ed. by H. H. Gerth and D. Martindale). Glencoe, Illinois: The Free Press

Weber, M. (1958). *The Religion of India.* (trans. and ed. by H. H. Garth and D. Martindale). Glencoe, Illinois: The Free Press

Wolfram, S. (1982). 'Anthropology and morality.' *Journal of the Anthropological Society of Oxford 13*, 262—74

2

Theological thoughts about evil

Donald Taylor*

INTRODUCTION

Our thoughts on evil are to some degree constrained and even directed by the language we use. Therefore, before looking cross-culturally at specific cases of evil elsewhere in this volume, it is appropriate that we search for the roots of the uses of the term in the Judaeo-Christian literary heritage. In this chapter, then, I outline some of the main features of the problem of evil and its related concepts as it is found first of all in the Hebrew Bible, and then in the Christian writings of the New Testament. I then illustrate how evil is viewed in both the Protestant and Catholic traditions in Christianity.

EVIL IN THE ANCIENT HEBREW TRADITION

The source of my reflections in this section is the Torah, or Law, which consists of the first five books of the Hebrew Bible: Genesis, Exodus, Leviticus, Numbers and Deuteronomy. These books are called collectively the Pentateuch, and were written originally in Hebrew. They form part of what Christians call the Old Testament. For my present purposes I prefer the expression 'Hebrew Bible' to 'Old Testament', because I want to distinguish them from the specifically Christian writings in the New Testament, which were written originally in Greek.

I have also called the traditional teaching found in the former scriptures 'the ancient Hebrew tradition'. This tradition arose among the early Hebrews who later were referred to as the Israelites, because they claimed descent from a common ancestor, Israel, also known as Jacob, the founding father of the

*I wish to record my thanks to my colleague Rabbi Isaac Newman at the Middlesex Polytechnic for his helpful discussions in the preparation of this chapter. Any errors in my presentation of the rabbinic point of view are my own.

twelve tribes of Israel. This early tradition must be distinguished from 'inter-testamental Judaism' which in this paper refers to the tradition that arose between the period of the Exile in Babylon (586—520 BC) and the Christian era which began with the birth of Christ. Modern Judaism developed originally out of inter-testamental Judaism, but must be distinguished from it because of the prominence of Rabbinic Judaism, which does not feature so much in inter-testamental Judaism. I will refer to Rabbinic Judaism only very briefly.

The preceding paragraphs are intended to do three things: first, to introduce the expressions 'Hebrew Bible', 'Law', 'inter-testamental Judaism' and others, and to note the way I intend to use them here; second, to distinguish the ancient Hebrew tradition from Judaism in general; third, to assure you that I am limiting myself to a reasonably small range of literature from the vast amount that is available on the subject.

The Hebrew word that is translated 'evil' in the King James's translation of the Bible is *ra. Ra* meant primarily worthlessness or uselessness, and by extension it came to mean bad, ugly or even sad. Thus *ra* originally meant evil in a weak sense, as suggested by Southwold in chapter 8 below. It meant simply bad as opposed to good. The truth is that the Hebrews did not discuss evil very much. Even today, the *Encyclopaedia Judaica* has no entry under the heading 'Evil'. For evil was never to them a metaphysical principle in opposition to God. The keynote of the early Hebrew religion, as we have it presented to us in the Bible, was ethical monotheism, and evil as a principle in opposition to God was basically contrary to this type of belief. It would be possible to say then that evil in the strong sense remains largely unverbalized in the Hebrew Bible.

But this does not mean that the early Hebrews were not aware of evil as something mysterious, the cause of harm, something to be feared. They were. Indeed, there seems to be evidence in these early writings that they thought about this type of evil animistically. For they seem to have believed in the existence of spiritual beings, some of which were good, such as 'the sons of God' or the Cherubim and Seraphim, and others of which were evil. These latter may have been spoken of collectively as *ruach* or spirit, and later, with the development of ethical monotheism among them, these spirits came under the control of God.[1] However, spiritual beings, even evil spiritual beings, do not necessarily have to disappear with the development of monotheism. Islam manages to have the strictest form of montheism while at the same time incorporating beliefs in spiritual beings such as *jinn*, a relic of the animistic religions of pre-Islamic Arabia.[2] And inter-testamental Judaism

[1] For a discussion of this development see Jacob (1958: especially 68—72).

[2] For further discussion on animism in an Islamic context, see Parkin, p. 235 below.

believed in the existence of angels and demons, beliefs that were taken over and even developed significantly in early Christianity and similar to the beliefs of Christian Pentacostals in south India today (see chapter 7 below).

My reason for saying this is not to wander into a discussion about evil spirits and demons, but to show that, even though people may not systematically isolate a concept of evil, very often their discourse on it is that of spirits and demons. Nor is it necessary for ideas of evil spirits to disappear when an abstract notion of evil is introduced. For at the folk level it is easier to talk in terms of evil spirits than to theologize about it. The latter becomes the prerogative of the theologians, who may or may not be in touch with the people for whom they are theologizing.

Let me here turn to the gradual institutionalization of the early Hebrew religion. Traditionally this began with Moses, the prophet and lawgiver, and with his brother Aaron, the priest, both of whom instituted the worship of God (known as Yahweh) during the course of a number of events that culminated at the foot of Mount Sinai. The form that this institutional religion took was determined by their belief that God had entered into a Covenant with them. Covenant in this particular instance meant an agreement between a superior and an inferior, as between a stronger and a weaker state, in which the terms of the relationship between the one and the other are formalized. The Hebrews naturally saw themselves as the inferior party, but now in a Covenant relationship with God, their superior, between whom the terms of the relationship were made explicit in the Book of the Covenant. In itself, the relationship was a good thing because it meant that they were under the special protection of God (that is to say, God would eventually bless them). But at the same time the Covenant imposed a responsibility upon them in that they had to keep to the terms that had been drawn up (the statutes and commandments, which came to be known collectively as the Law). And this was a difficult thing to do, because the Law covered every area of life, social, moral, juridical and ritual.

Indeed, there were so many ways of breaking this relationship with God that the Hebrews had about thirty words in all to refer to this possibility. Three of the most important words that refer to this breach are *ḥṭ, psh'* and *'awon*.[3] They are important for my exposition about evil in Hebrew thought so I will say a little more about each.

The root word *ḥṭ* meant originally 'missing a mark', especially missing or falling short of a target. It could also mean 'missing' as when sheep are

---

[3] *ḥṭ, psh', 'awon* are the root forms of the words to which I shall be referring. For the sake of convenience I shall use the root forms throughout this chapter, and omit the noun and verb forms derived from them.

missing from a pen. It came to be associated with failure to carry out the part expected of one in any relationship with another. As the failure of an obligation it meant an offence. When the failure was in the relationship with God it was seen to be particularly offensive. The word more often than not was translated into English in the King James version as 'sin'. This is unfortunate, because the word 'sin' in English has become marked in a religious sense, and could not today properly be applied to the failure to carry out an obligation between an inferior and his superior. Thus, if we wish to understand *ḥṭ* or 'sin' in the early Hebrew sense, we have to understand it within the context of the Covenant relationship. This accounts for later Hebrew thinking that there was no sin before the Covenant. In other words, before the Covenant or Law there was no formal relationship between God and them; hence there could be no breach (*ḥṭ*) of a relationship that did not exist. Only after the Law was given could it be breached, and with it came 'sin' (*ḥṭ*).

But an important consequence arises out of the marking of the word 'sin' in the Judaeo-Christian sense of offence against God, in that it cannot now be used cross-culturally without qualification. Obeyesekere (1968) wanted to reverse the marking process that has taken place in English and to make the word mean simply the breaking of religious rules and norms. In this way he felt he could use it in connection with Theravada Buddhism. A similar plea is implicitly made by Overing in chapter 14 below, when she finds that Ricoeur's marked use of the word in *The Symbolism of Evil* prevents her from applying it without qualification to Piaora society.

The second most important Hebrew word to refer to this breach in the Covenant relationship was *psh'*. It meant the breaking of a relationship, whether international or social. Hence it meant rebellious behaviour, and was often trasnlated as 'transgression'.

The third most important word in this connection was *'awon*, which meant crooked, twisted or wrong. It was often translated as 'trespass', since trespassing has the connotation of twisting or wandering off a path on to forbidden ground. The same ideas are to be found in the English words crook and twister, both of which refer to a person who does wrong. Even the word 'wrong' is related to the word 'wring', as in the wringing (hence twisting) of clothes that need to be dried.

All three words refer to the disruption of order (Parkin 1982 and chapter 13 below): either the failure to act in an ordered, expected way, or the breaching of the public order by means of revolt, or twisting off the straight, ordered path. Parkin has suggested (chapter 13) that evil, when verbalized as 'sin', as the disruption of order, needs to be dealt with by means of confession. This is certainly the case with the ancient Hebrews, and I refer to two instances of this type of confession in the Hebrew Bible. In the older texts the sinner was identified by means of the casting of lots (known as Ummim and Thummim). Once identified, he was expected to make a public confession, which was preceded by the ritualist expression 'I have sinned' (*ḥṭ*). Often the sin was confirmed by public enquiry before it could be dealt with. Later the casting of lots was dispensed with, and the sinner went before the cultic functionary and confessed his sin there. The functionary would then accuse him of his sin in the name of God. The second instance is that of the day of Atonement. On that occasion the collective sins of Israel, referred to specifically by the three words *ḥṭ, psh'* and *'awon*, were confessed by the High Priest, who first of all had to confess his own sins. Confession, therefore, was part of the process of re-establishing the right, that is to say, the ordered, relationship between Israel and God.

Evil was also regarded as impurity, and in this sense was regarded as a contagious blemish that affected the state of the person. Once affected, a person became unclean, impure or defiled. The idea of impurity, or defilement, is a very ancient one and is found in a number of religions. To understand it, we have to relate it to the notion of the sacred. Just as sin can be understood only in terms of the covenant (the *breaking* of a right relationship in terms of the *making* of this right relationship), so impurity can be understood only in terms of purity. But the polarity between purity and impurity goes back to an inner ambivalence in the notion of the sacred itself.[4] For the Greek word for sacred or holy (*hagios*) means consecrated, pure, holy, as well as dangerously desecrated, impure and damned. And the Latin word *sacer* shows a similar ambivalence. In Brahmanic ritual, too, this ambivalence between purity and impurity can be discerned, as for instance when special ceremonies dissolve the sins of the sacrificer, preparing him for the sacred rite, while at the end of the ritual a similar ceremony takes place to return him to ordinary life. And in Judaism today anyone who reads the Torah must do so only after certain ritual actions, since the Torah is so holy that it 'defiles the hands'.

As Parkin has pointed out in chapter 13, impurity is generally dealt with not by confession, but by ritual. In the case of the early Hebrews, the ritual of purification was generally that of having a bath, where water was used ritually to wash the impurity away. This was the case with the High Priest on the Day of Atonement. Before the full rituals could begin, the High Priest had to have a bath in order to purify himself of his own impurities or uncleanness. As Hebrew thought about impurity developed, so impurity tended to be given moral connotations. Thus, murder, idolatry and adultery were considered to be not only defiling, but immoral. One can see how these could be regarded as

---

[4] For the ambivalent nature of the sacred, see Otto (1917).

both, since they carry with them the idea of contagious contamination as well as the breach of a relationship. Moral impurities came to be included in the repertoire of sins, and on the Day of Atonement the High Priest confessed the impurities of Israel. The dual origin of the ritual on that day is reflected in the fact that both sins and impurities were disposed of by the High Priest, both by confessing the sins of Israel (*ḥṭ, psh', 'awon*) and by *ritually transferring* the impurities of Israel by laying his hands on the head of the scapegoat, which was later led out into the wilderness.

These two dimensions of evil, recognized both as sin or the breaking of relationship and as impurity, might be compared with what Hobart in chapter 10 has called the nominalist and the essentialist interpretations of contexts. It would appear that the Hebrew nominalist interpretation is that of sin, where sin is an attribute arising out of the context of the covenant; whereas impurity is an essentialist interpretation, where impurity is regarded as the essence of the human situation, and to say that a man is impure or unclean corresponds with the truth about man as he is. As we have already seen, however, early Hebrew thought allowed its two interpretations to interpenetrate one another. Some impurities were regarded as sinful, while some sins were regarded as impure or defiling.

This interpenetration of evil as defilement and as sin raises a number of interesting points. Overing, in chapter 14, provides evidence for the co-existence of defilement and sin in Piaora society. But in doing so she comes up against Ricoeur's 'evolutionary scheme that moves progressively away from a symbolism of defilement to a symbolism of sin', posited in his *The Symbolism of Evil* (1969). I agree with her conclusion that 'Ricoeur has not presented us with . . . an evolutionary typology of evil, but he has rather distinguished for us various ways in which evil can be experienced, symbolized, and judged — many of which can be incorporated within one and the same system of ethics' (p. 275 below).

However, Ricoeur has touched upon an important point in suggesting that a distinction can be made between one system, in which man is 'burdened' with 'fault' or defilement, and another, in which man suffers guilt as the author of sinful deeds. The change, Ricoeur argues, is from 'communal sin' to experiencing 'individual guilt'. This seems to be the case in the ancient Hebrew tradition. As the Hebrew religion became more and more institutionalized, and more areas of life came under religious control, so the religious functionaries made people more aware of their offences against God. This heightened awareness seems to have been accompanied by an increasing interiorization of guilt. Guilt seems to have become individualized, and the individual rather than the communal group became increasingly responsible for his or her own sin.[5] 'Sin here is being used in its marked Judaeo-Christian sense. But this example must not be taken to endorse a universal evolutionary scheme of ethics. For there is no reason to deny that sin, in the unmarked sense of breaking religious rules, can be experienced in any society where such rules, legitimated by any particular mythology or cosmology, are broken. Therefore, although I reject Ricoeur's evolutionary typology, I do believe that the distinction to which he has drawn our attention is important.

The early Hebrews had no doubt where sin came from. It came from man; especially by man's breaking of the relationship with God. Thus, sin was determined and defined by the religious institution and especially by the functionaries associated with the institution. Once the relationship was broken and defined as sin, punishment seemed to be inevitable, because the justice of God demanded that this be so. One might say that the inevitability of punishment was not unlike the inevitability of the effects arising out of previous causes in previous lives, formulated as the doctrine of *karma* in Hinduism. But there is of course a difference in that *karma* is taken as a . necessary law, whereas punishment in the Hebrew sense arises out of the breach of a personal relationship. And because this was so, it was believed that the sinner could plead for mercy and so be forgiven.

But not all sins could be forgiven: the sins of murder, idolatry and adultery were regarded as unforgivable and so punishable by death. They were also sins that defiled the land, and confession could not restore the relationship. The fact that some but not all sins could be forgiven led the early Hebrew priests and functionaries to classify sins. We have already mentioned three that were classified as punishable with death; they were not the only ones. Some were regarded as committed wilfully, 'with a high hand'; some were sins of commission; some were sins of omission; and some were involuntary. With this classification went discussion about the different reasons for punishment. One of the principal early reasons for punishment was to expiate God, who had been offended. Another reason was retribution, to which was related the 'Lex talionis' (eye for an eye, tooth for a tooth), the idea behind which was exact justice. More often than not the punishment was meant to 'put away' the sin. Some sins could be 'borne away' by sacrifice, and some could be transferred, as in the case of the scapegoat. Thus, although each person was meant to 'bear' his own sin, he could get another to bear it for him, as in the case of the sacrifice where there is no doubt that the sacrificed animal was regarded as a substitute for the sinner. And when God forgave sins he was believed to 'bear' them, in the sense of bearing them away, and covering them up so as not to remember them.

[5] The interiorization and individualization of guilt is made explicit at Ezekiel 18. But Israel continued to raise questions about corporate guilt and salvation after the Exile, as in Daniel 12: 1—4.

Punishment of individuals was rarely regarded as an evil, since it was looked upon as being just. However, when punishment came upon Israel collectively it was often referred to as evil in the weak sense. Thus, God sent evils upon Israel in the sense of bad things, as punishment for Israel's breaking of the Covenant. The bad things that were sent by God to Job were also called evil, but again in the weak sense. All the same, these evils remained within the province of God and so within the context of ethical monotheism.

However, in spite of the preoccupation with evil as sin, the priestly tradition in Israel realized that there was more to evil than sin. It was possible to blame man or Israel for sinning, but the question whence evil had to be faced. Part of their answer can be found in the Adamic myth of Genesis 1—3. According to this myth, the source of sin is man; but that which is prior to sin, depicted as temptation in the form of a mythological serpent, is outside man. Another early answer can possibly be found in another myth in Genesis 6: 3, 5. The myth appears originally to have referred to the fall of angelic beings, which seems to account for the evil ways of men. But neither of these two myths is developed, and the origin of evil remains an area of thought that is largely undiscussed in the Hebrew Bible and so is shrouded in mystery.

The later rabbis tried to theorize about this mysterious realm and developed the notion of the evil inclination, or *yeẓer ha-ra.* It was believed to be 'the force in man which drives him to gratify his instincts and ambitions'.[6] It was called evil because it could easily lead a man to wrongdoing. Yet it was regarded as necessary to life in that it provided life with its driving power.[7] So man is necessarily inclined to evil, yet this inclination has been created by the good God. The rabbis overcome this paradox in their various ways; but all of them argue that the evil inclination must be overcome by the antidote of the Law which has also been given by God. Thus, evil is overcome by the determined efforts of keeping the commandments of God, that is to say, the Law.

EVIL IN THE EARLY CHRISTIAN TRADITION

In this section I shall concentrate upon the Christian writings of the New Testament. However, in order to understand these with reference to evil I will have to draw upon some of the later writings of the Hebrew Bible, especially with reference to its apocalyptic literature. My reason for including this in the early Christian tradition is that, although apocalyptic literature originated in the Hebrew Bible, it was taken over with a vengeance by some

[6] Jacobs (1972). For a similar attitude among the Piaora, see p. 271 below.
[7] For a discussion about the necessity of evil, see p. 229 below.

Christian writers and eventually did much to influence Christian thought and the figure of Satan.

Apocalyptic literature stems from those writers who lived after Israel had returned to the 'holy land' from exile in Babylon in about 520 BC. During the exile the Jews had been influenced by Persian dualism, and so they tended to view the world in terms of good and evil. Evil was thought to exist in the strong sense, as the term has been used in this volume. The conditions under which Israel was living were regarded as being so terrible that no solution to the suffering and the persecutions was thought possible — at least by man. Thus, the world was believed to be irredeemably evil, and under the control of evil forces. God could do nothing with the world but destroy it, and bring about a new creation. All Israel could do was to remain faithful to God throughout this period of tribulation, and so eventually come to experience a blessed new creation.

The best known apocalyptic writer of the Hebrew Bible is Daniel, but by later Christian apocalyptic standards his apocalypticism is mild. What is interesting in Daniel is his use of animal symbolism to depict the evil nations that are bringing the terrible sufferings on Israel. The use of animal imagery to depict those who despoil Israel was not new; the psalmists had already done so. But from Daniel's use of it in the apocalyptic genre, it was developed to become the 'dragon' and the 'beast' in later Christian writings. Indeed, the Beast is alive and well in many forms of sectarian Christianity today. In Daniel the beasts depicting the persecuting nations are deliberately contrasted with the 'son of man' representing Israel. The humanity of the good is contrasted with the bestiality of the evil. It is hardly necessary to point out that we meet this tendency today when people try to verbalize about evil in the strong sense (see chapter 3 below).

Daniel does not make use of the figure of Satan. This is not surprising, as Satan did not have the same importance in Hebrew thought as he did in early Christianity. In early Hebrew thought Satan was regarded as an obstructor. The word 'Satan' (derived from a Hebrew word meaning 'oppose') was not the name of a person, but the function that a person carried out. This functional use of the word continued to be applied in the juridical sense, especially when he was taken to be the one who accused a person of a crime. A similar functional use of the word Satan is found in the book of Job (written about 400 BC). The Satan, or the Accuser, is one of the sons of God whose duty it is to test a person's faithfulness to God. Hence God gives the Satan permission to test Job to find out whether Job's dutifulness to God is simply a sham or whether it is sincere. And in doing so the author of Job unmasks another problem: the suffering of the innocent. Only at a late stage of Hebrew thought, especially during the inter-testamental period (say, 350 BC—AD 50) did Satan become identified with evil as such. During this period he was given a host of 'evil' names, such as Belial, meaning worthless. In later Jewish thought, Satan is the one who disrupts the relations between man and God. But at the same time, man is believed to be able to choose freely for or against evil, and so he is not under the control of Satan. Thus, by his own merit man can silence the Accuser. In the end the figure of Satan becomes dispensable and Satan loses his importance in later Judaism.

But in the Christian evolution of the idea of Satan, matters take a different turn. Christianity took over the apocalyptic world view, which was basically dualistic. Thus Satan came to mean all that was opposed to God. He was Prince of this world, and all the kingdoms of the world were under his control. Called by different names, he was known in the New Testament as Beelzebub, Beliar, Belial, the Evil One (the term used for him in the Lord's Prayer). He was the leader of the demons, tempter of Jesus in the wilderness, the murderer, the liar. He was also 'the strong man' who bound people with sickness and misfortune; yet Jesus, 'the one stronger than he', had overcome him (Luke 11: 14—23).

This last point, namely the overcoming of 'the strong man' by 'the one stronger than he', gives us a clue to the nature of the opposition between Satan and God. Here I will confine myself to two points, the first of which has a number of secondary points. In the first place, it shows that the dualism that the early Christians embraced in the apocalyptic literature was not an absolute dualism. Rather, it was a secondary dualism, if one might call it that. The two opposing personalities were Satan and Jesus. There were a number of reasons for this, but perhaps the most significant one was the ambivalent position of Jesus. As the Messiah or Christ, he was both a heavenly and an earthly figure. From this and other beliefs the Christians later developed a doctrine of the divine and human natures of Christ. They were thus able to incorporate Christ into the Godhead and at the same time remain monotheists; on the other hand, they were able to accommodate a secondary dualism between Satan and Jesus without relinquishing their acceptance of the ethical monotheism of the Old Testament. Thus Satan's opposition to Jesus could be interpreted both as an absolute dualism of radical evil against God, and as a secondary dualism of all that was opposed to the Messiah (as agent of God) that would ultimately be overthrown by the almighty power of God. This ambivalence between absolute and secondary dualism is reflected in the Book of Revelations, where Satan is allowed to continue to do evil for a while. Eventually he will be defeated by the Messiah and God will rule in a new heaven and a new earth. Absolute dualism is finally rejected, and the power struggle is portrayed in terms of Satan and Christ, with Satan being eventually overthrown. The appeal of the conflict between Satan and Christ was strong in the folk presentation of Christianity, where it seemed to develop a life of its own. It continued through to the Middle Ages in the Miracle Plays, and eventually came to be immortalized in Milton's poem *Paradise Lost*. It highlighted evil in the strong sense, and in fact did much to mark the word 'evil' as being that which is radically opposed to God in the English language.[8]

The second point I wish to make concerns the notion of power found in the Synoptic Gospels. Jesus' exorcisms were regarded as a power struggle between Satan and himself, in which Jesus was regarded as being the very presence of the power of God. The Evil One was overpowered by the presence of God's power in Jesus. Thus, Jesus was able to drive out demons and heal people's sickness simply by the power of his word, just as the power of the word of God had brought the creation into existence. The crucifixion was regarded as the power of Satan exercised through men. This was completely reversed by the resurrection, which was regarded as the power of God to bring life out of death, and to overcome the sum total of human wickedness against the will of God. Caplan, in chapter 7, notes how the Pentecostal Indian Christians still resort to the concept of power in dealing with demons and evil spirits, believed in by the poorer strata of south Indian urban society.

This opposition between Christ and Satan verbalized at a popular level the radical nature of evil, putting in mythological form the basic contradiction that radical evil was felt to be. In other words, it mythologized the existential experience of radical evil. But of course, Christianity was never prepared to leave matters at the popular level. Christian theologians soon began to theorize about the origins of evil. Whereas the rabbis had sought the origin in the evil inclination, Christian theologians sought the origin in the doctrine of Original Sin, derived from a Christian interpretation of the Adamic myth in Genesis 1—3. The Christian interpretation places the blame for Adam's sin on Adam himself, thus exonerating God from any responsibility of evil. It was Adam's Original Sin that was transmitted from him to all mankind, so that every person is born with the 'taint' of Original Sin. But the Adamic myth seems to imply 'an evil before evil'; a sort of unverbalized evil. For Adam's sin

---

[8] Milton probably drew upon Guillaume de Salluste, Seigneur du Bartas's *La Semaine* (1578), for the main features of *Paradise Lost*. This had been translated into English by Joshua Sylvester as *Divine Weekes and Workes* (1605). The fall of Adam had also been dealt with by Grotius in his *Adamus Exul* (1605), with which Milton was probably familiar. Macfarlane (p. 70 below) refers to Milton's treatment of good and evil in the radical sense in his *Paradise Lost*. This is in contrast to the infrequent use of radical evil in contemporary records in a parish in Essex between 1380 and 1750 (p. 62 below). It would appear, then, that evil in the radical sense was not much used in the ordinary course of events, but became a feature of reflection on evil, either in theology or in folk mythology.

would appear to be not absolutely the first, a fact that seems to be symbolized by the role of the serpent. This paradox worried some theologians in the early Christian period, and was taken up, like so many others, by St Augustine. He argued that this evil before evil was nothing other than the necessary fallibility of a finite creature created with free will as Adam had been. Adam therefore had the possibility of sinning because he was fallible though free. But fallibility was itself not evil, so no blame could be placed on God.

Other theologians have questioned whether this answer really does dispel completely the idea of evil prior to the fall of Adam. They ask whether it would not have been possible for God to make man free and yet always choose the good. Augustine's reply to this sort of question was simply that God did not want to create man so. But here of course one runs out of argument and rests one's case upon the incomprehensibility of God. The truth is that one is eventually confronted with mystery at this point. What this brief excursion into Christian argument about evil proved is that the question of evil sooner or later runs out of rational argument. In other words, it cannot be properly verbalized, and eventually has to appeal to mystery.[9]

PROTESTANT AND CATHOLIC VIEWS OF EVIL

The later Christian tradition cannot be regarded as a single tradition, and has to be distinguished between Protestant and Catholic. In this section I wish to note the distinction between the two, with reference not to doctrines, but rather to world views and their approaches to sin. But even here I must qualify what I am about to say with a warning about generalizations. This applies particularly to the Protestant tradition, because it is itself very diverse, and breaks up into segments, such as denominations, and later into sects, some of which in the end can be regarded as being only on the periphery of Christianity.

During the Middle Ages the Catholic tradition built up a world view based largely on an amalgam of Platonic and Aristotelian ideas of the cosmos. One of the most significant features of this world view was the Great Chain of Being, which was principally a static view of the universe. Each and every being was regarded as placed as a link on a chain between the Supreme Being, God, and the most inferior beings in the realm of matter. The place on the chain of any particular being depended upon the type of being it was. Man himself was between the angels and the animals, because he was believed to be part spiritual and part physical. The whole was a structured lattice which

---

[9] For an appeal to the positive value of mystery with regard to evil, see Hick (1967).

lent itself to the notion of hierarchy, with 'a place for everything and everything in its place'. The Devil's place was that of a rogue angel who wandered between angels and men, enticing men and women to sin, and causing them to become witches and practice their craft (power) on his behalf upon the innocent.

Men were born to their place on the chain, in relation to other beings. Since all men were born with Original Sin, sin as an expression of evil was deemed to be necessary. It will be noted that I have distinguished between Original Sin and sins in the last sentence, and I shall now try to show what this distinction is. I am suggesting that, just as the Hebrews made a distinction between sins, as the breaching of a relationship, and impurities or defilement, so we must distinguish between Original Sin and sins committed by individuals.

Original Sin, I am suggesting, must be seen as analogous to impurity. It is true that the Original Sin is depicted as a break in the relationship between Adam and God, but as we have seen, there has been much debate about the source of this sin. Not only is it to be traced to the wilful decision of Adam, but it can also be traced to something that is mysteriously outside the control of Adam. Some have suggested that it is to be found in the way that Adam was created, namely in his free will. Whatever the cause, Original Sin seems to refer to some deficiency in the nature or 'essence' of the first man, which was transmitted, by contagion, to all his descendants. The contagion I refer to here comes from the teaching of Saint Augustine, who, in the fourth century, said that it was to be found in 'concupiscence' (or sexual desire) that accompanies the act of procreation. In this way every person born was tainted with Original Sin.

That the Church seemed to think that Original Sin was equivalent to an impurity was to be found in the ritual of baptism. Baptism was regarded as an antidote to Original Sin, and the rituals themselves seemed to indicate that they were dealing with an impurity. For in baptism water was (and, of course, still is) used to 'wash away' Original Sin and so 'regenerate' the person being baptized. It is primarily a purification ritual, at which one is not expected to confess one's sins. It is true that in some traditions the person is asked to renounce 'the world, the flesh and the devil', but this is not a confession. It is a relic of the ritual act of exorcism, in which the Devil was exorcised from the individual before baptism took place. In the main Catholic tradition this was accompanied by a ritual that included salt, for salt was believed to be particularly terrifying to the Devil. Thus, once the person has been baptized, he or she is asked to make a confession, which takes place separately, usually on another occasion. It would seem therefore that the Catholic tradition at least regards Original Sin as an impurity, and baptism as a purification ritual.

Actual sins committed by the individual, on the other hand, had to be confessed. Out of this arose the institutional machinery for confession which was accompanied by the Sacrament of Penance. Sins here are regarded as the breaking of a relationship which has to be restored. It is a twofold relationship between God and the sinner on the one hand, and the Church and the sinner on the other. The sinner today must first of all confess and recognize his guilt by being penitent. He is assured of the restored relationship by the Absolution given by the priest, who is acting in a mediating position on behalf of both God and the Church. If the break with God includes a breach of social relationship (e.g. theft), the penitent must also try to restore the relationship by an outward act toward the injured party. An act of penance must be made to God by some ritual, usually the recitation of prayers. The forgiveness of sins, however, does not remove the guilt attached to the offence. The guilt must be removed by some further act. Thus, when a murderer is forgiven the sin of murder, he still has to pay for the guilt of murder by some form of punishment. From this developed the doctrine of purgatory. Here the individual is purged of his guilt before going on to the blessedness of heaven in the company of the redeemed. Thus, the 'crookedness' in the individual must be straightened out by confession, penances and purgation before he can be admitted to the ordered harmony of heaven.

Confession is a prerequisite to the taking of the 'Body and Blood' of Christ at the Eucharist. Thus at one time the penitent would go to confession before taking Holy Communion at Mass. Today many Catholics regard the corporate confession made during the introductory part of the Mass as sufficient. This tendency is being resisted by the bishops. But what is interesting is the fact that confession is required before the Mass; this therefore associates the Mass with those rituals that deal with men's sins. And that is so, for the Mass was regarded as an antidote to the wiles of the Devil. Anyone who took the 'Body and Blood' of Christ at the Mass was believed to have protection from temptations that may be sent his way. But in the Catholic tradition the Mass is regarded as more than confession. It is primarily a ritual that deals with man's basic condition, dealt with in baptism but needing constant attention through the ritual reception of divine grace in the sacramental elements of the body and blood of Christ. Although not regarded as a purificatory ritual, its function is very similar to such rituals and is regarded as necessary for the progressive purity of the Christian life.

There are a number of features in the Catholic world view depicted here which are similar to some in the African world view of the Mijikenda as depicted by Parkin in chapter 13. Thus, the Catholic view could quite easily accommodate spiritual beings, including evil beings, the notion of the necessity of evil through the doctrine of Original Sin and the practice of confession, which it retains. To say all this, of course, is not to imply that Catholicism is animistic, but that Catholicism can absorb animism probably more effectively than Protestantism can.

The Protestant world view is much nearer that of Judaism and Islam. But of course it must be distinguished from both of these. As a result of the Reformation, Protestant ideas swept away the Great Chain of Being, and in doing so removed the need for saints, angels and even spiritual beings. The only realities were God and his created world, in which man had pride of place. God and man were related to each other not by a latticed network of spiritual beings, but by God's grace and man's faith.

Each world view has a distinctive approach to the necessity of evil. Catholicism tends to the ambivalent. Evil as Original Sin or impurity is necessary because every one is born with this stain. Only baptism can wash it away. Evil, on the other hand, as 'sin', or the breaking of the relationship with God, is not necessary, since one can always turn to the grace of God offered by the Church, in the Mass, and so live in a loving relationship with God. But if sins occur there is always confession and the Sacrament of Penance to restore the relationship with God and other Christians.

The Protestant approach tends to be suspicious of the doctrine of Original Sin. All men sin, not so much because of Original Sin, but because all creatures are imperfect and it is in their nature to sin. Thus, baptism is regarded not so much as a purificatory ritual that washes away Original Sin, but as a confessional ritual which confirms man's decision to renounce the Devil and commit himself to Christ as his saviour. Hence the Baptists insist upon adult baptism only, since it is only an adult who has the capacity to make the confession. Here confession is both the recognition of the person as sinner and the declaration of commitment to Christ. Baptism is recognition that God has justified him, that is to say put him in the right relationship with God in spite of the fact that he was a sinner.

Actual sins after baptism are dealt with differently in the various Protestant traditions. Generally there is little or no institutional machinery for confession. Sins have to be confessed individually between the sinner and God. The general lack of such machinery has led many Protestants to seek other means of confession; hence, perhaps, the proliferation of psychoanalysis, especially in the United States. In some Protestant sects the sinner cannot remain within the community, and is often expelled. For such sects the world is divided into two: the world of sinners outside the congregation, and the world of the non-sinners (saints) who remain inside. Inside the congregation sin is not only not necessary, it is not allowed. But these are extreme cases that arise logically out of the premises of Protestantism, if viewed in a certain way. Generally, Protestantism acknowledges the paradox that sin is necessary because of the human condition, but unnecessary if man remains strong in his faith in God.

The paradox of the necessity of sin indicates that there is an unresolved mystery about evil, which neither Catholicism nor Protestantism, nor indeed any religion, has resolved. No theodicy, however intellectually satisfying, is existentially so. Perhaps I can finish this paper by referring to this unverbalized dimension of evil as mystery, by telling a story recounted by the rabbis in the Talmud. The story goes like this:

In the world to come the Rabbis decided they would catch the evil inclination, the Yezer ha-ra, and kill it. This they did. When the righteous saw it, it appeared to them as a mountain. And when the wicked saw it, it appeared to them as a hair. And the righteous said: If the evil inclination was like a mountain, how did we manage to overcome it? And the Rabbis said: This indeed is a surprise to us. And they turned to God, and God said: Is it a small thing that it is a surprise to you? For it is a surprise to me as well![10]

Indeed, maybe the mystery of evil *is* a surprise, even to God!

REFERENCES

Hick, J. (1967). *Evil and the Love of God.* Oxford: Basil Blackwell

Jacob, E. (1958). *Theology of the Old Testament.* London: Hodder and Stoughton

Jacobs, Louis (1972). 'Sin'. In *Encyclopaedia Judaica.* Jerusalem: Keter Publishing House Ltd.

Obeyesekere, G. (1968). 'Theodicy, Sin and Salvation in a sociology of Buddhism'. In E. R. Leach (ed.) *Dialectic in Practical Religion.* London: Cambridge University Press

Otto, R. (1917). 'Das Heilige', trans. John W. Harvey as *The Idea of The Holy.* Oxford: Oxford University Press (1923)

Parkin, D. (1982). Straightening the Paths from Wilderness: Simultaneity and Sequencing in Divinatory Speech. In *Paideuma,* 28, 1982, pp. 71–83.

Ricoeur, P. (1969). *The Symbolism of Evil.* Boston: Beacon Paperback

[10] Babylonian Talmud, Sukkah 52a.

3

Unruly evil

David Pocock

Chapter 2 has traced the Hebrew etymology of words for evil and shown how the so-called Semitic religions, including Christianity, codified the concept. In Western, or, more precisely, English, society there is folk usage that derives in part from the Teutonic tradition.

According to the *Oxford English Dictionary* (*OED*), the word 'evil' in the adjectival sense is little used in modern colloquial English, 'such currency as it has being due to literary influence'; and 'in quite familiar speech' it is 'commonly superseded by *bad*'. The dictionary tells us that the substantive is 'somewhat more frequent, but chiefly in the widest sense, the more specific senses being expressed by other words, as *harm, injury, misfortune, disease*, etc'. In the positive sense of 'morally depraved', 'bad', 'wicked', the usage is said to be obsolete as applied to persons.

I shall have to return to contemporary usage, but for the present I want to explore and try to explain the older sense from which the modern word derives. The word 'evil', together with the German *übel* and the Dutch *euvel*, derives from the theoretical Teutonic type *ubiloz*. The *OED* comments on this etymology:

usually referred to the root *up, over*; on this view the primary sense would be either 'exceeding due measure' or 'overstepping proper limits'.

At first sight this primary sense seems to be discontinuous with the modern word. I want to argue that, when we look at the ethnography of those cultures that have sought to explain events that affect humans adversely by reference to human agencies, we can see a continuity between the primary and the present sense. The first part of this essay will be devoted to this examination; I shall return to the question of contemporary usage in the second part.

I

In human affairs things must go wrong. This is not just because the natural environment is not completely under our control, or because accidents of all sorts may happen; it is not even because human beings are mortal, conscious of the fact, and do not like it. More fundamental than any of these is the human disposition to create ideals which make all human experience appear to fall short to a trivial or to a great degree, remediably or irremediably. We do not have to accept Schopenhauer's view of the essential negativity of happiness if we grant that there is truth in the proposition that 'the wish itself is pain'; this, or something like it, is what G. J. Warnock, with apologies for its portentous tone, calls the 'human predicament' (1971: 15).

Human beings are conscious of their predicament, and they try, with more or less vigour according to the circumstances, to explain its effects by seeking reasons; even the most sophisticated fatalist finds, I suggest, meaning in his fatalism. The diagnosis of any situation is not, of course, its remedy; nevertheless, any diagnosis makes any situation more tolerable, or less intolerable.

The cultures with which I am concerned in this paper are those that have sought the causes of misfortune in human malice rather than in (or as well as) the punitive or malevolent power of spiritual beings or (again, and) non-human, non-spiritual nature. I make this selection because such cultures are closer to ourselves than others to the extent that they have a reaction to misfortune that is, at least in part, moral and includes 'a *particular kind* of appraisal, or "evaluation", of people and their possible or actual doings' (Warnock, 1971: 10). Whether we ourselves do or do not *use* the word 'evil', it must surely be agreed that it belongs in the 'language of morals'. It is therefore more sensible to look at cultures in which there appears to be some connection between morality and misfortune rather than at those that are more interested in theodicy. This is not to say that the latter enquiry would be irrelevant, but rather that it would be a tough job to explain its relevance to the majority in our society who do, or do not, use the word 'evil'.

Anthropologists will recognize immediately that in speaking of human malice as the cause of misfortune I am referring to those cultures in which beliefs about 'witchcraft' and/or 'sorcery' are institutionalized and salient. I shall, however, avoid, whenever the ethnography allows me to do so, using these terms. Instead, I shall use the rather clumsy phrase 'spiritual malpractice' because, apart from other considerations, what one ethnographer calls 'witchcraft' another calls 'sorcery'; this terminological confusion springs from a pervasive tendency to concentrate upon the *modus operandi* and then to oppose the two classes of maleficence.

I think it is more profitable to look at all the ·attributes of spiritual malpractice in given cultures, and when we do so we find a set of oppositions that maintains remarkable consistency as a set, despite variations between cultures. It becomes then not a matter of whether 'witches' do or do not use material objects to produce their effects, but rather of the systematic opposition of material to non-material means. Similarly, we find that consciousness of evil intent is opposed to unconsciousness, remediable effects are opposed to irremediable effects, and maleficence thought of as coming from within the culture is opposed to maleficence thought of as coming from outside. There is possibly also an opposition between those who may be accused and those who may not even be named.

Anyone who is familiar with the literature will recognize here a familiar shape and at the same time know that it is not possible to identify one group of features as clearly constituting anything that has been called witchcraft or sorcery. In particular cultures the elements are variously distributed: the significant fact is that they are opposed.

In addition to what informants say, there is one opposition regularly made by the ethnographers, and that is the opposition of explicable maleficence to the inexplicable. There appears generally to be one kind of malice that, however heinous in its effects, springs from motives that are well understood, and another that is gratuitous, what Hume called 'disinterested malice' (1975: 226—7).

Understandable malice is related to jealousy (the desire to preserve) and envy (the desire to possess); jealousy here is to be understood as not necessarily having the pejorative connotation that it tends to have in contemporary English.[1] These two motives are not wholly absent from any human society, and it is not surprising that they have given rise to institutionalized beliefs in so many. They work upon each other, and it is expected that jealousy will, not may, engender envy, and that the fear of envy makes everyone jealous of what they value. Among the peasants of Gujarat — indeed, more widely — people are consciously jealous of their food and will eat even the simplest meal behind closed doors; otherwise they would be compelled by the fear of envy to offer food to anyone who might see them eating. Equally, the traveller who encounters labourers eating in the fields must (if caste regulations do not

---

[1] The failure of distinguished ethnographers to observe this distinction in their discussions of spiritual malpractice makes anything more than a superficial analysis of their material impossible.

disallow) eat a little of the food that they will press upon him to assure them of his goodwill.

The fear of envy is not limited to material goods. It can be extended to a skill or some physical feature, such as handsomeness, and thus those who possess such things will be, with good reason, jealous.

If being properly jealous of one's own good engenders envy, then envy is well understood by those who fear or suffer its effects. Even a man who is not conscious of envious feelings in himself understands them in others. Indeed, it may well be the case that, where goods are scarce or competitively achieved, their enjoyment depends to some extent upon the expectation, if not the hope, that others will be envious.

The relation between jealousy and envy in cultures where misfortune is preferably explained by human malice explains how it comes about that some misfortunes — indeed, the greater part of them — are regarded as understandable, which is not to say that they are forgivable.

Associated with this understandable human malice is a belief that there are also human beings who are moved by disinterested malice. In the African literature there is a remarkable uniformity in their supposed characteristics, which a few examples will indicate. Among the Gusii of Kenya they are called *abarogi* and have 'an incorrigible, conscious tendency to kill or disable . . . by magical means'; they run naked at night and indulge in necrophagy. Among the Kaguru of Tanzania the *wakindi* join a delight in incest to cannibalism and to dancing naked at night. Among the Gisu of Uganda the *balosi* walk naked at night without lights and meet to eat the corpses of those that they have killed, using human arms to stir their beer;[2]

> most Gisu, when asked to define a witch, will say that a witch is a man who sleeps with his daughter-in-law, which is the most heinous of all sexual transgressions. . . . For Gisu it is the epitome of evil and arouses feelings of horror and repugnance.
> Middleton and Winter 1963: 197

Various authors have made the point that such creatures are represented as the antithesis of normal human behaviour, but none have addressed themselves to the significance of this as directly as E. H. Winter (1963) in his study of the Amba of western Uganda, where he tries to explain why the Amba torture themselves with anxiety about these imaginary monsters.

Winter lists the seven characteristics of Amba witches and contrasts them with normal behaviour. Three of these call for no immediate comment: witches stand on their heads or rest hanging upside down; they quench their

---

[2] These references are from Middleton and Winter (1963: 225, 62).

thirst with salt; they transform themselves into leopards and eat people. They are also said to be active at night, which the Amba are not; they go naked, which the Amba regard as shameless; they invariably attack members of their own villages, which violates the norms that should govern the behaviour of villagers towards each other; finally, witches of different villages are said to be bound by reciprocity and obliged to invite each other to their cannibal feasts. This goes against the tradition that the relations between villages are those of potential enmity and the morality of the village is not extended to outsiders. Winter concludes:

> witches, then, are not only inverted physically but morally as well. They are much more than agents of misfortune; they are incarnations of evil. *Their death-dealing powers are merely the means by which their wickedness is expressed.*
>
> Winter, 1963: 293—4; my emphasis.

However, I want to go beyond Winter when he says that 'evil is a term which has meaning only within a world of morality'. I shall argue that, although the word 'evil' obviously has meaning in the language of morality, it has also distinctive ontological weight. But before doing so we may look at one way in which the belief in these monsters can be said to have a moral function.

Winter's account of Amba conceptions of village morality is idealized:

> The inter-village world is an amoral arena where people seek their own goals irrespective of the harm which may be done to others.
>
> The world of the village is different. Within it people should not use one another as means in the pursuit of their own personal goals. Their attitudes towards one another should be those of brotherly love and each should rejoice at the good fortune of his neighbour. Each man should aid and protect his fellow, even at the expense of his own welfare. . . . The village . . . is a moral universe and . . . the largest one to be found among the Amba.
>
> Winter, 1963: 293—4.

Such an ideal of how people should behave to each other could be replicated the world over, and one does not need to be cynical to suppose that the Amba villager is any less possessive or less desirous — less human, in short — than his counterpart in New Guinea or Gujarat. It is the belief in human monsters that makes such shortcomings tolerable; the Amba villager can accept that he is less than perfect because he knows that he is not, and cannot be, one of the inhuman monsters in which he believes.

Similarly, T. O. Beidelman tells us that the Kaguru believe that *wakindi* 'enjoy the things they do' and cannot renounce their incest and cannibalism;

they are 'bad until they die'. It becomes possible then for the Kaguru to imply sometimes 'that they are witches in order to make others fear and obey them' and even to 'publicly confess minor witchcraft' so long as they deny that they are *wakindi* (1963: 62).

Among the Azande the apparent ease and regularity with which accusations of witchcraft are made and purged by the accused would scarcely be possible if the accused were not confident that, whatever ill he may be unconsciously capable of causing, he is not a witch as this is normally understood by the Azande. Writing of the accused man's predicament, Evans-Pritchard says:

So far as he knows he has never visited the home of the sick man whom he is said to have injured. . . . Indeed, a man must feel that if it is true that he is a witch he is certainly not an ordinary witch, for witches recognise each other and co-operate in their undertakings, whereas no one has a secret understanding with him nor seeks his aid.

Evans-Pritchard, 1937: 120

In our own society it is well known, and prison authorities have to take account of it, that 'nonces' (child molesters), and sometimes rapists, are categorized as *'really* evil' by other convicts; the monstrosity of such crimes mitigates, by humanizing, the offences even of those who are thought to be evil by the public outside.

However, the ethnographic evidence on the ways that human beings have represented the very worst of all badness suggests that the symbolic inversion does more than define and in various ways validate the moral order. I suggest that it symbolizes the inversion of the ideal of order itself. The idea is not new:

A creature, absolutely malicious and spiteful, were there any such in nature, must be worse than indifferent to the images of vice and virtue. All his sentiments must be inverted, and directly opposite to those which prevail in the human species. Whatever contributes to the good of mankind, as it crosses the constant bent of his wishes and desires, must produce uneasiness and disapprobation; and on the contrary, whatever is the source of disorder and misery in society, must for the same reason, be regarded with pleasure and complacency. . . . Absolute, unprovoked, disinterested malice has never perhaps place in any human breast; or if it had, must there pervert all the sentiments of morals, as well as the feelings of humanity.

Hume 1975: 226—7

If we look again at E. H. Winter's list of the characteristics of Amba witches, we can see that it illustrates this point. There is nothing morally wrong by

Amba standards about resting upside down or quenching one's thirst with salt; taken out of their context, such notions are merely laughably absurd. However, in the context in which they are found they symbolize what human beings *are* not, and not only what humans *should* not do. The complex of the representation of disinterested malice expresses a paradox: a belief in creatures who are and are not human beings, at once within and beyond the limits of humanity. We may rephrase Winter's comment on the 'incarnations of evil' among the Amba and say that they are not monsters because they enjoy disinterested malice but that they enjoy disinterested malice because they are monsters.

This idea that there can be a wrongness that embraces and goes beyond moral considerations finds an echo in the traditional Christian distinction between mortal (deathly) and venial (forgivable) sin. H. Davis, SJ, quotes from St Thomas Aquinas:

The difference between venial and mortal sin is consequent on the diversity of that inordinateness which constitutes the essence of sin. For inordinateness is twofold; one that destroys the principle of order, and another that, without destroying the principle of order, implies inordinateness in the things which follow the principle.

Davis 1935: 210

To which we may add, by way of clarification, the author's comment:

Mortal sin and venial sin are not species of one genus. Mortal sin is sin strictly so-called: venial sin is sin by analogy.

Davis 1935: 204

In traditional Christianity the persistent mortal sinner is a human monster not because of the effects of his bad acts, but because he appears to enjoy a perverse will contrary to the divine order, which among other things defines the end for which he is created.

The modern, secular, sense of the world 'evil' refers almost exclusively to physical suffering. In the world of St Thomas, however, 'fault has more of the notion of evil than pain has', because fault is the product of a disordered will opposed to the fulfilment of the divine will. Moral and physical evil, unlike metaphysical evil, categorize the effects of this disordered will, the first being the voluntary deviations from the moral order and resultant actions, the second being social and natural defects in the human condition resulting from the original voluntary fault.[3]

---

[3] *Summa Theologica*, 1, Q 48, Art 6. See also, on *kinds of evil*, *The Catholic Encyclopedia*, New York, 1909, vol. V: 649. Metaphysical evil is described as 'the limitation by one

Humanity is not only governed by rules but recognizes itself as living in a rule-governed world, and it is my case that the peculiar strength that the word 'evil' retains in contemporary usage, when it is applied to human actions, derives from the judgement that such actions are unruly and therefore inexplicable: paradoxically, not human.

Anthropologists sometimes give the impression — sometimes, indeed, to themselves — that they have discovered the notion of order, whereas what they have done at best is to satisfy the demand in their own minds that all human behaviour, however exotic and even apparently irrational, makes sense. It is interesting in the light of this discussion to note that, just as cartographers progressively eliminated the monsters that inhabited the seas surrounding the ancient known world, so the precursors of modern anthropology moved from the physical monsters of Mandeville to the intellectual monsters of the enlightenment — the savages. Margaret T. Hodgen (1964) has documented this movement up to the seventeenth century, and Michèle Duchet (1971) has, magnificently, analysed the debates provoked in the eighteenth century by the opposition of civilized to savage man. Aptly, she quotes from Lévi-Strauss's *Tristes Tropiques* in her discussion of Rousseau to indicate that the conflict between one conception of order and another is endemic in the enterprise of anthropology:

je revivais donc l'expérience des anciens voyageurs, et à travers elle, ce moment crucial de la pensée moderne où, grâce aux grandes découvertes, une humanité qui se croyait complète et parachevée, reçut tout à coup, comme une contre-révélation, l'annonce qu'elle n'était pas seule, qu'elle formait une pièce d'un plus vaste ensemble, et que, pour se connaître, elle devait d'abord contempler sa méconnaissable image en ce miroir. . . .

Duchet 1971: 290

It is not as easy to generalize about contemporary usage in our own society as it is to generalize about the beliefs and practices of some remote culture which may indeed display the homogeneity so often represented. I have relied on two sources: the literary, and casual conversations with all sorts of people since I was first asked to address myself to the topic of evil.

---

another of the various component part of the natural world. Through this natural limitation natural objects are . . . prevented from attaining to their full or ideal perfection . . . the order [of nature] depends on a system of perpetual decay and renewal due to the interaction of its constituent parts . . . metaphysical evil does not . . . necessarily connote suffering. If animal suffering is excluded, no pain of any kind is caused by the inevitable limitations of nature; and they can only be called evil by analogy, and in a sense quite different from that in which the term is applied to human experience.' See also *Summa*, 1, Q 49, Art 2, and n. 5 below.

Apart from the anthropological works that I have already mentioned, my main reading has been works of theology and books by philosophers who have written on ethics. For the theologians the word 'evil' is clearly not obsolete, and I can add here that it was not obsolete for those of my 'informants' who were Christians. (The opportunity to discuss the matter with people of other religions did not present itself and, anyhow, I do not claim to have made a systematic survey.) Among philosophers, on the other hand, it does seem that the word 'evil' is obsolescent, occurring most often in the phrase 'good and evil', where it is not distinguishable from 'bad'. I have not come across any secular philosopher for whom the word 'evil' has distinguishing force.

In conversation, however, I find that there are differences between what I shall call minority and majority views. In the minority view there was a reluctance to use the word 'evil' of people, not because the word was obsolete, as, for example, 'miscreance' is, but rather, it seemed, because the word was too strong. In this minority view, invariably, the judgement 'evil' had to be held back because the actions that might be so judged could, or might, be explained. This attitude does, in its extreme form, come close to viewing the term 'evil' as obsolescent when the faith in the human capacity to explain is absolute. Thus, one 'informant' was confident that 'science is making such strides that, I guess, in years to come we'll just know so much about motivation, we shan't need to use the word'. The more general tendency was to hold the word in abeyance. A rather remarkable instance of this emerged in a discussion of a sexual assault by three men upon a boy of six which occurred in the summer of 1983. The response to the question, 'Would you not say that these men were evil?' was 'We don't know all the circumstances.' The implication here was not that the word 'evil' had lost its force, but that it was, on the contrary, so strong that it might be used only 'when all the circumstances were known'.

For the majority of the people that I spoke to, the word 'evil' is freely available both given the stimulus of a particular instance, such as the one that I have mentioned, and more generally: a variety of acts and classes of people were described as 'evil' with a vigour and emotion that made it clear that the substitution of the word 'bad' would have been wholly inadequate.

There are some things to be said immediately about these two views of evil. First, we note a difference in the relation between actor and act. For the minority, the doubts about the motives and mental condition of the actor make it impossible to categorize the act. In the majority view it is the act itself that defines the actor as evil. The second contrast is related to the first: it is the marked difference in attitude to explicability. The minority regard explicability as something to be sought, whereas for the majority, the actor having been defined as evil, any attempt to explain motives was regarded at best as misguided and at worst as participating in the very evil that, by explaining, it appeared to extenuate. Finally, it is clear that the word 'evil' has, for the majority, a totalizing force that, we can properly say, makes 'evil people' monsters in the sense that they are denied all admirable human attributes such as love or loyalty. The reaction to the evidence that such people are in all other particulars human beings like themselves is either the angry 'I don't want to know', or a heightened sense of their monstrosity. The minority require no such evidence, of course, and look rather to psychology or sociology to 'save the appearances' of humanity. But, and I return to an earlier point, in having recourse to such theories, the minority implicitly admit that the behaviour in question is not explicable by reference to 'normal' motives such as greed or lust.

Fundamental to these differences is a difference in the conception of the human, and before I examine this it may be necessary, for the benefit of readers who are not anthropologists, to explain what I mean. In speaking of definitions of the human, I am not calling in question the now probably universal recognition that humans constitute a distinct species. What I am referring to is the difference between and within cultures in the moral evaluation of this recognition. The Nuer of the southern Sudan clearly recognize the neighbouring Dinka as human beings, in that they intermarry with them and accept that many of their own lineages are of Dinka origin. This does not prevent them from refusing to accept that the Dinka are as fully human as themselves, although they concede that they are more human than more remote peoples. The Dinka, for their part, accept the Nuer within their own definition of humanity but exclude others. Although this difference between the two cultures remains a mystery for anthropologists, it exemplifies the way in which human socieites maintain cultural definitions of humanity that significantly modify, without denying, the recognition of the biological fact. The contrast between the Nuer and the Dinka is striking. In the Indian caste system the gradation of humanity is less dramatic but still clear. It is not unlike a view commonly held in nineteenth-century western society that human beings, while remaining human, can be graded on a scale of moral excellence such that some achieve a condition of refined humanity in relation to which the less advanced are not sub-human but, as it were, members of an inferior genus.

This kind of thinking is not so alien to our own as we might wish to suppose. Blatantly, in what we call racialism the paradox is apparent, because there the inferiority is located in the physical appearance of beings who are simultaneously recognized as human and denied full humanity. More general and subtle is the way in which, playing with a complex of similarities and differences, we create gradations of humanity distinguished by our own sense of ease and registered in degrees of sympathy: we deny humanity to no member of the species but behave as though some are more human than others.

When I say that I suspect that there is a difference in the conception of humanity held by those who do not hesitate to use the word 'evil', even if they do so only rarely, and those who are reluctant to use it, I should be more precise. I should say that for both it is a difference that operates only in the context in which they do or do not use the word 'evil'. Obviously, people who have recourse to psychological theory to explain events that are not explicable by common sense do not consistently feel the need to explain all events in this way; similarly, those who feel outraged by a psychological account of behaviour that they regard as evil are not necessarily resistant to a clinical diagnosis of, for example, their own irritability or their children's delinquencies. In what follows, this clarification of my intent should be kept in mind.

I suggest that, when my majority use the word 'evil' of people and use it with the force that I have described, their conception of the human is circumstantial, and is derived from their own knowledge and experience of themselves essentially, and of others whom they regard as like themselves. Hence the recurrence in conversation of such phrases as 'I have done a lot of bad things in my life', 'I have known some hard cases', or 'I can imagine myself doing most things' *but* 'I cannot imagine how anyone could do a thing like that'. Hence also the terms favoured by the popular press which do echo those that people actually use: 'beast', 'wild animal', 'savage'.[4] Parenthetically, I note that the often repeated 'hanging's too good for them', which obviously expresses the view that this form of capital punishment is only for human beings, also reveals the sense of paradox that I mentioned earlier: the evil act itself is beyond the comprehension of human justice and invites unspecified, inhuman penalites.

In the minority view the conception of humanity is not, and cannot be, circumstantial — the fact that there is something there to be explained precludes the possibility. The conception of humanity here lacks experienced social content; it is a theoretical humanity: more precisely, man as a construct of psychological science; more diffusely, man as he might in the future construct himself. This view seems to have interesting implications in that it should, but does not, affect the less dramatic moral judgements that those

[4] An example presents itself at the time of writing. The *Sunday Telegraph* for 11 December 1983 quotes a remark made in the *Spectator* three years ago by the Prime Minister's policy adviser, Mr Ferdinand Mount: 'Football hooligans are regarded as subhuman in the exact sense of the word: they are held to have forfeited the civil rights generally allotted to members of the human race.'

who hold this view make. I have suggested that the word 'evil' has ontic weight additional to its weight in the language of morality; but it does operate in that language to define the outer limits of the bad. Consequently, I do not see why the judgements 'bad' and 'good' are not to be withheld with the same delicacy and caution that, in the minority view, the judgement 'evil' is withheld. More forthrightly, I suggest that the scientific doubt appropriate to the observation of natural phenomena cannot be brought to bear upon one term of the moral complex without calling into question the whole. And were this to be done, something like the view of morality that G. J. Warnock has characterized as Thrasymachean would emerge:

What I call the Thrasymachean line would be more radical than [the Marxist]: it would be the contention that all moral concepts are intrinsically hollow — that what, for example, is officially regarded as 'just' is not merely a distortion of what in some sense is really just, but is a mere mask concealing a wholly amoral reality.

Warnock 1971: 155−6

Warnock goes on to suggest what, according to this view, might be held to be actually going on, and interestingly (I think unwittingly), he describes a position that will be familiar to social anthropologists:

Nothing really *is* 'morally' right or wrong; in reality there are only personal interests, more or less clearsightedly, tenaciously, and successfully pursued.

Warnock 1975: 155−6

But Professor Warnock, although no Thrasymachean, has a disposition to separate himself from the circumstantial world of my majority, and when he takes issue with anthropology he appears to share with my minority a conception of a theoretical humanity. It is worthwhile looking at the case he presents, first, because it is a rational expansion of a view that would otherwise be here represented by isolated comments and, second, because, as for many of our contemporaries, suffering, and indifference to suffering, is his evil, although he does not use the word.

'What', he asks, 'is the condition of moral *relevance?* What is the condition of having a claim to be *considered,* by rational agents to whom moral principles apply?' In answering the question it is important, and in his opinion easy, to dismiss 'closed' or 'tribal' moralities:

There have existed from time to time, and doubtless do exist, many curious instance of codes — often spoken of by anthropologists and others as moral codes — taken by their devotees to be of more or less sharply restricted applicability. . . . Thus there have been persons for whom, while it would be thought a very terrible thing deliberately to injure a fellow-tribesman, there was felt to be no objection at all to robbing with violence the occasional foreigner, and perhaps even great merit in killing him for the sake of his scalp; there have been white men who, loyal and considerate . . . to other white men, have seemed to recognise no such claim to consideration of other persons who happen not to be white.

Warnock 1971

Warnock will allow the term 'moral code' as one of convenience, but he continues:

such a code, while indeed it can be called *a* morality, is not morality — to see things so is not to see them from the moral point of view, and such notions, while wholly understandable, are not moral notions.

Warnock 1971: 148—9

Warnock justifies his position first analytically, on the grounds that the 'specialness' of the concept of morality precludes the possibility that any human being can be excluded from moral consideration. Second, he justifies it by considering what morality is for, and what it is for is to countervail the tendency of things to go badly in all sorts of ways, and to mitigate the harm that results from the indifference or hostility 'of persons to other persons'. Third, he argues that morality may not be restricted because the 'beneficiaries' or 'patients' of morality are defined by their capacity to suffer, and this raises the question, 'How far down the scale, so to speak, of the brute creation should moral relevance be taken to extend?' Warnock continues:

There is perhaps reason to say . . . that it extends just as far as does the capacity to suffer — though in practice we seem to be conscious of moral claims in non-humans in some sort of proportion, partly to the degree of their actual involvement (as with domestic animals and pets) in human communities, and partly perhaps to the degree to which they are, crudely, 'like us' — mammals in this way outranking birds and fishes, snakes and insects scarcely counting at all. But no doubt natural feelings on such points are often largely irrational; and certainly they seem to differ widely from one person to another. We need not, I think, fortunately, here try to adjudicate.

Warnock 1971: 151—2

Anthropologists nowadays are familiar with the kind of use to which philosophers put their material and the extreme cases of the unlovely practices of the headhunter, and the callousness of some colonial white men must not be allowed to distract us from the fact that all human beings live by such limited codes. And they are limited not by 'the limitation of human sympathies' but by the nature of human cultures, which variously define the human, and within the human the more and the less so, not only outside but inside the boundaries of the 'tribe'. No doubt these classifications and their implications for human action are complex, but they are not essentially different from the kind of thing that Warnock is dismissing. Even the headhunter is not indifferent to the fact that the person he has killed is a human being and not an animal, and the white man's lack of consideration for non-whites suggests nothing to the advantage of his white servants at home.

Moreover, Professor Warnock is himself, and I suggest inescapably, advocating a moral code, albeit an admirable one. In the closing pages of his book he pleads not for active sympathy but for non-indifference to suffering, and this is a plea for a definition of humanity that does not at present prevail. This definition rests upon a classification, as witness the unfortunate status of snakes and insects in his account.

The classification is somewhat concealed by the emphasis upon suffering, but this emphasis is eroded when we reflect that the irrational and differing 'natural feelings' of which he speaks are not limited to ascribing relative positions to birds and fishes, insects and snakes, but extend to the classification and ranking of human beings also. It is the conception of what is and is not human, and of the relations that exist within and between these two classes — in short, the conception of order — that precedes the very perception of suffering and the consequent judgements that it is unfortunate, a pity, or bad, or evil.[5]

I want, finally, to look at the emotional force of the word 'evil'. First of all, it seems that it has acquired added strength in relatively recent times, and this, rather than obsolescence, accounts for the fact that it is not commonly used. It may be that in our own culture in the past, and in others still existing, where a conception of cosmic order and, within that, moral order, was more secure, the judgement 'evil' could be more cooly made when its exercise depended upon a moral consensus. It may be that, in a society like our own, in which individuals devise, all unconsciously for the most part, their own conceptions of humanity, acts that violate this conception are repulsive not so much because they offend an agreed sense of order, but because they appear to

---

[5] Speculation about the moral significance of animal suffering is not new. *The Catholic Encyclopedia* refers to the view, held by some, that animal suffering was due to the fall of man. This notion is reflected in many paintings of the Garden of Eden, where predators recline in harmony with their prey, a representation that seems to derive from Isaiah 11: 6. Aquinas' view is somewhat different: he distinguishes the suffering that animals inflict on each other in accord with their proper nature and the suffering caused to animals by the needs of man's nature (*Summa*, 1, Q 96, Art 1, Reply Obj 2, and Reply Obj 3). On the later effects of the belief that man became carnivorous after the Fall, see Thomas (1983: 17–18, 287–300).

violate the boundaries of the self which is now thought to be the sole guardian of its own integrity.

In conclusion, I have suggested that, were the holders of the minority view of the word 'evil' to be rational, they might have difficulty in sustaining their right to make any moral judgement. The holder of the majority view, if it is one, is in a different state: to the extent that evil occurs beyond the bounds of his conception of the human, he may be prone to the vehemence of the self-righteous. I am very struck by the fact that in primitive societies evil is attributed ultimately to monsters that cannot exist, whereas in our society it is attributed to monsters that do.

A POSTSCRIPT

While this article was in proof a letter was received at the Mass-Observation Archive at the University of Sussex from one of its correspondents who is at present serving a prison sentence. He writes: 'people like looking down, you see, because it stops them looking inward . . . As a matter of interest . . . the term nonce is little used now apart from those in my age group and above, "beast" seems to be in vogue now.'

REFERENCES

Beidelman, T. O. (1963). 'Witchcraft in Ukaguru'. In Middleton and Winter (eds), *Witchcraft and Sorcery in East Africa*

Davis, Henry, SJ (1935). *Moral and Pastoral Theology*, vol. 1, London: Sheed and Ward

Duchet, Michèle (1971). *Anthropologie et Histoire au Siècle des Lumières*. Paris: François Maspero

Evans-Pritchard, E. E. (1937). *Witchcraft, Oracles and Magic among the Azande*. Oxford: Clarendon Press

Hodgen, Margaret T. (1964). *Early Anthropology in the Sixteenth and Seventeenth Centuries*. Philadelphia: University of Pennsylvania Press

Hume, David (1975). *An Enquiry Concerning the Principles of Morals* (3rd edn), P. H. Nidditch (ed.). Oxford: Clarendon Press

Middleton, J. and E. H. Winter (eds) (1963). *Witchcraft and Sorcery in East Africa*. London: Routledge & Kegan Paul

Thomas, Keith (1983). *Man and the Natural World*. London: Allen Lane

Warnock, G. J. (1971). *The Object of Morality*. London:

Winter, E. H. (1963). 'The Enemy Within: Amba Witchcraft and Sociological Theory'. In Middleton and Winter (eds), *Witchcraft and Sorcery in East Africa*

4

The root of all evil

Alan Macfarlane

As Pocock shows in chapter 3, the word 'evil' is of Teutonic origin. The *Oxford English Dictionary,* and also some other contributors to this volume, distinguish between a strong and a weak meaning. In the strong meaning, 'evil' is used to mean the antithesis of good in all its principal senses; morally depraved, bad, wicked, vicious. This strong sense of evil, the *OED* tells us, is 'little used in modern English'; when applied to persons it is 'obsolete'. Contrary to Pocock, I accept this view. The word is nowadays used only in the weak version, meaning to cause discomfort and/or pain, to be unpleasant, offensive and disagreeable, to be 'not good'. It is interchangeable with 'bad', 'unpleasant', 'harmful'. I shall be concerned here with the strong sense of 'evil': how, when and why did it become obsolete? The disappearance of evil as a concept is one of the most extraordinary features of modern society. That it is no longer generally possible to conceive of an abstract force of evil is clearly of great interest to historians and anthropologists.

The essence of evil lies in a combination of several features. First, it is shadowy, mysterious, covert, hidden, not fully understood; hence the association with night, darkness, black, secrecy. Second, it is an aggressive or, as the *OED* put it, a positive force. Evil tries to destroy the integrity, the happiness and the welfare of 'normal' society. It is aggressively, if insidiously, undermining, the worm in the bud. Witches would not be evil if they merely met and danced naked, but they also attack society, causing illness and death. These attacks are not justified; either they are motiveless, or the motives are perverted. God or the ancestors are not evil when they afflict man, for their ends are good: to improve the afflicted. They correct mankind as a loving father corrects a child. Yet when havoc falls out of a clear sky and strikes down an indiviudal or a society, there evil is at work.[1]

[1] I am grateful to Professor David Parkin and other members of the 'Evil' seminar for their comments on drafts of this paper. Among these was the suggestion that we still use 'evil' in

When misfortunes occur they tend to be explained by a set of factors. The causes are placed on a continuum, from an extreme of very human, personal, causes through rather abstract, half-human ones to the mechanical and inhuman. Among these are the following: ancestors, witches, fairies or other small spirits, God or the Devil, the stars, 'science', fate and chance. Usually a society will have available a set of two or three of these explanations. The choice of a particular explanation will reflect an individual's location in relation to the unfortunate event, for example whether there was thought to have been some earlier wrongdoing. One of the most puzzling problems for anthropologists has for long been why different societies should have opted for different sets of explanation and also why such sets should change. This essay is a brief attempt to suggest a few of the background factors that lie behind the choice of explanatory frameworks.

The nature of a world in which real evil is all around can be partially diagnosed. First, there is the secrecy. Things are not what they seem: the smiling face conceals hatred, the friendly gesture leads to downfall. The same person is both a neighbour and possibly a member of a secret, subversive, organization. This is a world of limited good, envy, the Evil Eye. Although the forms will differ with the religious system, if we survey all human societies, it does seem roughly to be the case that the strong concept of immanent evil flourishes in the middle range of human societies. Often the concept is weakly developed or absent in hunter—gatherer societies. In many tribal societies, in so far as there is evil, it is usually members of other distant groups who are evil, or abstract, non-human, spirits. It is in the densely settled agrarian societies that anthropologists have had to label as 'peasant' — China, India, parts of South America and Catholic Europe — that evil has developed as a massive moral and practical problem. Each of these civilizations has an intricate theodicy in which evil is given a formal place in the system of explanation, with the curious exception, perhaps, of certain forms of Buddhism (see chapter 8 below). Though the location and attributes of evil are infinitely varied, evil and the concept of evil are of central importance.

It could thus be argued that the moral economy of the peasant society has, as one aspect, the economy of evil. A great amount of energy is spent in trying to hold back and defeat evil through the use of that 'magic' that is built into

---

the strong sense, for instance to describe the Nazi holocaust, mass torture, sadistic crimes. This is perfectly true. Yet I would maintain that the *Oxford English Dictionary* is correct in saying that the word when applied to persons is 'obsolete'. The precise combination of horror, terror and condemnation that combines beliefs about supernatural as well as natural threats is almost, if not totally, extinguished at present in much of Western Europe and North America.

practical religion in Catholic, Hindu, Muslim and Confucian societies. Life and happiness are thought to be constantly threatened, by women, by death, by secret evil, by diffuse and invisible powers. There is a never-ending war, both within the indivdiaul and against external dark forces. An archetypical example of such a world can be seen in much of continental Europe between the fifteenth and eighteenth centuries. In the *Malleus Maleficarum*, or 'Hammer of Evil', written by Sprenger and Kramer and published in 1486, we are provided with a compendium of possible evil and a directory of how, through torture, interrogation and trickery, evil was to be eliminated. Throughout Catholic Europe the Holy Office of the Inquisition, in alliance with the state, set up an elaborate machine for seeking out and destroying secret evil. In that 'everlasting bonfire' (Maitland and Pollock 1952: ii, 659), thousands were burnt to death for their supposed evil works and many thousands of others were imprisoned and tortured.[2] The world later satirized by Goya, that world of constant threat and evil whose roots Norman Cohn (1975) has unmasked in *Europe's Inner Demons,* is one that is now becoming fully documented. There was believed to be a vast conspiracy of Evil abroad: relapsed Jews, gypsies, freemasons, witches, Lutherans — all were sought out as agents of Evil. Evil was then purged from them by fire and the rack. The Devil was alive and well and hovered over much of Europe. It is clear that, from rural peasant to Dominican inquisitor, few doubted the daily reality of Evil, the Evil One and evil beings. There was a Holy War for four centuries.[3]

Contrast this with the world of industrial, capitalist society in the later

---

[2] An early estimate by a Secretary of the Spanish Inquisition (Llorente 1827: 583) put the numbers punished by the Spanish Inquisition as follows: 'Number of persons who were condemned and perished in the flames — 31,912; Effigies burnt — 17,659; Condemned to severe penances — 291,450'. Even if, as later writers have argued (e.g. Bennassar 1979), these figures are likely to be inflated, the toll of the Spanish and Portuguese Inquisitions was still enormous. In Portugal there were reputedly almost 900 public *autos-da-fé,* in which approximately 30,000 persons were sentenced, over 1,000 of them being publicly burnt (Adler 1908: 169).

[3] It has been suggested that the sense of evil among the ordinary population of Europe may have been little developed, and that it was really only in the minds of a small number of the clerical elite and the persecuted heretics that evil was a daily reality. Clearly, the extremes of terror came in waves, and it would be unlikely that people could sustain a constant alarm. Yet a reading of the recent works by Baroja (1964), Cohn (1975), Henningsen (1980) and Larner (1981) will indicate how widespread the alarm was and how it penetrated to the lowest levels of the society. Symbolically, the expulsion of evil at the *auto-da-fé* involved not just the inquisitors, but the whole population, all of whom took part in the rite. I have here drawn on unpublished work on the Inquisition processes in Portugal, currently being undertaken by a joint project sponsored by the Gulbenkian Foundation in Lisbon and King's College, Cambridge.

twentieth century, the world of Benedorm and Monte Carlo, of 'Jeux sans Frontières' and the Eurovision Song Contest, the European Economic Community and butter mountains. Though 'evil' titilates in the films, television, science fiction and children's stories, in ordinary life the concept and the reality have largely been banished. Most people move in a one-dimensional world that has expelled Satan, witches, the Evil Eye and fairies. The supernatural dimension is dead, except as 'fantasy'. It appears that 'science' and 'chance' have largely replaced personalized explanation. As Keith Thomas has argued (1970, 1983), the reasons for this transformation are still a mystery. In many ways the world of evil and anti-evil, of witchcraft and magic are psychologically much more appealing than the acceptance of capricious fate. This, then, is the problem: how has evil, however temporarily, been almost abolished?

The conventional wisdom may be briefly summarized as follows. The world of evil was first abandoned in a part of north-western Europe, the same area where the rise of Protestant, capitalist, rationalistic societies emerged. This was part of Max Weber's 'disenchantment of the world'. The turning point was in the sixteenth to eighteenth centuries. There was then a revolutionary movement, from the mystical, magical universe of medieval Catholicism to the clockwork, mechanical cosmology of eighteenth-century rationalism. There was an expulsion of the concept of evil, first among the elite and then, increasingly, among the hitherto 'superstitious' folk. The process paralleled and was linked to other attacks on 'irrationality', the irrationality of despotic government, peasant ownership, familistic sentiments.

The causes of this massive change are notoriously difficult to establish. Once we have abandoned a belief in the necessary progress of 'enlightenment' and rationality, we are forced to argue that the social and other frameworks that had nourished the roots of the concept of evil had changed. Max Gluckman suggested a few of the possible underlying connections between a changing social and economic world and changes in the moral and explanatory theories (Gluckman 1963: chapter 4; 1965: chapter 6). He argued that there was a basic change from a world in which most good things arrive through other people (multiplex, face-to-face communities) to a world in which good arrives by way of impersonal forces, through the exchange of money, contracts, labour, short-term manipulative relationships. As good things come in this new form, it is no longer tempting to believe that evil also flows along personal networks. Thus, a change from a deeply rooted, multiplex, face-to-face community to those highly mobile, 'modern' societies would lead to the decline of witchcraft and evil. This is another dimension of that famous movement from status to contract, from *gemeinschaft* to *gesellschaft*.

Another interesting suggestion lies behind Keith Thomas's two major works, namely that it is increasing security, arising from greater control over the natural world, that frees men from terror and hence from evil (Thomas 1971; 1983). Through technical, technological, organizational and other changes, man's vulnerability is decreased. The mysterious is eliminated, or else is so contained that people can believe that one day all will be explained. Through improvements in the standard of living, through insurance, through the triumphs of exploration and discovery, men became confident. Risk was minimized, shocks were less frequent, logical patterns emerged. A planned, controlled, human-constructed world emerged. There is little place for evil in the polite, orderly world of Jane Austen and Capability Brown. The neat, systematic, mercantile world of the seventeenth-century Dutch landscape painters finally eliminated the demons that had infested Europe from the fall of Rome to Hieronymus Bosch. Though the romantic movement and Gothic revival tried to re-introduce the mystery and some of the horror, the world of Frankenstein, the Pit and the Pendulum and Sir Walter Scott was a fantasy world, a literary genre like science fiction today. Essentially, the argument is that the tree of evil was destroyed when the roots were exposed through the rise of bourgeois capitalism. The process was circular, for it was the elimination of 'evil' that enabled people to investigate the real causes of pain and misfortune. In other terms, 'Science' replaced 'Magic' in the older Frazerian formula.

There is something intrinsically attractive and plausible in this account. It feels like our own life-experience leading up to the present. There seems a natural progression from the childhood of the world, where men feared the dark, ghosts and witches, to the more prosaic world of adulthood, where caprice, chance and psychological or sociological explanations are offered for disaster. This is a world in which people believe that, if only one knew enough, all could be explained. The extension of the argument is that where the social and mental institutions of northern Europe were exported, and later reinforced by a similar ideology in northern America, there evil withered. There were pockets of resistance and accommodation, yet basically mobility, money, markets and improved technology would be more powerful than the missionaries. Much of anthropology's task has been to study and document this ripple effect.

Before accepting the chronology and the explanation, however, let us look a little more closely at the first European escape from this evil-threatened cosmology. This occurred in England. The first thing to establish is when evil as a practical possibility was abolished. This is not easy, for it is notoriously difficult to penetrate to the level of ordinary behaviour and belief in the past. All we can do here, when considering a country of four to five million persons over a period of four centuries, is to start by looking at one tiny microcosm, one parish. How did the situation there compare with that on much of the Continent, Scotland and some contemporary peasantries?

During the last twelve years we have assembled, transcribed and indexed all the known surviving records for the parish of Earls Colne over the period 1380—1750.[4] This was a parish with about 700 inhabitants, on average, situated near Colchester in Essex. It has very detailed records, manorial, ecclesiastical and civil, which enable us to begin to analyse ordinary village life and concepts (Macfarlane 1977, 1983). All these records have been put into a computer database system so that they can be searched instantaneously by word or subject from any direction. We may survey what they reveal about the concepts of evil and related topics.

The first striking fact is how infrequently the word 'evil' is used. In the 10,000 pages of transcribed documents, it occurs (if we include 'evilly' and 'evils') only 27 times. This is despite very full ecclesiastical and equity court records where people were frequently abusing each other. The word occurs 6 times in a set of ecclesiastical depositions concerning a case of adultery and only once elsewhere in the ecclesiastical courts. It occurs 12 times in three disputes over property in the Court of Chancery. Otherwise, there is a single reference in each of the following: in a manorial jury presentment, in minutes of a Friends Quarterly Meeting, in memoranda of the Quarter Sessions and in one or two other sources. In all of these sources, the word appears to have been used in the weaker and not the stronger meaning.

Although the records are much less ample in the fifteenth than in the sixteenth to eighteenth centuries, there is as yet no evidence of either a rapid increase or decline in the usage of the word over these centuries. Nor is there any evidence that it radically changed its meaning as the centuries went by. Its first use in the fifteenth century was in relation to people who broke into other people's property and were termed 'evil doers'. Its last use, in the eighteenth century, was when it was used to describe debtors who had fled to avoid paying their debts and who were called 'evil persons'. These two uses were characteristic, and they illustrate the most important conclusion of all. 'Evil' as a word was always used in the weaker, 'modern', sense of being synonymous with 'bad', 'criminal'. It was never used in the strong sense of

---

[4] I am grateful to other members of the Earls Colne project (a project funded by the Social Science Research Council), namely Sarah Harrison, Jessica King, Tim King and Charles Jardine, for the work from which these results are drawn. All the documents for Earls Colne have now been published on microfiche by Chadwyck-Healey Ltd and are available in a number of university libraries and the National Lending Library. The references to 'evil' and similar words are listed in the subject index included in that microfiche, where the full context of the use of the word may be seen.

being totally anti-social. This important conclusion can be illustrated by looking at the phrases in which it occurred.

A suspected adulteress was accused of leading an 'evil or dishonest life', and it was claimed that she never performed any 'evil or dishonest act'. A man was warned by the ecclesiastical court 'for keeping an evil woman in his house'. Intruders, persons who made wagers and defrauded others and those who failed to pay their debts — all were referred to as of 'evil conversation', of 'evil disposition and narrow of conscience' and as 'evil doers'. Evil was used to describe ordinary secular criminal acts. Thus, people were warned against 'felonies, trespasses and other evil acts. . . .'; people claimed that they had been 'very sore hurt and evil treated by the complainant', that riots had been caused by 'evil persons that are the secret authors or abettors of such tumultuous disorders', that people 'did assault and evil entreat' others. This is a use of the word 'evil' in its widest sense, just as we might today describe something as bad or wicked in a loose way. There is apparently nothing of the association with the Devil, with spiritual darkness, with another moral dimension.

It is always dangerous to work from absences in the records, since the documents were usually created in formal settings. Yet it is striking that, when the word was used, it was always used in the weaker sense. There is certainly no evidence here that evil in the stronger meaning was an important force in the life of the village. This first impression is supported by other related features. One of these concerns those associated concepts in Christian eschatology, the Devil and hell. It is likely that, if this was a world where evil was widely feared, the Devil would not have been far away and people would have been in constant mindfulness of the pains of Hell. This was particularly to be expected in an area of East Anglia that was famous for its strident puritanism. It is curious, then, that a search of the immense number of words that have survived in the records for Earls Colne does not reveal a single use of either the words 'Devil' or 'Hell' (or their derivatives). Never, it seems, did people in their bitter wrangling allege, at least in writing, that their opponents were in league with the Devil, that they would go to Hell. If we were to judge from local and legal records, this was a prosaic world in which evil, the Devil and hell were of marginal significance from at least the middle of the sixteenth century. Since the threat of evil, of the Devil and of hell is such a useful sanction in societies where it is strongly present, this seems strange. Yet again it fits more widely with other features of the society as revealed in the documents.

Where evil is an ever-present threat and reality, people are constantly seeking protection from it. They engage in a thousand forms of activity to ward it off, protecting their houses, their loved ones, their animals. Although Keith Thomas has documented a good deal of this activity in general (Thomas

1971), it is striking that so very little evidence survives at the village level for ritual and magical protection against evil. A certain amount of the burying of objects, hanging up of horseshoes, wearing of parts of the Bible round the neck as amulets would no doubt go unnoted in formal records. Yet it is significant that the church itself was very anxious to extirpate such magical protections, which were thought superstitious and unnecessary. Thus, in Earls Colne an astrologer who used magical books was prosecuted by the church authorities. It seems likely that, if there had been much magical activity, it would have been noticed in the church courts or by the Puritan vicar of Earls Colne, who has left a detailed diary covering the period 1640—83 (Macfarlane 1976). Ralph Josselin does occasionally mention superstitious practices, such as erecting a May Pole. Yet he never reports charms, amulets, magical words or signs that were designed to protect mankind against evil. The only protection was prayer and an upright soul.

While individuals do not appear to have had a wide repertoire of antidotes to evil, the formal authorities provided even less. Since the work of Robertson Smith (1889), anthropologists have been aware that, in a cosmology where evil is a constant threat, mankind tries to ward it off by various types of ritual activity that will avert the dangers. Among the most powerful of these are the rituals of sacrifice and exorcism. Sacrifice, the ritual destruction of an object and the giving of part of it, often the blood, to gods, ancestors or spirits, is a powerful technique in the battle against evil. Sacrifice acts as a lightning conductor, for the sacrificial animal takes upon itself the sins of the world and carries them away, thus diverting disaster. Man is protected from various evils, merited and unmerited, by sacrifice. It could almost be asserted that sacrifice and developed concepts of evil are necessarily intertwined. Looked at from this perspective, the total absence, as far as we know, of animal or other sacrifice in Earls Colne throughout the whole period is significant. Even the symbolic sacrifice of Christ on the cross was minimized by the Protestant emphasis on the fact that communion was not a ritual act, a sacrifice of blood and flesh, but merely a commemorative and communal act 'in remembrance of me'. There is no evidence that the rituals of the Church provided an effective shield against evil.

The weakness of ritual is also apparent in the absence of exorcism and possession. Although the rite of exorcism was available in the Anglican church and was sometimes used during this period, there is no evidence in these village records that it was of any practical importance. There is not a single case of diabolic possession recorded and no known instance of exorcism. Physical manifestation of the Evil One seems to have been minimal. The overwhelming impression from all types of documents is of a secularized world where people were concerned primarily with money, power and social

Marginal note: Not convincing — consider the N.T. references to Satan and evil. Clearly Jesus regarded these as real entities and yet never enjoined people to avoidance of them [by] ritualistic means.

relationships. It was not, as far as we can see at present, a world darkened by the overcasting shadow of menacing evil. Consequently it is not surprising to find an absence of any indication of evil times or evil places. There is no hint that certain days were evil in themselves, that the churchyard or other places were intrinsically evil. Of course, there were unlucky days; it was best not to set out on journeys on them, marry on them or undertake business on them. Yet bad luck and fortune are different from true evil.

Another apparent absence is the concept of the Evil Eye. Just as in Essex as a whole (Macfarlane 1970b), so in Earls Colne, there is no evidence for the developed belief that envy, in a world where good things are limited, endangers all life. In almost all other peasantries, it is believed that certain individauls are born with an evil eye; whenever they look with envy on a thing, it withers and dies. Such beliefs were strongly developed in parts of Scotland, Mediterranean Europe and elsewhere. Yet there is not a single hint, in all of our Earls Colne or wider Essex material, of such a concept, so closely linked to an idea of evil.

More complex is the reality and importance of witchcraft and fairy beliefs. In a general work I have surveyed witchcraft beliefs and prosecutions in Essex over the period 1560—1680, and there showed that Essex was one of the most witch-conscious of counties and that the sixteenth and seventeenth centuries saw the peak of beliefs and prosecutions (Macfarlane 1970b). Yet when we place witchcraft beliefs and accusations within the context of all the events within one parish, they become less impressive. In Earls Colne, there were literally hundreds of cases of recorded sexual misdemeanours, hundreds of accusations concerning economic affairs. Yet not a single person was condemned as a witch. The nearest to a formal prosecution occurred in the archdeaconry court in 1581, when Mary Green was accused by the churchwardens of Colne of being 'vehemently suspected of sorcery and witchcraft'. She failed to produce neighbours to swear an oath on her behalf and was thus excommunicated. We hear nothing more of her, so that she probably moved. The wording, alluding to 'sorcery', suggests that she was probably a 'white' witch, that is, someone who was illicitly curing people or searching for lost objects. Apart from several references to a local wizard or astrologer at the same period, this is all we would hear of witchcraft from the records. Nor is there any mention of any other evil or half-evil spirits. There is not a single reference in any of the documents to fairies, goblins, brownies or any of the host of spirits that peopled the high literature of Elizabethan England (Briggs 1962). There are no allusions to stories, myths, beliefs in the fairy world. It is a curiously flat, matter-of-fact world that is indicated by the local records.

Such a picture of practical life is a useful corrective to the exclusive use of literary sources. Yet there are clearly dangers in using only impersonal, often formal, records. Fortunately for Earls Colne, we are not just left with such material; for one of the richest sources on past beliefs, namely diaries and autobiographies, is well represented by the extensive 600-page diary of the vicar of Earls Colne, Ralph Josselin. The full diary has been analysed and published (Macfarlane 1970a, 1976), and we may mention some of the conclusions to be drawn from the source covering the middle of the seventeenth century. The projection of the distinction between good and evil into strong beliefs in heaven and hell does not show itself in this diary:

belief in the after-life does not play an important part in his private thoughts as recorded in the Diary. There is not a single direct reference to hell or to damnation. It thus seems that a Puritan clergyman, who might have been expected to use heaven and hell as threats or inducements to himself and his congregation, showed the most tepid interest in both.

Macfarlane 1970a: 168

Josselin was preoccupied with misfortune, illness and insecurities of various kinds. There are consequently many moving passages on death and disease. Yet what is striking in the Diary is the conviction that all suffering was derived from God. In Josselin's thought there emerges very clearly 'the principle that pain and evil came from God. There is no hint in the Diary that Josselin envisaged an alternative source of evil, Satan for example. Again and again he traces his own and the nation's troubles back to God' (Macfarlane 1970a: 173). Basically, 'Josselin seems to have accepted that pain was either divine purge, as in the story of Job, or a punishment' (p. 174). Guilt strikes us throughout the Diary, for Josselin blamed himself for much of the suffering of those around him; in the most famous instance, he linked too much chess-playing to illness and death. Thus, the roots of evil were ultimately in his own corrupt heart. It was no use blaming other people. The cause was either a loving God testing him, or his own, or the nation's failings. There is no suggestion that Josselin blamed witches, Satan or anyone else.

Interestingly, however, Josselin also believed in the possibility of diabolic intervention and of witchcraft. He never encountered the Devil himself, but he seems to have accepted the stories concerning two of his parishioners who had encountered the Devil. One had been tossed into a river by 'one in the shape of a bull', whom it was rumoured was the Devil. Another man visited Josselin to tell him that the Devil had appeared to him: 'the greediness of money, made him desire it, and God suffered it; he [i.e. the Devil] appeared in a black gown, and then in red; he took his blood on white paper.' A few days later Josselin was with the same man and there was a fear that the Devil might appear, but he failed to do so (Macfarlane 1970a: 190–1).

Josselin also believed in the possibility of witchcraft and reported two cases. In the first of these, 'one J. Biford was clamoured on as a witch, and Mr C. thought his child ill by it.' Josselin took the suspect 'alone into the field, and dealt with him solemnly, and I conceive the poor wretch is innocent as to that evil.' The following year he heard from a neighbouring minister that a woman was a suspected witch, who had acted in a suspect manner near a grave. Josselin 'pressed her what I could; she protests her innocency' (Macfarlane 1970a: 191 — 2). Josselin also believed in the power of cursing.

In this and other respects a personal diary helps to provide an added spiritual dimension to the local records. It shows a world of symbols, signs and visions that are absent from court records. Yet in many ways the Diary complements the other records in its central impressions concerning evil. Evil, the Evil One, the evil eye, the force and danger of evil, are largely absent. The world revealed by the Diary is not one of a constant battle between the forces of good and evil, of imminent destruction and threat from evil-minded persons or evil-minded spirits. Ultimately the individual, through his own purity of heart and through understanding God, can control the world. This is a world fully consistent with that we shall examine in relation to Josselin's great contemporary, John Milton, where evil and good are interchangeable. Josselin is primarily concerned with practical problems; with making money above all, and secondarily with establishing good relations with his neighbours, his family and God. The quality of this world can be most startlingly shown if we compare the atmosphere of this Diary, cosy and suburban in many ways, with the feeling portrayed by a fictional account of the mental world of another branch of Calvinism, the horrific account of the Devil and pure evil in James Hogg's *The Private Memories and Confessions of a Justified Sinner* (1824). There is portrayed a world where Hell, the Devil, real evil and darkness are a felt reality; that account leaves the landscape of Josselin's Earls Colne seeming a sunny, open and this-worldly one. Evil is never entirely banished, of course, but it is just a shadow on the edge of this English world, not a central pervasive feature, as it is in many cultures.

These are impressions based on one small example. Yet they are consistent with other contemporary evidence for the sixteenth to eighteenth centuries. Those familiar with the most detailed English diaries and autobiographies of this period, for example those of Samuel Pepys (Latham and Matthews 1970), John Evelyn (de Beer 1955) and Oliver Heywood (Horsfall Turner 1882), will know that there is very little in them about evil in the strict sense. Occasionally there are strange intrusions from another dimension — ghosts, poltergeists, the odd witchcraft trial. Yet the tone of all of the diaries is this-worldly, prosaic, not soaked in evil. The same is true of another genre, letters, which have survived in considerable numbers from the fifteenth century. The famous collections of the Pastons (Gairdner 1901), the Celys (Hanham 1975) and the Verneys (Verney 1970) have scarcely anything in them suggesting an interest in evil in the strong sense.

The absence of a horror and concern with evil is also clearly indicated by English proverbs. The various dictionaries of phrase and fable and handbooks of English proverbs contain very little about evil. For instance, the *Oxford Dictionary of English Proverbs* (1952) contains only a few proverbs under the title 'Evil'. In almost all of these it is clear that the word is being used in the weaker sense. For example, there is the proverb 'Evils (Harms, Ills, Mischiefs), of two / choose the least', which is first quoted for Chaucer (using the word 'harms'). Another is that 'Of Evil (ill) manners, spring good laws'. Hell is equally lightly treated. There are only 11 proverbs cited, including 'From Hell, Hull and Halifax, good Lord deliver us'; 'Hell and chancery are always open'; 'Hell or Connaught' and other frivolous ones. None is concerned with the horrors of Hell, how to avoid Hell and so on. Hell is a place that is 'full of good meanings and wishes', 'paved with good intentions'; 'He that is in hell thinks there is no other heaven.' The Devil receives more attention, but again is treated with a frivolous lightness which is significant. 'The Devil always leaves a stink behind him'; 'The Devil gets up to the belfry by the vicar's skirts'; 'The Devil is a busy bishop in his own diocese'; 'The Devil is an ass'; 'The Devil makes his Christmas-pies of lawyers' tongues and clerks' fingers'; 'The Devil will not come into Cornwall, for fear of being put into a pie' and many others. In sum, 'The Devil is not so black as he is painted'; he is a joker, God's ape, puny and weak, a trickster in a safe world.

Of course, the majestic prose of the Bible gives us a vision of a society where evil, hell, the Devil and all his works were very important. It would be foolish to overlook this dimension, and we can represent it here by one quotation. The Lord's Prayer included the phrase 'And lead us not into temptation; But deliver us from evil.' In his catechism, one of the sixteenth-century Protestants, Thomas Becon, quoted this slightly differently as 'But deliver us from the evil.' What was 'the evil'? It was 'Our arch-enemy the devil, author of all evil . . .'. Becon referred here to St Paul, who had equated the evil and the Devil. Satan, Becon tells us, brings about two major species of evil, of the soul and of the body. The evils of the soul include 'incredulity, misbelief, doubting, . . . uncircumcision of heart, corruption of judgement, error, heresy, schisms, controversies in religion, sects, pride of the mind, obstinacy in wickedness, fleshly lusts' and many others. There were also many evils of the body, including 'sudden death, plague, pestilence, unwholesome weather . . . famine, hunger, battle, dearth, beggary, loss of goods, infamy, shame, confusion, madness . . .' and a host of others (Becon 1845: 196). It is essential to remember that, at least nominally, this was a Christian civilization based on the premise that there were tangible evils, the Devil and Hell;

catechisms, sermons and much of education were founded on these beliefs. Yet, just as Keith Thomas has shown the amazing amount of religious ignorance and even stark atheism in this period and country (Thomas 1971: chapter 6), so it may be that, while people knew little of God and Christ, they also knew little of the Devil, and cared less.

A satisfying explanation of the absence of absolute Evil, the Devil and Hell will need a fuller treatment. It is clearly no coincidence, for example, that England was the only major European nation to have no Catholic Inquisition and no inquisitorial process under law. The terror of evil was not encouraged. Another part of the solution, as well as further evidence on the nature of the problem, is provided by two of those who wrote in England during the period under consideration. They have provided two of the best accounts of the problems of evil and good known to us, namely Shakespeare and Milton.

One of the most striking features of both authors, making them seem very 'modern' and relevant to us, is that they are concerned with a grey world where good and evil are interchangeable; where it is impossible to be certain, to have absolute moral standards; where nothing is entirely black or white. This is clearly the case in Shakespeare's treatment of all his central characters — Hamlet, Brutus, Prospero, Macbeth and even Iago. For them, the choices are difficult, there is no absolute standard, things are not what they seem. Shakespeare even suggests reasons why good and evil have become blurred. Money, he shows, could change one into the other. Here he is touching on a central paradox. In a capitalist society, evil becomes good, good evil. Karl Marx quoted Shakespeare approvingly because he had seen this central feature (Marx and Engels 1974: 102; Marx 1973: 163). A passage from *Timon of Athens* (Act IV, scene 3) is worth quoting at greater length than that in Marx's work. Timon digs in the ground and finds gold.

> What is here?
> Gold? yellow, glittering precious gold? No, gods,
> I am no idle votarist. Roots, you clear heavens!
> Thus much of this will make black, white; foul, fair;
> Wrong, right; base, noble; old, young, coward, valiant.
> Ha, you gods! why this? What this, you gods? Why, this
> Will lug your priests and servants from your sides;
> Pluck stout men's pillows from below their heads:
> This yellow slave
> Will knit and break religions; bless the accurs'd;
> Make the hoar leprosy ador'd; place thieves,
> And give them title, knee, and approbation,
> With senators on the bench: this is it
> That makes the wrappen'd widow wed again; . . . .

Thus, gold transforms everything, from black to white and back again; it brings together as equivalents things that are not really on the same plane and divides things that are naturally together. Man is no longer able to discriminate between what is good, what evil.

This confusion at the heart of life is echoed in Milton's greatest poem. The central theme of *Paradise Lost* is the battle between good and evil. Yet the struggle is not between two opposed sides, but within the same principle. The poem is an attempt to state the paradox that good and evil are entirely separate, yet also entirely the same. It grapples with the problem of how evil emerged at all, for it arose out of goodness. The problem is given one formulation in the myth of the garden of Eden, where evil was present even in a perfect Paradise. Once evil has emerged as distinct from goodness, having become separated, the problem for both is to prevent their mutual contamination and a tendency to become joined again. The attempt to foil God's attempt to bring them back into his mercy is the subject of many of Satan's famous lines in the poem. 'If then his providence/ Out of our evil seek to bring forth good, / Our labour must be to prevent that end, / And out of good still find means of evil' (book i, line 157). The world has to be redefined in order to achieve this. 'So farewell hope, and with hope farewell fear, / Farewell remorse: all good to me is lost; Evil be thou my Good' (book iv, line 108). Yet, just as evil has emerged out of the principle of good, so it is possible for good to emerge from evil. This is the constant threat to the fallen angels; that God may win them back and turn their evil into good, for the power of goodness is very great: 'abashed the devil stood, And felt how awful goodness is' (book iv, line 846). Ultimately, good and evil are not separable. Heaven and Hell, the Devil and God are in essence different aspects of the same power.

Milton's poem could be seen as the eloquent expression of the tragic recognition that the simplicities of a childlike black and white vision were not sufficient. It is all a matter of how we look at things, a subjectivist world in which man cannot depend on any external, eternal, objective, moral laws. Milton needed to justify the ways of God to man; as a result, each man would act as a judge upon God, rather than the reverse. Morality was in the eye of the beholder. As Pope would put it, 'Pleasure, or wrong or rightly understood / Our greatest evil, or our greatest good' (*Essay on Man,* epistle 2, line 91).

Pope, indeed, represented the culmination of a trend towards ethical relativism which argued from growing evidence that every civilization had its own appropriate moral system. Pascal had summarized this view in the seventeenth century. 'We hardly know of anything just or unjust which does not change its character with a change of climate. Three degrees of polar elevation overturn the whole system of jurisprudence. A meridian determines what is truth. . . . There is not a single law which is universal' (Pascal 1844: ii, 126ff.). Pope took the next step:

> All nature is but art, unknown to thee;
> All chance, direction which thou canst not see;
> All discord, harmony not understood;
> All partial evil, universal good;
> And, spite of pride, in erring reason's spite,
> One truth is clear, Whatever is, is right.
>
> *Essay on Man,* epistle 1, line 289

Beyond this lay extreme cynicism, as expressed for instance by Charles Churchill:

> Keep up appearances; there lies the test;
> The world will give thee credit for the rest.
> Outward be fair, however foul within;
> Sin, if thou wilt, but then in secret sin.
>
> Churchill 1970: i, 71

In a short essay such as this, it is possible only to raise a few questions and hint at an answer to the problem of the origins of the disappearance of pure evil. Both the answer and the problem are encapsulated in St Paul's warning that 'The love of money is the root of all evil' (1 Timothy 6: 10). This dismissal of avarice is one of the central pillars of that Judaeo-Christian tradition upon which western civilization is based. Yet, it could equally well be argued that the love of money — the famous propensity to barter, trade, accumulate — is an equally important pillar of this civilization. Adam Smith most clearly exposed this foundation of modern society, a feature without which modern societies would immediately collapse. As he put it, 'The division of labour, from which so many advantages are derived . . . is the necessary . . . consequence of a certain propensity in human nature . . . the propensity to truck, barter, and exchange one thing for another' (Smith 1976: book 1, chapter 2, 17). This division of labour and all that flows from it is thus based on a propensity that is, in the ethical terms laid down by the formal theology, evil. The foundations are laid on individual acquisitiveness, the love of money and pursuit of profit. Thus, good and evil are mixed in the roots of modern society.

Yet money, and all it symbolizes, is the root of all evil in a deeper sense than this. Viewed from outside the system, money can be seen to do something even more insidious. It subtly eliminates the very concept of evil. Or, rather, it makes it impossible to discriminate between good and evil, throwing people into that confusion that cast the angels from Paradise and afflicted Shakespeare's central characters. 'Money', which is a short-hand way of saying capitalistic relations, market values, trade and exchange, ushers in a world of moral confusion. This effect of money has been most obvious where a capitalistic, monetary economy has clashed with another, opposed, system. Thus it is anthropologists, who have worked in such areas of conflict, who have witnessed most dramatically the effect of the introduction of a monetized economy. They have noted how money disrupts the moral as well as the economic world. As Burridge, for example, writes of the effect of money in Melanesia: money complicates the moral order, turning what was formerly black and white into greyness. Money, he argues, 'reveals the vice in cultivated virtues, allows no vice without some virtue, concedes an element of right in wrong-doing, finds the sin of pride in an upright fellow. . . . money invites a complex differentiation and multiplication of the parts and qualities of man' (Burridge 1969: 45). More broadly, it is money, markets and market capitalism that eliminate absolute moralities. Not only is every moral system throughout the world equally valid, as Pascal noted, but, *within* every system, whatever is, is right.

The consequences of money and the mentality associated with it are equally apparent to the major sociological thinkers. One of the most eloquent descriptions of the way in which money destroys moral polarities, qualitative difference, is in Simmel's (1950) essay on the 'Metropolis and Mental Life':

By being the equivalent to all the manifold things in one and the same way, money becomes the most frightful leveller. For money expresses all qualitative differences of things in terms of 'how much?' Money, with all its colourlessness and indifference, becomes the common denominator of all values; irreparably it hollows out the core of things, their individuality, their specific gravity in the constantly moving stream of money. All things lie on the same level and differ from one another only in the size of the area which they cover.

Simmel 1950: 414

The consequences of this moral revolution were already apparent to people in the most developed capitalist economy, England, by the eighteenth century.

What had happened was that capitalism had fully triumphed: to modify Swinburne, 'Thou hast conquered, O pale Capitalism; the world has grown grey from thy breath.'[5] It has now become clear that what was considered to

---

[5] Swinburne's original (in *Hymn to Proserpine*) referred to Christ, 'O pale Galilean', rather than capitalism.

be the root of all evil, namely the love of money, was also the root of all that was good, namely the bargaining, market principle of Adam Smith. This paradox was so horrifying in its implications that, when it was pointed out starkly, there was fierce condemnation. The man who made the unspeakable truth known was Bernard Mandeville, a Dutchman who had settled as a doctor in London, in his *Fable of the Bees*. The sub-title of the work summarized the theme: it was 'Private Vices, Public Benefits'. The work, published in 1714, went alongside a doggerel poem entitled 'The Grumbling Hive: or, Knaves Turn'd Honest', first published in 1705. The theme of the poem was that it was out of the private passions and vices of the citizens — their lusts, acquisitive spirits and aggressive competition — that public benefits flowed. As Mandeville rhymed,

> Thus every part was full of Vice,
> Yet the whole Mass a Paradice;
> Flatter'd in Peace, and fear'd in wars
> They were th'Esteem of Foreigners,
> And lavish of their Wealth and Lives,
> The Balance of all other Hives.
> Such were the Blessings of that State;
> Their Crimes conspired to make 'em Great;
> And Vertue, who from Politicks
> Had learn'd a Thousand cunning Tricks,
> Was, by their happy Influence,
> Made Friends with Vice: And ever since
> The Worst of all the Multitude
> Did something for the common Good.
>
> Mandeville 1970: 67—8

Out of vice and evil passion came forth wealth and goodness. Evil lay at the heart of good in a capitalist society, just as evil had lain at the heart of good when the good angels had arisen to build a new world in the midst of Paradise. Mandeville's message was that, if one tried to be privately virtuous, the public world would collapse. Right at the end of the *Fable* Mandeville concluded that:

After this I flatter my self to have demonstrated that neither the Friendly Qualities and kind Affections that are natural to Man, nor the real Virtues he is capable of acquiring by Reason and Self-Denial are the foundation of Society; but that what we call Evil in this World, Moral as well as Natural, is the grand principle that makes us Sociable Creatures, the solid Basis, the Life and Support of all Trades and Employments without exception: That there we must look for the true origin of all Arts and

Sciences, and that the moment Evil ceases, the Society must be spoil'd if not totally
dissolv'd.

Mandeville 1970: 370

This was Mandeville's central message, and it was incorporated in the great
work that was written by the very moral Adam Smith, and which would
outline the basis of the capitalist system:

Without any intervention of law, therefore, the private interests and passions of men
naturally lead them to divide and distribute the stock of every society, among all the
different employments carried on in it, as nearly as possible in the proportion which is
most agreeable to the interest of the whole society.

quoted in Hirschman 1977: 110—11

Thus private vice, passions and interests have merged into public good.

Ironically, the foundations of Paradise were laid in Hell, and Hell in
Paradise. The serpent of desire propped up the tree of the knowledge of good
and evil. Or, to put it another way, the serpent was also the tree. By being that
tree, he led to the ultimate confusion, the inability to distinguish between
good and evil. When the fruit was tasted, it was found that, rather than
containing the new knowledge that enabled man to discriminate good from
evil, it contained the deadly knowledge that it was now impossible to
distinguish the two.

If the thesis advanced here has any truth in it, namely that capitalism and a
money order were fatally intertwined with an inability to distinguish good and
evil, it is clearly necessary to go further. We need to probe deep into the
origins of capitalism in order to seek out how it had eliminated the opposition
of good and evil. Such an adventure is for another occasion. What is clear is
that, at least at the popular level in England, the ambivalences and
contradictions were present back to the start of the sixteenth century. From
other work on related themes, it seems likely that they were present much
earlier, at least back to the thirteenth century (Macfarlane 1978). It is
possible to argue that ordinary people in England had for centuries been
accustomed to a world not of absolutes, but of relative good and evil, where all
could be changed by money. It is appropriate and hardly fortuitous that
Shakespeare should have provided the most exquisite expressions of that
uncertainty in the midst of the period, or that in its full flowering Pope should
have summarized the indecision and confusion so grandly:

Placed on this isthmus of a middle state,
A being darkly wise, and rudely great:
. . . .

He Hangs between; in doubt to act, or rest;
In doubt to deem himself a god, or beast;
. . . .

Chaos of thought and passion, all confused;
Still by himself abused, or disabused;
Created half to rise, and half to fall;
Great Lord of all things, yet a prey to all;
Sole judge of truth, in endless error hurled:
The glory, jest, and riddle of the world!

An Essay on Man, epistle 2

REFERENCES

Bennassar, B. (1979). 'L'Inquisition Espagnole XVe – XIXe Siècle'. Paris: Hachette

Adler, Elkan N. (1908). *Auto da Fé and Jew*. London: Oxford University Press

Baroja, Julio Caro (1964). *World of the Witches*. London: Weidenfeld and Nicholson

Becon, Thomas (1845). *The Works of Thomas Becon*. Edited for the Parker Society by Rev. John Ayre. Cambridge: Cambridge University Press

de Beer, E. S. (ed.) (1955). *Diary of John Evelyn*. Oxford: Oxford University Press

Briggs, K. M. (1962). *Pale Hecate's Team*. London: Routledge and Kegan Paul

Burridge, K. (1969). *New Heaven, New Earth*. Oxford: Basil Blackwell

Churchill, Charles (1970). *Poems of Charles Churchill* (ed. James Laver). London: Methuen

Cohn, Norman (1975). *Europe's Inner Demons*. New York: Basic Books

Gairdner, James (ed.) (1901). *The Paston Letters 1422 – 1509*. London: Archibald Constable

Gluckman, Max (1963). *Custom and Conflict in Africa*. Oxford: Basil Blackwell

Gluckman, Max (1965). *Politics, Law and Ritual in Tribal Society*. Oxford: Basil Blackwell

Hanham, Alison (ed.) (1975). *The Cely Letters 1472 – 1488*. London: Oxford University Press

Horsfall Turner, J. (ed.) (1822). *Autobiography, Dairies, etc. of Rev. Oliver Heywood 1630 – 1702*. Brighouse, Yorks: A. B. Bayes

Henningsen, Gustav (1980). *The Witches' Advocate, Basque Witchcraft and the Spanish Inquisition (1609 – 1614)* Reno: University of Nevada Press

Hirschman, Albert O. (1977). *The Passions and the Interests*. New Jersey: Princton University Press

Larner, Christina (1981). *Enemies of God. The Witch-hunt in Scotland*. London: Chatto and Windus (paperback edition, Oxford: Basil Blackwell, 1983)

Latham, Robert and Matthews, William (1970). *The Diary of Samuel Pepys*. London: G. Bell and Sons

Llorente, D. Juan Antonio (1827). *The History of the Inquisition of Spain* (2nd edn). London: Geo. B. Whittaker

Macfarlane, Alan (ed.) (1970a). *The Diary of Ralph Josselin 1616—1683.* London: Oxford University Press

Macfarlane, Alan (1970b). *Witchcraft in Tudor and Stuart England.* London: Routledge and Kegan Paul

Macfarlane, Alan (1976). *The Diary of Ralph Josselin (1616—1683).* London: Oxford University Press

Macfarlane, Alan (1978). *The Origins of English Individualism.* Oxford: Basil Blackwell

Macfarlane, Alan (1983). *A guide to English historical records.* Cambridge: Cambridge University Press

Macfarlane, Alan *et al.* (1977). *Reconstructing Historical Communities.* Cambridge: Cambridge University Press

Maitland, F. W. and Pollock, Sir F. (1952). *The History of English Law* (2nd edn). Cambridge: Cambridge University Press

Mandeville, Bernard (1970). *The Fable of the Bees* (ed. Philip Harth). London: Penguin

Marx, Karl (1973). *Grundrisse* (trans. Martin Nicolaus). London: Penguin Books

Marx, Karl and Engels, Frederick (1974). *The German Ideology* (ed. C. J. Arthur). London: Lawrence and Wishart

Oxford Dictionary (1952). *The Oxford Dictionary of English Proverbs* (2nd edn, revised by Sir Paul Harvey). Oxford: Clarendon Press

Pascal, Blaise (1844). *Pensées* (ed. P. Faugère). Paris

Robertson Smith, William (1889). *Lectures on the Religion of the Semites.* London: A. & C. Black

Simmel, Georg (1950). *The Sociology of Georg Simmel* (ed. Kurt H. Wolff). Glencoe, Illinois: The Free Press

Smith, Adam (1976). *The Wealth of Nations* (ed. Edwin Cannan). Chicago: Chicago University Press

Thomas, Keith (1971). *Religion and the Decline of Magic.* London: Weidenfeld and Nicolson

Thomas, Keith (1983). *Man and the Natural World.* London: Allen Lane

Verney, Frances P. (ed.) (1970). *Memoirs of the Verney Family During the Civil War.* London: Tabard Press

5

The seed of evil within

David Rheubottom*

In this chapter I consider some notions concerning evil as they are found in Skopska Crna Gora, a rural area in Yugoslav Macedonia. As a European community, we might see it as a possible test case for the presence or absence of a strong sense of evil. On the one hand, the material supports Macfarlane's view, expressed in chapter 4, that the concept is no longer that of a mystical, hidden and inexplicable malign force. On the other hand, villagers regard their fellows so suspiciously, and sometimes malevolently, that they show characteristics of the majority English view reported by Pocock in chapter 3. In some respects the notion of evil in Skopska Crna Gora is given a much wider extension than we would give to it, yet in others it is relatively undeveloped. To adopt a geometric metaphor, we might say that it has breadth but little depth. This lack of depth may be related to a relative poverty of theodicy within Eastern Orthodoxy. Linguistically, the situation is broadly similar to that of many parts of Europe. Macedonian, like other Slavic languages, has a triad of terms which we may translate as good (*dobro*), bad (*nedobro* — literally, 'not-good') and evil (*lǒs*).

I did not make any systematic enquiries into the notion of 'evil' while engaged in fieldwork.[1] The material for this chapter was collected haphazardly in the course of other enquiries. Indeed, I was unaware of 'evil' as an anthropological problem at the time. What I have done, therefore, is to concentrate on three sets of materials, each of which was labelled as evil by

* I am indebted to the Department of Anthropology of the University of Rochester and to the University of Houston Faculty Research Support Program for their grants. In 1966—7 I was affiliated with the Economics Faculty of the University of Skopje. I wish to acknowledge the many kindnesses extended to me by the (then) Rector Ksente Bogoev and by Dr Vlado Taneski. An earlier version of this paper was read at a seminar in the School of Oriental and African Studies.

[1] My fieldwork was conducted in 1966—7 and in the autumn of 1970.

informants. I then try to see what these three have in common. These are (1)
the evil eye, (2) certain properties of households whose standard of living was
appreciably greater than, or less than, the village norm, and (3) the division of
households. Before becoming immersed in the details of ethnography and
analysis, however, it is necessary to provide some background on Skopska
Crna Gora, the region where fieldwork was done.

Skopska Crna Gora is a rural area within Yugoslav Macedonia. Located just
north of Skopje, the capital of the People's Republic of Macedonia, it contains
11 nucleated villages. The inhabitants are primarily agriculturalists although
some households keep flocks of sheep in the mountains. A few men work for
wages in Skopje and commute daily between village and city. Ethnically, this
part of Yugoslavia is very mixed. Nearby villages contain Albanians and
Turks. Both are found in Skopje as well. While the Turks are all Muslim, the
Albanians are divided between Islam and Roman Catholicism. In the outskirts
of Skopje where the farthest fields of Skopska Crna Gora lie is a large
settlement of urbanized gypsies.

While Skopska Crna Gora lies within Macedonia, it is also very close to the
People's Republic of Serbia and the autonomous region of Kosovo-Metohija.
Some villagers claim to be 'Serb' and to speak 'Serbian' (Serbo-Croatian).
Others claim to be Macedonian and to speak Macedonian. Serbs refer to the
Macedonians as 'Bulgars'. While this distinction has considerable local
importance, it is ignored by outsiders, who speak of all the inhabitants of
Skopska Crna Gora as 'Crna Gorci'. I adopt this same convention in this
chapter.

All Crna Gorci with one exception are Eastern Orthodox.[2] Villagers are
very aware of the differences between religions. I was continually asked if I
was (in descending order of regard) Orthodox, Catholic, Muslim or an atheist.
The possibility of further categories was not recognized. They take great pride
in the fact that Sv Cyril and Methodius, the saints that translated and carried
the Gospels throughout the Slav lands, are thought to have come from
Macedonia.[3] The region, moreover, is richly endowed with churches and
monasteries of great antiquity. For example, the monastery of Sv Nikita near
the villages of Banjani, Gornjane and Čučer was established in 1307. The
church in the village where I lived had been established in 1348 by a certain

---

[2] One half of the village of Ljuboten contains Albanian Muslims who attend a small mosque.
I ignore them in this analysis. Several other villages are divided into Serbian and Macedonian
moieties. Mirkovci is an example, but in these other 'divided' villages there is only one
congregation of Orthodox believers.

[3] I adopt the convention of referring to saints in the local fashion: thus 'Sv Jovan' rather
than 'St John the Baptist'.

Lord Radoslav. The frescoes, by Mihail and Eutihij and members of their workshop, have been painstakingly restored by the Yugoslav government and are of great significance in the history of art (Nikolovski et al. 1961).

Crna Gorci belong to the newly autonomous Macedonian Orthodox Church. This is one of the national autocephalous churches of the Balkans. It is a recent offshoot of the Serbian church, which itself was granted autonomy by the Patriarch of Constantinople in 1931. 'Autocephalous' means that it became self-governing and equal to the other churches within the Orthodox-Byzantine tradition (Zernov 1961: 188). At the time of fieldwork the church was in decline. Church lands had been confiscated, religion was no longer taught in the schools, most villages did not have resident priests, and very few young men were training for the priesthood. Villagers felt themselves to be embattled by a militantly atheistic state. Religious beliefs and practices were mocked in schools, and it was clearly understood that open expressions of faith would be prejudicial to one's chances of a career in state institutions. The decline of the church and the advance of communism were taken as signs by some villagers that the Second Coming of Christ was at hand. When parts of Skopje were destroyed by a great earthquake on the feast day of Sv Arhangel in 1963, villagers interpreted this as a sign of warning to atheistic city-dwellers.

While both the 'Serbs' and 'Macedonians' of Skopska Crna Gora are Orthodox, the differences between them have considerable local significance. They are said to differ in dress, language, trustworthiness, level of civilization and so on. In the turbulent recent history of the Balkans, both Serbia and Bulgaria have dominated the region at various times. Local Serbs took advantage of Serbian ascendancy, for example, to victimize local Macedonians. The latter then took revenge when Bulgaria controlled the area. Each side, therefore, can relate a long catalogue of outrages which call for retaliation. The lines of division become self-perpetuating as memories of previous incidents lead to new ones at weddings, dances and other village festivities.

So far we have seen how villagers see themselves as a beleaguered community with hostile neighbours of differing nationalities and religions. These other religions are not regarded as being without efficacy. Crna Gorci will consult their specialists as a source for spells, amulets and other powers to further private ends. But they see other bodies of believers to be opposed to themselves. We have also seen that Crna Gorci regard the Yugoslav state as a hostile force whose interests are opposed to theirs. This opposition comes not only from the official atheism, but from a host of measures designed to limit and alter the nature of private peasant agriculture. Such measures are seen not merely as interfering, but as hostile in intent.

The Orthodox Church's view as it is locally understood can be stated as follows. Man is created in the image of God, the Creator of the World. As an image of God, Man is also a creator. But Man fell from God when, using his liberty, he disobeyed the commandment.

He became carnal, mortal. His character as a creature limited, imperfect, manifests itself in all his life and leads him towards evil and error. . . . Man is isolated in the world, for his direct relations with God are ended. He is obliged to *seek* God.
                                        Bulgakov 1935: 125; emphasis is original

Salvation is a pure gift from God. Here is no place for merit by which man might acquire a right to grace, 'for grace is incommesurable with any merit, whatever it may be. . . .' (Bulgakov 1935: 127). One can seek God and salvation only through the church.

Crna Gorci understand the church to be adherents of the Orthodox faith, living and dead. It includes the saints, prophets, angels and Christ. One can achieve salvation only by clinging to the church and its living faith. The corporate unity of the church is displayed within the church building. Internally it is divided by the *ikonostasis*, a wall or screen of icons behind which the Eucharist is performed. In the centre of this screen are the Royal Doors, which are opened and closed during the service to reveal and conceal the mysteries within. The screen itself contains icons of the saints. As Padwick says, these saints are true human fellow worshippers who have been lifted out of this world and who are now with Christ (Padwick 1934; quoted in Zernov 1961: 244). They mediate between living worshippers and the mystery of Christ's sacrifice for the salvation of the faithful.

Above the *ikonostasis* and on all the walls are frescoes depicting the saints and the life of Christ. Almost every surface is decorated. High above is Christ. Arrayed below him are the angels, prophets, fathers and saints of the church. They are arranged in acts of timeless worship. On the icons and frescoes the faces of the saints appear grim and expressionless. To believers they are depicted in a passionless eternity. The effect is powerful. Living worshippers are not only in a church building: they are encompassed within *the entire* church, living and dead. In contrast to the Gothic church, which reaches out and away from the worshipper through insurmountable distance towards the transcendent, the Orthodox churches of Skopska Crna Gora sit snugly around their worshippers, absorbing them within the body of the church (Bulgakov 1935: 151).

As the worshipper turns to leave, he is confronted with a large frescoe depicting the day of judgement. On it the saved are being raised into Heaven while the damned are herded into Hell by the Devil. It is a vivid reminder of evil and its consequences. Those who spoke to me about the matter claimed that there is much evil in the world. Indeed, the amount of evil is increasing. While this interpretation was often mocked by the younger, educated generation, their seniors argued that the progress of history has been from evil to greater evil. It began with Adam and Eve's betrayal with the fruit of knowledge. The life of Christ then offered hope to mankind until Christ, too, was betrayed. Once again evil was on the increase. Crna Gorci say that the early Serbian state offered new hope until it was defeated in the Battle of Kossovo and subjected to 500 years of tyranny under the Ottoman Turks. Interestingly, this Serbian defeat was triggered by the assassination of the Ottoman general by a member of his entourage. This act of treachery so enraged Ottoman forces that they hurled themselves against the Serbs. Some villagers gave a similar story of treachery to account for the rise of Tito and the foundation of the contemporary Yugoslav state.

As an embattled community threatened by forces outside, it is important to maintain harmony and cohesiveness among Orthodox believers. At the beginning of Lent villagers are expected to patch up differences and to beg forgiveness of one another for past wrongs. Among kin, affines and spiritual kin (*kumstvo*), juniors should seek out seniors and beg forgiveness. The ordering of relationships is important. No matter what the grievances, or even whether a grievance exists at all, in order to put affairs in order (*u red*) it is the responsibility of juniors to petition and of seniors to forgive. Significantly, as we shall see later, younger brothers petition elder, sons petition fathers and mothers, but wives do not petition husbands; nor do the wives of brothers petition one another. When Easter Sunday arrives the entire community should have purified itself through fasting and re-establishing harmony.

Just as the larger Orthodox community is surrounded by hostile elements, so too are the several units within it. Some villages are split into ethnic moieties, and even ethnically homogeneous villages are split into upper and lower sections. These provide lines of division for fights and local disputes. Within the sections of particular villages, the households of single clans tend to cluster together to form distinctive neighbourhoods. Their members see themselves in opposition to like constituted units (Rheubottom 1980: 225). Yet while the members of these exogamous, localized patriclans share a common surname and enjoy the protection of the same patron saint, their respective households compete with one another for wives and prestige. This competition is most in evidence on the feast day of the patron saint, the *slava* (Rheubottom 1976a).

The embattled nature of the household is clearly marked in its architectural layout. A well built domestic compound in Skopska Crna Gora is surrounded by a high brick wall. Walking through a village is like walking through a labyrinth. The walls are breached by gates which are kept closed. A vicious dog is chained just inside to make certain that no outsider gets in without an escort. Its barking heralds passers-by.[4] The house is normally built with its back abutting the wall and public thoroughfare, or perpendicular to the thoroughfare. If there are windows on the public-facing side, they will not be on the ground floor: they will be small and placed on an upper storey, so that insiders will be able to observe what passes by outside, but no passers-by will be able to see in. If the size of the compound does not permit, or if the household lacks sufficient means to build a protecting wall, the dwelling is placed perpendicular to the thoroughfare and situated so that it is not overlooked. Out-buildings are placed so that their entrances can be easily observed from the dwelling, but away from public gaze.

Careful site planning, however, is not enough to ensure protection. The household that I lived with, a unit that ordinarily contained seven members, was never left unattended during the year I lived there. This was standard practice. Calculations of domestic labour requirements always included one person to stay at home and guard the premises. It seemed unnecessary, and I chided my landlord for being overly cautious. The imperative nature of such precautions was made evident when a neighbour woman was taken to hospital. Although most of the household valuables had been removed to safer quarters, the house was ransacked during the hours it stood empty. Firewood and even the flowers placed outside the doorway were removed.

Everything, one's person and one's possessions, are constantly at risk to theft, vandalism and mystical attack. Even quite casual pieces of information may give comfort to those who would do one harm. Children are taught at a very early age to be guarded in what they say to outsiders, and they reply 'I don't know' to the most innocent requests for information.[5] This came to be extremely exasperating. The training process begins when the children are small. Games of teasing and torment teach hard but useful lessons. One favourite is to pretend that the adult has some choice sweet hidden in a pocket. The child has only to beg in a demeaning manner to be given it. The child is dubious about the sweet's existence and is goaded into begging with the threat that, if it does not ask, the adult will consume the sweet and the

---

[4] Villagers keep track of movements in the village at night by listening to the patterns in the barking. They are able to make shrewd deductions about who is visiting whom by listening to the 'trail' of barking and the way particular dogs bark.

[5] The usual greeting when adults meet along the road is for each to ask probing questions about the other's activities and intentions. Each person also responds with uninformative, evasive replies. At the end of an exchange each will be as ignorant about the affairs of the other as when they met.

child will get nothing. Eventually, in response to vigorous urgings and mouth-watering descriptions of the sweet, the child relents and begs. The adult then turns out an empty pocket and thumps the child for its gullibility. Onlookers mock it into tears. In such a manner children are taught that greed and trust lead one into trouble. The safe course is to be wary.

Given the ever-present danger as Crna Gorci perceive it, precaution is always in order. When crops such as grapes and melons stand ripe in the field, one household member remains day and night in the field until they can be harvested. At harvest time, when there is so much to do, the additional task of protecting crops presents severe strains on household labour resources. But, these exceptional periods apart, the precautions are habitual and routine. Because they are so scrupulous, Crna Gorci are seldom victimized and they appear neither timid nor fearful.

Similar precautions must also be taken within the household. At marriage each woman is given a wedding chest in which to store her family's valuables. The keys hang from a cord attached to her belt. These chests are never left unlocked and their contents remain a closely guarded secret. Generally there are very few accusations of theft, vandalism or attack within the household because there are very few opportunities. But when opportunity strikes, it is taken. My family heard the results of several incidents within our own household, and we were the victims of several others until we acquired a large chest and the habits of self-protection became second nature.

To prevent dissension in the household, there are elaborate rules governing the allocation of labour and reward. Every adult, for example, is given a turn to represent the household at weddings and christenings. Every child is given new clothes at Eastertime. Similarly, both unpleasant and pleasant tasks are rotated among the workforce. A good household head (*domaćin*) is particularly concerned with maintaining harmony, and he does this by ensuring that order is adhered to. No individual, and no nuclear family, should derive undue advantage or disadvantage. This does not mean equality, however: males are advantaged over females, and seniors are advantaged over juniors. But it does mean that personal favouritism should not be shown. If one nuclear family within the household should enjoy extra advantages, this is an unintended consequence of following customary procedures and those advantages will be averaged out through the passage of time (Rheubottom 1976b).

While the households of Skopska Crna Gora can differ from one another considerably in wealth, they contrive an appearance of uniformity — indeed, a uniformity of poverty. Ostentation in dress or habitat is deliberately shunned. Differences, particularly differences in apparent wealth, attract unwanted attention and appeals for a loan or assistance. Such appeals can decently be refused only by claiming inability to assist, never an unwillingness. And since such appeals are almost never made except when the applicant has convinced himself that there is no possibility of refusal, any appeal is extremely difficult to deflect. It is for this reason that, when someone stands outside the gate and calls to be admitted, those inside urgently confer over the possible motive. If it seems that some kind of appeal will be made, a child will probably be sent out to interrogate the caller about the purpose of his visit and then to deflect him by claiming that no one of any seniority is at home. If the caller asks where such persons are, or when they might be expected to return home, he will be faced with the usual 'I don't know'. If an adult goes to the gate, it is more difficult to turn the caller away without giving offence.

If the caller does get entry to the house, he or she is received hospitably, ushered into the kitchen and given something to drink. Only very special guests are allowed into the 'best room' (*prijemna soba*), where the household's prized furnishings are on display. If it seems at all likely that the caller has come to make an appeal, the conversation quickly turns to these bad times, difficulties with tax collectors, unpaid arrears, poor yields, badly deflated market prices and so on. This is accompanied by a long list of urgent, but unfulfillable, obligations. And, at long last, the host points to the poor rags he wears and the sad state of the house's contents and condition. With this armament any supplicant should be routed, although there may be a lengthy skirmish before he withdraws.

A household's fields and pastures are divided into numerous small plots and these are widely scattered. Some of the fields belonging to villagers in the place where I lived were located on the outskirts of the city of Skopje, over 15 kilometers away. Thus, while fellow villagers may make shrewd guesses about one another's land holdings, the exact amount and composition will not be known. I found, for example, that very close kinsmen of my village host did not know about all of his fields. And I am doubtful that I discovered them all, even though I took some pains to try to find out. Wealth, therefore, is guessed at, and knowledge about it is tempered by the fact that a large, apparently prosperous, household may be no better off on a per capita basis than a small, less prosperous one.

If thievery and vandalism can be forestalled through vigilance and sensible precautions, so too can some mystical attacks. Fertility of the fields can be vouchsafed by reciting the proper spells and burying certain ritual objects. The fertility of man and animals is protected by spells and amulets. The protective umbrella of the household's patron saint gives additional security. But all such devices offer only selective help. They operate only in so far as they have been properly constituted by observing the prescribed formulae, keeping the fast, abstaining from sexual relations and the like. And even when all of this is scrupulously adhered to, they operate only within limited provinces. The fertility of animals, for example, is secure only within the confines of the dwelling compound. On public paths or in open areas they are subject to attack. They may even be attacked at home if they can be seen. Borrowing a term from Favret-Saada, we may say that they are reasonably safe only if they are within the enclosed *domain* (1980: 196). By this term I mean more than physical space: it corresponds more closely to our sense of possessions and includes sites, things and people.

Yet for many this climate of distrust and suspicion is worrisome. I was frequently asked, for example, if such precautions were necessary where I came from. And many peasants spoke of their desire to emigrate for these reasons. People thought it would be better to rear their children in a place where people respected and trusted one another. Indeed, the dangers of theft, vandalism and attack were condemned by everyone, as was the necessity of having to take such extensive precautions.

But accompanying this loathing was a set of beliefs and practices that gave rise to, and maintained, this ethos of distrust and aggression towards others. This ethos holds that unusual success in many endeavours is merely the result of luck. If someone else is successful, he is lucky. If I do not enjoy similar success, or if I encounter a series of small disasters, I am not lucky. Notice that I have eschewed the idea of being unlucky to express the Crna Goran notion. For to be unlucky, as we perceive it, suggests a deficiency of luck, a negative amount. The Crna Goran view, if I understand it properly, is simply the absence of luck. In addition to this, the Crna Goran will contend that the difference between the lucky and himself (the not-lucky) is not one of worth or indeed of effort. The not-lucky will stoutly maintain that he is just as worthy, and has worked just as hard, as the lucky. It follows, therefore, that he is equally entitled to the lucky one's rewards. To help oneself to some of the lucky person's possessions, or to destroy some of what he has, is merely to re-establish an equitable distribution of reward.

But there is another side to this coin. If an opportunity to steal or destroy presents itself, and if there is no likelihood of being seen, then it would be wrong not to seize the chance. One day while returning to the village from the fields, my companion and I passed a melon patch belonging to unknown persons. Looking quickly around, he urged me to pick a melon and take it home. He picked one as I demurred and then, seeing that I refused, picked another for me and stuffed it into my rucksack. When I protested that this was just the kind of thievery that he so often condemned, he explained that if we did not take the melons then the next people coming along the path would do so. They would then be benefiting their household while our separate households would get no benefit. We, therefore, would be disadvantaged, and they were certainly no more deserving than we. We had the duty to be concerned with our households' welfare; we could not deliberately disadvantage our own. When we arrived at his house, my conduct was recounted to his wife and sister-in-law as further evidence of my naivety.

Since unusual success is undeserved, those who enjoy it have acquired it by evil means. This is particularly self-evident if the rise to fortune is rapid. Over several generations a household may prosper through continuing unity and careful husbandry. This permits the household to benefit from economies of scale in production and greater efficiency. But sudden success within a single generation can have no such explanation. The evil nature of inexplicable success is made obvious when others, seeing the manifest results, go to the household with requests for assistance. Their refusal, coupled with unlikely talk about hard circumstances, show the true reasons behind their success.

The theft of others' possessions, or their destruction through vandalism, thereby creates the uniformity of poverty that all espouse. But clearly, not all households are equally poor. Some people live in squalour and destitution while others are plainly comfortable. Does it follow, therefore, that the poor are left in peace while the affluent are brought down a peg or two? Crna Gorci strongly assert that it is sinful to attack the genuinely poor and increase their misery, but there can be some doubt about who the genuine poor are. Villagers say that children and grandchildren may be punished by God for the sins of their ancestors. The punishment for a sinful life is one hundred years of misfortune for the descendants. A village idiot who was thought to live incestuously with his half-mad sister was such a case. While his grandfather was said to have been quite prosperous, a long sequence of misfortune had depleted household resources, and with the death of this couple the grandfather's line would be extinct. No one claimed certain knowledge of the grandfather's sin, but equally, no one doubted that such a sin had been committed. For some, therefore, an attack on this household merely supported God's design. Others took a non-interventionist stance and a few, at one church meeting, advocated charity. But I have no doubt, although I cannot document it, that the unfortunate were heavily victimized. Therefore, weakness and vulnerability lead to further attacks, and the misfortune that ensues is retrospectively explained by others as divine punishment.

In these instances we can discern a dialectic between the unfortunate and the well favoured. Those who experience misfortune see themselves as being under attack. A couple, for example, who have no children, or whose children died in infancy, believe they have lost the protection of their patron saint and that their fertility has been mystically stolen. When a couple who have been childless suddenly have a child, other childless couples will believe that they have stolen their own fertility, and the happy couple believe that their magic has worked and restored the fertility that had been taken from them. Evil, therefore, is seen to reside in households that are unusually fortunate or unfortunate. Unusual fortune can only have an evil source. Unusual misfortune, too, has an evil source. Seen from the outside, misfortune is punishment for hidden evil deeds. To victimize such people surreptitiously is to carry out divine plan. For the unfortunate, they *are* victimized for no apparent cause. Therefore, their plight is best explained by the ill-gotten gains of the fortunate. The fortunate see themselves as deserving, but they are also continually threatened by those who, as they see it, are lazy, inept and jealous. These they regard with contempt. The fortunate must also go to great lengths to safeguard their domains from the importuning and attacks of jealous outsiders. But when these outsiders do attack, it is only to regain what had unjustly been denied them.

The second example of evil concerns the evil eye (*loši oči*). As Crna Gorci understand it, it exists only as a potential for evil. It is created in a child when its mother tries to wean it, but then relents at its cries and resumes breastfeeding.[6] This temporary lapse in resoluteness creates a potential for evil. Crns Gorci say that many people have the evil eye. As the doctrine suggests, the holder of the evil eye may be either male or female. Most holders are well-known in the villages and freely acknowledge their power. Some of them are also properly circumspect. They restrain themselves from commenting favourably on something the first time that they see it and, as a consequence, they do not activate the power for evil within them. A few people, conscious of their power, deliberately use it to harm others. But most with the evil eye, if they do not intend evil, are sufficiently negligent from time to time unwittingly to cause trouble. If the source of the trouble is diagnosed in time, the person with the evil eye will be asked to spit over the affected item, or at least to spit into a glass of water which can then be applied to the item. In this way the evil influence is removed. Babies and young children are especially vulnerable to attack, as are young animals.

Deliberate attacks can come at any time, but they are particularly likely when the domain is open. The domain is open when some aperture is left open, if the boundaries have not been properly sealed off, or if some part of it must temporarily be outside. For this reason the household goes to great lengths to keep the contents of its domain hidden. This applies particularly to new contents or those that are especially vulnerable. A field standing alone may be vulnerable, but ownership is likely to be known only to those who own

---

[6] The same pattern has been described by Stein for Slovak-Americans, where it is also associated with teething and toilet training (1976: 196—201). Stein presents a psychoanalytic interpretation of this association. In Skopska Crna Gora weaning generally occurs some time after teething and is not associated with toilet training.

adjacent fields. Furthermore, it is likely that anyone who knows the owners and wishes them harm will not be seeing the field for the first time. Shepherds exchange flocks of young lambs so that first-time onlookers will not know their true owners. But even established flocks, because of the long periods that they are away from the villages, are brought down to the villages so as to arrive just as night falls. This reduces the likelihood that they will be seen for the first time by someone who intends evil. If follows that the longer something has been in the village, the greater is the chance that those with the evil eye will have already seen it. This reduces the likelihood of attack from this source. But those who live some distance away might well be seeing something for the first time. Therefore, the more socially distant a person, the more of a threat he can be, especially when, because of this distance, it is not likely to be known whether he possesses the evil eye or not.

The third and final example concerns women. Crna Gorci do not regard women as being evil by their nature. Rather, it is women's weak nature that leads them easily into evil. By their nature women are thought of as being selfish, wilful, lazy and concerned with creature comforts. It is this short-sighted hedonism that leads to trouble. Women are thought to want to sit by the fire at home all day, to eat what they want, to sleep in the afternoon, and to look after their own children and spoil them. There is very good reason for these desires since a beautiful woman is considered to be a white-skinned, fat woman. There is nothing beautiful, as Crna Gorci see it, in being lean from hard work and deeply tanned by the sun. To be 'dark like a gypsy' is to be ugly. Whiteness represents goodness and beauty (Rheubottom 1976a: 22). If a woman can lead a life where she can grow fat and fair-skinned, she attains a condition that is highly admired. Furthermore, it is the mark of a successful man to have a plump wife. Her indolent life and sleek physique testify to his abilities as an excellent husband and provider. Therefore, the cultural system presents a two-sided image. One side extols beauty and success. But attempts to achieve this ideal result in the other side of the image, which presents women as lazy, selfish and indolent.

The wilful nature of woman must be tempered by a man. A good woman is restrained and hard-working, but these latter characteristics are inculcated by men, first her father and brothers and later her husband and father-in-law. As one person explained, a woman needs to be 'tamed' by her husband. The image of domestication is apt, for a woman's improper behaviour reflects more on her husband or father and his ability to control and direct her actions. She is not held directly responsible. A neighbour woman who was unusually quarrelsome and obstreperous was generally given wide berth. When I remarked on her behaviour, my informants shrugged their shoulders and pointed out that her husband was away from the village for days at a time collecting firewood in the mountains. Women are also held to talk more easily and fluently than men. Like the devil, women have a facility with language, and baby girls are thought to learn to speak more quickly than boys. But this is not interpreted as female superiority: on the contrary. An intelligent man is measured in his speech and weighs his words with care. Woman's facility with speech merely demonstrates her intemperate nature, careless and impetuous. But the connection between women and evil lies in another, if related, direction.

Women are held to be evil not in themselves, but in the consequences of the actions that they cause. Household division is the most frequently cited example. Crna Gorci hold that men could live together in harmony in a single household for ever were it not for the divisive nature of their womenfolk. Indeed, Crna Gorci say that in the past men did live together without division. There was less evil then and men were stronger in character. If women prompt division nowadays, it shows that men are weak. In the past they would have kept their womenfolk in check. When I explained to villagers that I was interested in studying why the large households (*zadrugas*) of the past had declined, I was told that the answer was obvious. Households divide because women prod their menfolk into it. This was repeated so often by men and women alike that it smacked of dogma. And, of course, it was true — incomplete and misleading, but true.

Why do households divide? The answer that Crna Gorci provide is simple. It also fits with what they believe about the nature of women. A woman does not like working in the fields while her mother-in-law or sister-in-law remains at home by the fire and looks after the children. Furthermore, the rules governing work and reward disadvantage junior wives and their nuclear families. A young woman sees her husband and herself working at least as hard as her husband's brother and his wife while the latter's larger family gets a larger share of the rewards. This leads to unresolvable arguments about child care, work and reward. Gradually, as doctrine has it, a man gives in to his wife's hectoring and initiates division. As a consequence, she becomes the mistress of her own home and is now able to stay home and cook and look after her own children. The fact that division almost always brings hardship in its wake does not concern her. Because of division, important economies of scale are lost. Land, house, livestock, tools, crops — all the substance of the household is divided. Each of the resultant units is worse off after division. Each unit is now also more vulnerable, since illness or death is more serious in a smaller household where there are fewer people to fill out the work roster, tend the sick or care for children whose parents have died. Furthermore, the menfolk must face the village having failed to live as brothers, fathers and sons are expected to live. They have also shown themselves to be weak in dealing with their women.

In considering these three examples of evil, we have seen that Crna Gorci feel themselves to be at risk from a variety of outside forces and agents. In the limited scope of this chapter, it has been possible to mention only a few. Government, strangers and a variety of other agents (material and mystical) may bring harm. If they can not be completely warded off, at least they can be held at bay by carefully maintaining the boundaries of village, household and person. The boundaries of any of these 'nested' units has implications for the integrity of the others. The single person seeks salvation but is prone to error and sin. The village congregation, as the local embodiment of the church, is the only true source of guidance. The household mediates between person and village. Its members bring it into the congregation of believers at baptism, sustain it throughout its life; and, through food taken to the grave on the Days of the Souls and through prayer, they help ease its way into Heaven and then sustain it there.[7] The prayers of living descendants can reduce the time that a soul suffers for its sins. The three units of person, household and village are bound together in a 'spiritual economy' of salvation.

Only the person can sin, but the integrity of the person, household and village come mutually into jeopardy. Villages become disordered when households become unnaturally poor or well-to-do. This unlikeness among otherwise similar units both creates evil and exemplifies it. The household becomes disordered when constituent nuclear families become unequal and seek division. This too, as we have seen, creates evil and exemplifies it. Similarly for the person. The child, improperly separated from its mother, carries latent evil in its evil eye. It can create illness, death or destruction among others. Evil, therefore, has two dimensions. It can come from outside and attack a person and his domain. Crna Gorci talk as if evil such as this is always present. The best safeguard is to maintain boundaries and keep things bounded. But evil can also be created. This happens when an element contained within the confines of a bounded village, household or person breaches the boundary. In doing so it creates evil. This is the common thread linking our three examples. It also links Crna Gorci notions about the history of evil, for in each instance it was the trusted dependant, the contained element — Eve, Judas, the member of the Ottoman general's entourage — that betrayed the whole of which it was a part.

---

[7] A fuller discussion of these feast days of the dead will appear separately.

REFERENCES

Bulgakov, S. (1935). *The Orthodox Church.* London: Centenary Press.

Favret-Saada, J. (1980). *Deadly Words.* Cambridge: Cambridge University Press.

Nikolovski, A., Čornakov, D. and Balabanov, B. (1961). *The Cultural Monuments of the People's Republic of Macedonia.* Skopje: Nova Makedonija Press.

Rheubottom, D. (1976a). 'The Saint's Feast and Skopska Crna Goran Social Structure'. *Man* (NS) 11, 18–34.

Rheubottom, D. (1976b). 'Time and Form: Contemporary Macedonian Households and the Zadruga Controversy'. In *Communal Families in the Balkans* (ed. R. Byrnes). Notre Dame: University of Notre Dame Press.

Rheubottom, D. (1980). Dowry and Wedding Celebrations in Yugoslav Macedonia. In *The Meaning of Marriage Payments* (ed. J. Comaroff). London & New York: Academic Press.

Stein, H. (1976). 'Envy and the Evil Eye: An Essay in the Psychological Ontogeny of Belief and Ritual'. In *The Evil Eye* (ed. c. Maloney). New York: Columbia University Press.

Zernov, N. (1961). *Eastern Christendom.* London: Weidenfeld and Nicolson.

6

Confucian confusion:
the good, the bad and the noodle western

*Brian Moeran**

INTRODUCTORY REMARKS

This chapter is about notions of 'good' and 'bad' in modern Japanese society, as interpreted through television samurai period dramas known as *jidaigeki.*

I ought to start by making it clear that Japanese concepts of 'good' and 'evil' differ — fairly naturally — not only from those found in the Judaeo-Christian tradition that has been the subject of previous chapters, but also according to whether they are used in a Shinto, Buddhist or Confucian context within Japan. There are three points to be made here.

First, neither the Japanese nor — so far as I can judge — the Chinese make any distinction between 'bad' and 'evil', between what Southwold in chapter 8 refers to as 'evil' and 'radical evil'. A single Chinese character (*o, aku*) is used to express 'badness', and this character appears to connote 'disgust', rather than 'wrong'. Although I may, like Shelley's skylark, blithely speak of 'good' and 'evil' during the course of this paper, I should stress here that my use of the latter word is primarily to satisfy those who believe in the efficacy of cross-cultural semantics.

Second, concepts of good and evil are perforce relative. What Shinto deems good, Buddhism might regard as evil; and what Buddhism regards as evil, Confucianism might see as good — although Shinto and Confucian concepts of good here will not necessarily coincide. Similarly, in the midst of a wet winter a farmer prays for sunshine, whereas in the midst of summer he may well pray for rain. Sun and rain, therefore, can be good or bad depending on

* I would like to thank Dr James McMullen, of the Oriental Institute at the University of Oxford, for taking the trouble to constructively comment upon an earlier draft of this paper.

circumstance. For someone stumbling home late at night from the local pub, a cloudy night is 'bad' because it prevents him from seeing his way; for the mugger hiding in the bushes, however, there is nothing worse than moonlight. This point about the relative nature of good and evil is made elsewhere in this book, but perhaps needs reinforcing here, since the Japanese have not one, but three, modes of religious thought with which to contend. Good and evil are not absolutely opposed; rather, they are shifting categories. The purpose of religious or moral thought would appear to be to mask this fact.

Third, before moving on to my main theme of Confucianism and *jidaigeki*, I should perhaps give some indication of what these differences are concerning the notion of evil. In the mythologies of Japan, written in the eighth century after Christ and designed to uphold the authority of the imperial family, evil connotes pollution and death. We find that Izanami, one of the two founding deities in the Shinto religion, became polluted when she ate a cooked substance in the land of darkness (*yomi*), home of the dead. She was prohibited from returning to the world above and became the goddess of evil and wickedness (cf. Motoori in Tsunoda, De Bary and Keene 1964: 25). In Shinto thought, good and evil are connected with purity and impurity, with life and death.

Death is one of the three evils of Buddhism, along with old age and sickness. In tenth-century Japanese literature, written when Buddhism had enormous influence on the Japanese court, we find that good refers to nobility, long life, wealth and prosperity, while evil refers to low rank, illness, poverty and failure. Those who understand *mono no aware*, the sorrow of human existence and the transience of things, and who are sympathetic and in harmony with human sentiments, are good. Others are more or less evil.

While there are clearly various notions of good and evil, I wish to suggest that it is in terms of Confucian, rather than Shinto or Buddhist, ideals that we should consider people's interpretations of morality in modern Japanese society. In the following analysis of *jidaigeki*, noodle westerns, I argue that the essentially Confucian relationships depicted in the dramas not only focus on the ambivalent relation between group and individual in Japanese society, but also enter into a wider cultural debate on the relative importance of tradition and modernization, of oriental 'spiritualism' *vis-à-vis* western 'materialism'. I then suggest that the Confucian cultural debate within Japan is carried over into anthropologists' interpretations of the way in which Japanese society is organized. Hence we have 'good' theories and 'bad' theories, depending on which side of the group/individual irrigation ditch we prefer to squat.

CONFUCIANISM, PRINCIPLE AND ETHER

Although we use the term 'Confucianism' in English after the name of Confucius — the man who is popularly believed to have taught the doctrine — we might perhaps start by noting that the Chinese term is *ju chiao* (*jukyō* in Japanese) and strictly means 'the doctrine of the literati'. It is, therefore, perhaps incorrect to call Confucianism a 'religion' as such, since its concerns are essentially secular and centre on rules of conduct according to social proprieties and political principles. Weber has written that:

In the absence of all metaphysics and almost all residues of religious anchorage, Confucianism is rationalist to such a fargoing extent that it stands at the extreme boundary of what one might possibly call a 'religious' ethic. At the same time, Confucianism is more rationalist and sober, in the sense of the absence and the rejection of all non-utilitarian yardsticks, than any other ethical system, with the possible exception of J. Bentham's.

Weber 1947: 293

Although Weber's version of Confucianism is in certain respects idealized (as we shall soon learn to our cost when we discuss neo-Confucian metaphysics), in general it can be said perhaps that Confucianism is an ethico-political system which has shaped Chinese civilization for more than two millenia, and which has been alive and well — although occasionally slipping into uncharacteristic disguises — in Japan for the past 1,500 years. In particular, perhaps, it should have suffered from its latest escapade when — like the wolf in the *Tale of Little Red Riding Hood* — Confucianism decided to hop into Grandma Shinto's bed. From there it leaped with pearly teeth, harbouring bombastic designs upon us children of the Occident, who were saved only by the tenacity of a gum-chewing lumberjack. The question is: did Confucianism die with the wolf? Or did it manage to escape into another, less provocative disguise?

Confucianism's main focus of attention has been its social philosophy that man should live in harmony with the laws of heaven by maintaining what are known as the Five Fundamental Relationships (*wu ch'ang*, or *gojō* in Japanese): between ruler and minister, father and son, husband and wife, elder brother and younger brother, and friend and friend. These relationships are accompanied by certain duties and obligations. The ruler should be righteous and his minister loyal; the father affectionate and his son filial; a husband harmonious and his wife submissive; an elder brother friendly and his younger brother respectful; and friends mutually sincere. These are the keywords of Confucian thought, and to them are added the four (occasionally five) virtues of benevolence, righteousness, wisdom, decorum (and sincerity). Hence, Confucianism espouses a moral doctrine that is primarily concerned with the ordering of the state by government. Men of superior qualities at the top of the social hierarchy are supposed to set a good example and so influence the popular masses under their control. Men have distinct roles which they should perform for the sake of society, and society itself is arranged in an orderly manner. If those in charge of government apply the moral principles inherent in the four virtues, social harmony will ensue. Morality is instilled in others by virtue rather than by force.

Alas! L. R. Mauré's Law of Opposition does not apply here, for Confucianism is not as unconfused as the last paragraph might lead us to believe. During the Sung Dynasty (960—1279), Confucianism in China underwent fairly radical re-interpretation as philosophers tried to answer some of the intellectual problems raised by Buddhist thought. While Buddhism emphasized transience and impermanence, Confucianism insisted on the reality of the self and of the universe. If a black hole existed, it was not in space (the Buddhist void), but in Calcutta (Confucian reality). Somehow the two modes of thought had to be reconciled, and it was this realization that forced Chinese intellectuals in the Sung period to think Confucian ethics into metaphysics. Western philosophers will no doubt be as sceptical of their methods as physicists are of professional spoon-benders, but I shall proceed because neo-Confucian explanations of the universe happen to coincide with my interpretation of the workings of Japanese social organization.

Neo-Confucianism is the title given to what was essentially a synthesis of Buddhist, Taoist and Confucian ideas.[1] The most famous of the neo-Confucian scholars was Chu Hsi (1130—1200) who, adopting some of the ideas of his predecessors, distinguished between metaphysical 'above shapes' (*keijijō* in Japanese) and physical, concrete 'below shapes' (*keijika*). What existed above shapes had, as its name implied, neither shape nor form; it transcended both time and space. This Chu Hsi called *li* (*ri*, in Japanese), or 'immaterial principle'. What existed below shapes he called *ch'i* (*ki*), 'material force' or 'ether'. *Ch'i* lay within the bounds of space and time, and so had actuality and form.

Chu Hsi argued that *li* had no creative power of its own and had to rely on the transformations of *yin* (quiescence) and *yang* (movement) within *ch'i* to give it form. Yet, at the same time, *li* had *a priori* existence over *ch'i*. Chu

---

[1] In the following paragraphs I have relied particularly on Chang (1957: 243—83) and Fung Yu-lan (1953: 533—71).

Hsi's duality of immaterial principle and material force thus strike me as being somewhat similar to de Saussure's distinction between *langue* and *parole*. Both *langue* and *li* can exist in an ideal vacuum, but they rely upon *parole* and *ch'i* to give them substantial form.[2] This is what might be called a 'Blue Flame' theory: the genie may be hovering somewhere around, but he is not allowed to make an official appearance until Aladdin rubs his lamp.

Li is a supremely good, normative principle — equivalent, at the metaphysical level, to Aristotle's Prime Mover and, at the level of moral values, to Plato's Idea of the Good. *Ch'i*, however, would appear to be potentially imperfect; for when it combines with *li* to form things and people, it produces clever people and dull people, kind people and cruel people, and so on. This suggests that *li* can lose perfection when it is activated by *ch'i* — in much the same way as we can imagine a perfectly round circle, but tend to end up drawing a somewhat elliptical wobble.

Nevertheless, Chu Hsi argued that man's essential nature was good, and so adopted Mencius's position rather than that of Hsun-tzu, who said that human nature was evil, or that of Han Yu, who suggested that there were three kinds of human nature — good, bad and a mixture of both. For Chu Hsi, human nature had to be good because principle was good and human nature was principle. Where there was imperfection, this was in man's *physical* nature as a result of *ch'i*.

The distinction between essential and physical nature coincides with that between *li* and *ch'i* and gives rise to certain moral values. Man's sense of filial duty, loyalty, honesty and so on (attributes connected with the Five Fundamental Relationships), together with his understanding of the Four Virtues, all came from his endowment of *li*. However, his physical nature produced feelings, and feelings in themselves gave rise to selfish desires (*yü*, or *yoku* in Japanese). It would thus appear that an excess, or insufficiency of, desire is responsible for evil, since it leads man away from the perfection of principle which is in his essential nature.

The relation between *li*, principle, and *ch'i*, ether, has been the subject of considerable debate on both sides of the China Sea, for neo-Confucianism was to some extent adopted by the Japanese when Tokugawa Ieyasu (1542–1616) set about unifying the country at the beginning of the seventeenth century. From then on, two types of neo-Confucian thought have existed, one stressing principle (*ri*, in Japanese) and the other ether (*ki*) (de Bary 1979: 19).

I do not wish to dwell too long on historical facts, but it might be pointed out here that each of the major thinkers of the Tokugawa period (1603–1868)

---

[2] *Langue* differs from *li* in that it *can* be generative, but I still feel that the parallel is worth making.

was concerned with human nature and its inherent goodness or evil. Fujiwara Seika (1561—1619) saw emotions as the source of selfish desires and hence potentially evil. Hayashi Razan (1583—1657) felt that physical nature was not necessarily evil and that principle could hardly exist unless embodied in ether. Yamaga Sokō (1622—85) followed Mencius in thinking that man was by nature good. If selfish desires were bad, then it implied that the actual self was also evil; so Sokō proceeded to distinguish between desire permitted by heaven (public desire) and desire that was merely personal (private desire). Itō Jinsai (1627—1705) tried to separate man's essential nature from principle, for he felt that Sung Dynasty neo-Confucianism had allowed the individual too much self-expression and not enough restraint. Spontaneity, in Jinsai's opinion, could destroy social morality if it were too subjective. Finally, Ogyū Sorai (1666—1728) agreed with Jinsai, but felt that human nature could be perfected only by becoming involved in society, rather than by cultivating an inner moral growth, as Jinsai had suggested (de Bary 1979: 127—86). Is all this an idle con, a fusion of ideas, or plain confusion?

Behind each of these slight shifts in neo-Confucian thought in Japan seems to lie one basic concern: to what extent is the individual bound by Confucian ethical principles, or duties, known as *giri* ('socially contracted dependence'), and how much can he allow his spontaneity, *ninjō* ('human feelings'), to affect his social relations? In other words, as principle (*ri*) is to ether (*ki*), so is society to the individual and *giri* to *ninjō*. What is more, this dialogue between *giri* and *ninjō* (which is, after all, merely the social application of the dialogue between the metaphysical principle and the physical ether) still goes on and is to be found at the heart of Japan's internal cultural debate.

It is perhaps surprising to find that Confucian ethics have survived the lumberjack's felling of Grandma Shinto at the end of the not so Pacific War. After all, at one stage Confucian ideals were looked upon with some scepticism, and the widely propagated and accepted statements of Confucian-cum-Shinto ideology that sustained Japan's military nationalism before the war came to be seen as part of a 'feudal' past which could scarcely contemplate courtship with the postwar bride of Western industrial capitalism. I would suggest, however, that Confucian ideals are still important in modern Japanese society and that they form part of the country's internal cultural debate over such problems as the relationship between tradition and modernization, between an 'oriental spiritual civilization' and a 'Western materialist civilization', between society and individual and — ultimately — between concepts of good and evil. In order to illustrate this argument, I want to take a look at what I shall here refer to as the 'noodle western' (or 'spaghetti eastern', depending on one's culinary and geographical tastes).

CONFUCIAN ETHICS AND THE NOODLE WESTERN

The television genre known as *jidaigeki*, to which I have irreverently referred as the 'noodle western', consists of films about samurai. *Jidaigeki* literally means 'period drama' and refers to any film whose story takes place prior to the Meiji Restoration of 1868. Films can be full-length features for cinema, as with Kurosawa Akira's *Kage musha* or Kobayashi Masaki's *Hara-kiri*, but here I will be talking about the somewhat less intense and more frivolous television films shown almost nightly on one of Japan's many television channels. These films are generally about 50 minutes long and centre on Robin-Hood-type heroes who perform miraculous deeds for the benefit of society. In both content and methods of direction, the *jidaigeki* are comparable to the spaghetti western, and a number of American films have either copied, or been parodied by, their Japanese counterparts. *The Magnificent Seven*, for example, is a straight copy of *Shichinin no samurai* (*The Seven Samurai*); the *Sambiki no samurai* parodies the western gunfight that concludes *The Good, The Bad and The Ugly*.

In the noodle western television films, what might be termed the 'semiotics' of good and evil are made abundantly clear, and are similar to what we have come to expect of spaghetti westerns. Thunder, lightning and heavy rain, for example, signify danger (and rain, occasionally, acts as a metaphor for the tears of despair). A night-watchman patrolling the streets and clapping his wooden sticks rhythmically, as he calls out dolefully 'Take care of fires!' (*hi no yōjin*), almost invariably signifies the peaceful prelude to action — a swordfight or, more probably, a robbery. If it is a moonlit night, it is more than likely that the break-in will be conducted by magical *ninja* spies, who can do standing jumps ten feet into the air, run soundlessly across tiled rooftops and hurl sharp metal stars with the accuracy of expert dart players. A man eating buckwheat noodles at a noodle vendor's store is a 'goody', as is the kimonoed girl with flower in her hair and leaning very slightly to one side as she trips along in her wooden clogs — like a reed bending in the breeze. At the same time, her very fragility is a premonition of her luckless fate. The unkempt *rōnin* samurai, with sake bottle slung from hip or over his shoulder, tends to be cast as the 'baddy' — as is the bald priest, the merchant or the lord who is filmed consulting his cronies with a candle's flame flickering in front of his face.[3]

---

[3] The anthropological literature on hair and hairlessness suggests an equation between self-abandon and self-control, respectively. I find it interesting, therefore, that the notion of the

These oppositions of day and night, light and dark, clean and dirty all support the basic contrast of good and bad. Heroes are well washed, clean-looking, closely shaven. They wear well-barbered wigs and well cut kimonos with bright and tasteful designs. They emanate purity. Villains, for their part, have oily skins and sweat freely. They dress in dark robes of cotton or luxurious silk, depending on their social status, and have menacing — so obviously evil — laughs. They are neither polite nor humble like the heroes, but rough and rude, and occasionally obsequious. It is as easy for the viewer to feel immediate revulsion for the bad as it is for him or her to identify with the good. The system of signs used in *jidaigeki* demands very little in the way of *parole*-like interpretation.

The plots of noodle westerns are similarly simple and demand little intellectual concentration. A young girl is murdered for accidentally witnessing a robbery; a hardworking young apprentice is tricked into betraying his master; a crooked policeman is bribed by a merchant or feudal lord to overlook certain irregularities. In every case revenge is taken by a heroic samurai, an honest policeman or down-to-earth citizens turned magically, like Cinderella's mice, into merry men in the service of a Tokugawa-period Robin Hood. Every film starts with society being disordered in some way or other — by murder, robbery or other forms of violence. Every film ends with a return to normality. Like ritual, it conjoins two initially separate people or groups of people (both or all of whom end up on the side of the good) (cf. Lévi-Strauss 1966: 32).

But what, you may ask, has all this got to do with Confucianism? Earlier on, I mentioned such concepts as the Five Fundamental Relationships and the Four Virtues, by which Confucian scholars have argued that society should be organized. These social relationships and moral virtues are an essential part of the noodle western. They form the very moral foundation upon which characters are expected to build their social contacts. It is according to whether they do or do not behave according to the Four Virtues, do or do not respect the Five Fundamental Relationships, that they are distinguished as 'good' or 'bad'.

It is our old friend 'principle' (*ri*) that underlies almost all action in the *jidaigeki*, for it is according to principle that social laws are seen to be natural laws. You have only to behave according to these natural laws of socially contracted dependence, or *giri* — which is defined by the virtues of

---

shaven head seems frequently to connote evil, and sexuality, in films. Yul Brynner may have been a model of good behaviour in *The King and I*, but actors like Telly Savalas and Donald Pleasance frequently find themselves in the role of evil gangster, desperado, villain or spy. Balding academics should, perhaps, beware.

humaneness, righteousness, wisdom and decorum — and you know precisely how society will react towards you. If you behave well and follow *giri*, society will treat you well and all will turn out well. If you disregard these laws, however, you will be treated unfavourably by others and will in the end get your just desserts. Good will *always* prevail; evil will *always* be defeated. If one of the goodies does get killed, he or she will be avenged by others. Whatever a baddy's status in society, he will be caught and punished.[4] Thus society, as depicted in the *jidaigeki*, is a well-knit organism which invariably rectifies its faults. By following principle, people can become perfect social beings.

If *everybody* followed principle, of course, there would be no baddies in the noodle westerns. This is where ether (*ki*) comes in, in the form of human feelings (*ninjō*). Provided that *ninjō* remains in accord with the Four Virtues, then it perfectly balances *giri* and suggests that each individual is a well-oiled cog in the harmonious wheels of Japanese society. But once somebody somewhere decides not to observe social decorum, humaneness or sincerity and allows his human feelings to follow the path of selfish desire, the cog wheels hiccup and grind to a halt.

And thereby hangs a tale. Just as Pooh and his friends persuaded an enlightened Owl to hand over his new bell rope so that it could be nailed back on to Eeyore's rump, so do characters in *jidaigeki* see the wisdom of the Five Fundamental Relationships.[5] In the small group that forms the basic entity in Japanese social organization, each member respects and is loyal to other members. People help one another as friends; and yet, at the same time, because the Japanese tend to frame their relations hierarchically, this friendship frequently takes the form of an elder brother—younger brother, or father—son, relationship. This can be seen with the two runners attached to

---

[4] To some extent, of course, television dramas in the West use the same contrasts for the same didactic ends. In the noodle westerns, incidentally, baddies are almost invariably men, even though the Tendai and Shingon sects of Buddhism have taught that women are inherently evil and are able to attain salvation only by first being reborn as men. In fifteenth-century Japan women were accused of being agents of the devil whose aim was to prevent their husbands from following the way of the Buddha (cf. Paulson 1976: 9).

[5] Some might think that the reference here to a slightly obscure British upper-middle-class children's story is out of place in an article such as this, but my reason for including it stems from more than a desire to betray my childhood reading habits. In many ways, the world of Pooh Bear is a Confucian world of the kind idealized in Japanese noodle westerns. It may not be so violent, perhaps, but its actors are basically kind and generous, and soon recognize the errors of their ways when they do, inadvertently, like Owl, upset their neighbours. They live in a harmony with one another, which we, and the Japanese, find impossible to emulate in real life.

the policeman, Zenigata Heiji; with Sukesan and Kakusan in the service of the disguised feudal lord, Mito Kōmon; or with the fire chief, Megumi no kashira, and his followers in *Abarembō Shōgun*.

There is a general emphasis in *jidaigeki* on kinship. A certain food will remind a heroine of her dead mother's cooking; a locket will remind a hero of his sister in childhood, and plots are filled with tales of lost sisters, of the search for a daughter, of the discovery of a missing brother, and so on. Women are compliant — unto death if needs be — and hence fulfil their fundamental social role of faithful mother, daughter, wife or sister.

These familial relationships are an important aspect of Confucian thought, which emphasizes that a state can be well run only if people behave to strangers in the same way that they treat their nearest and dearest. It is perhaps not surprising, therefore, to find that in *jidaigeki* strangers are almost always taken into a family-type group and are given help and affection: the hungry are fed, the sick nursed back to health and the deprived taken into people's homes. And, in return, those who are helped are always prepared to repay what is seen to be social obligation.[6] No relationship between two people, once begun, by whatever stroke of chance, can ever end, except in death. Yet even by death the Japanese household is continued, and it is perhaps not surprising to find numerous scenes in *jidaigeki* of the goodies visiting graveyards. These are not quite such frightening, haunted places as they can be made to be in other types of film (both in Japan and in the West), but are places where people join together to respect the dead and look after their ancestors. It is the good who are buried; the evil dead are left to rot in the dust on which they fall.

The relationship between sovereign and people is another of the Five Fundamental Relationships given great importance in the noodle western. A number of film series has people from the highest echelons of society mingling with the masses. These characters are based on historical figures and include such eminent men as the 8th Shogun, Tokugawa Yoshimune (in *Abarembō Shōgun*), Ieyasu's grandson, Tokugawa Mitsukuni (in *Mito Komōn*), and nephew of the 3rd Shogun Iemitsu, Matsudaira Chōchichirō (in *Tenka Gomen, Chōshichirō!*). Other characters, such as Momotaro Samurai, supposedly twin brother of one of the Tokugawa shōguns, may be based less on historical fact and more on a fanciful imagination which likes to suggest that sovereigns rule best when they fully understand the problems of their subjects.

---

[6] One might note here the frequency with which such phrases as 'I have been utterly indebted to you' (*sukkari o-sewa ni narimashita*) and 'the return of obligation' (*ongaeshi ni*) occur.

These heroes lead double lives, infiltrating the lower levels of society and helping to keep order as they follow the Confucian precept of *kanzen chōaku*, encourage good and punish evil. Unrecognized, of course, by the simple townspeople with whom they consort, they prevent the spreading of corruption and the flouting of authority. They tangle with villains who come from the lowest stratum in the Tokugawa *shi-nō-kō-shō* four-class system (the merchants), and even from outside society altogether (*yakuza* gangsters and masterless *rōnin samurai*). But the very worst of the villains are those who, like the heroes themselves, come from the very top of society — feudal lords and senior samurai in government bureaucracy — and who make use of their elevated status to take advantage of innocent people and indulge in private profit, extravagance and luxury. They are assuredly evil, not only for their corruption and misuse of an authority entrusted to them by the shōgun, but because they fail to lead lives of frugality espoused by Tokugawa Confucianism.

Dutifulness and loyalty remain the virtues that are practised by the good and that form the single path to redemption for the wayward villain. Obedience is demanded of people; even the baddies do as they are told, and the retainers of an evil lord will attack without question the samurai hero, even though it is apparent that the hero just happens to be their overall lord and master! Immediate loyalties take precedence over more distant, and hence more impersonal, ones. These retainers never run away, even though 30 of them may have already been slashed to death by the hero's flailing sword. Cowardice is unmanly and contrary to the ethics of *bushidō*, or the way of the warrior. Death is an honour, especially at the hands of the high and mighty!

Another aspect of *jidaigeki* morality worth noting is honesty. Honesty always pays. In the end, someone will realize that the wronged goody is not telling lies, that he is in short a goody, and will come to his aid. Submissiveness and humility, too, are vital — particularly for women. The humble woman may be defiled (*watakushi no yō na kegareta onna*) — and note here how Shinto beliefs creep in to an essentially Confucian system — but her humility simultaneously makes her good, and we know that, in the end, she will be able to conquer the evil of her defilement and find an equally humble, 'harmonious' man to look after her.

Finally, trust is another major theme in the noodle western. 'Believe me' (*shinjite kure*) is a phrase used frequently by strangers, and even though there may not be any reason at this particular stage of the development of the plot for anyone to believe anyone else, characters are saved or damned by their capacity to trust the right or wrong person. Trust is thus ambiguous; it is good because it is close to sincerity (one of the Virtues when inflation increases them from four to five in number), but it can lead to suffering. All in all, however, society is seen to be safe and people find safety in social relations that are based on trusting one another.[7]

CONFUCIANISM AND JAPAN'S INTERNAL CULTURAL DEBATE

Noodle westerns are not simply entertainment. Like all forms of entertainment, they contain within them certain social ideals. In particular, they advocate Confucius's notion of the Five Fundamental Relationships and the Four Virtues. But why should people in present-day Japan be amenable to such ideals, given the disastrous consequences of Confucianism's alliance with Shinto nationalism in the 1930s? The answer to this question lies, I think, in Japan's response to westernization and to modern industrialization. Just as in Tokugawa times Confucian ethics tried to deal with the role of the individual in Japanese society, so now they are used to combat what is seen to be the purely negative ideal of Western individualism. Confucian ethics remain at the heart of a continuing dialogue between individual and group in Japanese social organization (cf. Moeran 1984).

First of all, it is clear that *jidaigeki* create a world that is purely Japanese. All films are set in an age when Japan was still isolated from Western influences. Moreover, they generally depict life during the Genroku era (1688–1704), a 'golden age' when — as in Tudor England — internal trade, the arts and other cultural activities flowered. It was during this era that the Tokugawa shoguns were at the zenith of their power and the samurai class was fully conscious and proud of *bushidō*, the way of the warrior. The country

---

[7] In Confucianism there seems to be a complete lack of what Pocock in chapter 3 refers to as 'gratuitous malice'. This may well have something to do with the fact that Confucian morality concentrates on the actor, rather than on the act, in trying to explain evil. When first preparing this paper, I asked a number of Japanese acquaintances living in London to write down what they felt to be the worst (most 'evil') possible act of which a human being was capable, and why they felt so. The 14 replies could be analysed rather neatly into two groups, one centring on the betrayal of trust, the other on the taking of human life. In 70 per cent of the cases, the reasons given as explanation of why such acts were seen as 'evil' were *social*. For example: 'The corruption of politicians. It is unforgivable when someone betrays the trust of the people and thinks only of his own advantage'; 'betraying someone's trust. Trifling with other people's feelings (*kokoro*) is the worst thing of all'; 'killing somebody. . . . By depriving someone of life, you also deprive his or her family and relatives of all happiness.' Somehow, it seems as though the perpetration of an 'evil' deed has to be explained in terms of social relations. To do otherwise would be to suggest that society as a whole is to blame for its failure to encompass an individual. It would seem to me that Pocock's 'minority view' is in fact the 'majority view' in Japan.

had been closed to foreigners for several decades (with the exception of a couple of trading posts in the south-western island of Kyushu), and the Japanese were discovering the glories of their own cultural achievements. Noodle westerns, then, depict a 'pure' Japan, untainted by the 'barbarism' of the 'red-haired devils' of the West. People wear kimonos and clothing with Japanese family crests. They have Japanese hairstyles. They eat Japanese food and drink Japanese *sake* or *shōchū*. They live in Japanese-style wooden houses, sleep in Japanese bedding laid out on *tatami* straw matting, and bathe in Japanese baths. They visit Japanese temples and speak a language that is pure and uncontaminated by foreign words.

All of this presents an immediate contrast with present-day Japan, where people wear Western suits and dresses, have Western-style haircuts, frequently eat Western food and drink Western alcohol. They may now live in earthquake-proof concrete blocks of flats (generally referred to as 'mansions') and sleep in beds on wooden floors. Although they may still visit Japanese temples and shrines and bathe in Japanese-style baths, the modern Japanese will speak a language that frequently uses more English than Japanese vocabulary, so great is the number of foreign loanwords in vogue.

Second, while *jidaigeki* seek to remind modern Japanese that deep down they are 'different' from their Western counterparts in London, Paris or New York, they also point indirectly to problems that are seen to accompany westernization. One of these is the relationship between industrial capitalism and private profit. As I pointed out earlier, it is frequently the merchants who are depicted as being the baddies in noodle westerns. According to Confucian ideals of the Tokugawa period, merchants were placed at the lowest end of the four social classes because, unlike the farming peasants and artisans above them, they did not produce anything. Rather, they dealt with the products of other people's labour and were seen to be interested in little more than profit. This method of making a living has always been regarded by the Japanese as somewhat suspect. Yamaga Sokō, for example, the mid seventeenth century neo-Confucian intellectual mentioned earlier, suggested that for the sage — and by implication the samurai — personal gain and a large salary should be as fleeting an attraction as 'a snowflake and a red hot stove' (Tsunoda *et al.* 1964: 394). In *jidaigeki*, it is the samurai who disregards this admonition by getting involved with merchants, and whose downfall is finally brought about by his lust for gold, who is most roundly condemned. Now, given the role of the samurai in Tokugawa society as setting an example to the people, this attitude is understandable. What is not so easily grasped is the fact that money should still be seen as 'the root of all evil' in modern Japan, where the production and marketing of commodity goods, together with the growth of the nation's GNP, have been publicly proclaimed as important social goals over the past 30 years.

Macfarlane, in chapter 4 above, has talked about the ambivalence of money and has suggested that money eliminates the concept of evil because it ushers in a world of moral confusion. While I am inclined to agree with the idea that money is morally confusing, I am not convinced that 'it is money, markets and market capitalism that eliminate absolute moralities' (p. 72). Confucian ethics, like the Protestant ethic, have always highly valued work, as can be seen in such phrases as *hataraku sugata wa utsukushii* ('how beautiful the figure of someone working'). This means that the division of labour is not seen as being necessarily 'wrong' in Japan, because group ideals at the company or factory level unite workers and managers. Work is especially good when it is done on behalf of others. A similar attitude prevails towards money, which *in itself* is seen as evil. Fujiwara Seika's comment made around the turn of the seventeenth century still holds good: 'Commerce is the business of selling and buying in order to bring profit to both parties. It is not to gain profit at the expense of others' (Tsunoda *et al.* 1964: 340). This attitude goes some way towards explaining why the Japanese 'economic miracle' has occurred and why, perhaps, our own economy is so depressed. Christianity warns us that the pursuit of money is evil' Confucianism stresses that people are allowed — indeed, ought — to make money, but that they should then put it to proper social use. Noodle westerns reinforce this ideal. They remind the present-day businessman that it is not just entrepreneurial skill that matters: he must make some contribution to the welfare of others (cf. Vogel 1963: 160). The continued emphasis on this attitude to money-making partly explains, I think, why modern businesses plough back their profits into sporting competitions, art exhibitions and other cultural activities. They must be seen to be making money for the benefit of the Japanese nation as a whole, not just for themselves.

Third, noodle westerns also touch on the problem of urbanization and its accompanying impersonalization. Urbanization in Japan, of course, is not new. The *jidaigeki* depict society in Edo (present-day Tokyo), which by 1733 had a population of 1.4 million people and was probably the largest city in the world (Yazaki 1968: 134). But Edo in Tokugawa times was somewhat different from Tokyo today. Starting from the shōgun's castle, the city was carefully laid out, with feudal lords living in one area, samurai retainers in another and the common people in wards that were guarded and sealed off at night. What the noodle westerns portray, therefore, is a city of inherent order in which each citizen is allotted his station in life and knows how to act accordingly. They intimate that modern Tokyo-ites may end up in chaos if they fail to observe this order and ignore the personal connections (*tsukiai*) by which people organize their social relationships. Consequently, *jidaigeki* portray a society in which the anonymity of modern Western urban society does not exist. Not only do they emphasize the importance of kinship groups, neighbourhood associations and mutual friendship, but they also suggest that neither the sovereign nor the law is aloof, and that those who govern Japan always have their eyes and ears open to the needs of the people. However high their social status, rulers are at one with the ruled. Together they form a united group which is the Japanese nation.

At the same time, there is a neat oriental twist of fiction to make life coincide with fact. The urban society that is portrayed in the noodle western is that of the Edo townspeople (*chōnin*). It is the culture of the common people, and not that of the samurai, that is eventually held up as an example to present-day Japanese. Here some concession has had to be made to reality. The four-class system of samurai—peasant—artisan—merchant is sacrificed to some extent to a — I dare not say 'the' — notion of democracy. Just as one people's power can be another's Exide battery, so is democracy in Japan interpreted in a specifically Japanese manner, and so does it depend on the important principles of social obligation and human feeling, *giri* and *ninjō*.[8]

Here we come face to face with the masked bandit of Japanese thought. Westernization, capitalism and urban anonymity are three of the unacceptable faces of individualism that, unlike Batman or Dynatron rods, fails to do anybody any good at all. The Japanese are wary of the notion of individualism because they feel that its adoption will merely serve to lead Japan down the straight and narrow path to social chaos. In stressing the importance of familial relationships, therefore, *jidaigeki* are merely echoing the very real apprehension of intellectuals, businessmen and politicians. Anthropologists talk of the household group as being the basic element in Japanese social organization; businessmen proudly proclaim that their company is 'one happy family'; and politicians like Mr Nakasone, the most recently elected Prime Minister of Japan, can make an inaugural 'policy' speech with the question: 'Wherein lies the happiness of the people? It is when the family hurry home and, joined around the dinner table, are together in an aura of contentment' (quoted in *The Times*, 4 December 1982).[9]

---

[8] It is of interest to note here that the Japanese had no word for 'democracy' until they came into contact with the West, whereupon they hit upon the loan creation *minshushugi*. Recently, however, an English loanword, *demokurashī*, has come into use. *Minshushugi* now refers to a specifically 'Japanese' style of democracy and has positive connotations; *demokurashī* refers to Western-style parliamentary rule and has somewhat negative connotations.

'GOOD' AND 'EVIL' INTERPRETATIONS OF JAPANESE SOCIETY

I have already suggested that Chu Hsi's metaphysical distinction between immaterial principle and material ether is paralleled in Japan by a social distinction between ties of obligation (*giri*) and spontaneous human feeling (*ninjō*). What I now wish to argue is that an emphasis on either *giri* or *ninjō* leads social anthropologists to adopt one of two models by which to explain Japanese social organization. Just as neo-Confucian scholars of Tokugawa Japan emphasized *ri* or *ki*, and so came to interpretations of Japanese ethics that saw man as naturally good or naturally evil, so do modern anthropologists emphasize either a 'group' or a 'social exchange' model of Japanese society and come to similar conclusions about the nature of Japanese social organization through *giri* and *ninjō* (see figure 1).

Figure 1

Group model	Social exchange model
li (*ri*) immaterial principle	*ch'i* (*ki*) material ether
keijijō, above shapes	*keijika*, below shapes
perfection	imperfection (desire *yoku*)
essential nature	physical nature
society	individual
giri, socially contracted dependence	*ninjō*, human feelings

The so-called 'group' model of Japanese society assumes that people prefer to act within the framework of a group and that such a group will be hierarchically organized and run by a paternalistic leader. It is the *ideally balanced* combination of *giri* and *ninjō* which permeates all social relationships, in particular those between leader and subordinate in a group.

According to this model, members of a group are expected to conform and cooperate with one another, to avoid open conflict and competition. The emphasis, therefore, is on harmony, and behaviour tends to be ritualized and

---

[9] I am grateful to my colleague, Lionel Caplan, for pointing out that it is probably precisely because the despised merchants of Tokugawa times have emerged as a new class of capitalists that present-day society seeks to constrain and control them by resorting to such ideological notions as that of the conflict between group and individual. The question that remains unanswered here is, Are we really witnessing the rise of individualism or the growing class character of Japanese society?

formal in order to reduce or eliminate conflict or embarrassment. Ideally, in this kind of situation people are supposed to subordinate individual interests to group goals and to remain loyal to group causes. In return for their loyalty and devotion, the leader of the group treats his followers with benevolence and magnanimity (Befu 1980: 170—1).

The 'social exchange' model points out that the group model fails to deal with a number of paradoxes. Not all forms of social organization are hierarchical in Japan; paternalistic leaders do not necessarily look after the welfare of their subordinates; people do behave in ways that go against group norms; the ideology of harmony does not explain the conflict and competition rife in Japanese society.

As an alternative means of explaining these paradoxes, the social exchange model assumes that the individual has certain resources, such as wealth, knowledge, skills or influential friends, which he can exchange with others for resources that he does not possess. In other words, the individual maximizes opportunities by a strategic allocation of resources. Thus, while the group model is motivated by altruism, the social exchange model is motivated by self-interest (Befu 1980: 179—80).

The idea that we consider social exchange when analysing Japanese society is sensible, for it allows us to consider the role of personal networks (*tsukiai*), which have been almost totally ignored by anthropologists espousing the group model. The thing is that one frequently finds people making use of *tsukiai* to break down the altruistic morality of their own in-group and to threaten the solidarity of an outside group. In other words, spontaneous human feelings take precedence over socially contracted dependence. This the group model of Japanese society is unable to explain because, in spite of its insistence on a balanced reciprocity between *giri* and *ninjō*, it is really concerned with *ninjō* only in so far as it obeys the rules of *giri*.

So, in Japanese anthropology, there are — although they may not realize it — followers of Mencius and followers of Hsun-tzu. Those who believe that Japanese society is essentially good adopt the group model, while those who believe it is evil adopt the model of social exchange. Needless to say, the Japanese themselves prefer to be seen as good and so tend to adopt the group model (as espoused by Nakane, 1970, for example). At the same time, I suspect that foreigners studying Japan ultimately regard their own Christian societies as evil and look to Japan (as other anthropologists, indeed, look to other 'primitive' societies) for the good that they themselves have never been able to experience back home. Anthropology itself thus yearns for the Garden of Eden before the apple tree bore fruit.

REFERENCES

Befu, H. (1980). 'The Group Model of Japanese Society and an Alternative'. In *Rice University Studies*, 66: 169—87.

Chang, Carsun (1957). *The Development of Confucian Thought.* New York: Bookman Associates.

de Bary, T. (1979). 'Introduction' and 'Sagehood as a Secular and Spiritual Ideal in Tokugawa Neo-Confucianism'. In de Bary and Bloom (eds) *Principle and Practicality: Essays in Neo-Confucianism and Practical Learning.* New York: Columbia University Press.

Fung, Yu-lan (1953). *A History of Chinese Philosophy*, vol. 2 (trans. Derk Bodde). London: Allen and Unwin.

Lévi-Strauss, C. (1966). *The Savage Mind.* London: Weidenfeld and Nicolson.

Moeran, B. D. A. (1984). 'Individual, Group and *seishin* — Japan's internal cultural debate'. *Man*, 19: 252—66.

Nakane, C. (1970). *Japanese Society.* London: Weidenfeld and Nicolson.

Paulson, J. (1976). 'Evolution of the Feminine Ideal'. In Lebra, Paulson and Powers (eds) *Women in Changing Japan.* Colorado: Westview Press.

Tsunoda, R., de Bary, T. and Keene, D. (eds) (1964). *Sources of Japanese Tradition,* vol. 1. New York: Columbia UP.

Vogel, E. (1963). *Japan's New Middle Class.* Berkeley: University of California Press.

Weber, M. (1947). 'The Social Psychology of World Religions' in *From Max Weber — Essays in Sociology* (ed. C. Wright Mills and trans. H. Garth). London: Kegan Paul, Trench and Trubner.

Yazaki, T. (1968). *Social Change and the City in Japan.* Tokyo: Japan Publications Inc.

7

The popular culture of evil in urban south India

*Lionel Caplan**

INTRODUCTION

Theologians and historians of religion frequently point to a fundamental distinction between the way in which Hinduism and Christianity approach the 'problem of evil'. The former, if we can oversimplify O'Flaherty's extremely subtle and complex argument, tends towards — though never quite achieves — a monistic stand. Everything is an aspect of God, although his responsibility for evil is explained differently in Brahmanic, ascetic and devotional mythology. In Hindu India, she writes, 'the solution offered by Manichean dualism is seldom invoked because . . . the ambiguous nature of the demons makes them unsuitable to bear the blame for the origin of evil' (O'Flaherty 1980: 57). While in some early Hindu myths demons are left unredeemed, demonic, to maintain a force of evil and distinguish themselves from the gods, in most myths, and especially the later ones, evil is the fault of the gods, a result of their malevolence against virtuous demons and virtuous humans. And in a passage that reveals her Lévi-Straussian sympathies, O'Flaherty writes: 'The opposition between gods and demons is purely structural: they are alike in all ways except that, by definition, they are opposed' (p. 64).

In a recent work on south Indian Tamil temple myths, David Shulman (1980) interprets the god—demon relationship in a somewhat different

* Fieldwork in 1981—2 was made possible by a grant from the School of Oriental and African Studies, for which I am greatly indebted. During my stay in south India I was affiliated to both the Christian Institute for the Study of Religion and Society, and the University of Madras, and I thank these institutions for their academic hospitality. David Parkin, Brian Moeran and Pat Caplan were kind enough to read and comment on an earlier draft of this chapter.

manner. In contradistinction to the Saivite tradition in northern India, Tamil Saivism, he argues, asserts the purity of the God, devoid of evil. Yet, while the demon symbolizes the evil within humankind, it is also an ambiguous figure. For in the Tamil devotional literature, the demon itself becomes a devotee, and, as a surrogate sacrificial victim in place of the God, is reunited with its Lord. So the demons, like those who propitiate them in south India, are ambivalent: obsessed with self — the very epitome of evil — yet longing for the goodness and purity of God.

By contrast, Christianity, it is argued, is a semi-dualist religion. The conflict between good and evil, Russell suggests, stands at the centre of New Testament theology. Christianity rejects totally the near-monist position of pre-prophetic Judaism, and approaches, but ultimately draws back from, the full dualism that asserts the opposition of two eternal cosmic principles. The unity and goodness of God are preserved, while his creature, the Devil, is given vast scope for evil. Satan is not only God's chief opponent, but has under his command all opposition to the Lord. The wide powers assigned to Satan in Apocalyptic Judaism were not only accepted by Christianity but extended even further, with the Devil increasingly removed from his divine origins (Russell 1977).

Against such a backdrop of contrasting scriptural theodicies, I want to examine the ways in which ordinary Protestant Christians in a predominantly Hindu south Indian metropolis conceptualize and deal with evil in their midst.

Shulman (1980) uses 'evil' variously to connote the concern with self, as the opposite of righteousness, as unlimited violence and as a synonym for sin, vice, misfortune and suffering. He employs it, in other words, in both its 'weak' and 'strong' senses (see chapter 8 below). Although Shulman renders several Tamil words as 'evil' (including *pavam, titu*), he offers no single term that conveniently or consistently translates the concept. The *Dravidian Etymological Dictionary* identifies at least a dozen words, any one of which, in the appropriate context, could convey some aspect of the wide semantic field covered by the English 'evil'.

Gustav Oppert, who was Professor of Sanskrit and Comparative Philology at Madras University towards the end of the nineteenth century, noted that the original meaning of *peey* — the common term for demon or malevolent spirit — 'is evil, bad; it is in this sense also applied to wild or obnoxious plants' (Oppert 1893: 559). In contemporary rural Tirunelveli (in southern Tamilnadu), according to Reiniche, *peey* 'encompasses all kinds of evil/bad (*mauvaises*) influences and demoniacal supernatural beings' (1979: 185). Another author, writing of the same district, refers to *peey* as 'hideous and gigantic demons' (Good 1978: 495), while a recent study of a village in the northern part of Tamilnadu state describes *peey* as 'low, impure, blood-thirsty and maleficent beings' (Moffatt 1979: 113).

In Madras city, the locus of this study, *peey* is the colloquial term for those spirits who, to recall Oppert's description, 'persecute, seduce and destroy' humankind, and whose 'malignity' is 'unbridled' (Oppert 1893: 515, 554). In the crowded neighbourhoods of the lower class, *peey* are thought to bring all manner of illness and misfortune, from infertility to cancer, unemployment and even examination failure. In addition, human failings of every kind — anger, lust, envy, violence — may be personified as *peey*: Ziegenbalg (1869) listed dozens of these 'devils', as he called them.

Thus, I begin by noting the presence of a notion of 'radical' evil (see chapter 8 below) among those — Christians and non-Christians alike — who are, by education, occupation, income and situation in the productive sphere, far removed from the centres of power and privilege. The ideas they hold and practices they follow constitute a species of popular culture that is hardly, if at all, shared by those in the upper reaches of the urban class order. The theological distinction between moral and natural evil, to which Kiernan (1982) has drawn attention, seems not to be applicable here. Moral evil resides, he writes, in outward conduct, and is experienced as some form of social deviance, while natural evil expresses itself as suffering, illness or misfortune — a physical incapacity. Among the people with whom this paper is concerned, a more significant distinction lies between those indications of evil that are humanly motivated and those that arise from non-human and largely gratuitous malice. Most typically, the former is attributed to sorcery, one form of which is the control and manipulation by sorcerers (*suniakaran*) of *peey* (see Caplan, forthcoming). The latter kind centres on the capricious acts of these spirits, outside human control. Both forms of evil may be experienced as physical suffering. A comment by Ricoeur seems to put succinctly how evil is here fused with misfortune: 'The ethical order of *doing* ill . . . is not distinguished from the cosmo-biological order of *faring* ill: suffering, sickness, death, failure' (1967: 27; author's emphasis).

Binsbergen identifies a similar dichotomy in his Zambian study. There are manifestations of evil that express social conflict and are thus 'largely predictable and almost justifiable' ('evil with a human face'), and others that are impersonal or unpredictable and comprise 'the most abhorred, diabolical incarnation of evil conceived of in the region' (1981: 142). Pocock, in chapter 3 above, distinguishes 'explicable' and 'inexplicable' forms of evil along similar lines.

It is on the personification of evil as occult forces beyond most forms of human control that I want to focus. It must be emphasized that I am not attempting to deal with every way in which evil is objectified or explained, or with every means employed to deal with it, though I would guess that the *peey* have a more prominent role in the dramaturgy of evil than any other single category of being or mode of explanation. The discussion divides into three sections. The first outlines briefly the ideas about evil spirits held by most people in Madras, Hindus and Christians alike. The next section relates these ideas to the divine hierarchy of local Hinduism. The final part turns to the Indian Christian context, to examine how these ideas about *peey* are accommodated within both the orthodox missionary version of Protestantism and the more recently introduced Pentecostal views.

THE PEEY[1]

In some of the literature on south Indian popular Hinduism (e.g. Ziegenbalg 1869; Whitehead 1921), the *peey* are said to be the ghosts of those who were bad characters or committed crimes in their lifetimes. But most writers, and certainly all my own informants, both Hindu and Christian, suggest that they are, in the main, ghosts of persons who died untimely or inauspicious deaths, and so roam the earth in search of humans against whom to vent their anger and frustration at having been denied their full measure of life and happiness. Whereas in the rural areas of Tamilnadu — and certainly in the district that surrounds Madras — the *peey* are said to live outside the village, in the city itself they are everywhere, although their concentration is greatest near trees and wells, cemeteries (and to a lesser extent cremation grounds) and railway tracks.

Although it is possible to be affected simply by the nearness of a *peey*, or to be 'slapped' or struck by one, generally it manifests itself by possession of a victim, and so must be cast out.

Women are said to be more susceptible to attack by the *peey*, a fact explained by their greater fear (*bayam*[2]). The notion of fear is frequently coupled with that of weakness, generally meaning weakness of mind, and since women are thought to be weaker than men, they are thereby more liable

---

[1] *Peey* are also sometimes referred to as *pisasu*, or *peey-pisasu*.

[2] The term *bayam* connotes a range of feeling from mild apprehension to painful emotion generated by a belief in impending danger. Numerous individuals recounted to me their experiences involving serious illness or other misfortune (their own or that of close relatives, usually children), attributed to the machinations of *peey*. In so far as I was able to judge, such events had been extremely disturbing at the time, and even the recollections were often very upsetting. A number of people I met, moreover, reported being meticulous in taking elaborate ritual precautions when going out in the dark or on retiring to bed in order to obviate demonic attacks, the thought of which they found intensely frightening.

to become possessed. A complementary view is that evil spirits are bloodthirsty, and therefore are drawn especially to menstruating women. Some *peey* — especially the ghosts of young unmarried women — are reputed to be attracted to pregnant women, whose unborn foetuses they want to take away. Women whose pregnancies are aborted are thought to have been possessed by such a spirit.

Although the *peey* form a category of unnamed ghosts of prematurely deceased persons, there are other kinds of possessory being who behave in similar ways and are equally referred to as *peey*. These, however, are non-human or at least not invariably human in origin, and have a somewhat ambiguous status in the divine hierarchy of local Hinduism.

PEEY IN THE HINDU CONTEXT

With some slight modifications I utilize Moffatt's (1979) model of the hierarchy in a village close to Madras, which, in turn, is based on Wadley's (1975) scheme for a north Indian rural community. The names of divine beings mentioned here are common to both rural and urban Tamilians. Where the same divinities appear at different levels of the hierarchy, their precise location is either ambiguous or varies from place to place.

1 At the highest level God is pervasive, and unembodied. It cannot be transacted with. Common terms for God in this sense, in both rural and urban places, are Kadavul and Devam.

2 At the second level God is embodied and worshipped. These deities are pure beings, with general, wide-ranging powers over the whole world order. They are basically seen as beneficent. Siva and Parvati are the main Hindu divinities worshipped in south India at this level, though Vishnu has his followers as well.

3 The third level contains the regional gods — mainly the sons of Siva and Parvati, i.e. Vinayagar or Ganesh (the elephant-headed deity) and Murugan. They are lesser but more popular beings among the Hindu masses, regarded as intermediaries to the higher gods, and equally beneficent, though liable to punish lapsed devotees. They are also seen by their votaries as able to defend them from the threats of maleficent beings. Those who follow Murugan, for example, pray regularly for his protection from the *peey*.

4 At this level, we find the 'fallen' forms of Parvati: Moffatt refers to them as 'quintessentially intermediate beings' alternately beneficent and malevolent, peaceful and angry (1979: 233). Their powers are specific and concentrated, but are regarded as considerable for just that reason. In south India the Goddess is widely worshipped in her many forms — as Amman (mother),

Sakti (divine power or energy), or occasionally in her fierce aspect as Kali. It is to the Goddess more than to any other divinity that ordinary Hindus turn for protection from the *peey*, and for assistance when they have fallen victim.

5 At the fifth level are the guardian gods, who also protect the villages from the *peey*. According to Moffatt, some of these gods may themselves come from the ranks of the *peey* who have been subdued and domesticated. The implication is that the guardian deities do not possess people, though they may find ways of harming those who neglect them. But in the city their role may be interpreted differently. Muniswaran, for example, is regarded in villages near Madras as a 'low' but protective being, so he will often have a temple at the entrance to the settlement. He is also worshipped as a lineage god and additionally placated by many households, especially if he has revealed his power to them. This also occurs in Madras. But in the city, Muniswaran is sometimes thought to be the chief of the *peey*, and is identified frequently as a possessory evil spirit by both Hindus and Christians.

6 Which brings us to the occupants of the sixth and lowest level in the hierarchy. These are the ranks of the undomesticated demons, the *peey*, who, though consisting mainly of ghosts, in Madras at any rate are supplemented by other beings, like Muniswaran, who are ambiguously placed in the hierarchy. Mohini is another example. She appears in several Mahabharata myths, when Vishnu takes the guise of an enchantress — on one occasion to distract the demons and turn their minds away from thoughts of capturing the ambrosia (*amrita*) of immortality. In south India she is sometimes Siva's consort, and, as a female form of Vishnu, the mother of the popular god Aiyanar (see Dumont 1959). According to Shulman (1980: 311–12), Mohini is worshipped in Tamil villages, although he does not indicate what form the devotion takes, or at what 'level' of the hierarchy. The fact that in some myths Mohini is identified with the Goddess (Shulman 1980: 311–12) suggests that villagers may regard her, in Moffatt's classificatory scheme, as a 'fallen' form of Parvati. None of my urban Hindu informants ever spoke of propitiating her. In Madras, Mohini is the spirit of females who commit suicide out of disappointed love. She appears occasionally to young women of whose good fortune she is envious, but mainly she appears to young bachelors, most typically on their way home from a late night film, wearing a white sari and flowers in her hair. She seeks to lure such a man in order to 'live' with him as his wife, take his strength and finally kill him. In Madras, among both Christians and Hindus, she is generally referred to as 'Mohini-*peey*'.

There are several points that emerge from the narrative so far. The first is that, in the popular culture of Madras, evil is commonly projected and symbolized, by Christians and Hindus alike, as *peey*. This tendency to attribute wrongdoing or 'wrong-faring' to maleficent occult agents external to the human actors is what Southwold, chapter 8, following a theme initially pursued by Lienhardt (1961), labels 'theism'.

Second, it is difficult to assimilate the *peey* of popular culture to the demons of certain Hindu mythologies who are said to be barely distinguishable from the gods. Nor can they be easily joined to the demon devotees of the Tamil temple myths, who are redeemed by their sacrifice and ultimately united with their god(s) (see above). In the beliefs and discourses of the ordinary people, the *peey* are wholly maleficent and without redeeming features.

In this connection, Inden, in chapter 9 below, identifies a set of texts (the Pancaratras) that reveal a very clear conception of evil within Hinduism, and acknowledge that it is an integral and indispensable part of the world. There are, moreover, embodiments of evil that are free, rebellious and/or refuse to submit to their overlords. And while they can be overcome and subjugated by the superior forces of good, they can never be eliminated. In the Madras context, too, the divine order is perceived hierarchically. Lower beings are ultimately controlled by higher ones. By objectifying evil in the *peey*, it can be dealt with through recourse to the deities whose powers are greater, and generally more beneficent. But the divinities already discussed operate only on behalf of their Hindu devotees, which of course leaves out practising Christians. The next section turns to the wider religious context in which Protestants conceptualize and deal with the *peey*.

PEEY IN THE CHRISTIAN CONTEXT

Although there were Protestant missionaries in peninsular India from the beginning of the eighteenth century, the expansion of Protestant Christianity in British south India began in earnest only in the first decades of the nineteenth century, when the East India Company was compelled by Parliament to recognize the principles of introducing Christianity to its territories. The missionaries who journeyed to India during the early period of evangelical activity were in little doubt about the goals they had come to realize. The widespread assumption was of a divine purpose in the western conquest of the sub-continent, and that they were there to play a part in its fulfilment. The kind of thinking that was typical is represented by this quotation from the writings of a missionary who worked in south India during the latter part of the nineteenth century:

We have taken their country and we owe them this debt; or, rather, God has given us this country and demands from us that we shall do our duty. . . . The Church exists to evangelize the world and God has given India to us instead of to Holland, Portugal or France . . . and we may be sure of this, that if we English fail to do our duty, God will take — and rightly so — our empire from us and give it to some worthier nation.

Sharrock 1910: 329

This kind of imperialistic evangelism went along with a feeling of disdain for Hinduism on the part of many if not most missionaries of this period. The Gospel, suggests one modern church historian, 'was presented against the background of errors, weaknesses and abominations of Hinduism' (Estborn 1961: 26), while another remarks on the extent to which it was accompanied by denunciation, in 'abusive language', of Hindu faith and Indian culture (Shiri 1969: 10).[3] One missionary wrote contemptuously of 'the opposition to truth, the love of idolatry in the Hindu' (Mullens 1854: 39), while another warned his colleagues that 'it is to consciences thus cramped, into lives thus enervated and depressed (by Hindu philosophy, religion and caste) that the message of the Gospel must be brought' (Mylne 1908: 39). An American medical evangelist, a legendary figure in Indian missionary circles, whose family established the world-famous hospital and medical college at Vellore in south India, is quoted by Houghton as stating that '[all the works] in which [Hindus] so fondly believe, are nothing else than lying fables, wickedly concocted by false and designing men' (see Houghton 1981: 111—12). Well into this century such attitudes had not disappeared entirely. Gandhi records how when he was a young man Christian missionaries 'used to stand in a corner near the high school and hold forth, pouring abuse on Hindus and their gods. I could not endure this' (1964: 33). Their 'homiletic' methodology, as Houghton terms it (1981: 107—10), involved the denigration of all things Hindu in order to demonstrate the 'superiority' of Christianity.

The growth of Indian nationalism, coupled with the serious and scholarly study of Hinduism by later missionaries no less than by secular academics, led gradually to the emergence of a more generous attitude towards the religion of the majority. The earlier contempt and ridicule gave way to greater understanding and respect, especially for the cosmic themes revealed in the sacred literature, as this was translated and examined. Christianity, in the increasingly liberal atmosphere of the late nineteenth- and early twentieth-century missionary world, was no longer seen as the only light shining in the darkness of Hindu India, but rather as the fulfilment of Hinduism's ideals — its 'crown', as the title of Farquhar's famous work would have it (Farquhar 1913).

[3] According to Marshall, opinions on Hinduism hardened towards the end of the eighteenth century, with the rise of the Evangelical movement in Britain (1970: 41—3).

While respect grew for the literate or 'great' tradition, missionaries associated with all the major Protestant societies continued to be as dismissive of popular religious notions and practices as had their predecessors. They denied the 'existence' of *peey*, and regarded as nonsense people's convictions about them. They assumed that conversion to a religion with 'simple affectionate teaching' (i.e. Christianity) would displace beliefs in the 'malignant spirits who peopled [the converts'] world in the past' (see Richter 1908: 248). Clearly, the Europeans who had come to convert India and the indigenous clergy they trained could not accommodate such ideas in their own theologies. Dougall's remark on western missionaries in Africa, i.e. that 'they faced the power of the spirit world with unbelief', applies in the south Indian Protestant context as well (Dougall 1956: 260).

The missionaries of the eighteenth and nineteenth centuries had long since rejected their own thaumaturgical legacy. Hill argues that it was the Calvinist theologians rather than the scientists who banished miracles, exorcism, magic and the like from everyday Protestant religion in seventeenth-century England, assigning them to 'the distant past, to the age of Christ and the Apostles' (Hill 1983: 182–3).[4] Macfarlane, in chapter 4 above, traces the beginnings of the decline of a pervading 'cosmology of evil' even further back, to the previous century, attributing this development to the emergence of 'capitalism and a money order'.

Protestant missionaries in south India were very much products of this new orthodoxy, which regarded the earlier theodicies as at best old-fashioned, and at worst ignorant and superstitious. Thus, a popular tradition that externalized evil and sought thaumaturgical solutions was met by a western Protestant tradition which urged instead individual responsibility and the notion of personal guilt — what Hill calls the 'internalization of the struggle against the forces of evil' (1983: 183) and Taylor, in chapter 2 above, calls the 'interiorization of evil'.[5] In the event, Indian Christians were compelled either to suppress their deeply held beliefs and inclinations or, as apparently happened on occasion, to turn to a variety of Hindu ritual specialists to help them cope with the evil in their lives. Bishop Diehl, writing about the situation in parts of south India barely 30 years ago, noted that 'Protestant Christians must either change their means of solving their problems or trust in the old helpers' (1965: 138).

---

[4] Though presumably they were not eliminated altogether from the experience of ordinary Protestants. Hill observes that, since people could no longer find protection in the church, they turned to the 'cunning man' or lay magician (1983: 183).

[5] Referring to the diary of a seventeenth-century English minister, the Rev. Ralph Josselin, Macfarlane notes in chapter 4 above that Josselin blamed himself for much of the suffering of those around him.

Since independence, and especially during the past 20 years, the Protestant community in Madras, like that in many parts of the Third World, has been profoundly influenced by the growth of what has come to be called the New Pentecostalism. This movement emerged on the West Coast of the United States at the beginning of this century, and gradually spread throughout the Christian world (see Harper 1965). Although such sects have been reported in south India for as long as 70 years, they attracted little attention and few adherents until around 1960 (see Nelson 1975).

Pentecostalism covers a multitude of dogmas, and its boundaries are by no means clearly delineated (see Hollenweger 1972). The proliferation of schismatic groups attests to just how much scope there is for rival exegeses: there are hundreds — some say as many as 500 — small and large Pentecostal congregations in Madras city alone. But whatever the variations among them, they all place the greatest doctrinal stress on the significance of the Holy Spirit in the Christian trinity, and isolate for special attention the gifts of the Holy Spirit, as set out in Paul's first Letter to the Corinthians (1 Cor. 12: 4–11). Two of these are especially prominent for these Christians: one is 'speaking in tongues' — a form of ecstatic utterance (which is thought by many to be the initial evidence for the manifestation of the Holy Spirit) — and the other is the gift of healing.

The timing of this efflorescence is not wholly fortuitous. While this is not the occasion to detail the history of the movement, I think that two important developments — one indigenous, the other international — have to be at least acknowledged, if we are not to conclude that the spread of such ideas is, as the official Pentecostal view would have it, simply evidence of an 'outpouring of the Holy Spirit'.

The international aspects of Pentecostal growth in the Third World during the past few decades is a phenomenon that has been much commented on, though hardly, if at all, analysed. What does seem clear is that these groups are often American-led and funded. They mount an aggressive attack on 'liberation theology', which has strongly influenced many of the clergy in Asia and Latin America, and has its supporters within the World Council of Churches. These assaults generally go along with a strong anti-Soviet, anti-socialist and anti-Marxist rhetoric. In the south Indian context, where a radical theology is almost totally absent, the Pentecostal leadership provides an ongoing critique of the liberal 'social gospel' (or 'modernism'), which has been the mainstay of the orthodox Protestant churches during most of this century, and is still so today. Most people are, however, attracted not by the movement's political philosophy, the implications of which are, in any case, not fully appreciated, but by the manner in which it accommodates the popular culture of evil.

Within south India itself, and especially in the area of Madras, the 25-year period between the Second World War and the mid-1960s was one of considerable economic and demographic change. During these decades the city and its environs became an important industrial region, which encouraged large-scale migration into Madras. The numbers of migrants more than outstripped the pace of economic growth, and, as the rate of expansion levelled out in the 1960s, the situation for those at the lower end of the class order grew increasingly difficult.

For the Protestants among them, the difficulties were exacerbated by the refusal of the central or state authorities to grant them the special concessions available to other 'backward' communities. Within the Protestant fold, moreover, the missionary institutions that had provided education and training to a wide cross-section of converts in the past became increasingly the preserve of the emergent middle class. The majority, meanwhile, found it increasingly difficult to acquire or maintain the benefits previously available through missionary patronage and the protective umbrella of colonialism. With the end of the brief period of expansion and opportunity, these ordinary Christians have little chance against the well-to-do, who hold on desperately to their newly won advantages in educational and occupational fields. Disprivileged Christians therefore feel an ever-growing concern for their own future and that of their children. Their prospects seem, if anything, less bright than in the past; their material conditions have, and are felt to have, deteriorated. It is predominantly among such people that Pentecostalism has won its adherents.

Protestants from the main orthodox churches flock to worship in Pentecostal halls and assemblies — generally after attending services in their own churches. Many take second or immersion baptism in defiance of the teaching of the denominational churches, and not an insignificant number endeavour, by 'tarrying', to receive the Holy Spirit. Most importantly for the present discussion, they seek out ritual specialists from within the Pentecostal fold to deal with the adversities wrought by the *peey*. For the first time, there is accessible to Indian Protestants a Christian rationale for and response to such traditionally recognized symptoms of evil in the world. The last part of this paper examines the ideas and procedures now available to the community.

PENTECOSTALISM AND THE *PEEY*

Pentecostal views are wholly consistent with popular ideas about evil spirits, and for 'proofs' of their existence Pentecostals regularly point to instances of possession and exorcism in the Bible (e.g. Luke 8: 27—32).[6]

There is some disagreement about how to accommodate the widespread notion that suicides and other persons who die prematurely provide the bulk of the spirit population. One tendency is to fortify this belief by seeking scriptural justification. Evidence is found in the words of Ecclesiastes 3: 1−2 that 'to everything there is a season, a time to every purpose . . . . a time to be born and a time to die . . .'. And if the allotted time is not lived out in full, the argument goes, then a person is condemned to roam the earth as an evil spirit until the date appointed for death by the heavenly diarist (Dhinakaran 1979: 33).

Some Pentecostals find this particular argument somewhat fanciful and assimilate indigenous ideas about the *peey* more directly to the Judaeo-Christian notion of the Fall. This tendency to absorb other traditions is of course not unusual. Biblical demons and devils are themselves an amalgam of various elements found in the folk religions of those societies with which both the Israelites and early Christians came into contact (Russell 1977: 252).[7] The untimely dead, in this approach, are regarded as the victims of Satan and/or the spirits they leave as his maleficent servants. To this category of evil forces are added the Fallen Angels, whose main role, in the Pentecostal view, is to deceive the majority of people in this heathen land by appearing to them in the guise of Hindu deities and demons, so keeping them from the True God.

Despite the many doctrinal differences among Pentecostal sects in south India, they are unanimous in characterizing Hinduism as 'paganism', 'idolatry' and 'the worship of Satan'. (The epithets they use to describe Hinduism are very reminiscent of those employed by the early European missionaries mentioned above.) The ecumenical note sounded increasingly by the main Protestant churches (for example, in their inter-faith dialogues) is also bitterly attacked as tantamount to cooperation with the 'forces of darkness', and even attempts to indigenize forms of worship in these churches are interpreted as Hinduization, and so considered compromises with the anti-Christ.[8]

---

[6] Margaret Egnor quotes a Hindu Tamil 'priestess' as remarking that 'those people who say hallelujah, who don't wear jewels or anything, they too have belief [in demons]' (Egnor 1977).

[7] Hill observes that 'the ability to absorb into the popular faith elements from pagan and other non-Christian sources had always been a feature of Roman Catholic thought' (1983: 182).

[8] This aspect of Pentecostal activity is especially disapproved of by the orthodox Protestant churches. The Church of South India's Bishop in Madras writes: 'It is a pity that sometimes one hears in the street corners even today, fiery preachers preaching not the love and peace of Christ, but . . . the wrath of God on idolatry and on certain other beliefs sacred to men of other faiths' (Clarke 1980: 96). While I was in Madras in 1981−2 some violent incidents took place in a town about 80 miles away following remarks made about Hinduism during a public meeting organized by one of the fastest growing Pentecostal groups in south India.

So Hinduism is 'devil worship', and the Hindu pantheon an array of malevolent spirits under the control of Satan. Such views are commonly held, but for obvious reasons seldom appear in the writings of Pentecostal theologians, and when they do they are left somewhat vague. For example, the historian of one large fundamentalist group based in Madras remarks that 'the demons which we cast out . . . identify themselves as the deities which are much worshipped in neighbouring places' (Daniel 1980: xv). As I have noted, the *peey* are common to both Hindus and Christians. But the Pentecostal specialists who ascertain the identities of the possessory spirits are not constrained by the divisions within the Hindu divine hierarchy between the evil spirits and the various higher, more beneficent and more powerful deities who are enlisted to confront and neutralize, if not defeat, the *peey*. While Pentecostal healers appear never to attach blame directly to the highest embodied gods — Siva and Parvati — they make no distinctions among the lesser Hindu divinities and between them and the *peey*.

Murugan, Ganesh and the Goddess, in her various forms and especially as Kali, as well as all manner of demons, are said to possess people as evil spirits. Thus, while popular Hinduism in Madras involves the recognition of a hierarchical order of divinities with gradations of benign and malign powers, popular Christianity — as it finds expression in Pentecostalism — in effect eliminates the hierarchy by regarding all non-human beings in the Hindu pantheon as undifferentiated. Just as the early Christians made demons of the gods of Greece and Rome (Russell 1977: 58), the Pentecostals absorb and relegate Hindu divinities in their own pantheon. The latter are all equal and unequivocally evil.

Earlier I noted that vulnerability to attack by the *peey* is enhanced by fear. This notion is somewhat extended in the Christian context so that it includes the fear of Hindu supernatural beings. The overcoming of fear involves accepting Jesus Christ as personal saviour, and being filled with the Holy Spirit. For until one is thus imbued, it is argued, there is an 'empty space' which Satan can easily occupy.[9] Those not so endowed, i.e. non-Christians as well as the 'nominal' Christians attached to the main Protestant churches, must seek the assistance of ritual specialists from within the Pentecostal fold to deal with all manner of adversity resulting from attacks by the *peey*.

---

[9] The question that then arises, and it is one frequently debated in the Pentecostal literature, is whether a 'true' Christian can be possessed by an evil spirit (see Penn-Lewis 1973). The latest thinking in the wider Pentecostal world seems to be that someone can be tormented or afflicted in some area of his/her life and still be a sincere believer (Basham 1971). But among my informants in Madras the predominant view was that, with the Holy Spirit, a person is invulnerable to the threat of evil forces.

Just as Pentecostals classify all Hindu divinities as evil spirits, so they dismiss Hindu exorcists — whose power frequently derives from the gods or, more usually, goddesses — as tools of the devil. There are several different types of Hindu specialist using a variety of ritual techniques to deal with possessory *peey*, but among the most common is the 'god-dancer' (*samiadi*), a shaman-like figure who becomes a medium for the Goddess, who then drives out the *peey* either by appeasing it with a sacrifice or threatening it with her superior power, or both (see Moffatt 1979: 241 — 2).

Since the power of the Hindu deities is regarded as satanic, the rituals these 'god-dancers' perform cannot, by definition, be protective or benign. The ritual objects they give the victims to ward off further attack, say the Pentecostals, in fact contain evil spells and evil spirits — the very forces they are meant to guard against. It is only the power of the Holy Spirit that can overcome the *peey*. And while all those who receive the Holy Spirit may also obtain one or more of its gifts, only those especially chosen by God are granted most if not all the boons, the most important, as I've already said, being the gift of healing. Today in Madras there are many such persons, and those who are thought to be the most powerful — and so enjoy a wide popularity — draw thousands to their public meetings and have large followings not only in Madras and the rest of south India, but among descendants of south Indian emigrants to Sri Lanka and parts of South-East Asia.

Pentecostal exorcism calls on the power of the Holy Spirit to confront and defeat the evil spirits, and ritual specialists usually fast and pray prior to performing such rites in order to enhance and concentrate their divinely given powers. The procedure involves identifying the possessing *peey*, not to strike a bargain with it — one offers nothing to the *peey*, says the Pentecostal specialist — but only to know its origins and character. Here the gift of 'discernment' is important since, it is said, some evil spirits may come as 'angels of light' to confuse and trick victim, healer and congregation alike.

The *peey* is roundly abused and finally driven out by the power of Jesus, which is manifest in the very name of Christ or in His word as contained in the Bible; both (name and word) are said to be feared by Satan's agents, i.e. the *peey*. Sacred oil, blessed by the exorcist in the name of Jesus, is commonly given to the victim; the Bible may be placed on the latter's head; and commands to leave the body are issued in the Lord's name — all to frighten and assist in driving out the *peey*. The exorcist occasionally speaks in 'tongues', giving evidence of the presence of the Holy Spirit.

There are no further rites to cast out the spirit, or accompany it to its place of origin, and Pentecostals generally point out that, while the *peey* driven out by Hindu specialists are free to attack again — possibly even the same victim — the spirits exorcised by Christian healers are driven into the Abyss (*badalam*), the reference being to Revelations 20: 3, where the vision of the Last Days has Satan chained up for a thousand years and driven into the Abyss, where he can no longer seduce the nations. Even then, however, the victim may be attacked by other *peey* unless baptism in the Holy Spirit takes place to effect total immunity.

So the divine hierarchy of Pentecostalism is two-tiered. Below are the forces of evil — which include not only ghosts but the demons and deities of local Hinduism. Above stand the forces of Good — the Holy Spirit and the Son of God. Unlike liberal Christianity spread by late nineteenth- and early twentieth-century missionaries of the principal denominations (and still found today within the leadership of the orthodox Protestant churches and community), which denied the 'reality' of evil spirits in the everyday lives of their followers and potential converts, Pentecostalism not only acknowledges their existence, but continuously demonstrates the power of the Holy Spirit to vanquish them.

CONCLUSION

If we examine the particular context of a south Indian metropolis, we can detect a wide area of overlap in popular notions of evil as between those divided by formal religious affiliation. Ordinary Hindus and Christians objectify in a strikingly similar way the hostile and malevolent forces that impinge on their lives, and employ similar ritual procedures to oppose and neutralize them. These procedures share a conception of divine beings as imbued with differential spiritual powers, so that the ritual becomes in effect a power contest. The whole notion of power in world religions has received relatively little attention from anthropologists, although several south Asianists have recently sought to rescue it from its 'encompassment' by ritual status in the Dumontian model (Dumont 1970), and to redefine it as both a material and a moral or spiritual quality present in all beings (see Wadley 1975; Marriott and Inden 1977; Moffatt 1979).

If nothing else, Pentecostalism has drawn attention — and this explicitly — to the significance of power in early Christianity as well. In Russell's view, the figure of Satan is comprehensible only when it is seen as the 'counter-principle of Jesus Christ'. The saving mission of Christ must therefore 'be understood in terms of its opposition to the power of the devil. That is the whole point of the New Testament' (1977: 237, 248).

Pentecostal practices and discourses have enjoyed a considerable success among the Protestant urban lower class, largely because they are seen to provide an authentic biblical justification for popular beliefs about the nature and sources of evil, as well as a means of deliverance from it. Control over malign forces in the world is the privilege of all True Believers, and requires only what is regarded as within the reach of anyone — surrender to Jesus. Those who have already become devotees stand ready to protect and assist others as yet unable or unprepared to dedicate themselves.

But the Pentecostal 'option' is of relatively recent vintage, and not the only one available to south Indian Protestants. As we have seen, western missionaries for centuries offered (and the orthodox churches by and large still offer) a different mode of interpreting evil: namely, to become aware of its origins in personal sin, and to cope with it not by 'external projection' but 'interiorization' of guilt (see Taylor, chapter 2 above). To employ the terminology used by Southwold in our symposium discussions, both 'theistic' and 'psychologistic' anthropologies are to be found within a single cultural community. It seems to me, therefore, that we must resist the temptation to conclude from first principles how the adherents of a particular religion (like Christianity) conceptualize and deal with the problem of evil. In chapter 9 below, Inden suggests a similar conclusion, challenging, on the basis of one set of texts, the view — based on quite different ones — that evil is absent in Hindu religions. That one tendency and not another should prevail at any moment (see chapter 4 above) or among a particular segment of the population and not another (see chapter 10 below) suggests that attention must be paid to the social frameworks and historical conditions within which notions of evil are nourished and transformed.

REFERENCES

Basham, D. W. (1971). *Can a Christian have a demon?* Monroeville, Penn.: Whitaker House.
Binsbergen, W. M. van. (1981) *Religious change in Zambia: exploratory studies.* London: Routledge and Kegan Paul.
Caplan, L. (forthcoming). 'Popular Christianity in urban south India'. *Religion and Society.*
Clarke, S. (1980). *Let the Indian Church be Indian.* Madras: Christian Literature Society.
Daniel, J. (1980). *Another Daniel.* Madras: The Laymen's Evangelical Fellowship.
Dhinakaran, D. G. S. (1979). *Healing Stripes* (revised and ed. D. S. G. Muller). Madras: Christian Literature Society (first published in Tamil in 1972).
Diehl, C. G. (1965). *Church and shrine: intermingling patterns of culture in the life of some Christian groups in south India.* Uppsala: Hakan Ohlssons Boktryckeri.
Dougall, J. W. C. (1956). 'African Separatist Churches'. *Int'l Review of Mission,* 45: 257–66.

Dumont, L. (1959). 'A Structural Definition of a Folk Deity of Tamil Nad: Aiyanar, the Lord'. *Contributions to Indian Sociology,* 3: 75—87.

Dumont, L. (1970). *Homo hierarchicus* (Engl. transl.) London: Weidenfeld and Nicolson.

Egnor, M. (1977). 'A Tamil Priestess' (Manuscript).

Estborn, S. (1961). *The church among Tamils and Telugus.* Nagpur: National Christian Council.

Farquhar, J. N. (1913). *The Crown of Hinduism.* London: Humphrey Milford, OUP.

Gandhi, M. K. (1964). *The Collected Works of Mahatma Gandhi,* vol. 39 (an autobiography, Part 1). Delhi: Publications Division, Ministry of Information and Broadcasting.

Good, A. (1978). *Kinship and ritual in a south Indian micro-region.* Durham University Ph.D.

Harper, M. (1965). *As at the beginning: the twentieth century Pentecostal revival.* London: Hodder and Stoughton.

Hill, C. (1983). Science and Magic in Seventeenth Century England. In *Culture, ideology, and politics.* R. Samuel and G. Stedman Jones (eds). London: Routledge.

Hollenweger, W. J. (1972). *The Pentecostals.* London: SCM Press (first published in German in 1969).

Houghton, G. (1981). *The Development of the Protestant Missionary Church in Madras, 1870—1920: the Impoverishment of Dependency.* University of California, Ph.D.

Kiernan, J. P. (1982). 'The "Problem of Evil" in the Context of Ancestral Intervention in the Affairs of the Living in Africa', *Man,* 17: 287—301.

Lienhardt, G. (1961). *Divinity and experience.* Oxford: OUP.

Marriott, M. and Inden, R. (1977). 'Toward an Ethnosociology of South Asian Caste Systems'. In *The New Wind: changing identities in south Asia* (ed. K. David). The Hague: Mouton.

Marshall, P. J. (1970). *The British Discovery of Hinduism in the Eighteenth Century.* Cambridge: CUP.

Moffatt, M. (1979). *An Untouchable Community in South India: Structure and Consensus.* Princeton: University Press.

Mullens, J. (1854). *Missions in South India.* London: W. H. Dalton.

Mylne, L. G. (1908). *Missions to Hindus: a contribution to the study of missionary methods.* London: Longmans, Green and Co.

Nelson, A. (1975). *A New Day in Madras: a Study of Protestant Churches in Madras.* South Pasadena, California: William Carey Library.

O'Flaherty, W. D. (1980). *The Origins of Evil in Hindu Mythology.* Berkeley: University of California Press.

Oppert, G. (1893). *On the Original Inhabitants of Bharatavarsa or India.* Westminster: Constable.

Penn-Lewis, J. (1973). *The Warfare with Satan* (based on addresses given in 1897). Poole: The Overcomer Literature Trust.

Reiniche, M. L. (1979). *Les dieux et les hommes: étude des cultes d'un village du Tirunelveli, Inde du Sud.* Paris: Mouton.

Richter, J. (1908). *A history of missions in India* (transl. S. H. Moore). Edinburgh: Oliphant, Anderson and Ferrier.

Ricoeur, P. (1967). *The Symbolism of Evil.* Boston: Beacon Press.

Russell, J. B. (1977). *The Devil: Perceptions of Evil from Antiquity to Primitive Christianity.* Cornell: University Press.

Sharrock, J. A. (1910). *South Indian Missions.* Westminster: Society for the Propagation of the Gospel.

Shiri, G. (1969). *The Indian Government Policy on Missionary Activities since 1947.* B.D. Thesis, Serampore University (Union Theological College, Bangalore).

Shulman, D. (1980). *Tamil Temple Myths: Sacrifice and Divine Marriage in the South Indian Saiva Tradition.* Princeton: University Press.

Wadley, S. (1975). *Shakti: Power in the Conceptual Structure of Karimpur Religion.* Chicago: University Press.

Whitehead, H. (1921). *The Village Gods of South India* (2nd rev. edn). Calcutta: Association Press.

Ziegenbalg, P. (1869). *Genealogy of the South Indian Gods* (trans. G. J. Metzger). Madras: Higginbotham and Co.

8

Buddhism and evil

Martin Southwold*

There is no concept of evil in Buddhism: so I concluded on the basis of my fieldwork among Sinhalese Buddhists in 1974—5.[1] But the literature implied that this must be wrong. Ling had published a book with the title *Buddhism and the Mythology of Evil* (1962), and Boyd another, covering similar ground, entitled *Satan and Māra: Christian and Buddhist Symbols of Evil* (1975). Obeyesekere's distinguished paper, 'Theodicy, Sin and Salvation in a Sociology of Buddhism' (1968) mentions notions of evil among Sinhalese Buddhists, and can easily be read as discussing them at length. It was not to be supposed that such eminent scholars had enlarged on mere figments of their own imagination: more probable that my own fieldwork had been negligent.

Closer scrutiny revealed that the contradiction was more apparent than real. The key terms, 'Buddhism' and 'evil', are so ambiguous that it can be truly said both that there is and that there is not a concept of evil in Buddhism. Such ambiguity screens reality from view. When it is resolved, by clearly distinguishing the different senses of the terms, there comes into view a more nuanced and interesting scene. There are some concepts of evil in Buddhism; but there is no concept of evil in the strongest and most distinctive sense in which we use this term. Some Buddhists — and this is also significant — have notions that approach it more closely than do those of others.

The term 'Buddhism' itself suggests a more unitary phenomenon than actually exists. In this paper I consider only Buddhism of the Theravāda variety, and not Māhāyana. My first-hand evidence in fact is only of Sinhalese Buddhism, but I shall assume, as others have, that the Buddhisms of Burma and Thailand will differ only in minor ways (see particularly Spiro 1971: 16).

Within Theravāda Buddhism I distinguish two main interpretations, which

* This fieldwork was supported by a Research Grant (no. HR 2969/1) from the late SSRC, for which I am grateful.

[1] The fieldwork, lasting just over a year, was conducted in the Kurunegala District of Sri Lanka; I give more details in Southwold (1983).

do differ in some rather basic ways.[2] In what I have termed Meditation Buddhism, the goal is to attain Nirvana soon; this is to be done by withdrawing from the world and pursuing a life of austerity and intense meditation; it is assumed that this can hardly be done except by members of the Sangha, or clergy, and among these only by 'forest monks' (see Carrithers 1983), living in monasteries or as hermits in the wilderness. In what I have termed Ministry Buddhism, Nirvana is an ultimate goal, not to be attained in ordinary time; the vocation of clergy is to serve the laity, especially by teaching, contributing thereby to their own spiritual progress as well as to that of those they serve.

It seems clear that Ministry Buddhism is now, and was in the past, the version preferred by most Buddhists, clergy as well as laity, and is thus the greater part of the ethnographic reality. This has too often been missed because most scholars have based their studies on the scriptures, in which Meditation Buddhism has a much larger place. The scholars also exaggerated the importance of the scriptures: partly because they had studied them; partly because they imagined that in them they found the words of the Buddha himself; partly because they overestimated the extent to which the scriptures are authoritative for Buddhists. In consequence, on matters where Meditation and Ministry Buddhism diverge, the accounts of scholars who have studied the scriptures differ from those of ethnographers who have studied people. On the present topic, this accounts for some differences of emphasis; more impressive, I think, is the fact that neither among the Meditation Buddhists of the scriptures nor among the Ministry Buddhists of real life is there to be found an entire concept of evil.

I have been helped by Kenneth Grayston's brief article on Evil (1950) in Alan Richardson's *A Theological Word Book of the Bible*.[3] Strictly, Grayston discusses the meanings of the Hebrew and Greek words that are translated as 'evil' in the Authorized Version of the Bible. The fact that they were so translated implies that 'evil' had a similar range of meanings in the English of that period — and this can be readily confirmed from other sources.[4] Grayston distinguishes between the 'descriptive' and the 'moral' meaning of the terms. The latter is of course familiar — broadly, it refers to conduct that is morally wrong or bad. The former is less familiar, and is best explained in Grayston's own words:

---

[2] I summarize here what I have set out at length in Southwold (1983: chapter 9).

[3] The implication that I have not been helped by other books I have consulted is mostly true. I except works discussed in this paper; and also Doob (1978), an admirable discussion which is rich in empirical material.

[4] E.g. Shakespeare's plays, of which some typical usages are summarized in Onions (1949: 73).

The Hebrew term *ra'* conveys the factual judgment that something is bad (e.g. figs, cattle), displeasing (e.g. a woman in the eyes of her husband), or harmful (e.g. wild beasts, poisonous herbs, disease). Quite generally it means anything that causes pain, unhappiness, or misery, including the discipline of punishment sent by God.

Grayston 1950: 73

This descriptive meaning may have a moral connotation, i.e. the implication that the harm is due to someone's moral fault; or it may have no such connotation, in which case I would speak of the purely descriptive meaning. Grayston's account clearly implies that the purely descriptive meaning of *ra'* was the earliest, that at some period the word was normally used without any moral connotation (see chapter 2 above).

The descriptive meaning does survive in modern English: most familiarly as a noun, used to refer to such characteristic human afflictions as disease and death. It can still, just, be used adjectivally, as when an ugly face is termed an 'evil countenance'. But these are literary rather than colloquial usages, and usually, I think, deliberately archaic.[5] In modern English the moral has become the primary, indeed unmarked,[6] meaning, and this makes it difficult to use the descriptive meaning without risk of misunderstanding. It is impossible now to use the purely descriptive meaning. Does one read 'evil countenance' as merely 'ugly' without understanding also 'malevolent'? Could one read of an 'evil wife' as merely unattractive to her husband, without supposing she is morally wicked?

There has been a shift in meaning of the word 'evil' since Jacobean times; hence we tend to misinterpret passages in the Bible, or in Shakespeare, where it was used with the descriptive meaning. Anthropologists who write about the traditional religions of other peoples have a tendency to resort to biblical idiom, and this may produce misunderstanding. It is not always perfectly clear whether or not the word 'evil' carries a moral connotation or meaning.

There is a further ambiguity, less widely recognized but more harmful than this: an ambiguity within the moral (or, as I would rather say, 'ethical') meaning of 'evil'. When used with this meaning, 'evil' is a term of ethical judgement or condemnation. It may be applied to an act of wrongdoing, to a course of such acts or a disposition or tendency thereto, or to the wrongdoer himself; especially as a noun, it tends to reify or personify a supposed principle

---

[5] The *OED* also remarks that what little use the word has in colloquial English is due to literary influence (see p. 42 above). Is it possible that the concept of evil, especially radical evil (see below), has always flourished more in writing than in speech?

[6] I.e. the meaning that is understood in the absence of any specification of the intended sense.

or force of wrongness. There are differences of connotation between some of these applications. More basic, however, is a distinction between two major senses, which have notably different implications and consequences. I distinguish them as the 'weak' and 'strong' senses of the moral meaning.[7]

As an ethical term, 'evil' sorts with a family of such terms, e.g. 'immoral', morally 'bad' or 'wrong', 'wicked', 'sinful'. In the weak sense, 'evil' is no stronger in condemnation than these, is effectively synonymous and interchangeable with at least some of them. This sense is plain in the common expressions 'good and evil', 'good or evil', applied particularly to acts. Here the assumption is that, of acts to which moral judgement applies, and neglecting the band of the morally neutral, the universe divides between those that are good, to be approved, and those that are evil, to be disapproved. The term 'evil' here has the same wide scope as 'bad': whatever is not good (and not neutral).

In the strong sense, however, 'evil' is far from synonymous with 'bad', etc.: it expresses condemnation that is markedly more severe. If we order wrongdoings on a scale of gravity or heinousness, the range of application of 'evil' tends toward the graver end. It is unacceptable to use it of a peccadillo, and uncomfortable to use it of a venial offence. At the other end of the scale, for a gross moral enormity 'evil' is not only acceptable but almost required: perhaps only 'wicked' will do as an alternative. If one were to describe and discuss what the Nazis did at Auschwitz and elsewhere in pursuit of their Final Solution, and conclude with the judgement that such conduct was 'bad' or 'wrong' or 'immoral', one would outrage one's readers. Judgement in those terms would be perceived as quite inadequate, as close to condoning the conduct. Pocock's observation (p. 42 above) that 'evil' is cognate with 'over' in the sense of 'excessive' seems apt for this strong sense of the term. The bias towards the more severe end of the moral scale is still more marked when the reference is to the wrongdoer, not just wrongdoing: to term a person, or set of persons, 'evil' is very severe — indeed, fighting talk.

There is plainly a notable difference between the weak and strong senses of 'evil' as an ethical term. There is a simple test to distinguish between them: where we encounter the term 'evil', can we, or can we not, substitute such other terms as 'bad' or 'immoral' without loss of meaning? In too many cases there is no certain answer; in others it becomes evident that an author slides, no doubt unawares, between one sense and the other. Sometimes he suggests, or leaves the reader to suppose, that the people he describes have a concept of

[7] This is not the distinction that Macfarlane (chapter 4) draws between a 'strong' and a 'weak' meaning; in his usage the latter is close to my 'descriptive' meaning. Nor is it equivalent to the *OED*'s distinction between 'positive' and 'privative' senses.

evil in the strong sense, while the evidence presented warrants only the conclusion that they have a concept of evil in the weak sense.

We should understand other cultures, and indeed our own, better if we gave up using the misleading term 'evil', or at least always qualified it. Instead of 'evils' in the descriptive sense we might speak of 'afflictions'; for 'evil' in the weak ethical sense we should substitute the terms 'immoral', morally 'wrong' or 'bad'. I want to keep 'evil' in the strong sense, the better to point to the problems that arise: I shall therefore specify this as 'radical evil'.

So far I have suggested that 'radical evil' is like 'bad' only more so — which does not make it obvious why it is important to distinguish. The important differences lie in the images and associations of the two concepts, and still more in the responses each tends to evoke. The notion of radical evil is notably associated with demonology, with the imagery of hosts of malignant beings. But demonology need not entail this notion, which is more strictly associated with demonology of the Iranian (Zoroastrian) dualist kind. For obvious reasons, notions of hell may be, but need not be, indices of radical evil. More significant, I think, is the dogma that 'there can be no compromise with evil.' The other side of this is our feeling that to describe as 'bad' what should properly be termed (radically) 'evil' is to condone it. The radical evil is that which must not be condoned or admitted to compromise: and since we must oppose it, this is indeed fighting talk. My own very restricted explorations do indeed indicate a strong association of notions of radical evil with war. They seem to be favoured by the militarist and the bellicose, and the categorization of adversaries as evil is unmistakably a call to arms. This is probably the basis of their associations with demonology: evil demons or devils, in my view (and that of Buddhists[8]), are projections of the ill-will and pugnacity of those who suppose them.

The word 'evil' is often used by anthropologists, as by others, with little or no attempt to distinguish its various senses. In consequence it is often impossible to be sure what concepts are being designated by it. Worse, it is all too easy to suppose that certain concepts (ours, usually) have been attributed to another people, when there is no sound evidence for it in the text. I am especially conscious of this because of the way that I, and some others, have misread Obeyesekere's (1968) paper. It is very easy to suppose that here we have an account of Sinhalese Buddhist concepts of evil broadly similar to our own. But it is not so. Obeyesekere does say something about Buddhist ideas of 'evil', but this is always 'evil' in the descriptive sense. He says more about ideas of moral wrongs among contemporary Sinhalese Buddhists, but he never uses the word 'evil' in presenting them (mostly he terms these wrongs

[8] Ortner (1978: 99); Southwold (1983: 52, 196).

'sins').[9] There is no evidence here that Sinhalese verbally link afflictions and moral wrongs, as is done by our word 'evil'. Still less is there any evidence for a concept of 'evil' in the strong ethical sense — indeed, I suspect that it is because there is no such concept that Obeyesekere avoided the word in describing moral views.

It would be consoling if Obeyesekere's paper were unusually obscure. On the contrary, it is remarkably clear once one thinks to look for the distinctions between various senses of 'evil'. My point is that we rarely do, and in consequence we fall all too readily into the trap of attributing our concept of evil to other cultures, without warrant.

What, then, are Sinhalese Buddhist notions about wrongdoing and about affliction, and do these form a complex sufficiently similar to our own to warrant our saying they have a concept of 'evil'? I should say at once that I did not examine this question while I was doing fieldwork, and do not find much material in my notes or elsewhere that bears at all directly on it. I am moderately confident that what I say is sound, since there is much else that confirms it indirectly. But more research is needed.

Among the Sinhalese the word *naraka*, which means 'bad' in a very wide sense, is applied to wrong acts and dispositions, and also sometimes to afflictions. But apart from this, it seems that one set of terms is used of wrong acts, etc., and another of afflictions and suffering. In my experience there is no word commonly used to link these two areas of reference as our word 'evil' can. I do not think this is important, since the two are very strongly linked conceptually. According to the doctrine of *karma*, all one's afflictions are the consequences of one's own former misdeeds — which does not, in practice, exclude alternative etiologies. The commonest term for suffering and unhappiness is *duka*, or Pali *dukkha*, and in Buddhist analysis *dukkha* is caused entirely by one's own wrongness.

Affliction, physical 'evil'[10] and wrongdoing, moral 'evil', are then linked by the Sinhalese, and to that extent they have a concept like ours, if not a word of similar application. They are probably unremarkable in this, since it is likely that most peoples make some such link. Grayston writes, referring to the descriptive meaning of *ra'* among the early Hebrews, 'the development of a moral connotation is very natural; a harmful action, as viewed by the injured

---

[9] There are four passages (pp. 23, 33, 34, n. 4) that seem to be exceptions; but in none of them does Obeyesekere unequivocally impute to living Sinhalese the use of a term translatable as 'evil' in the ethical sense.

[10] My distinction between the descriptive and ethical meanings is close to that in traditional moral theology between physical and moral evil; but as mine makes no space for metaphysical evil, the two schemas are not the same.

party, is a wicked one' (1950: 74). Equally, in most ethical systems an act is identified as wrong because it is harmful, especially to others. It is likely, further, that the experience of punishment conditions people to think of affliction as a response to the victim's wrongdoing.

Examined more closely, the thinking of the Sinhalese may be significantly different from what I suggest is commonplace in human cultures. Grayston's remark assumes that the wrongdoer and the victim are different persons; and the harm that people anticipate from wrongdoing is mainly harm to others. But the theories of *karma* and *dukkha* that the Sinhalese use do not make that distinction: the stress is on the harm to oneself from one's own wrongdoing. For the same reason their theories are not, cognitively at least, extrapolations of the experience of punishment. Wrongdoing is not an offence against the command or authority cr sacredness of some godlike being, for there is no such being. It is seen as a matter of natural law that suffering follows wrongdoing, much as smoke follows fire.

This is the basis of the fact that forbids us to attribute a concept of 'evil' to Sinhalese Buddhists: the absence of any concept of radical evil. If one regularly blames others for one's misfortunes, it is easy (but not necessary) to come to see them as radically evil, meet to be destroyed. It is rather unlikely that one will see oneself in the same way — though some of the austerities of the more extreme Meditation Buddhists could be considered self-destructive.

It is, of course, always difficult to be certain of the absence of anything. I say that there is no concept of radical evil among Buddhists partly because all the words I have encountered, in fieldwork and in literature, that might be or might have been translated as 'evil' quite clearly do not carry the strong sense, and partly because examination of the cultural contexts in which such a concept might more probably lurk fails to uncover it.

It is necessary to hold in mind the distinction between Meditation Buddhism and Ministry Buddhism, as I have termed them. I assume that this correlates strongly (but not perfectly) with the distinction between Buddhism as it appears to those who study scriptures, and Buddhism as it is found by those who study people. I further assume that, by his distinction between 'monastic' and 'lay' Buddhism, Ling had something similar in mind. I should further remark that, in studying the concepts of Buddhists, one ought to make the distinction they themselves make, between the Buddhist and the non-Buddhist parts of their culture; however, with regard to 'evil' at least, the two are consistent.

In writings about Buddhism, the term 'evil' is notably used in reference to the mythological figure of Māra. Māra is often called 'the Evil One', and compared with Satan in the Christian tradition. If anywhere, it is here that we might expect to find a concept of radical evil among Buddhists.

Ling (1962: 43 and *passim*) remarks that the scriptures contain many references to Māra, who is thus an important figure within them. He is represented as the tempter, who tries to divert the Buddha and his followers from their quest. In particular, he sought to divert Gotama from attaining that Enlightenment by which he became a Buddha; then he sought to obstruct the teaching of that Enlightenment. He seeks every opportunity to destroy whatever insight has been gained by disciples of the Buddha, and especially opposes the practice of meditation (pp. 51–2). He is the upholder of false views arising from ignorance (or delusion) — *avijjā*; he seems like a symbolic image of ignorance (pp. 61–2).

What this evidence from the scriptures shows is that the figure of Māra was important for those Buddhists who produced the scriptures, whose views, I have suggested, were mainly those of Meditation Buddhism. He may be important today for those who take a similar view, and for those who read the scriptures much — which categories, in my experience, seem largely coincident. Ling also points out that Māra is unlikely to have been important in the popular instruction given to laymen. 'Māra is almost entirely disregarded' in the non-canonical Jātaka stories, which laymen know much better than the canonical scriptures (Ling 1962: 73), while, according to the canonical scriptures, though ordinary villagers might be possessed by Māra, they would not perceive the fact (p. 75).

On the basis of my observation, I can say that the figure of Māra is more familiar to villagers than Ling's account suggests. He is mentioned in sermons, but is most familiar from imagery: notably in the statues and pictures in many temples which present Buddhist themes to the public in visual form. Pictures of him are also quite common on postcards, religious pictures and book illustrations. But it would be a gross error to infer from this that Māra the Evil One is a significant element in the religion of ordinary Buddhists. He is hardly ever spoken of, except by clergy in sermons and by people actually seeing his image in a temple. Nothing suggests to me that anyone imagines he might actually encounter Māra; on the contrary, Māra is simply a stock character in the scene of an event of long ago in the experience of that superhuman person, the Buddha. The scene is always the same: that in which Māra appeared with his three voluptuous daughters in a vain endeavour to tempt the Buddha-to-be from achieving enlightenment. I am rather sure that this scene is so often depicted because it gives the artists, and their clients, a religious pretext for relishing the depiction of voluptuous women. I would guess that, if any villager ever does imagine himself in such a scene, the emotion evoked is by no means fear. Māra, to be blunt, is a sort of pimp.

Ling's view of the matter (1962: 72–6), that Māra is a prominent symbol in monastic rather than in popular Buddhism, seems to be correct; though in my terms I would say that he sorts with Meditation rather than Ministry Buddhism. If, as we saw above, Māra is particularly opposed to meditation, this is understandable — I found that villagers were commonly indifferent to, if not disdainful of, meditation. Ling, apparently alluding to the scriptures, writes of 'the frequently emphasized idea that only the Buddha sees Māra and recognizes him, and after him, those others who like the Buddha have become awakened, those who are devoted to the Dhamma and walk in the Buddha's holy path' (p. 75). The figure of the Evil One, it seems, occurs in the context of the quest for perfection.[11]

But is Māra properly termed 'the Evil One'? Ling (1962) so frequently uses the expression that the identity is fixed in the reader's mind before there is any discussion of the indigenous term. On p. 47 he mentions, and on p. 56 begins briefly to discuss, the Pali term *pāpimā*, which has been translated as 'evil'. Though he asserts that it indicates 'moral evil', his discussion strongly suggests that its sense is mainly descriptive, to designate 'evil, an ill'. Neither here nor elsewhere where the issue comes up is Ling clear. Similarly, though use of the word 'evil' and the comparison with Satan would suggest to many readers that this is 'evil' in the strong ethical sense, Ling fails to clarify the distinction, while presenting evidence that counts against this sense. As Ling points out, in all the scriptural passages, bar one, in which Māra confronts the Buddha, there is no real conflict. Simply 'to recognise Māra is to deflate him', and the Buddha always immediately recognizes, deflates and then dismisses him (p. 50). Other Buddhists are counselled to do the same (pp. 63—5).

Boyd's discussion of the terminology is very much to be preferred. On the first page of that section of his book which deals with Māra he has a note:

The rendering of the Pali and Buddhist Sanskrit term *pāpa* as 'evil' is not done without hesitation, for though the English term 'evil' is an accepted rendering . . . it runs the risk of retaining implicit Christian meanings which do not necessarily belong to the Buddhist understanding of *pāpa*.

Boyd 1975: 73 n.1

Boyd goes on to note that Rhys Davids related the term to Greek *pema*, which translates as 'misery, calamity'. Repeating this latter observation on p. 157, he continues: 'The basic meaning of the term *pāpa*, therefore, most probably is: that which is essentially miserable, full of suffering, and inferior.' He contrasts the meaning of *pāpa* with the connotations of the English term 'evil', and suggests that the term 'bad' may be a better rendering than 'evil', as 'The

---

[11] In the course of our discussions, Pocock suggested that the concept of (radical) evil seemed to be evoked by the desire for perfection.

English word "bad" in contemporary usage does not as readily carry the moralistic and strong malignant connotations as does the term "evil"' (p. 158). Noting that there are contexts in which *pāpa* connotes moral wrong, as well as having (what I call) the descriptive sense, he writes, 'Because the English term "bad" embraces both connotative levels more readily than does the more forceful term "evil", it appears to be a more appropriate general rendering of the Buddhist meaning of *pāpa*' (p. 159).

Finally, Boyd remarks another contrast between Christian and Buddhist concepts. For the Buddhist the source of *pāpa* as moral wrong is within the person, but for Christians the source of *ponēros* (evil) is external to man: 'the early Christians understood the nature of *ponēros* to be ultimately an extrinsic power foreign and hostile to the rightful conditions of human existence.' There is thus a 'difference between the Christian affirmation and the Buddhist rejection of the externality of the source of "evil" . . .' (Boyd 1975: 159—61).

In summary, then, Boyd considers that to render *pāpa* as 'evil' is likely to be misleading, partly because the meaning is primarily descriptive rather than moral, partly because, to the extent that it is moral, it is without the strong sense; and he links this latter observation to the fact that the source of *pāpa* is within oneself, not external. This is so similar to my own analysis that I should point out that I had formulated mine before I read Boyd. On this point at least, analysis of modern ethnographic reality and analysis of the scriptures converge towards the same conclusion.

There is more evidence to be found in the Sinhalese notions concerning demons (*sing: yaksa*). For want of space I must refer the reader to Gombrich's account (1971: 160—3). In brief, there are at least three categories, of which only one might reasonably suggest a notion of radical evil: these are the named demons, such as Mahasōnā, which are 'distinctly malevolent' and are, in the low country of Sri Lanka mainly, the objects of exorcism rites (p. 162).[12] The Sinhalese consider these to be no part of Buddhism, and in any case they are not radically evil: both because, as Kapferer (1983) makes clear, the rationale of the exorcisms rests on the assumption that the demons do not really have power to harm, and because, as Gombrich points out, *yaksas* and gods are not clearly distinguished (1971: 162). Sinhalese notions of *yaksas* are similar to those of *yakkhas*, as found in the Pali scriptures (pp. 160—2); but also, as Ling shows (1962: 44—6), the notions of Māra closely resemble these latter. Hence the lack of a concept of radical evil in both cases is unsurprising.

Again, if space permitted, Sinhalese notions of hell (or rather, hells —

---

[12] On these rites see especially Kapferer (1983).

apāya) might be explored. My impression, among the villagers I knew, was that no one took these very seriously. People would sometimes say, of someone they considered unusually wicked, that he deserved or was likely to go to hell; it did not seem to me that anyone had ever supposed this might be his own fate. Carrithers points out that forest monks (in my terms, those most committed to Meditation Buddhism) often have an unusual fear of hell and fascination with hell-fire preaching (1983: 17—18, 78—9). This fits my suggestion that there is more that resembles our own notions of evil in Meditation than in Ministry Buddhism.

There is no concept of radical evil in Buddhism: does this matter? What does not exist is of no interest in itself, but only in a comparative context; and our discussion makes it uncertain what the comparative context is. People have talked and written confidently enough about notions of evil in Buddhism: more careful and critical scrutiny shows that the term is seriously misleading. The same may well be true of other cultures to which people have carelessly attributed concepts of evil. Is Buddhism unique, or unusual, in having no concept of evil in the full sense? Or is Buddhism normal in this regard, and our own culture of Christendom the odd stream out? One comparison at least I can make with some confidence, and it is that between Buddhendom and Christendom.

The widespread complacency of liberal intellectuals notwithstanding, the concept of radical evil is alive and festering among us — not least among the most educated and influential. The speech of President Reagan at Orlando, Florida, in which he described the Soviet Union as the 'empire of evil' is a notorious instance. A more daunting example is in the first leader of *The Times* of 20 May 1982, pontificating on the imminent British invasion of the Falkland Islands; it is quoted, together with an analysis of its 'tremulous repetition of "evil"' in Barnett (1982: 98—100). A sadder instance occurs in *The Church and the Bomb* (Church of England 1982), the report of a working party of the Church of England. Much of the argument hinges on a crucial passage of ethical analysis on pp. 99—101: close attention will show that its plausibility rests on equivocation between the weak and strong senses of 'evil'.[13]

How could we account for the fact that some cultures (also some sub-cultures, some individuals) use the concept of evil in the strong sense, others

---

[13] I regret that I do not have the space to demonstrate this. Were space more ample, I should discuss at length the use of the term 'evil' in this report. Passages in which the term is frequent and the strong sense plain are markedly contrasted with those where the usage is infrequent and the sense 'weak'. They indicate very different theologies which are imperfectly harmonized in the report.

only in the weak sense? I suggest that the practical difference between the two senses reflects less or more readiness to forgive. 'There can be no compromise with [radical] evil'; to call the radical evil merely 'bad' seems to condone it. What, then, might cause some to refuse to forgive what others would forgive? I have space to mention only a few factors in a very complex manifold. (1) To forgive is to re-admit the wrongdoer to community; to refuse is to exclude him. We might therefore expect indisposition to forgive, manifested in openness to a concept of radical evil, to be more marked among the more asocial. This clearly fits the difference between Ministry and Meditation Buddhists. (2) Forgiveness, I guess, is commonly in the spirit of 'forgive that ye may be forgiven': hence those who are most aware of their own need for forgiveness, of their own proneness to sin, should be most forgiving. The stiff-necked and authoritarian would be unforgiving, and most ready to speak of radical evil. This fits many facts.

But, further (3) self-awareness of this kind might vary according to where the culture locates the source of wrongdoing. As Lienhardt pointed out in *Divinity and Experience* (1961), the Dinka tend to project on to supposed external occult agencies much that we attribute to the inward workings of mind (pp. 149—55). There is evidence that this is characteristic of 'primitive' cultures;[14] whereas the tendency to reduce all occult agencies to inner psychic phenomena goes further among Buddhists than among ourselves. Buddhists are therefore taught to see the roots of wrongdoing within oneself. In other cultures these are blamed on external occult agencies, which can easily then be seen as alien in themselves, and as possessing the evildoers; which facilitates seeing the evildoer as an enemy to be destroyed.

This is why, as I have suggested, radical evil is associated with demonology, which itself is associated with theism. But the association is imperfect: the concept of radical evil seems to be more closely associated with monotheism.[15] Monotheism seems to me to be quite strongly associated, as both cause and effect, with intolerance. What is it that associates both of these with the Middle East, while both, with their bedfellow radical evil, are virtually absent from India?[16] Could it be that the much-maligned caste system, by producing

---

[14] See, for example, Hallpike (1979: chapter 9). However bizarre in parts, Jaynes (1982) also contains much that points to the infrequency of notions of subjective consciousness like our own.

[15] Professor Roy Wallis first pointed this out to me, in discussion when I presented an earlier version of this paper in Belfast.

[16] O'Flaherty notes that 'Indologists have long maintained that there is no problem of evil in Indian thought. . . .', and quotes several writers (1976: 7, 4). She disagrees, choosing to translate the word *pāpa* (Boyd's discussion, of which I cited in the text) as 'evil'. There

a series of closed but interdependent communities, gives rise to polytheism and religious pluralism, hence the religious tolerance and the self-awareness that find no place for radical evil?

REFERENCES

Ahern, M. B. (1971). *The Problem of Evil.* London: Routledge and Kegan Paul.
Barnett, A. (1982). *Iron Britannia.* London: Allison and Busby.
Boyd, J. W. (1975). *Satan and Māra: Christian and Buddhist Symbols of Evil* (Studies in the History of Religions, xxvii). Leiden: E. J. Brill.
Carrithers, M. (1983). *The Forest Monks of Sri Lanka.* Delhi: Oxford University Press.
Church of England (Board for Social Responsibility) (1982). *The Church and the Bomb.* London: Hodder and Stoughton.
Doob, L. W. (1978). *Panorama of Evil: Insights from the Behavioral Sciences.* Westport and London: Greenwood Press.
Gombrich, R. F. (1971). *Precept and practice: traditional Buddhism in the rural highlands of Ceylon.* London: Oxford University Press.
Grayston, K. (1950). 'Evil'. In Alan Richardson (ed.), *A Theological Word Book of the Bible.* London: SCM Press.
Hallpike, C. R. (1979). *The Foundations of Primitive Thought.* Oxford: Oxford University Press.
Jaynes, J. (1982). *The Origin of Consciousness in the Breakdown of the Bicameral Mind* (first edition, 1976). Harmondsworth: Penguin
Kapferer, B. (1983). *A Celebration of Demons.* Bloomington: Indiana University Press.
Lienhardt, G. (1961). *Divinity and Experience: the Religion of the Dinka.* London: Oxford University Press.
Ling, T. O. (1962). *Buddhism and the Mythology of Evil.* London: Allen and Unwin.
Obeyesekere, G. (1968). 'Theodicy, Sin and Salvation in a Sociology of Buddhism'. In E. R. Leach (ed.), *Dialectic in Practical Religion* (Cambridge Papers in Social Anthropology, 5). Cambridge: Cambridge University Press.
O'Flaherty, W. D. (1976). *The Origins of Evil in Hindu Mythology* Berkeley: University of California Press.
Onions, C. T. (1949). *A Shakespeare Glossary* (first edition, 1911). Oxford: Clarendon Press.
Ortner, S. B. (1978). *Sherpas through their rituals* (Cambridge studies in cultural systems, 2). Cambridge: Cambridge University Press.

---

seems to be confusion here, O'Flaherty affirming the use of weak and descriptive senses, the Indologists denying the use of the strong sense. Ling refers to some of the same authors in support of his claim that India has a 'mythology free from Iranian dualism' (1962: 25—6); evil in the strong sense seems to be closely linked with Iranian dualism.

Plantinga, A. (1974). *God, Freedom and Evil.* London: Allen and Unwin.
Southwold, M. (1983). *Buddhism in Life.* Manchester: Manchester University Press.
Spiro, M. E. (1971). *Buddhism and Society: A Great Tradition and its Burmese Vicissitudes.* London: Allen and Unwin.

9

Hindu evil as unconquered Lower Self

Ronald Inden

INTRODUCTION

My intention in this essay is to explicate the concept of 'evil' held by one of the major orders of Hinduism, that of the Pancaratra Vaishnavas. What I wish to say about this topic will perhaps seem strangely 'activist' in its outlook, but there is a reason for this. Discussions of good and evil in India's religions have been dominated largely by a scholarly discourse that has placed the civilization of the 'West' in a relationship of opposition to that of India (and that once served to justify the rule of the former over the latter). Europe (with North America) is portrayed as fundamentally 'materialistic', 'realistic' and 'optimistic'. India, by contrast, is seen as 'spiritualist', 'idealistic' and 'pessimistic'. Scholars (Farquhar 1912: 38—43; Eliot 1922: I, x—xvi) have, accordingly, tended to assume that the one school of Brahmanism that was indeed idealist and quietist in its views was also the one that was central to Indian culture, its religious 'essence'. They have, correspondingly, tended to assume that the realist and activist philosophies of Hinduism, including those loosely affiliated with the Pancaratra Vaishnavas, were, somehow, peripheral.[1] Historically, quite the reverse was the case, at least down to the advent of Islamic rule.[2]

---

[1] The school centred in this way was, of course, that of Advaita ('non-dualist') Vedanta ('end of the Veda'/'completion of gnosis'), as propounded by Sankara around AD700 (Thrasher 1979). The schools that actually occupied the middle ground between the Advaita and the Dvaita ('dualist'), the view radically opposed to it, were the (earlier) Bhedabheda ('different yet not different') of Bhaskara and the (later) Visistadvaita ('qualified non-dualist') of Ramanuja.

[2] The 'idealist' school of Buddhism, called Yogacara or Vijnanavada ('conceptualist'), formed itself in and rose to prominence at a time (fifth and sixth centuries) when Buddhism as a whole had lost its place as the premier religion of India's hegemonic states. The idealist school of Advaita Vedanta arose as a response to that school of Buddhism. Both found themselves outflanked by the Vaishnava and Shaiva theistic orders of temple Hinduism.

Two views of good and evil were held to derive logically from the pantheism and idealism characteristic of Brahmanism and attributed to Indian religion as a whole. One is the 'pessimistic' view, epitomized in Buddhism, that existence is itself evil (Niven 1914: 321). The other is that evil, or evil in a 'strong' sense, does not (along with sin) really exist. The appearance of evil is illusory, the result of ignorance of the oneness of the world with the Absolute/ God (pantheism). Evil exists, if at all, only in a weak sense, and is conceived of naturalistically; that is, moral evils (sin) and physical evils (suffering) are not distinguished. Ethical acts are, therefore, largely purificatory. They are but a prelude to those meditative or ascetic practices by which a man will realize his unity with the One, an Absolute entirely good or, perhaps, even 'beyond good and evil' (Hopkins 1927: 112—20). Southwold's view (chapter 8) that Buddhism lacks a strong sense of evil because it is psychologistic and lacks an 'authoritarian' political component would seem to be a variation on the first position.

These accounts of good and evil may or may not (Radhakrishnan 1959: 58—114) adequately represent the views of idealist schools of Buddhism and Brahmanism, but they are almost totally inadequate representations of the orders of both Shaivas and Vaishnavas that actually predominated in Indian states and of the schools of thought associated with them. These orders of Hinduism all called for action in the world. Indeed, they called for their royal and householder devotees to constitute the world as a theophany, one that centred on monumental temples and on the doctrine of 'participatory devotion' (*bhakti*) and the 'honouring of images' (*puja*). None of these orders was more activist in its orientation than that of the Pancaratra Vaishnavas, the subject of this paper.

To begin with, I present a sketch of the Pancaratra ontology and anthropology of good and evil. Then I turn to the explication of a particular 'history', that of the evil King Vena, as a device for exploring two issues. The first of these is the 'cause' of evil and the closely connected question of power, the power to decide what is evil and what to do about it. The second is the theme with which the history ends, the 'subjugation' of evil and its constitution as a 'lower self' of India.[3]

The outlook depicted as typical of Indian religion was thus, if anything, the perspective of two schools of thought that were *themselves* defensive and peripheral in relation to the increasingly successful theistic orders of the Vaishnavas and Shaivas.

[3] I do not rehearse here that classic chestnut of European theology, the 'problem of evil', which was not, as Herman (1976) shows, an Indian problem. Adherence to a doctrine of transmigration of souls focused attention more on the question of what to do about evil than on why it existed in the first place. Nor do I reopen the ancillary question, the 'origin of evil', a topic recently explored by O'Flaherty (1976).

The Pancaratras (the rule 'of the five nights', probably referring to the major annual festival of the order, the 'awakening' of Vishnu) flourished in north India for some ten centuries. After the establishment there, in the thirteenth century, of the Delhi sultanate, Pancaratra Vaishnavism as a practice centred on Hindu imperial temples virtually disappeared.[4] The major text on which I rely here is the *Vishnudharmottara* (1912), a text on cosmology, theology and kingship from the eighth century. The text is in Sanskrit and was (most probably) 'disclosed' in Kashmir at the court of Lalitaditya Muktapida; the King of Kashmir and the paramount king of the North, he performed the seemingly impossible feat of conquering the quarters and becoming the paramount overlord of all India in the middle of the eighth century.

METAPHYSICS OF EVIL

The concept of evil put forward by the Vaishnavas was known as *papa* or *tamas*, either of which may be translated loosely as 'badness' or 'evil'. It is opposed to *punya* or *sattva*, both of which may be translated by the single term 'goodness'. The meanings and usages of these terms was (and is) complex. As substantives, the paired terms *papa* and *punya* meant 'trouble', 'misfortune' and 'inauspiciousness', as well as badness or evil, and 'virtue', 'rightness' or 'auspiciousness' as well as goodness. These words could refer as adjectives to the moral quality of a person, his (or her) 'acts' (*karman*) and 'soul' or 'essence' (*atman*). They could even be used to denote the acts themselves, *punya* as a 'good work', *papa* as an 'evil deed' or 'sin'. The same two terms could also designate atomistically the 'demerits' or 'merits' a person accumulated in his soul as a result of the acts he/she performed. The term *tamas* meant 'darkness' and, thence, 'ignorance' or false knowledge/consciousness (*ajnana*) and 'badness' or 'evil', all of which were held to be closely connected. False knowledge was the cause of evil, darkness was its visible sign. The term *sattva*, prolific in meanings, derives from the verb 'is' or 'be' (*as*). It meant existence, essence, presence and fixity and, simultaneously, goodness. It also had the sense of true knowledge or consciousness (*jnana, caitanya*), the cause of goodness, and of 'light' or 'brightness' (*tejas*), its visible sign. These two terms could also denote the active power to do good and evil as well as the passive attributes or conditions of good and evil. Here, *tamas*

---

[4] A southern transformation of the earlier Pancaratra order, the Srivaishnavas, had risen to prominence by this time (Gonda 1965, II, 140—52, 160—7), and continues to flourish.

had the sense of 'delusion' (*moha*) and of disintegration or destruction, while *sattva*, in this context a synonym of *tejas*, meant 'courage', 'valour' or 'glory'.

The terms *tamas* and *sattva* tend to come to the foreground in Vaishnava discourse because they were used to construct the theory of the three 'strands', to which I now turn. The cosmos was thought to be a living thing. The primordial stuff of which it was made was conceived of not as mere physical matter but as a kind of ever-changing protoplasm. The theory of the three 'strands' (*guna*) presumed to account for the fluctuating conditions of this protoplasmic stuff. Indeed, one might say that this theory constituted matter as alive. (In order to capture the double contrast implicit in the use of these terms, I translate them, below, with two English words and provide alternate renderings.) The three strands or substrata of matter were *sattva*, 'quiescent goodness' or 'enlightened existence'; *rajas*, 'restless activity' or 'passionate energy'; and *tamas,* 'inert badness' or 'benighted lethargy'. A triad of gods, Vishnu the preserver, Brahma the creator and Shiva the destroyer, each a manifestation of Vishnu as Cosmic Overlord, embodied the fullest expression of this triad of strands.

The first of these strands, and the one considered the highest, was the propensity that matter had for order, for essence; that is, for enlightened as opposed to mere existence, for becoming/completing oneself as a moral being, for attaining one's proper end. At the risk of pushing modern biological metaphors too far and mixing them too much, it was the propensity of the cosmic protoplasm for homeostatic growth. Vishnu, the god of protection who fostered the cosmos after its creation or emission and before its destruction or retraction, and who led his devotees to the goals of cosmomoral order and release from the world, was the embodiment of this strand of quiescent goodness or enlightened existence, the highest of the three.

The second of these substrata, the middle one, was the propensity or tendency in the primal protoplasm to procreate, to move, to energize, to clash, to acquire or consume and, in general, to renew itself. Brahma, the manifestation of the Cosmic Overlord, who was charged with the emission of the world at the beginning of a cosmic period, was the fullest embodiment of this middle strand, that of restless activity or passionate energy. The third of these strands and the lowest of them, inert badness or benighted lethargy, was the propensity of the protoplasmic matter for degeneracy, dispersal and exhaustion. It entailed, in a word, the tendency to destroy itself. Shiva was the member of the divine triad who was destructive in nature; his mandate was to bring about the retraction of the world, to cause its dissolution and destruction at the end of a period in the life of the cosmos.

Already one can see that this third and lowest strand, the strand productive of evil and made to predominate over the other two by evil acts, was conceived of as an integral part of the material of the cosmos and of its processes as a living thing. Let us continue with our lesson in Hindu moral biophysics.

Among human beings, the three substrata, always in themselves invisible, were to be known by certain sensible properties. The strand of enlightened existence displayed, for example, the physical properties or signs of lightness and transparency, while the strand of benighted lethargy exhibited the opposite qualities of heaviness and opaqueness. Critical among these were the internal attribute — knowledge — and its external property and sign — light. The invisible propensity for knowledge (*jnana*) of Vishnu and its accompanying purity (*nirmalatva*), two of the major attributes of enlightened existence, the highest of the three strands, were 'illuminating' or 'resplendent' (*prakasaka*). The colour signifying this best of the strands, consistent with its tendency to enlightenment, was white. Its propensities were, first and foremost, functions of the intellect (*buddhi*), of the philosophical reasoning faculty of a person. By contrast, the ignorance (*ajnana*) of the lowest strand, benighted lethargy, was perceptible by its property signs of darkness and dullness. The colour signifying it was, appropriately, black. Its propensities were primarily functions of the senses (*indriya*) which, unguided by mind and intellect, produced the degenerative doldrums and category mistakes characteristic of this strand.

The strand of passionate energy stood between the highest and lowest strands. Its life-promoting passions (*raga*) and movement (*pravrtti*) were opposed, on the one hand, to the deadening slackness (*pramada*) and holding back (*niyama*) characteristic of the substratum of benighted lethargy. On the other hand, those same passions and ceaseless movements were also opposed to the knowledge and calm demeanour of the highest strand of enlightened existence. Not surprisingly, the identifying colour of this middle strand was neither white nor black, but red. And its activities were functions neither of the intellect nor of the senses but of the organ situated between those two, the mind (*manas*), the faculty of desire or will and of hesitation, the faculty moved by the passions and pulled this way and that by its not-so-rational choices.

The inclusion of a middle strand in this theory of matter and morality brings to the surface the problem of power that is usually masked by the paired terms 'good' and 'evil'. For the Pancaratras (and other Hindus), the power to do the good or the wicked were, wherever they appeared in the cosmos, the result of the operation of the three invisible strands in tandem with one another. The Pancaratras held that neither *sattva* nor *tamas* could operate in the world without the energy (compare Freud's idea of libido) of the strand that stood between them, *rajas*. They called for the restless activity of the middle strand to be taken up by and included in the first strand, that of quiescent goodness, and separated from the third, the strand of inert badness.

The result was a new entity, *tejas*, the power of gods and men to do the good, their power to uphold Dharma, cosmomoral order. A synonym of *sattva*, I translate *tejas* as 'luminous power' or 'triumphant glory'. It consisted of two aspects. One was light, the other heat. The light aspect of it was grounded in the higher substratum of enlightened existence, the strand of pure, still goodness, while the energy or heat aspect was grounded in the middle substratum of passionate energy, the strand of motion and conflict, of what Western philosophy might refer to as 'will'. Fused together, both stood against the darkness and death of the lower substratum, benighted lethargy. To say that a person was endowed with luminous power or triumphant glory was to say that he was commanded by a higher self. His intellect, the faculty of enlightened existence, directed his mind or will, the faculty of restless activity, and both together dominated over his senses, the faculties of benighted lethargy.

If the strand of quiescent goodness could capture the passionate energy of the middle strand and transmute it into triumphant glory, it was possible for *tamas* to do likewise. The result was a new and dangerous power that posed itself as the direct opposite of *tejas*, the luminous power of the gods and of enlightened, virtuous men. It was, like the third strand itself, usually called *tamas*, but in this more virulent form the lethargic aspect of benighted lethargy was reversed. Darkness and false knowledge became an active, evil force, the power used by the demons, atheists and barbarians to mislead and overwhelm men. It was the 'weapon' wielded by the malevolent 'seizers' or 'possessors' (*graha*) whom the gods dispatched to punish men for their offences. The *peey* so well described by Caplan can be seen as the ontological descendants of those seizers in modern Madras. This form of *tamas* I translate as 'dark delusion' or 'evil darkness', since these phrases imply an active attempt either to deceive or do harm. To say that a person was filled with dark delusion was to say that he was dominated by a lower self. His actions were guided not by an enlightened intellect but by the deluded senses.

One cannot, of course, approach the Vaishnava concept of evil without looking at the concept of Vishnu, the highest god and universal absolute of the Pancaratras, styled the 'cosmic overlord' (*sarvesvara*), and at his relationship to the world. The Pancaratras, like many other Indic thinkers, equated badness and its more active form, evil, with ignorance and darkness. Goodness, and its active form, triumphant glory, they equated with knowledge and brightness. These same Vaishnava theologians thought of the god Vishnu as a 'transcendent' (*para*) 'man' (*purusa*), out of whose 'body' he caused the entire cosmos to emanate. Through a number of mediating 'manifestations' (*pradurbhava*), epiphanies or 'incarnations', Vishnu created or emitted, protected or fostered, and destroyed or retracted the sequences of formations of which the cosmos was constituted. Now, the god Vishnu himself was, in his transcendent form, absolute, eternal and unchanging. His conscious knowledge was also absolute and unchanging. The brightness or splendour (*tejas*) he possessed was, as a result, 'infinite' or 'unlimited' (*amita*). Correspondingly, his goodness (*sattva*), forever quiescent, was also unbounded.

The world that emanated from Vishnu was a part of him. It participated in him. Yet it was not absolute, infinite and unchanging. It was just the opposite. It was impermanent and continually in flux, going through endless births and deaths. Knowledge in the world, like the world itself, was relative, finite and changing, as was its correlated brightness. Quiescent goodness in the world was, correspondingly, also finite and subject to changes. The world, moreover, did not consist solely of knowledge and brightness and the quiescent goodness with which they were equated. These comprised only one of the three strands that constituted the world. It contained the two lower strands as well: 'restless energy', the middle strand, and 'inert badness', the lowest strand. Devoid of these, the world could not have existed in a recognizable form.

It was, therefore, a major presupposition of Vaishnavism that evil, in the form of the lowest of the three strands, is an integral part of the empirical world, which is itself a part of God. He 'emitted' (*srj*) it from his body (emanationism), and it continues to participate in him without yet exhibiting his completeness (panentheism). People could not construct a world in which evil did not exist; nor did there ever exist a time in the past when evil did not occur. There was no 'fall' from a state of pure grace and no Adamic myth to tell of it. Since evil was an integral part of the world, kings of the earth and their householder subjects could, if they followed Vishnu's orders, keep the constituents of evil separate from those of the good and keep the latter in a position of inferiority and subjection to the former. But they could never do away with evil.

The three strands were integral to the Vaishnava theory of action. Human beings were born, according to the Pancaratra theodicy, with differing proportions of good and bad in their souls and bodies. These varying proportions not only determined their places in the Hindu 'chain of being', they also determined their higher and lower competencies to act in the world. They determined the extent to which a person participated in the construction and sustenance of the Vaishnava version of *dharma*, cosmomoral order.

Human acts, *karman*, had consequences or results (*phala*, 'fruit'), both for the actors and for the world around them. Vaishnava theologians used a number of paired terms, all synonyms of the terms *punya* and *pāpa*, to describe the moral qualities of humans, their souls, their acts and the consequences of those acts. Some of the more common were *su-*, 'good', 'well', and *dur-*, 'bad', 'ill'; *sat-*, 'good', 'true', 'pure', and *asat-*, 'bad' or 'wicked', 'untrue', 'impure'. Other terms were *mangala* and *subha*, meaning primarily 'auspicious' or 'bright' (and their opposites) and such terms as *dusta*, meaning 'defective', 'faulty', 'wrong', 'wicked' or 'offensive'. Good acts, those in conformity with dharma, could cause the soul or body of a person to become 'pure' or 'bright' (*sauca, sukra,* etc.) by making *dharma* in the sense of 'merits', particles of *sattva,* to increase. Bad or evil acts, or the parts of good acts that were bad, could cause 'filth' or 'spots' or 'impurity' (*mala*), 'dirt' or 'taint' (*kalmasa*), or 'defects' or 'faults' (*dosa*) to arise in the soul and body by making *adharma*, 'demerits', or particles of *tamas* to increase in them.

The point about this vocabulary of good and evil, with its equation of the divine, the bright and the pure and of the demonic, the dark and the impure, is that it is not simply metaphoric or symbolic. The idea was that actions changed the ontological content of a person's body and soul. Vishnu continually responded to acts of devotion and infused his devotees with his inexhaustible luminous power. Those who offended him and his *dharma*, however, he caused to be punished by the evil darkness inherent in the world. The agency of god and man thus made a person more divine or more demonic, brighter or darker, more truly conscious or more deluded, more glorious or more vile.

Badness, evil in the 'weaker' sense, was an integral part of the world, part of its life, death and rebirth. Evil acts brought about evil consequences, to be sure; but even good acts necessarily had bad 'side-effects'. In so far as the world of flux (*samsara*) continued to reproduce itself, there would be badness and even evil in the world. No Utopia in which evil would be for ever eliminated was considered possible. Yet, the Pancaratra Vaishnavas were no Stoics. They were men of both knowledge and action. By adhering to 'true' knowledge, that of the Pancaratras, a king and his people could dispel the ignorance or false knowledge on which evil thrived. They would, by following the orders of Vishnu contained in that knowledge, gain access to the infinite luminous power or *tejas* of Vishnu, his triumphant glory. With that, they would be able to overpower the bad in themselves and in others and keep the bad at bay. They would be able to prevent it from acquiring the *rajas*, the restless energy or undirected power inherent in the world, and from going on the rampage.

The idiom in which confrontations of good and evil took place was not, therefore, that of a battle between Self and some totally evil, unified and externalized Other. It was, rather, one of a conflict between a 'higher self' and a 'lower self', the 'civilized' people of India and the 'uncivilized'. A variety of embodiments of evil in the form of antigods or demons from the underworld and barbarians from the wastes and borders, the mountain fastnesses and swamps of India are made to rebel against their overlords. After a verbal clash and a trial of armed strength, the demon or barbarian either submits or is slain. Sometimes, however, a lower self appears among the civilized and among their kings. This is what happened to King Vena.

CONTESTED CAUSES OF EVIL

Discussions of evil typically argue that the people of a community tend to agree that certain conditions — poverty, disease, illiteracy, mental disorder, cruelty to children and animals, wife abuse and so on — may be called evil. Disagreement arises, however, when different schools of thought try to explain *why* those conditions of suffering exist. The intrepid moral philosopher, not wishing to be caught in a relativist trap, then proceeds, against all odds, to see if he can establish a common ground for these varying views (Niven 1914: 318—20). Anthropological theories of culture also tend to be consensualist (Bourdieu 1979). It is, hence, assumed that a community will have a single, shared explanation of evil, or, if not, that the anthropologist will be able to infer a single 'underlying' explanation from apparently diverse views. The position taken here is quite different. Following Gallie (1968), I hold that it is more productive to see explanations of good and evil as 'essentially contested concepts'. Explanations of good and evil (and the discrepant ontologies presupposed by them) necessarily take their shape and reproduce themselves in a continuing dialectical relationship with other, opposing explanations.

The 'history' (*itihasa*) of the paramount king of India, Vena, and his son, Prthu, provides an interesting confirmation of this 'contestation' hypothesis.[5] Contained in the section of the Purana on 'genealogies' (*vamsa*), this history marks the transition from the previous Epoch of Manu (*manvantara*), the Caksusa, to the present one, that of Vaivasvata Manu. It begins, appropriately enough, with a synopsis of Vena's parentage. The progenitor of Vena's royal lineage was, we are told, Dhruva (the 'fixed one'), the Polestar. Considered a direct manifestation of Vishnu himself, his place was at the centre of the sky and his material sign was the globe of quiescent goodness around which the

[5] The history or legend of Vena appears, in somewhat differing version, in the 'great epic' of India, the *Mahabharata*, and in most if not all of the Puranas ('ancient narratives'), including the *Vishnudharmottara* (1912: I. 108—9) whence all but one of the passages cited below; also used were Brahmanda Purana in Kirfel (1927: 233—50) and *Vishnu Purana* (1910: I.13).

cosmos revolved. Our text does not hesitate to call him, therefore, the 'soul' (*atman*) of 'cosmomoral order' (*dharma*).

The paternal grandfather of Vena made the mistake, however, of marrying his son, Anga, to the daughter of Mrityu ('death'), called Sunitha (the 'well-conducted one'). It was as a result of the 'faultiness' or 'wickedness' (*dosa*) of his maternal grandfather that Vena was born 'faulty' or 'wicked' (*dusta*) 'by nature' or 'inherently' (*nisargad*). Such is the explanation offered for the evil that Vena is about to do. It is assumed that a lineage, like a person, could commit a sin — here, the sin of accepting the daughter of Death in marriage — whose results would be physically transmitted and would appear in a later generation. Clearly, also, the theory of the three strands is presupposed. The 'evil darkness' of which Death is primarily constituted has entered the line of Dhruva and given that constituent of his lineage the upper hand. Yet this explanation itself is not seen as problematic. The major reason for this is that a cosmic life, an Epoch of Manu in this instance, was drawing to a close. So it was quite 'natural' for Vena, called the grandson of Time (*kala*), to appear on the scene and bring about the death of the Epoch. This does not detract from the hypothesis of Herman (1976) that Hindu ethical systems were oriented more towards the problem of counteracting evil than towards the problem of 'explaining' how evil and an infinitely good, omnipotent god can co-exist. It was not just that, for the Hindu, the evil inherent in the world was an integral part of the 'life' of the cosmos. Pancaratra discourse implies again and again that the evil in the world was more powerful than the good. Without repeated acts involving the acquisition of divine power — the 'luminous power' of Vishnu — 'evil darkness' would violently and prematurely bring death to the cosmos as an ordered world. Dramatic affirmation of this ontological proposition is indeed forthcoming in the history of Vena.

The very first thing we learn about Vena, his ancestry provided, is that he is an 'unbeliever' who adheres to the teachings of a 'school' of 'sensationalists':

The son of Anga was Vena, an unbeliever (*nastika*) devoid of *dharma*. He was unswervingly (*nitya*) loyal to the untrue/evil (*asat*) teachings (*sastra*), the best of sensationalist/materialists (*lokayatika*).

One could be an 'unbeliever' or *nastika* (one who says, 'There is not') in the sense of not believing in the validity of the Veda, not believing in the existence of the gods or not believing in the existence of life after death. The Vaishnavas, like other Hindus, believed in the validity of the Veda and in the existence of gods and of life after death. Two of the philosophical schools of ancient India, the Mimamsa and Sankhya, did not believe in the existence of the gods, but accepted the validity of the Veda and believed in the existence of life after death. The Buddhists and Jains neither accepted the validity of the Veda nor believed in the existence of gods, but they did adhere to the proposition that there was life after death. The Senstionalists, also known as Carvaka (apparently after the name of the school's founder) were unbelievers in all three senses (Chatterjee and Datta 1954: 5). Of all the 'world views' advanced in ancient India, theirs was thus the most radically opposed to that of the Pancaratras.

The term that people used to designate the holders of this extreme view, *lokayatika*, means one who says, 'Everything is confined/limited to (*ayata*) the visible world (*loka*).' It succinctly describes the Carvaka ontology and epistemology. Only that which is immediately perceptible by the senses is real, and the only sure means of knowing is direct perception (*pratyaksa*), since verbal testimony (*sabda*), inference (*anumana*) and analogy (*upamana*) are unreliable. Another term, *svabhavavadin*, 'proponent of the doctrine of inherent nature', locates their materialistic but anti-deterministic explanation of the varying conditions in which people live. Humans do not obtain the invisible (*adrsta*) results of moral or immoral acts performed in past lives. They enjoy only bodily pleasures (*sukha*) and pains (*duhkha*). These are the result neither of the operation of any *dharma* in the sense of a cosmomoral law nor of any 'cause' or 'agency' (*karana*) (the gods) situated outside of their bodies or of substances (transmigrating souls) within their bodies. Rather, people live as they do because of the highly volatile natures inherent in the material elements that constitute their bodies (Sinha 1956: I, 229–76).

The Carvakas apparently held the same presupposition that the Vaishnavas and others held, namely, that ontologies were to be practised and not merely theorized about in the form of epistemologies. The person who decided which ontology was most true was the king, who, after he had decided, should cause the state to be an actualization of the chosen ontology. This, we may presume, is why Vena is said to have proclaimed, after his coronation, that the ritual acts concerned with the invisible entities of *dharma*, the rites by which the king and his subjects reproduced India as a cosmomoral order, were henceforth not to be performed:

Opposed to *dharma*, the overlord of men (*naradhipa*, 'king') confined the goals of conduct (*maryada*) to the visible world (*loka*): 'The Prime Cause (*kārana*) of *dharma* is not to be sacrificed to (*yastavya*), not to be offered to (*hotavya*), and not be given to (*deya*).'

Hindus conventionally held that there were four 'goals of man' (*purusartha*). These were: (1) *kama*, personal pleasure; (2) *artha*, the accumulation of wealth and followers; (3) *dharma*, the acquisition of 'merit' (also called *dharma* and consisting of *sattva*, 'quiescent goodness', first of the three strands) so that one could journey to heaven and be reborn on earth in a higher life form; and (4) *moksa*, final release of the soul from the world of ceaseless change. The Sensationalists denied the existence of anything beyond the material world of the sense perceptions and attributed the variability of the human condition to their anti-deterministic view of human nature. They were, therefore, not only materialists, but also amoral psychological hedonists who deemed it pointless to pursue the two latter goals of *dharma* and *moksa*. For them, the only goals worth pursuing were the accumulation of wealth and personal pleasure, for which the wealth that a Sensationalist obtained was to be spent. The people who were attracted to these views, apart from the savants who espoused them, appear to have been the 'urbane householders' (*nagarika*) for whom texts on personal pleasure such as the *Kama Sutra* of Vatsyayana were composed (1962: I.2, I.4).

The *dharma* to which Vena opposes himself, though unnamed in the text, is, of course, the *dharma* of the Pancaratra Vaishnavas, and the Prime Cause of it is none other than the god Vishnu himself. The Pancaratras considered their *dharma* to be quite comprehensive. It not only embraced the *dharmas* of the Pasupata Shaivas and the Vedists, but even claimed to include the *dharma* of the Buddhists. Each of these had its place, albeit an inferior one, within the Vaishnava chain of being.

Vena prohibited the performance of rites to Vishnu, but he did not call a halt to the performance of the rites themselves. Vena was the paramount king of India, the paramount overlord of the earth, the highest person in the visible world. Vishnu, the supreme god of the Pancaratras, was taken by them to be the overlord not only of Vena's domain, the visible world, but of the entire cosmos, of both its visible and invisible realms. The Carvakas, however, claimed that there was no Vishnu. This left Vena as the overlord of the entire cosmos. So he ordered that the rites formerly directed to Vishnu be directed to himself!

The sacrifices, oblations and gifts to Vishnu and the other gods that Vena had forbidden were not merely rites that symbolized the commitment of the king and his people to the *dharma* of Vishnu. They were also presumed by the Pancaratra Brahmans and their followers to have ontological effects. These rites caused the power of Vishnu to infuse the king and his devoted subjects, thereby enabling them to reproduce Vishnu's order in the world and to produce it where it did not exist. The banned rites were thus not only the *signs* of the world's goodness, but also the formal *cause* of it. Vena's redirection of these rites was an unmistakable expression of the evil, inherent in the world, that had become predominant in the soul of the paramount king of India. At the same time, it was, in the eyes of the Vaishnavas, both the omen and cause (*nimitta*) of the evil disasters (*upadrava*) about to befall the earth. What was the response of the Pancaratras to this cosmic evil? What could they do against the most powerful man on earth, the paramount king of India? To begin with, the Brahmans assemble, go before the king of kings and try to dissuade him from his course of action. Their dialogue with Vena consists of two long exchanges of view which together take up the major part of the first chapter in which the history of Vena and Prithu is narrated. It soon becomes clear, however, that this is not a 'dialectical' exchange, in Collingwood's (1971: 181—2) sense of the term. The Brahmans and Vena are not going to move from a position of non-agreement to one of agreement. Their exchange is, instead, 'eristical' in form. Each is going to try and vanquish the other as an enemy; each is going to use provocative language against the other. The Brahmans open the debate, boldly declaring to the King's face that he cannot bring about the changes he has ordered. They then present what amounts to a classic Hindu explanation for the existence of bad or evil in the world, that is not accounted for by one's moral or immoral acts as a 'responsible' agent. This is, of course, the explanation by rebirth:

The sages approached him at one point and made this statement: 'You are not able here and now to strike down the goals of conduct, set up in the past by those before us and engaged in by those before them, with your materialistic commands. Living beings obtain well-being/pleasures (*sukha*) here by acts that are good (*su-*), and living being obtain distress/pain (*duhkha*) as a result of acts that are bad/evil (*dur-*). Those who consistently worship (*yajna*) the gods, serve their elders (*guru*), are fond of honoring the Brahmans, are intent on pilgrimages, perform penances (*tapas*) and are ever devoted to truth (*satya*) and to gift-giving (*dana*), obtain pleasures in the next world (*para-loka*), o king. You, however, deserve to go to those worlds of men that are stripped of pleasures.

The Hindu theodicy rehearsed in brief here states that people who perform the acts enjoined in the Vaishnava teachings obtain good results. It will be noticed here that it is evil as distress, suffering or pain (*duhkha*) that is explained by the doctrine of rebirth. It is opposed to *sukha*, which for Hindus was a condition of well-being both with respect to the soul and body and to the domain of which was a person was master (or mistress). For the Sensationalist, however, this same term denoted an immediate condition of the senses, one of material pleasure.

Vena, good logician that he is, wastes no time in picking holes in this Brahmanical theodicy. He begins his retort on an insulting note:

Vena said: 'How useless are you Brahmans with your incoherent chatter! Those who are dead are all dead. Whence do the dead originate? Certainly, the occupation of a body by a soul (*prana*) consisting of wind (*vayubhuta*) that has left a body is not proven (*upa-pad*) by rational inquiry (*yukti*).

He continues his attack:

Penances are [simply] year-long forms of torture (*citra*), the practice of self-restraint (*samyama*) [consists of nothing more than] cheating oneself of sensual enjoyments (*bhoga-vancana*). Those rites beginning with the Agnihotra are to be regarded as the games of children. Swindlers (*dhurta*) coveting the wealth of villagers whose minds are deluded (*mudha-citta*), of women wearing garlands, and of others who are wealthy string together injunctions (*sastra*) of many kinds: 'Give continually! Sacrifice thusly! The gods are favorably disposed toward you! You shall acquire wealth and overwhelm your enemies! Well-being (*sukha*) is yours!' Thus are the deluded defrauded by swindlers who want to rob them of their wealth.

Thus does our sharp-tongued monarch parody the Brahmans and the Vedic sacrificial cult (in which the Agnihotra, a daily sacrifice to the Sun in fire, was the first of the 'extended' rites to be carried out). Consistent with the non-deterministic theory of action adhered to by the Sensationalists, Vena then states his position as a psychological hedonist:

So long as you live, live as you please (*sukham*), for there is nothing to be experienced beyond death. Whence is the return of the deceased once they have been turned to ashes? There are no recipients (*nasti*) of that which is given, offered, or sacrificed; there exist neither gods nor sages. I have obtained kingship and a multitude of other enjoyments here on earth; why should I give up what I have obtained [for the performance of rites] merely on your say-so?

The Brahmans respond by pointing to the good and evil conditions in which people live and asserting that these conditions come about as a result of good and evil acts. The overlord of the earth answers with a devastating attack which they, yet again, attempt to refute.

So far, neither side seems to have gained the upper hand in this debate. Toward the end of this, the final response of the Brahmans, the situation suddenly changes. The Brahmans sarcastically ask Vena, committed as he is to his Sensationalist epistemology, if he can see that the Brahmans are going to turn their penitential heat against him. They conclude by pointing to inconsistencies in the conduct of the Sensationalists:

Do you not, o overlord of the earth, directly (*pratyaksam*) perceive (*pas*) the curses (*sapa*) about to be pronounced by Brahmans using their fully heated penitential heat (*tapas*)? . . . Do you not directly perceive the vision of *dharma* in the world (*loka*)? Men obtain the seeds (*bija*) [consisting of their past acts] at the time of their conception (*bija-kala*) and are directly perceived to share their fruits in the world. Observe that those very men [the Sensationalists] who have as their highest object the harassment of the Brahmans themselves employ mantras to remove poison and then consider: *dharma* does indeed exist. Even those men whose speech is mean and for whom the next world does not exist are themselves afraid of evils (*papa*) (that might befall them). Do you, therefore, abandon *your* evil course (*papa*).

With this criticism, the debate ends. Vena has no comeback. Yet, he does not change his mind:

After he heard this statement of the sages, whose souls were transformed (*bhavitatman*) [by participation in Vishnu], the miserable one (*dina*), left without an answer, gave no reply. He [none the less] thought to himself: 'The words spoken by the Brahmans, whose highest goal is adherence to the *dharma*, are false, there is no doubt about it.'

The Brahmans have already hinted that their power to see is greater than that of the Sensationalists and their royal spokesman, Vena. The visible sign of goodness was light. The good possessed luminous power. It radiated out from their bodies, especially from their eyes. People could perceive it 'directly' through their eyes in the form of their healthy and handsome appearance. But goodness was not simply a constituent of a person's body; it was, even more, a constituent of a person's soul. A person who had performed good acts in his previous life accumulated more 'merits' or 'goods' (*punya* or *dharma*), conceived of as invisible particles of 'quiescent goodness' (*sattva*), than 'demerits' or 'bads' (*papa, adharma*), invisible particles of 'inert badness' (*tamas*). These were the 'seeds' he took with him into his next life.

Men such as the Pancaratra Brahmans had been born with a preponderance of goodness in their souls. They had, in addition, continually performed the rites of devotion to Vishnu and the lesser gods under him, rites of participation in which they came to be infused with the quiescent goodness of the gods' souls. The luminous power of their souls was, thus, very great. This is what the text means when it refers to the Brahmans as men whose souls had been transformed. People who possessed the 'inner eye' of knowledge, the knowledge of the Veda and of Vishnu, could see the inner goodness of men such as the Pancaratra Brahmans and the great power that it commanded. But Vena could not. His power to see, true to his Sensationalist metaphysics, was confined to what was palpably and directly before him! The visual power of the Vaishnava Brahmans, however, was a double vision, a strengthened mode of perception. Equipped with the 'eye of true knowledge' (*jnana-caksus*) and the luminous power of Vishnu entailed in that transcendent knowledge, they were able to see beyond that which was immediately present to their senses.

They could gaze into the ordinarily invisible souls of other men and they could see into the normally inaccessible future:

The foremost among the Brahmans perceived the intent (*abhipraya*) of the king: 'The universe consisting of the three worlds (heaven, the atmosphere, and the earth) together with their moving and non-moving things is', they observed, 'destroyed.' Thus had the gods caused the intellects (*buddhi*) of the mighty-souled (*mahatman*) Brahmans to penetrate the heart of the evil-souled one (*duratman*) because of his intention to destroy.

CONQUEST OF EVIL

The life of the last Epoch of Manu was drawing to a close. Evil was an integral part of the world according to Hindus. It was, if one will, an inherent limitation of the universe. As a living thing, defined by its constant activity, it underwent birth, growth and death. Each of these three activities was an attribute, in Pancaratra metaphysics, of one of the three strands of matter, and each was embodied in one of the three manifestations of Vishnu as cosmic overlord.

Shiva, god of destruction (death), was the embodiment of 'inert badness' (*tamas*). At the beginning of one of the immensely long Cosmic Formations (*kalpa*), Brahma emitted from his body the entire visible world, and at the end of that period Shiva destroyed it. At the ends of the shorter lives of the world contained within a Cosmic Formation, lesser manifestations of Shiva carried out the task of destruction. That god was, we might say, following Leibniz and other Western moral philosophers, the divine embodiment of metaphysical evil. Clearly, the King, Vena, was taken to be a lesser manifestation of Shiva whose destiny was to destroy the earth at the end of the last Epoch of Manu. One of the other versions of Vena's history indicates this when it has Vena say to the Brahmans:

I may, as I will, set fire to the earth and flood it with water, and I may block communication between heaven and earth as well, do not doubt it.

The question is, why not simply let Vena get on with his task of destroying the world? The answer is that discretion has to be used in this process of dismantling the cosmomoral order. Destruction was not supposed to be complete. The souls of people were eternal. They remained for the duration of an entire Cosmic Formation. So enough of the earth and its things had to be preserved from one life to another so that its inhabitants could build *dharma* anew. Death was, in this metaphysics, not total annihilation; it was, rather, a period of retraction and rest, a period of gestation out of which the world would be reborn.

Now, it was not just that Vena lacked discretion. As I stated earlier, the goodness that was inherent in the world was no match for the bad. Without the regular and repeated infusion of Vishnu's divine goodness, the badness in the world would not remain intact. It would gain command of the middle strand of 'restless energy' and transform itself into 'dark delusion', evil on the march. Vena had begun to do just this. By his senseless redirection of the rites, he was causing the inert badness inherent in the world to become dark delusion. That is why the Brahmans saw the total destruction of the world in the immediate future. It is also the reason why the gods, who had given the Brahmans the power to see into that future, themselves requested the assistance of their overlord, Vishnu. The gods begin by informing Vishnu of what the Brahmans are about to do to Vena:

The gods then made a request of Vishnu, the overlord of the universe (*sarvesvara*), the power in everything (*sarva-sakti*), the gazer on everything (*sarva-drk*), and the realization of everything (*sarva-sadhana*), regarding the kingship over the earth: 'O god, the Brahmans shall cause Vena who, though born in the line of Dhruva, has committed a royal transgression (*kilbisa*), to be killed by using sacrificial grass (*kusa*) brightened (*puta*, 'purified') with *mantras*. Then the Brahmans, acting together, shall cause his arm to be whirled rapidly back and forth (in the manner of the stick used to start a sarificial fire).

The gods continue, requesting Vishnu to make a direct manifestation of himself on earth:

As they do that, do you, out of a desire for the welfare of the people (*loka*), cause a birth (*sambhava*) to take place and, immediately you have done so, cause the three worlds to be protected — assume the form of a man and protect us from suffering (*tapa*).' The God replied: 'Thus shall I do it.'

Power as an active force now comes into the centre of the picture. Hindu polities were hierarchically constituted. The Vaishnava Brahmans, construed in the *Vishnudharmottara Purana* as the rightful masters of knowledge relating to *dharma* in its highest and truest form, were taken to be the highest persons in India. They were responsible for, among other things, the teaching of *dharma* to others and, above all, to princes. So when Vena prohibited the performance of rites dedicated to Vishnu, the Brahmans properly warned him against it. They even entered into a debate with him. The Brahmans are presented as the winners, in logical terms, of this debate, but to no avail.

Vena, himself a champion of the logical methods of the Sensationalists, persists in his beliefs. Such was the power of 'dark delusion' once it had captured the mind.

It is at this point in the discourse that the question of displaying the power of divine goodness in the world comes to the foreground. The reason for this is that the dispute between Vena and the Brahmans was not simply a disagreement over *who* was evil; it was a dispute about what *constitutes* evil. The very rites that, for the Vaishnavas, comprised the greater good were seen by the Sensationalists as a greater evil, fraudulently motivated and wasteful. These radically opposed constructions of the Vaishnava rites were due to the radically opposed ontologies of the two sides. The dispute was, thus, not primarily moral; it was, at base, ontological. The differences between the Vaishnava Brahmans and Vena could not be resolved by words of reason in a debate that was, by its very nature, eristical in tone. It was, thus, time for a test of strength. Note that it is not a question in what follows of 'might makes right': rather, it is a question of which of the two contending ontologies is able to prove itself by producing in the world what it claimed as its *summmum bonum*. The right *ought* to possess the might.

For Vena, the confinement of the goals of conduct to the visible world entailed the prohibition of rites dedicated to the invisible gods, and this had been necessary to his establishment of a materialistic, hedonistic world order. For the Brahmans, the removal of King Vena, their implacable foe, as the ontological centre of India was necessary to the survival of the world. If the gods really existed and wished to save the world from total destruction as it underwent death and rebirth, they had better show their hand. So the gods are made, in this theistic discourse, to prove their existence through the acts of the Brahmans themselves. The gods had already given the Brahmans the power to see the impending ruin of the world, and they had stated what action they would take against Vena. Now, we learn, they move them to that act by inspiring them with divine anger:

Fully angered (*samkruddha*) by the anger of the gods, the Brahmans killed the king with sacrificial grass brightened with *mantras*. Next, they rotated the left thigh of that evil-souled one back and forth and a son of that one — dwarfish (*hrasva*), ill-proportioned (*atimatra*), black of body, cruel, and terrible (*daruna*) in appearance — came into being.

The Brahmans have performed the extraordinary act of beating the evil king, Vena, to death with blades of sacrificial grass. They were able to do this because the grass had been filled, by way of the words of the Veda, with the divine power of Vishnu. The Veda and its sacrifice, which Vena had attempted to de-ontologize, have, when wielded by the Brahmans, killed him instead. What follows, however, is even more unusual. The Brahmans may have killed Vena, but they did not by this act cause evil to disappear. Indeed, they did not make it disappear at all. No sooner had they struck the King down than they took hold of his left leg. Rotating it back and forth in its socket, as though trying to start a fire, they caused a 'son' to emerge from Vena's body. We soon discover that this son, Vena's first to be given him by the Brahmans, was an embodiment of the King's evil:

The Brahmans, skilled in the Veda, said to him, 'Sit down!' (*nisida*) and as a result of this command of the sages, he whose source (*sambhava*) was the taint (*kalmasa*) of Vena became the progenitor of the Nisada genus and of the Nisadas in all living beings.

After the Brahmans finished with the left leg of Vena's corpse, they seized his right arm:

The twice-born then rotated the right arm of that one back and forth. From it, Vishnu, assuming the outward appearance of a man, was born as his son. Those bulls among the twice-born named him Prithu (the 'broad one').

The history of Vena ends on a cheerful, if somewhat sarcastic, note. A Hindu householder was supposed to discharge the 'debt' he owed to his ancestors by begetting a good son, a *putra*, so-called because he 'rescues (*tra*) a man (*pum*)', his father, from Hell. Vena did not, of course, perform the act of procreating a legitimate heir. None the less,

As a result of the birth of that son, Vena was released from his evil (*papa*). Because he had obtained a good son, Vena, the evil-souled one who had himself committed every evil act (*sarva-papa*), went to the third heaven, (that of Indra, king of the gods). Moreover, when the sages saw the prince who had been born, they thought: 'This world (*loka*) has fulfilled itself.'

Here in this birth of Vena's sons we can see the operation of the Hindu theory of good and evil. This first son of Vena arose, we are told, from his father's *kalmasa*. I have translated this term as 'taint', but it also means stain, dirt, dregs and settlings; that is, it denotes a substance that is unwanted, one that has no further use. He is also described (in another text) as resembling a burnt/blackened stump of a tree. He is the charred remains of a fire, not fire itself, which the Brahmans have produced. Not only is this Nisada black of complexion, he is ill-proportioned and fierce — in a word, ugly. Appropriately, this dregs of a son was brought forth from a lower limb, the leg, on the inauspicious (death-related) side of the body. Prithu, the son born of Vena after his body is 'purified' by the removal of the Nisada, is produced in the same manner as his 'elder brother', but from a higher limb of Vena, his arm, and from the auspicious (growth-related) right side of his body. This time, the priests succeed in starting a fire. Prithu is described as being possessed of glory/splendour (*pratapa*), shining brightly (*dipyamana*) and burning, by way of his own body, like a fire. These are also ways of saying that he was fair of skin, tall, well-proportioned of limb, gentle and friendly in appearance.

The names of the two also display a sharp contrast. Prithu, the name given to the second son of Vena, means 'broad' or 'extensive'. It refers to the fact that King Prithu is going to exercise overlordship over the entire, broad earth, which will be named *prithivi*, 'the expansive one', after him. He will pursue her, armed with his immense, divinely bestowed bow. She will turn into a cow and flee, but to no avail. He will corner her and threaten to kill her and 'extend himself' to make the earth if she does not submit. Which she does. The name bestowed on Vena's first-born was Nisada. It was a name borne by one of the peoples of India who were here constituted as an 'untouchable caste' of fishermen, there as a 'forest tribe' of hunters. The Brahmans gave the Nisada that name because he sat down (*ni-sad*) when they commanded him to do so. His royal parent had refused to heed the words of the Vedic priests. The Nisada extracted from his body is, however, by his very nature, submissive.

The event recounted here presupposes the theory of the three strands, operating in a Vaishnava theistic milieu. The sharply contrasting appearances and demeanours of Prithu and the Nisada were nothing but the visible signs of the invisible 'goodness' (*sattva*) and 'badness' (*tamas*) constituting the souls (as well as the bodies) of the king and the tribal, respectively. But note that the relative strength of the two that had obtained in Vena is reversed in his offspring. The badness in the soul of King Vena was clearly predominant. It had taken command of the strand of restless energy. He was, therefore, evil in the active, deluded sense. His mind, the organ of restless energy, which ought to have been under the direction of his intellect, the organ of goodness and illumination, had been overcome instead by his senses, the organs of deluded darkness. Now that the Brahmans have 'operated' on him, it is goodness that has gained the upper hand. Prithu, the good son of Vena, has command of restless energy, while the Nisada, the bad son of Vena, does not. The goodness in Prithu's soul not only predominates, it has become active. It has transmuted into 'triumphant glory', with which Prithu will subdue the earth and constitute her as a cosmomoral order. Meanwhile, the badness separated out of the body of Vena is no longer evil in the active sense. No longer in command of restless energy, it has been rendered passive and inert.

Yet we are not permitted to believe that the Brahmans have alone effected this reversal of the relative strength of the good and bad by the use of the power they possess, that of the Veda. Prithu does not shine so intensely simply because the Brahmans have *removed* the 'darkness' in his body with their Vedic *mantras*. The Nisada, to be sure, consists of nothing more than the dark stain of his father. Prithu, however, contains more than the purified goodness of Vena. Vishnu has, at the request of the gods, entered his body and soul with the 'unlimited luminous power' (*amita-tejas*) of his soul, with his inexhaustible goodness. He has, we are told, made a partial manifestation of himself in Prithu. It is this timely, direct appearance of the divine that enables Prithu and the people of India together to produce a cosmomoral order on earth, one in which evil can be reduced to inert badness by its constant submission to the good. In that Order, a divine Higher Self (wherein intellect directed mind) would dominate over a demonic Lower Self (wherein the senses or passions misguided the mind). The successors of Prithu, the Arya kings of India and their people, those who would constitute that cosmomoral order, could be virtuous devotees of Vishnu. They could make themselves into the Higher Self of India, but they could accomplish this only by conquering the bad in themselves, separating it out of themselves and constituting it as India's Lower Self, the descendants of Vena, the Nisadas.

The Nisadas themselves were one of the many peoples of India that inhabited the Vindhyas, the vast area of mountains, hills, forest and scrub that divides the north of India from her south. Hindu discourse classed them not as Aryas, the 'honourable' men, the Higher Self of Hindu India, but as Mleccha (they utter sounds like 'mlich' instead of speaking properly), the 'barbaric' or 'savage' men, the Indic Lower Self. Designated as 'fallen' and 'excluded', these people were engaged in bad/evil occupations (*papakarman*) associated with death, killing and pain, with the dead, the dirty and discarded, with the wild and unwanted. They were the living (sic!) results of the evil acts of the Aryas of the past. Left to themselves, these Lower Selves would be overcome by their senses. It was, therefore, only by subservience to the Aryas of the present that these people could work off the badness in their demonic souls. The manifestation of triumphant, divine goodness, a Higher Self, in a unitary, cosmic theophanic order also required, it would seem, the manifestation of its dialectical opposite — a submissive, degraded, demonic badness.

Vaishnava ideology conceived of the *dharma*, the Order that the kings and peoples of India were supposed to build and maintain, as a hierarchy of contrasting, relatively good and bad zones inhabited by relatively good and bad people. Since the good was divine in relation to the bad and the bad demonic in relation to the good, one could also say that the Vaishnavas called for the earth to be organized as a vast theophany. India was, thus, to be organized into a superior middle region and inferior directional regions. Each of these was to be organized into a foremost country and a number of peripheral countries. A 'country' or 'nation' (*desa, janapada*) itself was to consist of a capital or royal city (*nagara*) and a surrounding countryside. This latter was further divided into provinces, each with its garrison market town and hinterland, and so on, down to the level of the single village. At each level in this hierarchy roughly the same pattern was repeated: a commanding residential centre was surrounded by a zone of choice cultivated fields. The centre at each level was supposed to be inhabited by a Prithu, a virtuous and powerful lord together with his image of Vishnu, his court and a purveying market. The fields beyond the walls of this headquarters were to be worked by Prithu's people, the loyal, obedient, taxpaying householders of the countryside.

Together, these lords and their people constituted the Aryas of India, her Higher Self. At each level in the hierarchy of places, however, there was an outer rim. It consisted of inferior, waste land, of mountains, hills, swamp or desert. There, on the outskirts of every city, town and village and in the wastelands surrounding every province, country and region and, at the highest level, the whole of India, dwelt the Nisadas and other Mlecchas, the Lower Selves of India. Just as the gods, the Higher Selves of the cosmos, resided, in their earthly forms, on top of the supreme Mount Meru in the centre of the world while the demons or anti-gods, the Lower Selves of the universe, were confined to the underworld, so, too, the divinely inspired Aryas properly dwelt in the better parts of India while the demonic Nisadas and their ilk 'justly' eked out an existence on her inferior margins.

So long as the Higher Selves of India remained devoted followers of Vishnu, the god would continually replenish their entropic goodness, their evanescent luminous power, with his own. Should these Vaishnava kings and their people disobey Vishnu, however, his infusion of the Aryas with his virtue and glory would cease, and the theophany that their forebears had thereby produced and reproduced would turn into demonic chaos. The Lower Self of India, hypostasis of badness ever-ready to rebel and overturn *dharma*, would turn into her Evil Other. The barbarians of the mountains and deserts, the tribes of the hills and jungles and the untouchables of the suburbs and hamlets would turn on their betters, the kings and people of the cities and villages of their Arya lords. Having transmuted into the feared and hated Dasyus, cruel *dacoits*, they would set aside their approved occupations and leave their assigned places to invade the plains, plundering, raping and burning as they went. Indeed, the senses, the Nisadas found in all living creatures, would conquer their erstwhile masters, the minds and intellects of the Aryas themselves.

Might we not also say, in conclusion, that the present-day world, a theophany of Mammon dominated by the United States and challenged by the USSR, Reagan's 'evil empire', stands similarly at risk within the framework of its own ontology? The moral ambiguity that Macfarlane attributes to the contemporary world is also characteristic of such values as Scientific Progress. Considered the highest good of modern economism, the scientific transformation of the world may also have as its worst 'by-product' the greatest evil ever to exist — the near-total annihilation of human life itself.

REFERENCES

Bourdieu, Pierre (1979). 'Symbolic Power', *Critique of Anthropology.* IV. 13—14, 77—85.

Chatterjee, S. and Datta, D. (1954). *An Introduction to Indian Philosophy.* Calcutta: University of Calcutta.

Collingwood, R. G. (1971) (1st edn, 1942). *The New Leviathan.* New York: Thomas Y. Crowell.

Eliot, C. (1954). (1st edn 1922). *Hinduism and Buddhism: An Historical Sketch.* New York: Barnes and Noble.

Farquhar, J. N. (1912). *A Primer of Hinduism.* London: Oxford University Press.

Gallie, W. B. (1968). 'Essentially Contested Concepts'. *Philosophy and the Historical Understanding.* New York: Schocken.

Herman, A. L. (1976). *The Problem of Evil and Indian Thought.* Delhi: M. Banarsidass.

Hopkins, E. W. (1927). 'The History of Hindu Ethics'. *The Evolution of Ethics as Revealed in the Great Religions* (ed. E. Hershey Sneath). New Haven: Yale University Press.

Kirfel, W. (1927). *Purana Pancalaksana.* Bonn: K. Schroeder Verlag.

Murti, T. R. V. (1955). *The Central Philosophy of Buddhism: A Study of the Madhyamika System.* London: Unwin.

Niven, W. D. (1914). 'Good and Evil'. *Encyclopaedia of Religion and Ethics* (ed. J. Hastings), VI.

O'Flaherty, W. D. (1976). *The Origins of Evil in Hindu Mythology.* Berkeley: University of California Press.

Radhakrishnan, S. (1959). *Eastern Religions and Western Thought.* London: Oxford University Press.

Sinha, J. (1956). *History of Indian Philosophy.* Calcutta: Sinha Publishing House.

Thrasher, A. W. (1979). 'The Dates of Mandana Misra and Samkara'. *Wiener Zeitschrift für die Kunde Südasiens,* XXIII

Vatsyayana (1962). *Kama Sutra,* trans. R. Burton. New York: Medical Press of New York.

Vishnu Purana (1910). Bombay: Srivenkatesvara Steam Press.

Vishnudharmottara Purana (1912). Bombay: Srivenkatesvara Steam Press.

10

Is God evil?

*Mark Hobart**

Enquiring into the nature of evil is a little like the Hunting of the Snark. It calls for great ingenuity and exertion, only for the object to vanish or become something else altogether. Commentators, seizing upon different aspects, often land up at cross-purposes, and all but the most skilled are prone to find that 'the bowsprit got mixed with the rudder sometime.'

A discussion of evil would be dull were someone not to question what we are doing. So, for the sake of argument, I shall play Devil's Advocate and ask if evil is something — be it a state, property or predicate — that can coherently be defined for any culture, let alone be compared between them. To put it bluntly, I suspect that those who start out searching for what evil really is anywhere will have looked in vain, no matter whether

> They sought it with thimbles, they sought it with care;
> They pursued it with forks and with hope;
> They threatened its life with a railway-share;
> They charmed it with smiles and soap.
> The Hunting of the Snark, Fit 5, The Beaver's Lesson

The grounds for my scepticism are briefly as follows. To ask what is the essence of evil in any culture may well be to beg the question of its having one. It is also to take the ways in which words like 'evil' are used out of their settings, which may be social, moral, cosmological or epistemological, among others. Cultures differ anyway in the importance that their members attach to ideas of evil, or the degree to which they agree as to its interpretation. Nor can evil be equated with what is confused or inexplicable in the human

* I am grateful to Professor David Pocock for stimulating my thoughts on the links between evil, explanation and order, in chapter 3 above and in the preliminary discussions between contributors. I would also like to thank Professor David Parkin and Dr Brian Moeran for their invaluable comments and criticisms on the original draft of this chapter.

condition. To do so is to run the risk of ignoring the point that order and explanation are themselves cultural — and possibly disputed — constructs. Instead of searching for objective standards by which to tell real 'evil' from ordinary 'badness', an exercise in correlating evil with the limits of taxonomies, perhaps we should consider how classifications are actually used. After all, neither culture nor classification is a thing, nor do people necessarily agree on how they should be interpreted. Ideas and explanations of behaviour are asserted, questioned and denied. So we need to look at how and when different views are put forward. Evil as assertion or explanation itself has to be explained.

The point will be made by looking at Bali, a society often cited as a dramatic case of ideas of evil run rampant. If one does not skim lightly over the ethnography, however, it emerges that, not only may different interest groups proffer different interpretations, but also different styles of judging thought and action are found in the cultural repertoire. Evil cannot be dismissed so easily, though. After all, in some societies some people swear by, or indeed at, its existence. I shall suggest that the existence of good and evil is a claim with important social and political implications. Such claims are often linked to an 'essentialist' style of argument which is powerful but, as a look at Western theories of morality shows, may dangerously distort our representations of what people do.

Our lines of debate about evil seem to have been laid down long ago. Before Augustine and Thomas Aquinas, the impact of eastern ideas such as Zoroastrian dualism on early Greek thinkers spawned a host of arguments. Often we do not know exactly what the origins were, or what the authors said, so much as how they were interpreted, but the arguments in different guises have bedevilled discussion since.

So it is worthwhile for a moment to look reflectively at our own intellectual tradition to see how far it may influence us in the ways we look at other cultures. Socrates, for instance, seems to have held the intellectualist stance that no one would willingly stray from *agathón*, the good, except out of ignorance. His disciple Plato, by contrast, shifted his ideas to see good and evil, *kakón*, not as value judgements so much as hypostatized realities (or forms, *eide*), objects potentially willed by the soul (*Laws* 896d, Plato 1961: 1452), identified at times as World Souls (*Laws* 896e). In a few strokes good and evil became real, dual and either moral or cosmic. Evil was thought to be removable from the soul by purgation, *kathársis*, by analogy to bodily disease (*Sophist* 227–8, Plato 1961: 970) — a theme destined for many variations. The notion of imbalance from the Pythagoreans comes to the fore in Aristotle's treatment of evil as excess (*Nichomachean Ethics* 1106a, Aristotle 1941: 958) and also as *ápeiron,* as indeterminate, inexplicable, 'Other' (*Ethics*

1106b). The potential link of matter, *hýle*, and evil in his writings was developed by Numenius, leaving the Epicureans to equate evil with pain and the Stoics with the puzzle in theodicy of how evil could exist in a world ruled by a good God. The stage — strewn with dichotomies and ambiguities — seems substantially set for later heroes and clowns.

It is a moot point whether the seeming convergences between our own and other cultures' ideas of evil are not a fancy born of unthinking translation and the export of our cultural presuppositions. Pocock, in chapter 3 above, shows neatly how much we rely on dichotomies when we try to explain forms of mystical maleficence like 'witchcraft'. For instance, evil intent is split according to whether it is conscious or unconscious, from internal or external agents, and is held to spring either from explicable or inexplicable malice (p. 44 above). The problem is that such ideas are hard enough to pin down among ourselves before we can start finding out if other peoples have the same at all.

So how do we view evil? Pocock suggests the English have two contemporary folk attitudes. The minority view regards the attribution of evil to deeds or people as due to lack of knowledge of the context. The majority are more Aristotelian — although it might surprise them! — in seeing evil as inexplicable excess, to the point that it is no more a moral judgement but an ontological assertion: there are truly evil acts which show the perpetrators to be inhuman (pp. 50—3 above). If evil is so extreme, then the dubious doings of ordinary people pale by comparison with such monsters. Most English then stand Terence on his head:

> Homo sum, alieni nil a me humanum puto!

Talk of evil is marked by peripeteia, a feature used to effect by La Rochefoucauld on the theme that our virtues are usually vices in disguise. Mystical evil-doing is not always so remote, but may be recognized as springing from all-too-human motives like greed, envy or love of power. And, far from conveniently inhuman outsiders being responsible, the source of trouble is often uncomfortably close to home. The real threat, to reverse de Béranger's famous remark, is likely to be *les ennemis, nos amis*. The kaleidoscopic nature of representations of evil suggests we reconsider whether the inverted behaviour associated with 'witches' and other inhumans are symbols of their essential 'otherness'. Perhaps evil, for all sorts of reasons, is paradoxical. Signs, after all, do not just refer to the world; they may be reflexive, or poetic, and refer to the discourse of which they part. Might it not be that the perversions and inversions claimed of evil-doers are ways of saying something about the nature of judgements about evil itself?

It is tempting to treat the topsy-turvy forms that evil takes as ways of trying to cope with its sheer inexplicability. Whether or not the reasons or motives (see Skinner 1972: 142ff., on the difference) for actions are explicable (and so understandable?) may depend on how a culture casts its ideas about the world and human nature. Evil may have many kinds of explanation, such as among South American Indian groups (see chapter 14 below) or in Buddhism (chapter 8), where it is seen as stemming from ignorance. In such worlds, in Wilde's words, 'There is no sin except stupidity.'

As Parkin notes in chapter 13, human frailties are more tolerated in societies with inchoate ideas of evil and are set apart in those with clear-cut classifications. This raises an intriguing possibility. Some societies, as Pocock points out (pp. 44ff.), may have more than one set of ideas about evil. When and why one scheme is used rather than another will be a major theme of this chapter. But it cannot then be that evil is necessarily inexplicable universally or even in a single culture. So, where evil is held to be beyond explanation, is this because it is too awful to be allowed in, or because the styles and scope of classifications vary?

Might there not be reasons — as much political as philosophical — for using taxonomies to leave some kinds of act out? An intellectualism is much in the air, exemplified by structuralism, in which it is axiomatic, if counter-factual, that disorder is anathema to the human mind. Now, disorder is not the strict antithesis of order (even if the Greeks postulated a dichotomy of *chaos* and *cosmos*); nor need it be equated with the inexplicable. Some cultures, as some people (usually academics, one suspects!), express more concern over order, or explanation, than others. So perhaps we should start to ask why some taxonomies leave evil as inexplicable and others not? Also, are the reasons people do good any less in need of explanation than the reasons they do bad?

According to one classical anthropological view, evil is inexplicable in philosophical terms because its real referent is, in some sense, society. The argument is as follows:

If indeed we can relate philosophical dualism [the doctrine of two kinds of humanity, good and bad, found in small bounded communities] to certain kinds of social structures, then some re-examination of the history of ideas is called for. No longer should it be permitted for historians to write as if philosophies move automatically in a social vacuum, one idea hitting another, splitting it, growing, decaying and being taken over.

Douglas 1970: 119

Evil is to be understood either as symbolizing the problems of social structure or as a means of evaluating social roles. Both suffer shortcomings.

The first version treats the pattern of beliefs about mystical malefactors as a projection on to a cosmic or theological plane of the structural features, and weaknesses, in society. So 'witchcraft beliefs are likely to flourish in small enclosed groups, where movement in and out is restricted, where interaction is unavoidably close, and where roles are undefined or so defined that they are impossible to perform' (Douglas 1970: 108). Even were the mass of social causes unentangled and each made precise, the problems it raises are by now familiar. Raw correlation says little about the analytical categories or their relation (Needham 1963: xi—xxix). Social structure is represented as reified and mechanical with no reference to the situations in which beliefs are invoked (Turner 1964) or to the participants' problems in interpreting alternative possibilities.

Another version has recently been resurrected by a philosopher, Alistair MacIntyre, to try to keep theories of ethics from falling into relativity. The confusion in moral philosophy, he suggests, comes from failing to locate morality in its social context, as the simple fulfilment of roles. In heroic Greece, for instance, according to the Homeric epics, *agathós,* good, denoted the qualities of being kingly, courageous and clever (MacIntyre 1967: 6). Either a man had those attributes, or he hadn't. The nasty gulf between performance and judgement, or fact and value, had not yet opened (MacIntyre 1981: 54—7, 114—22). The fuss over senses of 'good' or 'evil' comes about simply because we have lost sight of the kind of society in which the terms originally applied. Ancient Greek society is conveniently not documented in enough detail; but there seem to be few cultures so closed or simple as to rule out more than one interpretation of an act or event. Appeal to context does not help, as deciding what is relevant in any instance is open to different ideas and claims (Hobart forthcoming; cf. Sperber and Wilson 1982). For the social moralist context is the devil in disguise.

Finally, should 'good' and 'evil' properly be linked to what is socially approved? In Bali, I shall suggest, this is a delicate question. In general it is empirically unsubstantiated and rests on a naive view of language. Ethnographically, societies differ over whether such terms apply only to social roles. For the Japanese, as portrayed by Moeran in chapter 6 above, use of the terms is a simple function of social models (Buddhist or Shinto, p. 92; and 'group' against 'social exchange' conscious models, p. 107). As Overing makes clear, though, in chapter 14, it is hard to apply such Durkheimian criteria to the Piaroa, where culture is poisonous and may cause madness; for the intricacy of shamanistic speculation has little to do with social roles. The drawback of identifying the socially approved with the moral is that it becomes impossible to question social ideals, except clumsily in terms of other social ideals, which still leaves the ideals themselves largely unexplained.

Perhaps we need to distinguish between uses of 'good', 'bad' and 'evil'. Some may evaluate social roles, others may allow a degree of reflexivity. Where it is recognized that acts may be accounted for by different reasons and motives,[1] more than one criterion is needed. Further, what kind of adjectives are we talking about? Geach's distinction between predicative and attributive adjectives is important here. To say 'x is a red book' implies that x is red and x is a book; but to say 'x is a big flea' implies that x is a flea, but *not* that x is big (Geach 1956: 33). Here 'red' is predicative, 'big' attributive. Geach suggests that 'good' and 'bad' are always attributive ('x is a good cricketer' does not mean that x is good and a cricketer). 'Evil', however, may arguably be predicative ('x is an evil leader' may imply that x is a leader and evil to boot), which raises interesting questions of possible differences even within the class of moral adjectives in English. The point is neatly put by G. K. Chesterton:

> The word 'good' has many meanings. For example, if a man were to shoot his grandmother at a range of five hundred yards, I should call him a good shot, but not *necessarily* a good man.

Only fools rush in where angels fear to tread.

Let us turn then with due caution to the subject of good and evil in Bali. On few matters is a simple summary so impossible. For the Balinese have absorbed Hindu, Buddhist, Tantric, Old Javanese and other, including apparently indigenous, religious ideas and have mixed them into a textual and practical tradition which has so far baffled description. Any account of evil alone would take many monographs (see for a start Hooykaas 1963, 1973, 1977, 1978). My treatment of cosmological and moral doctrines must needs be cavalier, and I shall look mostly at ideas in daily use rather than at priestly knowledge.

In Bali many forms of evil are held to stem from (the Hindu—Balinese deity) Siwa in his destructive aspect: as Kala (Sanskrit Bhaṭṭāra Kāla, the noble Lord Kāla),[2] who is allowed by mythical charter to eat humans (Hooykaas 1973: 170—87; cf. O'Flaherty 1973), or Durga, who in Bali is invested with many attributes of another of Siwa's consorts, or *sakti*, Kali (Kālī the Black One). Among other forms, evil may spring from Buddha as Siwa Maha-Barawa (Śiva Mahā-Bherava) and the Buddhist goddess Vairocana as Yama-Raja. In village representations such aspects of divinity are often spoken of as

[1] For example, 'Sin grows with doing good' (Eliot 1935: 33)
[2] Wherever possible, I use Balinese spelling in the text and keep the Sanskrit spelling for parentheses.

buta (*bhūta*) and *kala*. These may be lumped together as *buta-kala*, a distinctly unpleasant class of greedy, destructive spirits who must be propitiated to leave humans in peace. They may also be seen as different kinds of invisible agent or principle.[3] In the ritual invocations during temple ceremonies in Bali, *buta-kala* may be bought off collectively or be subject to quite different identification (Hooykaas 1977: 83—4, 90—2). In purificatory rites, known as *caru*, Durga may also be linked separately with *buta* and *kala* (pp. 76—8). The subject is complicated: there are probably hundreds of different sets of invocations for temple ceremonies in the island, and there are thousands of different rituals.[4]

Other ideas bear more immediately however on human evil. Sets of texts deal with how humans may obtain power, (*ke*)*sakti*(*an*).[5] Such texts are many and varied but are mostly secret and often esoteric (Hooykaas 1978; Pigeaud 1967: 198—201, 265—73; Weck 1937). Knowing too much, or learning too fast, leads easily to madness, as my informants who had tried such ('Tantric') paths were willing to testify. The agency behind this in village thought is usually the goddess Durga (the Inaccessible, the Unattainable), often known simply as Batara Dalem ('Insider', an epithet given because she is too dangerous to name casually). It is she who tangles with the human world, for it is from her one obtains power to assume different forms or learn techniques to help or attack others. It would be convenient to split people according to whether they know 'black magic', *pengiwa*, and are *léyak, dèsti,* or *manusa sakti* — terms that may very loosely be rendered as 'witches' — or 'white magic', *penengen*, and are *balian*, 'doctors'. (Translation is fraught with misleading connotations here, and the English words are used merely to avoid too many Balinese words.) Unfortunately, mystical expertise is not so easily controlled and the labels fail to account for the practitioners' inclinations on different occasions. Also, what is harmful to one person may be good from another's point of view!

The kinds of mystical power are classified in different ways. Commonly there are eight (known as the *aṣṭa-śakti, aṣṭa-guna* or *aṣṭa-siddhi*, eight powers, qualities or abilities). Two versions are given in table 1 (from

---

[3] In Sanskrit *bhuta* is 'that which exists', '(material) element', and in Old Javanese a 'class of demons, demon (in general)' (Zoetmulder 1982: 278). *Kala* has many senses: 'wicked, evil, base, false', possibly from Sanskrit *khala*, a mischievous man (Zoetmulder 1982: 767).

[4] There is no space to give examples here. A comparison of the Darma Pawayangan and the Kala-Purana (Hooykaas 1973) with the invocations, *mantra*, in an ordinary temple ceremony, *piodalan* (see also Hooykaas 1977) will show how different usage and reference may be in just two texts in common use.

[5] The senses of the term are close to the Sanskrit: 'power, ability, strength, might; regal power, energy or active power of a deity personified as his wife' (Zoetmulder 1982: 1607). It may also connote mystical as opposed to political power, *kekuasaan*.

TABLE 1 *Two versions of the eight supernatural powers known in Bali*
(*The* Asta-śakti, Asta-guṇa, Asta-siddhi, Astaiśwarya)
Version (a): the Wrhaspatitattwa

		Wrhaspatitattwa (14: 66)	Balinese popular knowledge
1	*aṇiman*	The power of becoming as small as an atom	The ability to become small at will
2	*laghiman*	The faculty of assuming lightness at will	To be able to levitate (25 – 50 cm is the hallmark of *léyak*, 'witches')
3	*mahiman*	The power to increase size (the power to change form)	The former is unknown; changing form, *ngelekas*, *masiluman*, is the most basic ability of all
4	*prāpti*	The power of obtaining everything	Often treated as the goal of the other powers
5	*prākāmya*	Freedom of will, irresistible will	Thought to be possible only for very advanced specialists
6	*waśitwa*	Power to subdue to one's own will	Why people cannot run away on meeting a 'witch'; they lose the ability to will their bodies
7	*iśitwa*	Superiority; supremacy	What specialists fight about; if one wins the other is found dead in bed the next day
8	(*yatrakāmā*) *wasāyitwa*	Power of transporting things (Z); ability to suppress passions (H)	Both are known but villagers are rather vague about them

TABLE 1 (*contd*)
Version (*b*) : *the* Kalima Usada

		Kalima Usada	*Balinese popular knowledge*
1	*dūra-darśana*	Power of seeing what is distant or hidden	Ability of specialists with a fairly high degree of knowledge
2	*dūra-śravaṇa*	Power of hearing at a distance	A common ability which makes it very unsafe to talk anywhere about such specialists
3	*(dūra)sarvajña*	Power of knowing at a distance (Z), omniscience (H)	Subsumed by villagers under the first two entries above
4	*asasañcara*	Faculty of not needing sleep	A necessary attribute if one is to spend the night abroad and work normally the next day
5	*ambaramarga*	Ability to move through the air; ability to fly	Proper flying requires greater expertise than levitation
6	*adṛśya*	Power of being invisible; power to make invisible	A fairly common ability, and much easier than making other things or people invisible
7	*awakaromaya*	Faculty of spatial extension (?)	Usually identified with changing shape, but also being in bed and abroad at the same time
8	*dūra-grahana* (*dūra-wedha*)	Ability to seize objects (or attack) from a distance	Long-distance theft is rarer than ability to attack enemies from afar, which is common

Sources: Hooykaas (1963) (H); Punyatmaja (1970); van der Tuuk (1897); Zoetmulder (1982) (Z).

Balinese editions of the *Wṛhaspatitattwa* and *Kalima Usada*; see Weck 1937; also Hooykaas 1963: 86—8; and van der Tuuk 1897: 221). Interestingly, the words are Sanskrit and carry something close to their classical senses with one or two exceptions. (These are *mahiman,* which in Old Javanese denotes the ability to change shape (Zoetmulder 1982: 1090). In Balinese the term is *ngelekas* or *masiluman,* the most common proof of spiritual powers. *Yatrakāmā-wasāyitwa* has two senses, which are given in table 1.) How full the knowledge of most adult villagers is, as against that of experts, turns out to be rather striking (an outline is given in the right-hand column of the table). Such powers are attributes of divinity in the form of Siwa (Punyatmaja 1970: 32—6), obtainable by humans through supplicating, *nunas ica,* his active aspect, Durga. The importance of these potentialities may perhaps be gauged by my having had to take my informants to Java before they felt safe to talk without the fear of being overheard by those with *dura-srawana,* the ability to hear at a distance. People with such powers are thought rather dangerous, if for no other reason than that it is hard to tell what they are up to!

What are the popular representations of these mystical practices? Balinese make widespread use of various kinds of doctor or spiritual specialist when ill, for protection against suspected attack, or in the hope of attaining dubious ends: potions to kill others, become rich, make people fall hopelessly in love and many others (see Weck 1937). Villagers quite often report meeting frightening manifestations at night in the roads or speak of battles where rival camps turn into (*ngelekas*) detached limbs, giant snakes, burning trees or, in one instance of one-upmanship, a helicopter. Mystical activities, usually at night, are a theme on which Balinese imaginations run gently riot.

The most famous form evil takes, however, is in the figure of Rangda. She is often identified as the historic widow, Queen Mahendradatta, mother of the Balinese prince, Erlangga, who became king of Java in AD1019 (being herself Javanese may not have helped her reputation). More questionably, she is identified as Durga, in her form of Mahisasuramardini, in the temple, Pura Meduwé Karang, in north Bali (Grader 1940: 16). In paintings, statues and as a mask and dress worn by an actor she is bulbous-eyed, canine-toothed, dangling-breasted. In popular accounts of Bali, Rangda is best known from 'trance dances' in several villages on the tourist track near the capital, Denpasar. There she confronts another giant puppet, Barong Kèkèt (sometimes, and rather doubtfully, identified as Banaspati Raja, the Lord of the Forest), in what tourist guides describe as 'the eternal fight of good and evil'. In the village of Tengahpadang,[6] where I worked, the mask is used by

---

[6] The name is a pseudonym of a settlement in North Gianyar, where I carried out fieldwork in 1970—2, 1973, and 1979—80, financed by a Leverhulme scholarship and a grant from the School of Oriental and African Studies, University of London.

itself in a dance drama, Calon Arang (de Zoete and Spies 1938; Poerbatjaraka 1926), to protect the welfare of the community. The mask is also used, as are those of various kinds of Barong, to cure illness.

A little more prosaically, but more usually, Rangda is thought to act as the leader, or source of power, for persons wishing to learn various unpleasant arts. Something like one in ten villagers, mostly women, are thought to have inherited or learned the ability of becoming witches. At night these adepts are held to leave their bodies behind in bed, to congregate in the graveyard, where they transform into hideous old hags or men, under the aegis of Rangda. There they dig up the newly dead and, after a hearty supper on rotting flesh, titivate themselves using intestines as necklaces, lungs as earrings and so on, before setting off to harass or kill the living. Geertz sums up the popular image as follows:

In Rangda, monstrous queen of the witches, ancient widow, used-up prostitute, child-murdering incarnation of the goddess of death, and, if Margaret Mead is correct, symbolic projection of the rejecting mother, the Balinese have fashioned a powerful image of unqualified evil.

Geertz 1973a: 180

If we hack through the textual thickets, do we not have here a coherent vision of the cosmic and moral forces that give meaning to suffering and misfortune — 'the Symbolism of Evil', in Ricoeur's (1967) terms? The argument has indeed been advanced, using Balinese and Javanese ethnography, by one of Ricoeur's main disciples as follows:

The so-called problem of evil is a matter of formulating in world-view terms the actual nature of the destructive forces within the self and outside of it, of interpreting murder, crop failure, sickness, earthquakes, poverty, and oppression in such a way that it is possible to come to some sort of terms with them.

Geertz 1973b: 130

For it is

in essence the same sort of problem of or about bafflement and the problem of or about suffering. The strange opacity of certain empirical events, the dumb senselessness of intense or inexorable pain, and the enigmatic unaccountability of gross iniquity all raise the uncomfortable suspicion that perhaps the world, and hence man's life in the world, has no genuine order at all. . . . And the religious response to this suspicion is in each case the same: the formulation, by means of symbols, of an image of such a genuine order of the world which will account for, and even celebrate, the perceived ambiguities, puzzles and paradoxes in human experience.

Geertz 1973c: 107—8

The problem of evil, once again, is the problem of the inexplicable and of disorder.

It would make our problems much easier if we could encapsulate, and so study, evil in terms of a set of symbols that would help to make sense of the human predicament. How adequate, though, is the approach? There are both theoretical and ethnographic grounds for questioning its usefulness.

At first sight the argument has a self-evident ring of truth to it. May this not come, however, from begging the question? The suspicion in any culture that the world is unordered and inexplicable gives rise to symbols. Where, though, did the suspicion come from in the first place? It was made possible by the symbols themselves! The elaboration of ideas of evil is not a function of the highly variable 'objective' incidence of misfortune (see Turner 1964 on this point), but is at least as much a question of what kind of classification a culture has. Much suffering in Bali is brought about by other people pursuing goals by means defined by such 'symbols'. Anyway, suffering — unlike pain, perhaps? — is culturally defined.

There is a way out of the circularity, but its implications are unpalatable. Suppose we postulate a basic human need to understand, of which anxiety over disorder is a manifestation. If this be so, as Geertz is clear, it must hold for all humans. If not, we require an explanation of its variability. Apart from being open to empirical disproof, we are committed to a universal theory of human nature which does little to explain why symbolism should vary across cultures. There are also good arguments against such a universal view (Collingwood 1946: 81—5). The implicit psychological hypothesis is also causal. A need to explain produces symbols. Also, we still need an account of how symbols successfully resolve human anxiety. There is an implicit assumption that the human mind is a *tabula rasa*, such that the existence of an explanatory symbol in a culture *ipso facto* is a sufficient condition to satisfy the anxiety or need. It is unclear how a symbolic assertion of how the world ought to be solves the problem of people in the world as it is. (The dichotomy of symbol and reality here is not of my making, or to my liking: it is an assumption of the approach.) A properly cultural analysis would, by contrast, have to start with a study of indigenous ideas of order, human nature and different classifications of the world for the society in question in order to find out what kinds of disorder were feared or treated as inexplicable. It could not start from dubious general assumptions about the human condition.

Let us consider with a little more care, then, Balinese representations of order, good and evil. In Indonesia widely, order is glossed as (*h*)*adat* (an Arabic word). The *locus classicus* is Shärer, for whom *adat* is more than usage: it is, firstly, divine cosmic order and harmony, and secondly . . . life and actions in agreement with this order. It is not only humanity that possesses *hadat*, but also every other creature or thing (animal, plant, river, etc.), every phenomenon (e.g. celestial phenomena), every period and every action. . . .

Shärer 1963: 75

Adat is at once descriptive and prescriptive. In Bali, order (usually *tata*) depends upon *désa, kala, patra* (place, occasion and situation). So it varies between villages and kingdoms, by historical periods (sometimes identified with the Hindu cycle of *yuga*) and according to particular circumstance. Each kind of being has its own code. It is the task of tigers to eat people, the task of crows to warn of impending death, and the task of witches to attack others. To the Balinese, it is conflict that is to the fore, and how conflicting codes achieve harmony God only knows. What is appropriate, *patut,* for humans is triply contingent, and, on a common reading, order is the *de facto* recognition of how things are here and now. As a solution to the problem of suffering, I wonder how much it helps to know that it is just someone else's way of doing things.

There is a further twist. There are at least nine well-known causes of personal misfortune. Gods may directly afflict the living for all sorts of reasons, most often for forgetting to carry out rites, sometimes very unusual ones. Ancestors are prone to interfere in their descendants' lives for good or bad. The souls of those who have died bad deaths, *tonyo,* are likely to attack people trespassing (to get water, plants and so on) in ravines where they have their villages. *Léyak,* 'witches', may cause trouble, as in a rather unspecified way may *buta* and *kala*. Specialists may be hired by relatives or enemies to make one ill by spell or medicine (*pekakas*). The living may curse a family member, or someone may swear a false oath, and it may last or take generations to fulfil itself. The Hindu doctrine of *karma pala,* the effects of (previous) actions, may affect one in a later incarnation or may strike immediately within a lifetime. If the deed was bad enough, the whole family may suffer the effects. Another common explanation is fate, *ganti,* which it is doubtful even the gods can control. Where a victim may attribute suffering to one of these, others may see it as plain stupidity or culpability. Privately, one may suffer from bad thoughts, *manah jelé,* for which one may hold oneself or other agencies responsible. One adolescent I know developed a desire to flash his genitals and went, very ashamed, to pray and purify himself at a temple. Everyone else treated it as just the pains of sexual maturing. So culture may turn what some regard as normal into a heinous offence: it may create evil. The main point, however, is that Balinese culture, with so many possibilities to choose from, does not eliminate bafflement. It may encourage confusion, or at least convert it into the delicate difficulty of choice and interpretation.

Sadly, space prevents me from looking at the subtleties of Balinese eschatology, as more needs to be said about the *dramatis personae* already introduced. The primary sense of *buta* in Bali is 'blind' (metaphorically, used of someone blinded by pride). It is also said of a shrine where offerings have not been made for a long time. Significantly, it refers as well to 'elements', as in *pañcamahabuta*, earth, water, fire, air, ether.

Kala is more complex. Among its homonyms — I avoid speculating about etymology — are 'wicked', 'scorpion', 'snare', 'noose', 'time as inescapable fate' and the name of the god of death and annihilation, besides the attribute, or class term, for the Hindu spirits known as *rākṣasa* (cf. *rakṣaka,* guardian). In compound words like *niskala* and *sekala, kala* denotes invisibility and visibility, respectively. It may also mean 'raw energy'. In high Balinese 'bad' is *kaon,* which also means 'to be defeated'; in low Balinese the term is *kalah.* The room for play is immense. *Buta* may be 'demon', but also human blindness and so ignorance. In ritual it is often spoken of as returning complex entities to their constituents. *Kala* are often treated as the negative aspects of high deities, or the inevitable entropy of all visible forms; while the pun on *kalah* allows all manner of interpretation. Even as demons, the most striking attribute of *buta* and *kala* is not that they are destructive, but they are polluting. They may be vile, but are they evil?

Speculating about spirits is difficult for the Balinese because, being invisible, any evidence is indirect. The doings of 'witches' at least deals with human motives and actions; but ideas about them show an odd paradox. Speaking generally, most Balinese assert that they bring illness and death. When such misfortunes occur, however, the same people often are quite firm that the most witches can do is hang around in the vague hope that people will die, perhaps egging them on by making nasty faces or frightening them. Causing fear and showing off are the stock in trade of 'witches', but they are hardly alone in this. Further, they are only a nuisance if they live in the same compound (i.e. are immediate family). Most accusations are made by the victim or close kin and are often dismissed by other villagers as excuses for their own ineptitudes. As it turns out, most Balinese are 'hot', *panes,* and temperamentally unable to see, or feel, the presence of witches, and some are downright sceptical of their existence. Stated belief in doctors' powers is, quite reasonably, prevalent. Almost everyone I spoke to admitted to using them for sundry nefarious purposes. And one day, sitting in a coffee-stall, the most feared specialist in the area asked me, as one scholar to another, quite publicly, if I would like to learn the techniques and offered to take me to Geriya Delod Peken, the accepted centre of such expertise (in the heart of the main tourist village on the coast)!

The theological status of Durga is also extremely complex, as suggested above. The gift of unusual powers is not hers alone: it may come from almost any deity, as may assistance in all malfeasance. Thieves, for instance, pray to, and may be made invisible by, Batara Désa (sometimes identified with Brahma). Durga further protects people in time of pestilence, especially cholera; but it is far from clear that this is because she is the original cause. In my village her temple, the Pura Dalem, is known for bringing peace of mind, and, if one sleeps there, it is extraordinarily refreshing. It is also said that holy water and prayer at her shrine induces an unparalleled tranquility — an assertion I can confirm from experience, for what it is worth. The title 'Dalem' is used of royal princes, and in many ways Durga resembles them. She is a dangerous enemy but a caring patron of those who seek her help. She is, after all, an active aspect of Siwa himself.

Impersonations of powerful figures also occur in dance and drama. Masks of Rangda and the various kinds of Barong appear in gentle comedy and burlesque but rarely in knock-about farce. Both are given their power, *sakti,* by invocation at night on the cremation mound, *pemuun,* in the graveyard, and must be treated afterwards with care. The character for real slapstick is the *celuluk,* similar to Rangda but with a squarer head and slightly less extreme features. In popular theatre (*derama*), she or he plays a buffoon, part frightening, part touching, and pops out of the wings to howls of anticipatory laughter. *Celuluk* come up behind the low-caste servants unexpectedly, or when they are asleep, and stroke them fondly, nurse them or make coy amorous overtures. After a double take the servants leap up, into one another's arms, rush off or look generally panicked, while the *celuluk* sets off in a pursuit halfway between anger and disappointment, although sometimes the scene is reversed and the *celuluk* flees from the clownish servants. As Rangda's main adjutant, whatever it be, the *celuluk* is hardly an 'image of unqualified evil'.

Can the *celuluk's* antics be dismissed as simple catharsis, or making the world safe from demogorgons? I think not. Over 40 years ago, Bateson and Mead remarked that Rangda 'is not only a fear-inspiring figure, but she is Fear' (1942: 35). In the figure of the *celuluk,* who may be as much sinned against as sinning, I suggest the Balinese are as much as anything laughing at themselves — at their fear, at the impossibility of a creature so different wanting to cherish or to be lovable to human beings. The notion of catharsis makes little sense of much of the *celuluk's* cavortings and caresses (the actors certainly did not see it as merely inspiring horror). I suspect too that catharsis is a term from a particular theory of mind, whether Greek or Freudian, which is at odds with Balinese ideas. Prima facie, to apply it to Bali would be a category mistake. Could it not be that such ambiguous figures, rather than depicting evil beings, are poetic reflections on the ambiguities of fear, danger and difference?

In what does the difference lie? We are, I think, back to the problem of order. For neighbouring Java, Becker has argued that the worlds of the gods, heroes, clowns and demons in the shadow play illustrate the coincidence of different epistemologies, by which he seems to mean 'world views' (Becker 1979: 219ff.; cf. Hobart 1982: 10−13). Taken literally, however, it is as good a reading as any. The meeting of different kinds of being, with different metaphysical presuppositions, ideas of knowledge, reason and aims in life, is an important theme in Bali. The incommensurability of different forms of life, expressed in theatre and supernatural beings − in the terrifying but sad figure of the *celuluk,* for instance − makes more sense of the ethnography than reducing it to mere symbols of evil. If we are content to trundle out dog-eared stereotypes, like the French all eating garlic and snails and the English struggling endlessly through peasoup fog in bowler hats, then there is evil in Bali a-plenty. If we are not, then is it not perhaps time we delved a little more deeply?

Apart from cosmological, or theological, representations of good and evil, there are also moral standards for judging behaviour. In order to understand these, it is helpful to sketch in the outlines of Balinese society. The vast majority of Balinese are, or were, peasant rice farmers who supported an elite of princes and priests that made up less than 10 per cent of the population. The idiom of relationships was caste, and this was justified by Hindu dogma. Political authority over villagers, mostly *sudra,* lay in the hands of local − often, indeed, village − aristocrats who styled themselves *satriya.* Religious, textual and juridical matters were the preserve of brahmanical priests, who also sat as judges in royal courts, the most famous being the *Kertagosa* in Klungkung, the notionally most senior of the island's eight kingdoms. The legal and moral basis of the caste system was laid down in Hindu and Old Javanese texts in which the idea of *d(h)arma* was critical. In Balinese, *darma* stands for 'true', 'calm' and 'patient', as well as 'morality' and 'duty'. The Brahmans gave it a more classical gloss as divinely ordained rules of conduct, but also virtue itself, as well as one's nature (see Zoetmulder 1982: 367−9). A perennial problem therefore arose as to whether moral codes could be defined exclusively by caste or whether they held good for all Balinese, or all humanity.

Some of the differences in moral codes are adumbrated in the first two examples below. Space does not allow a fuller consideration. So, if the reader feels dissatisfied, it makes my point that one needs to know a great deal about a culture before one can start to assess moral issues (the background to the first two cases can be found in Hobart 1979: 35−47 and 522−72).

Case 1   *The royal suicides in front of the Dutch army*

The Dutch finally conquered South Bali between 1906 and 1908 after meeting heavy resistance. When the main armies in several kingdoms had conceded defeat, the royal families with their entourages marched out, dressed in full regalia, and men, women and children committed suicide (the children were often stabbed by their parents) to the reported astonishment of the Dutch soldiers. Several royal dynasties were drastically reduced in numbers as a result.

Among the best-known caste duties of *satriya* is to be courageous in face of death. Running away in battle is not to live to fight another day but to besmirch one's reputation, the memory of which clings to the fugitives' descendants for generations. One of the purposes of dynastic chronicles, *babad,* is to record which families in history have lost legitimacy this way. Now there are two senses of *satriya*. Besides evaluating observed characteristics, like bravery, the term is used ascriptively of an entire caste group, many of whom may well prove notorious cowards. In order to remain *satriya* in the strong, achieved, sense and to preserve the integrity of the descent line, the royal families chose to adhere to the strict moral code that held for their caste.

The conflict of moral codes comes out in the next case.

Case 2   *The problem of the orator's underpants*

The Balinese aristocracy kept some of their power after colonization both through their large land-holdings and by becoming administrators under successive regimes. During the Second World War the island was invaded by the Japanese, with whom the courts cooperated in varying degrees as at least liberators from the Dutch.

What the Japanese termed 'the Greater East Asian Co-Prosperity Sphere' entailed the removal of surplus produce, so the Balinese had little to eat and still less access to consumer goods. Cloth, for example, was tightly rationed. In my village the allocation was funnelled through the local princely family who served as the Japanese amanuensis. Almost all cloth found its way into the hands of the prince and his close clients.

One young villager, a man of great oratorical skills but from a poor family, found wearing the substitute of barkcloth as underpants rather chafing. So finally he decided to persuade a friend of his, the rations clerk in another village, to write him an extra allowance. Later that day the villagers swarmed out to watch an extraordinary sight. The orator was strolling up the main road swathed in five metres each of red, white and blue cloth, which he allowed to trail behind him in the dust, as he sauntered in front of the local court.

This extraordinary episode, which 40 years later still brought amusement to many and chagrin to some, has meanings I cannot deal with here, such as the colours of the cloth. First, the orator was drawing attention publicly to the court's failure to fulfil its social obligations to redistribute resources, however scarce, to its subjects. That this is the *darma* of a successful king is reiterated for the populace in shadow theatre and other media. As Worsley put it, 'the realm exists not only for the good of the monarch but also for the sustenance of its population. The king was required to furnish the needs of his people and was dutybound to listen to their grievances' (1972: 45). The orator was making public their deviance from caste *darma*, by caricaturing their greed (and, by letting the cloth trail, ensuring it was unfit for high-caste use). Was this all? Implicitly, the orator was touching on a second issue, that of a universal morality. Another sense of *darma* deals with the moral obligations incumbent on all human beings in dealings with others, which among other things condemns selfishness and greed. The court was painted as falling short both in caste and universal *darma*.

How universal is 'universal' here? The villagers, if not the priests, recognize five exemptions. One is not sanctioned should one lie to, or cheat, enemies, traders, lunatics, sexual partners and children. The first of these colours attitudes to strangers in an island that has known centuries of internecine warfare: but the Balinese rarely go as far as many people seem to in treating outsiders as barely human and fair game for duping. The moral code indeed may stretch beyond humans (something that appears to have escaped Kant), for many people are reluctant to take animal life, preferring to leave that for butchers who suffer for this breach in hell. So, already we have at least three senses of good and bad. A person may be a bad *satriya* in the weak sense by being of dubious birth, by contracting a mis-caste marriage and so on; or in the strong sense by falling short of caste morality; or in terms of more general codes. The exceptions embody a further twist in recognizing that there are many contexts where what is good for you is likely to be bad for someone else.

If it be indeed that 'there is nothing either good or bad, but thinking makes it so' (*Hamlet* II, ii), then Balinese imagination has still more to exercise it, as the next two cases suggest.

Case 3   The punishments of Hell

In the Kertagosa, the supreme criminal court in Klungkung, presided over by high priests, the ceiling is decorated with vivid paintings of the punishments in Hell for wrongdoing in life. Apart from the more obvious crimes, the scenes depict aborted foetuses pushing their mothers off wobbly bridges into well-stoked fires; butchers' heads being sawn open by the animals they killed; the indolent inverted in mortars to have the behinds, on which they sat while others worked, pummelled by giant pestles; and fornicators having their genitals scorched by flaming brands.

Case 4 Possession by kala

If a Balinese engages in behaviour that is abnormal or inexplicable by their usual standards — if someone runs amok, or if a normally calm man comes home and starts hitting his wife — he is said to be *kerangsukang kala*. If one enquires of a priest what this phrase means, one is likely to be told that the person has been entered by a *kala*, some kind of demonic influence or being. One sense of *rangsuk* is indeed 'to enter'; another is 'to manifest'. In a survey of my village most adult villagers, however, interpreted the expression as '*kala* manifesting itself'. When asked what *kala* denoted here, the answers ranged from 'badness' to 'uncontrolled emotion', from 'impulsiveness' to 'uncontrolled energy'. It was rare for a villager, on being asked what *kala* was, to speak of an external agency. The Balinese agree on the diagnostic label; they disagree over what it implies.

At the risk of pushing the distinction too far, there are interesting differences between the styles of interpretation of villagers and the elite. The punishments in Hell suggest that wrongdoing results in clear, unambiguous consequences. Likewise, priests tend to support the view that there are real, and essentially destructive, forces at work called *kala*. Put simply, there are kinds of agency and act that may be judged to be bad. For villagers the clarity of the classification is sometimes puzzling. Some acts, like murder, are agreed to be bad, if understandable; others, like sexual intercourse outside marriage, are commonplace and hardly deserve to be put in the same class as serious offences. Rather than *kala* being something nasty in the woodwork of life, they are ways of talking about how people may behave on occasions, to be explained in terms of control and balance. The two views are not exclusive: priests and princes often use explanations similar to villagers in everyday life. None the less, it is curious to find the elite endorsing rather literal interpretations as against the peasants' proclivity for abstraction.

A similar disjuncture of interpretive styles occurs over the link of ritual purity and moral judgement. Differences in caste duties are justified by the view that birth confers innate differences in purity and so determines one's appropriate role in the social order. Together with this is a stress on actions as purifying or polluting, and the handling of adventitious dangers, in the form of *buta* or *kala*, in terms of ritual responses such as purificatory offerings. According to the ascriptive code, high-caste persons, barring certain permanently polluting acts, are always purer than low-caste ones. By contrast, according to the universal code, moral judgements depend on the act, not upon the actor's status. In caste dogma, goodness is implicitly linked to ritual purity and birth, a connection that the other code questions.

How far can the differences in interpretations of such codes be linked to social structure? The idea that 'evil' or 'pollution' denote essential qualities, real things in the world, which one social group understands and can control, lends itself to political use. Essentialism is a trusty standby for all sorts of elites, from academic to political. The advantages of claiming that one knows what the world is truly like are pretty obvious. In contemporary terminology, this is described as 'false consciousness', which mystifies people as to the actual state of affairs. If pushed, one might then argue that essentialism is essential (sic) to an elite to avoid 'true consciousness' of the situation — in other words, that 'evil', 'pollution' and so forth were merely names. Nominalism would then be the style of revolutionaries and essentialism the style of those in power.

It would be comfortable to be able to stop at this point, having linked ideas of good and evil to the conditions of social differentiation and political stability. Good and evil, to the elite, would be stated as really existing, as solid a set of predicates as any, and used to judge fulfilment of given social roles. There is some evidence to support this view, and it can easily be adapted to take in different contexts of use of evaluative terms. How such a scheme might work is laid out in table 2, in the left-hand column.

The argument is weak, however, on several scores. Ethnographically, it leaves much out. Most speculation about evil comes from high priests and other literati who, as Bali is a village society, share many village values. Social explanations of evil tend, further, to be functional. At best, they account for how ideas about evil may be used to one kind of end, but little more. When people take decisions, they must choose between possibilities: so definiteness may have more to do with the particular circumstances of action than with social structure *per se*. Opponents of a regime may be just as dogmatic as its proponents, each backing a different essential definition. And arguments about 'true' or 'false' consciousness merely move essentialism from something to be explained to the false status of an explanation itself. Social life is about rival claims, questions and uses, where to speak of 'objective' yardsticks, let alone about as tricky a term as 'consciousness', is not just misleading but begs the interesting questions.

If use of evaluative terms cannot entirely be reduced to social structure, is it perhaps part of an 'internal cultural debate' (see Parkin 1978: 286—336)? After all, the Balinese do talk about good and bad; and the theme crops up perenially in theatre and ritual. The trouble is that some people use such terms more than others for some purposes, and ignore them on other occasions. There are as many metaphors for the nature of society as one has ingenuity and time to dream them up. Some are more illuminating for some problems than others, but they are perspectives, not keys to society's essential nature. 'Internal cultural debate' implies a bounded entity, with a shared

TABLE 2   Descriptive summary of some Balinese uses of 'good' and 'bad'

Context	Essential attributes		Nominalist problems	Overlap of use
1 Cosmic forces	batara : kala (god)	: : creative : destructive	Problem of ontological status of gods	Subject to 3 in sense of darma I
	batara : buta	: : benign : malevolent	Avoidance of personifying/ hypostatizing ideas	Evaluated by 4(a) darma II or 4(b)
		: : abstinence : greed complex : elemental		
2 Limits of normality	witch : human	: : extraordinary : ordinary (faculties and appetites)	Many sources of power, not just witches have sakti Question whether witches act intentionally Question whether witches exist	Ability comes from 1 May be judged by 4(a/b)
3 Social roles (darma I)	darma : adarma	: : good : bad (role fulfilment)	Conflicting texts over what is proper role-set Different ontological bases of purity Different epistemological interpretations of purity	Established by 1 Liable to conflict with 4(a)
4 Universal roles (darma II)	(a) Deontic good — bad intentions reasons	(b) Utilitarian good — bad acts consequences	Problematic status of karma: does it apply to 3 or 4? No necessary link of intention/ act or reason/effect	4(a) and 4(b) may take account of 3
	Digital* truth functional textual signification referential		Analog* no truth functions contextual meaning connotative	

* Adapted from Wilden (1972: 191–5).

'language' and agreement over assumptions, means and ends. It may well be useful to designate a political response (as Parkin intended), but it is misleading applied to Bali, where villages differ so much and confusion and conflict may prevail as often as debate. Society may be treated *as if* it were a language, a code, a debate, a dance or a fight; but it *is* none of these.

Again, might it be that ideas of good and evil only look many and jumbled, but are in fact ordered by some underlying keys or 'paradigms'? This is merely to jump out of the Durkheimian frying-pan into the Platonist fire. One essentialism replaces another. In describing some of the most often stated difficulties in defining good and evil as 'nominalist' in table 2, I do not suggest there has to be some alternative, articulated framework. Rather, ostensibly unambiguous definitions ('digital' ones in Wilden's terms, 1972: 155—201) obscure all sorts of puzzle implicit in the classifications themselves, and any switch (to 'analog' perspectives) threatens to tear away the mask of order.

It would be slightly surprising to find ideas of good and evil neatly ordered anywhere, least of all in Bali, granted the various historical influences it has absorbed and the formula for diversity built into the notion of custom. So where do the regularities, if any, lie? There are preferred styles of argument which the Balinese recognize as appropriate. The label 'playful pragmatism' catches some of these, but it is perhaps best brought out by examples. So I shall finish by tidying up some left-over ethnographic points and contrast Balinese styles with recent Western philosophic approaches to morality.

Earlier I suggested that some senses of good and bad might be more reflexive than others. For all but die-hard substantivists, to use the term 'good' is to invite questions like: 'for whom?', and 'by what criteria?' To the extent that attributive adjectives may raise more questions than predicative ones, they encourage not just reflection but an open field. The Kantian solution, for instance, may be seen as two ways of closing down the possibilities. In hypothetical imperatives, the injunction implicit in 'good' is directed to a particular person for the criteria of fulfilling particular ends (if x wishes to achieve y, doing z is good). The categorical imperative holds for all persons, and good becomes an end in itself, by way of the criterion that 'good' for one person shall not be 'bad' for another (z is good in itself for all xs). The former implies a certain utilitarianism; the latter is deontic. Arguably, such implications are inevitably faced when one uses words like 'good' or 'bad'.

What implications does the term '*darma*' have for the Balinese? As it lays down duty regardless of ends, prima facie it is categorical and deontic (about binding obligations): for whom differs between the caste and universal senses. Following or ignoring *darma* has, however, consequences in bringing happiness or pleasure (*suka*, from Sanskrit *sukha*) as against misery and pain (*duka*, from Sanskrit *duhkha*). The recognition of consequences invites consideration of the distinction between intended and unintended effects of action; and for whom. Thomas à Becket observed that 'The last temptation is the greatest treason: to do the right deed for the wrong reason' (Eliot 1935: 32).

Balinese pragmatism gives this a curious twist. While they are quite clear that there are different intentions for action, it is often impossible to know what these are without looking at the consequences. A hard-nosed empiricism requires that intentions may have to be ignored for many purposes. (It is the stress on sense-data which I suspect accounts for much of priests' preference for speaking of abstractions as potentially perceptible.) The drift of Balinese attitudes to intention comes out clearly in the term they use, *tetujon,* which has in its primary use a sense of 'direction' or 'goal'. So they might endorse Balzac's remark that 'Evil, no doubt, is a form of good of which the results are not immediately manifest.'

The range of interpretation of evaluative terms is curtailed by the need to achieve a degree of coherence with other sets of terms. The Balinese use the word *becik* (*luwung* in low Balinese) in most contexts where we would say 'good'. There are many words used predicatively to talk of things they dislike: rotten, coarse, ugly and so forth. The term used attributively is *kaon* (or *jelé* in low Balinese). One word, *corah,* looks promising, as dictionaries usually render it as 'wicked', 'evil'. It connotes, however, wanting something belonging to someone else, being greedy. So, if we are to ask for whom something is good or bad, we must look at what is presupposed by the terms the Balinese use.

As the link of 'evil' and 'greedy' suggests, judgements commonly refer back to a theory of human nature, which the Balinese have borrowed and adapted from Indian philosophy. Both aristocracy and villagers agree that humans have divergent goals. (This view is used to explain why one person's prayer may not be answered: divinity cannot satisfy everyone!) They are known as the *triwarga: darma,* a disposition to do one's duty; *arta,* the pursuit of wealth; and *kama,* the search for sensual pleasure. Whereas *darma* brings good to others as well as satisfying oneself, in pursuing *arta* and *kama,* the good or pleasure one obtains may well be only for oneself and is likely to be at the expense of others. The diverse forms of good are justified by a theory of human nature that recognizes conflicting aspects, the *triguna: sattwa,* the disposition towards purity or knowledge; *raja,* towards passion; and *tamas,* towards desire or ignorance. Where the Balinese give this Indian model an interestingly pragmatic turn is in questioning that good lies in the ideals of duty and knowledge (cf. chapter 9 above). As human nature has several aspects, they are all of value, and excess in any direction is bad, and endangers not only happiness but sanity. It is the pure man who is liable suddenly to

lapse, and, as villagers would often remark, the local thief (a one-time
murderer) could be generous and kind. They tend to be suspicious of views,
like Augustine's, that 'To many, total abstinence is easier than perfect
moderation' (*On the good of marriage*, xxi).

Finally, how do the Balinese link the stress on balance and the pragmatic
nature of good with the nature of God? The following story from my
fieldwork may help.

Case 5   Is God evil?

Late one evening after a long discussion with a group of villagers, in which they
commented on how many contradictions and inconsistencies their beliefs seemed to
contain, I remarked that we too had our puzzles. In Christianity there was a paradox
that, if God were good, omnipotent and omniscient, how could evil exist? To my
surprise I was met with hoots of laughter. White people seemed so clever. How could
they find difficult what was so obvious, even to simple villagers who could not read or
write? One of them explained the matter to me, to mutters of agreement from the
others. Of course God — in Bali Sang Hyang Widi, the highest, all-embracing Divinity
— was bad (*kaon*). How else could there be bad in the world? Were he not bad as well
as good, we could never know if an action, or thought, were good as we would have
nothing to compare it to. It is only because God is both that humans are able to say that
something is good or bad at all.

On further enquiry with Balinese from different social strata similar views
turned up, and they all seemed quite satisfied that the style of argument was
'good'. It is interesting to see how their answer to the problem of theodicy
(from *theós*, god, and *díkē*, justice) works. Traditionally, the problem stems
from three premises being mutually incompatible:

  1 God is almightly and all-knowing;
  2 God is perfectly good;
  3 Evil exists.

The elegance of the Balinese solution to my mind, though probably to few
Western theologians, is to elaborate the second premise such that, in allowing
humans the capacity to discriminate, God allows the existence of badness. On
one reading God becomes in fact the possibility of discrimination and choice.

Earlier I suggested there is a sense in which order, for the Balinese, is the
way the world is. The point may be made by contrast to a problem in Christian
theology. Once the existence of Satan, or evil, has been admitted, the tables
have to be turned so that God must always win in the end (cf. chapter 2
above). The Balinese give a similar argument a flavour all of their own, by

arguing backwards. If the good always win, then who wins is good. For example, in the Balinese version of the Indian epic, the Mahabarata, upon which much theatre and cultural commentary draws, the five 'good' Pandawa brothers, who defeat the horde of 'evil' Korawa, are often no more honourable in the means they use than are their opponents: the difference is that they win. It is not that Brutus is an honourable man, in Balinese parlance, in overthrowing the tyrant Caesar, but rather that Brutus is alive and Caesar lies stabbed. The logic, whether one likes it or not, is impeccable.

Given the tenor of my argument, it would be contradictory to try to sum up the 'essence' of Balinese approaches to evil more than loosely to use a label such as 'pragmatic'. So perhaps I might be allowed to conclude by drawing a contrast between Balinese and Western styles of approaching morality.

To an outsider, Western philosophers have a striking tendency to try to pin down the 'essential nature' of the good or the moral. Unfortunately, different schools of thought seize upon different essential features. Is there method in their apparent muddle? It is possible that there is and that it is language — not as I tried to use it to look at culturally recognized implications, but in its different functions.

The point may be made by a quick inspection of Jakobson's model of the functions of language (1960). As I understand him, speech has many functions at the same time, but these may be distinguished analytically none the less. What is important is that speech does not just *refer* to things in the world. In differing degrees, depending upon speakers, listeners and context, different aspects of language come to the fore. The speaker's attitude to what is being said may be crucial. This is the *emotive* function ('How lovely to see you!'). Or the stress may be on the listener, as in vocatives and imperatives, which is the *conative* function (as in the command 'Drink!', cited by Jakobson himself, 1960: 355). The better-known *phatic* aspect may serve to check that the medium is working ('Good morning, how are you?'). Rather differently, the *meta-lingual* function is about confirming that the same code is being used by those concerned ('I don't follow you — what do you mean?'). Perhaps the hardest function to grasp immediately is the *poetic,* or *aesthetic,* which focuses 'on the message for its own sake' (Jakobson 1960: 356; Tennyson's 'And murmuring of innumerable bees', quoted by Lyons 1977: 54; or perhaps 'Frailty, thy name is woman!'). In describing the Balinese *celuluk* as reflecting the ambiguities of fear, danger and difference, I was hinting at something like the poetic function. The possible connection between these functions and theories of ethics is given in figure 1.

The parallel between Jakobson's functions of language and kinds of ethical theory is almost uncanny. Philosophers are described as 'naturalists' if they

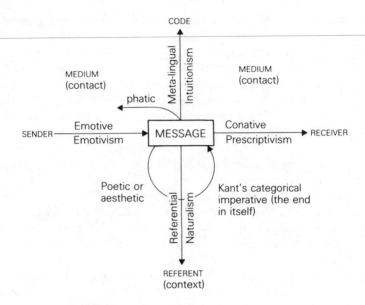

FIGURE 1   *The connection between Jakobson's functions of language
and theories of ethics*

try to describe 'good' by *reference* to supposedly objective, observable features
of the world (e.g. Herbert Spencer or R. B. Perry). Naturalism implicitly
assumes that reference is the key function in the language of moral
statements.

'Non-naturalists' come, like Snark Hunters, in many shapes and sizes.
'Emotivists', such as Russell and A. J. Ayer, hold that moral statements do
not so much assert truths about the world as express attitudes. By contrast,
'Prescriptivists', of whom R. M. Hare is perhaps the best known, regard such
statements as a species of prescriptive discourse, of which the classic case is
imperatives (cf. the *conative* function). 'Intuitionists', such as G. E. Moore,
argue that moral terms like 'good' are like properties such as 'red' in being
ultimately undefinable, but that they differ in being non-natural. Either one is
simply aware that something is good or one is not: one cannot be shown it. I
am tempted to paraphrase this as implying that either one understands the
code or one does not (which would parallel the *meta-lingual* function).
Somewhere between a stress on the code and the medium lies MacIntyre
(there is a shared basis of some rather unspecified kind in social judgements).
It is anthropologists who come near to elevating the *phatic* function of
communication to the status of a theory of morality. For instance, F. G.
Bailey's notion of 'moral community' is not so much a matter of understanding,

or agreeing to, the code (the double sense of code in 'moral code' should be obvious) as of recognizing that people share contact above all (Bailey 1971: 7–8). Finally, in Kant, or at least in the way Kant was interpreted by the Romantics, the connection between morality and aesthetics is pretty explicit. If the moral is what is an end in itself, the aesthetic was to become something very similar.

In trying to find out what morality really is, it looks as if philosophers searching for its 'essence' have unwittingly sounded out only the functions of language, and have confused words with their imagined objects. If the Balinese, as I suggest, stress the contextual and pragmatic use of evaluative words, then applying well-worn Western distinctions, designed to catch the essential nature of moral concepts, may be fruitless and ill-conceived. I suspect it makes a category mistake. The Balinese seem to work with quite different presuppositions and styles of argument. Any discussion of evil requires for a start so detailed and particular a knowledge of cosmology, theology, ideas of human nature and of social relations used by people in a culture that one wonders whether strict comparison would ever be possible. Worst of all, such an endeavour commits the essentialist fallacy of presupposing that there is something there to be compared. One recalls what happened to the hunters who thought that finally they had caught a Snark:

> He had softly and suddenly vanished away —
> For the Snark was a Boojum, you see.
> Fit 8, The Vanishing

REFERENCES

Aristotle (1941). *The Basic Works of Aristotle* (ed. R. McKeon). New York: Random House

Bailey, F.G. (1971). 'Gifts and Poison'. In *Gifts and Poison: the Politics of Reputation* (ed. F. G. Bailey). Oxford: Basil Blackwell

Bateson, G. & Mead, M. (1942). *Balinese Character: a Photographic Analysis.* New York: Special publication of the New York Academy of Sciences, vol. 2

Becker, A.L. (1979). 'Text-Building, Epistemology and Aesthetics in Javanese Shadow Theatre'. In *The Imagination of Reality* (ed. A. L. Becker and A. Yengoyan). Norwood, NJ: Ablex

Collingwood, R.G. (1946). *The Idea of History.* Oxford: Clarendon Press

Douglas, M. (1970). *Natural Symbols: Explorations in Cosmology.* London: The Cresset Press

Eliot, T.S. (1935). *Murder in the Cathedral.* London: Faber and Faber

Geach, P.T. (1956). 'Good and Evil'. *Analysis* 17, 33–42

Geertz, C. (1967). 'Tihingan: a Balinese Village'. In *Villages in Indonesia* (ed. R. M. Koentjaraningrat). Ithaca, NY: Cornell University Press

(1973a). ' "Internal conversion" in contemporary Bali'. In *The Interpretation of Cultures.* New York: Basic Books

(1973b). 'Ethos, World View, and the Analysis of Sacred Symbols'. In *The Interpretation of Cultures.* New York: Basic Books

(1973c). 'Religion as a Cultural System' in *The Interpretation of Cultures.* New York: Basic Books

Grader, C.J. (1940). 'De Poera Medoewé Karang te Koeboetambahan: een Nord-Balisch agrarisch heiligdom'. *Djawa* 6, 1—34

Hobart, M. (1979). 'A Balinese village and its field of social relations'. Ph.D. thesis, University of London

(1982). 'Is Interpretation Incompatible with Knowledge? The Problem of Whether the Javanese Shadow Play has Meaning'. *Second Bielefeld Colloquium on South East Asia.* Westphalia: Bielefeld University

(forthcoming). 'Thinker, Thespian, Soldier, Slave? Assumptions about Human Nature in the Study of Balinese Society'. In *Context and Meaning in South East Asia.* (ed. M. Hobart and R. Taylor). London: SOAS

Hooykaas, C. (1963). 'Yama-Rāja: the Lord of Judgement'. In *Āgama Tīrtha: Five Studies in Hindu-Balinese Religion.* Amsterdam: North-Holland

(1973). *Kama and Kala: Materials for the Study of Shadow Theatre in Bali.* Amsterdam: North-Holland

(1977). *A Balinese Temple Festival.* The Hague: Nijhoff

(1978). *The Balinese poem Basur: an Introduction to Magic.* The Hague: Nijhoff

Jakobson, R. (1960). 'Concluding Statement: Linguistics and Poetics'. In *Style in Language* (ed. T. Sebeok). Cambridge, Mass.: MIT

Lyons, J. (1977). *Semantics* (2 vols). Cambridge: Cambridge University Press

MacIntyre, A. (1967). *A Short History of Ethics: A History of Moral Philosophy from the Homeric Age to the Twentieth Century.* London: Routledge & Kegan Paul

(1981). *After Virtue: a Study in Moral Theory.* London: Duckworth

Needham, R. (1963). 'Introduction' to E. Durkheim & M. Mauss, *Primitive classification* (trans. and ed. R. Needham). London: Cohen and West

O'Flaherty, W. (1973). *Asceticism and Eroticism in the Mythology of Siva.* London: Oxford University Press

Parkin, D.J. (1978). *The Cultural Definition of Political Response: Lineal Destiny among the Luo.* London and New York: Academic Press

Pigeaud, T.G.T. (1967). *Literature of Java: Synopsis of Javanese Literature 900—1900 A.D.* The Hague: Nijhoff

Plato (1961). *The Collected Dialogues of Plato Including the Letters* (ed. E. Hamilton and H. Cairns). New Jersey: Princeton University Press

Poerbatjaraka, R.N. (1926). 'De Calon Arang' *Bijdr. Taal-, Land- Volkenk.* 82, 11—180

Punyatmaja, I.B.O. (1970). *Pancha Çradha.* Denpasar: Parisada Hindu Dharma Pusat

Ricoeur, P. (1967). *The symbolism of evil.* Boston, Mass.: Beacon

Shärer, H. (1963). *Ngaju Religion: The Conception of God among a South Borneo People* (trans. R. Needham). The Hague: Nijhoff

Skinner, Q. (1972). ' "Social Meaning" and the Explanation of Social Action" in *Philosophy, politics and society* 4th series (ed. P. Laslett, W. G. Runciman and Q. Skinner). Oxford: Basil Blackwell

Sperber, D. and Wilson, D. (1982). 'Mutual Knowledge and Relevance in Theories of Comprehension'. In *Mutual Knowledge* (ed. N. V. Smith). London and New York: Academic Press

Turner, V.W. (1964). 'Witchcraft and Sorcery: Taxonomy versus Dynamics'. *Africa* 34: 319—24.

van der Tuuk, H.N. (1897). *Kawi-Balineesch-Nederlandsch woordenboek Vol 1.* Batavia: Landsdrukkerij

Weck, W. (1937). *Heilkunde und Volkstum auf Bali.* Stuttgart: Enke

Wilden, A. (1972). *System and structure: essays in communication and exchange* (2nd edn). London: Tavistock

Worsley, P.J. (1972). *Babad Bulèlèng: a Balinese Dynastic Genealogy.* The Hague: Nijhoff

de Zoete, B. and Spies, W. (1938). *Dance and Drama in Bali.* London: Faber & Faber.

Zoetmulder, P.J. (1982). *Old Javanese—English dictionary* (2 vols). The Hague: Nijhoff

11

Good, evil and spiritual power: Reflections on Sufi teachings*

John Bousfield

The Divine Beauty includes Predispositions of all that is good, and the Divine
Majesty includes Predispositions of all that which is evil . . . . (By both his
hands) is meant Power and Will . . . . According to one expression by His two
hands is meant Beauty and Majesty; Beauty is likened to the right (hand) and
Majesty to the left (hand). All that is good comes into being from the right
(hand; all) that is evil . . . from the left.[1]

Al-Attas 1970: 374, 384

Hamzah Fansuri, the great Malay Sufi, affirms here the teachings of 'extreme'
Sufism (*tassawuf*) or, as many contemporary Muslims would prefer to have
it translated, Islamic spirituality. I refer to it as 'extreme' both because at
various times the Sufi tradition of which Hamzah is a representative has
been damned as heretic and fanatic by the Muslim community, and because it
develops themes in the spiritual encounter with God to an explicit and

---

* The following discussion is based partly on research carried out in Malaysia (mainly
Kelantan) and Indonesia (Sumatra) in 1979. The texts referred to are written in Malay,
although they draw heavily on Arabic terminology. Similarly, all of my discussions then and
since have been with Malay intellectuals and mystics in Malay or English. The Arabic
terminology was learnt via Malay, and it is Sufism in Malay culture that is discussed here,
although I do not believe this constitutes a departure from the Sufi tradition as such. Most
terms referred to in the text are Arabic but are part of the global language of Islamic
mysticism. The idea of a 'global vocabulary' is mentioned in this paper but not examined.

[1] All quotations are taken from Naguib's translation of two texts by Hamzah Fansuri, *The
Secrets of the Gnostics* (Asrarul—Arifin) and *The Drink of Lovers* (Sharabul—Ashiqin),
romanized editions of which (and one other text) are included in the above work. Naguib's
lengthy introduction to and commentary on Hamzah's Sufism is seminal and remains the
best introduction to the texts.

ultimate point. I want to discuss these teachings because of the way in which they articulate the theme that everything comes from God, typical of the spiritual affirmation found among those Muslims who would call themselves moderate and orthodox in their Sufism.

The teachings stand in the great tradition of Sufism and go back at least to the twelfth or thirteenth century and earlier certainly in inspiration. The texts and biography of Hamzah Fansuri (sixteenth century) still arouse controversy in the Malay world today, and the ideas I will present are familiar to those practising their Sufism both within the orders (*tariqah*) and outside. There is a continuity between the more cautious statements of orthodox Sufis now and the 'extreme' followers of Hamzah who in the seventeenth-century Sumatran kingdom of Aceh were persecuted and executed for their ideas and practices. Rather than getting embroiled in the controversy, I hope that the way in which the Sufis characteristically attempt to place their experience of the Unity of Being within the Islamic framework will emerge. I will present what I take to be their 'theodicy' and end with suggestions on how these ideas can be related to other cosmologies of South-East Asia as well as Europe.

We see already that good (*baik*) and evil (*jahat*) are said to be from God and that the pathway from the Divine Essence to the theatre of their manifestation which we inhabit as actors and audience is mapped with precision. As I attempt to place the discussion within the contours of the Sufis' own vision, a cautionary note is called for.

I return to these teachings time and again because of the power with which they present one solution to the problem of evil. This time I made my return because an apparent contradiction in Hamzah's version was drawn to my attention. It seemed as if, in wanting to have it both ways, he ends up trying to slither over an embarrassing source of incoherence. Yet might it not be that for him there was no solution because there was no problem? That I had from the start demanded a formal solution to the problem of evil which might exist for me but not for mystical Muslims of the sixteenth century? It could be that the meaning and force of *baik* and *jahat* were not the same as those of 'good' and 'evil' for me, and that the relation between their presence in the world and God's power could not be construed as we characteristically do in thinking of the Christian and post-Christian dilemmas. But instead of seeing a severe problem of translation, which would close us off from the world of Sufism altogether, it seems that the encounter with that world can shed light on what *we* mean by 'evil' (and, indeed, who 'we' are), anyway. That has become one of the main ethnographic concerns of these discussions.

What I will try to show is that the force of the Sufi teachings derives precisely from the way in which they confront a religious problem in the Quranic Revelation and, by taking up one side of the contradiction in an extreme way, change the force of that contradiction without obliterating the religious core in which it arises.

Before we enter this world, one more caution needs to be sounded. The texts from which I quote are manuals of spirituality. The force of the words is to be grasped not just intellectually, but as part of a disciplined journey along a path (*tariqah* in the esoteric sense) to the state of gnosis (*ma'arifah*). I will return to this later because a circularity in the argument is not so much broken as rendered self-sufficient, self-guaranteeing only through the claim to a series of transcendent and redemptive experiences.

What the Sufi experiences is that all comes from God and from no other source, neither human agency nor the seductions of Satan. It is the unswerving pursuit of the meaning of this idea in the context of Islam and its implications that give Sufism its particular character in relation to other mystical ways. The Sufis follow a path that leads from the realization that everything depends on God for its existence through to the realization that, not only is there no God but the One God, but there is naught *but* God. And beyond this knowledge the Sufi as a knowing subject is obliterated like a moth in that Divine Unity. Gnosis is not knowledge as we take it but a threshold before a state beyond individuality and distinction. That state is extinction (*fana*) when there is no longer one who experiences and loves God but only a Unity of Being and Consciousness.

At the heart of the teachings lies the utterly controversial idea of the Unity of Being (*wahdat al-wujud*): controversial because it seems to affirm pantheism. God and the universe are one. More than that, God is 'in' everything equally and wholly. The teaching is frequently articulated in outrageous and ecstatic utterances: 'I see nothing except I see God in it'; 'Verily I am God!'; 'There is nothing in my cloak save God!' (Al-Attas 1970: 386, 395, where traditional attributions are given by Hamzah). A Muslim lawyer said, 'They say that God is here in my pocket.' To affirm this identity is heresy; it constitutes the ultimate sin. It undermines Islam.

Islam is the relation between God and man, between lord and servant. The whole duty and privilege of humankind arises out of this acknowledgement, this acceptance of the ultimate relationship. To assert that lord and servant are the same is to undermine the point of *ibadah,* devotion and service. The pantheistic teaching of the so-called *Wujudiyyah,*[2] followers of Hamzah Fansuri, is what got them killed (see Al-Attas 1966). It seems as if the implication is that anything goes and whatever, it does not matter. Constantly the charge of heresy involves specific charges that members of the *tariqah* are no longer bothering to pray, to carry out their ablutions, that they have illicit

[2] The 'existential monists'.

sexual contact and in general abandon their duties as Muslims. Yet constantly Sufis protest their orthodoxy, and through time and cultural space the orders have maintained their presence and influence, have succeeded in dissociating themselves from 'deviant' teachings and have proven their point by having in their ranks leading members of the devout community.

The Sufis can be seen to be trying to give space to a realm of experience threatened by the emphasis on personal responsibility and salvation on the one hand and by Divine Omnipotence on the other. The spiritual path then looks like an escape route from the double-bind of the injunction to follow the Law (*shariah*) and the impossibility of human agency. The force of the Sufi response, however, lies in remaining right within the Quranic revelation.

Instead of a spiralling out, as seems suggested by the idiom of extinction (*fana* being like a violent path to *nirvana*), the traveller (*salik*) on the path aspires to an experience that establishes in a redemptive moment, somehow out of time, not so much a mediation as a totalization, a complete occupation of the site of the contradiction. The confrontation with Divine Power *and* the Divine Injunction, both constantly reinforced in the Quran, is the experience of Islam, establishing the whole range of religious experiences — fear, awe, trust, love, comfort and nourishment as well as pain and yearning. And the Sufi finds a ground upon which a unity of experience can be established which renders that contradiction essential and necessary. So we are not confronted with a formal theodicy that exposes antinomies ultimately doomed to play their role in the downfall of religion (a sense that these problems have acquired especially in Christian apologetics). An experience is offered the flavour of which involves the intense appropriation of that contradiction. It is as if the tension becomes a part of the mode of perception structuring a vision (*shuhud*) of the Real (*al-Haqq*). We then see how the Sufis do not explain away the differences between good and evil and between human power and Divine Power but use the force of these disjunctions to articulate and achieve the experience of unity. We do not get sophistry, which defuses the problem, but more an exaggeration of the difficulties, which functions as a detonation device.[3] The texts offered as meditational aids, setting up, preparing the way for, the achievements of the Sufis' devotional exercises, make use of a specific rhetorical structure.

First, let us look at the savage determinism that Hamzah constantly pushes at us:

One He causes to believe; one He causes to disbelieve; one He causes to be rich; one He causes to be poor; one He allows always to transgress; one He allows always to do

---

[3] Ronald Inden pointed out that my use of terms like 'explosion' concurred with his intuition of Sufism as 'eruptive' (while, e.g., Buddhism is 'interruptive').

good; one He allows to do evil; one He causes to enter Heaven; one He causes to enter Hell; one He allows to do many devotional acts and then causes him to enter Heaven; (one He allows to commit many sins and then He causes him to enter Hell); one from the believers He causes to disbelieve; one from the unbelievers He causes to believe.

Al-Attas 1970: 394

No agency, no choice. What God puts into effect here is a drama of belief (Islam) and infidelity (*kekafiran*); devotion (*ibadah*), sin (*masiah*) and treason (*derhaka*). In that drama lies the entire sphere of sin as it exists for Hamzah. *Baik* (good) and *jahat* (evil or wicked, or even naughty) are the Malay terms that Hamzah uses. They are adjectival or, perhaps better, indifferent in their use between adjectival and substantive. Descriptive, they do not imply evil as a being or force. Nor do they mark out a distinction between on the one hand metaphysical or physical evil as opposed to human evil, and on the other a descriptive, naturalistic use and a morally evaluative one (see chapters 2 and 8 above). Hamzah restricts their use paradigmatically to sin, as we shall see. But the answer to the question, 'Why are there sinners?' turns out also to answer the question, 'Why is there suffering?' Just where we might expect a distinction between evil in general and sin in particular, we are given an account that does not distinguish natural or metaphysical evil from the evil of human agency. The fundamental categories of being are from the start ethical, bluntly the same. It may be that Hamzah is reasserting this unity in experience against the separation being pushed by the Doctors of the Law.

The sin to which the texts constantly refer us is that of being *kafir,* the sin of 'disbelief'. 'Belief' and 'disbelief' are ambiguous terms and inadequate here; it is better to understand *Islam* in a pristine sense as submission and *kekafiran* as rebellion, treachery of the ultimate degree. The Sufis present us with a cosmic drama in which human existence as such may be construed now as good and righteous in itself, and now as by its very nature sinful. The rest — the fruits of the earth, the pleasure of company on the one hand, and the suffering that we endure on the other — all take their place in relation to this drama.

Yet having iterated and reiterated that the whole drama is from God, Hamzah elsewhere says:

According to the Law, although good and evil are from God, yet God Most Exalted wills (and approves) only good, and does not will and approve evil. The meaning of these words is most recondite and it cannot be conceived by the People of the Path, for since Divine Majesty is His Attribute and Divine Beauty is His Attribute, how can He not will and approve His Attribute? But if we consider this in respect of the Primordial Potentialities, then it is possible (to grasp the idea), for both of them (i.e. Divine

Majesty and Divine Beauty) are present (to Him) *there.* Although He causes both of them to come forth *there,* He wills and approves only good, and He does not will and approve evil. But this is an eternal question!

Al-Attas 1970: 390

Eternal indeed! It was this passage that was taken to be the source of the embarrassing incoherence, unless it was just Hamzah not wanting to tread on the toes of the People of the Law, the '*shariah*-minded',[4] the straight *ulama.* It looks as if everybody moves constantly round in the same circle. The People of the Law say that, while God is omnipotent, nevertheless He wills only the good, and unless we can attribute freedom to people, there can be no justice in the Law. However prepared the theologians are to explain away prima facie cosmic evil, this sense of justice coupled with human responsibility is clung to tightly. The People of the Path deny any freedom but have no desire to assert 'God is not just.' More important, they constantly affirm, if they are claimants to orthodoxy, that we must always remain within the bounds of *shariah.* Little mercy seems extended to those who are determined not to. How can God permit suffering in general, and evildoing in particular, if He yet wills only good? At this point, we have to leap into the Sufis' world of radical necessity.

In attacking the theologians and philosophers, Hamzah rejects any notion of the universe being created if newness in order of substance or of time is implied — just as much as he rejects any notion of the universe being co-eternal with God. The latter position, the philosophical one, denies the movement of Divine Power, the heave of the Compassionate Sigh on which all is dependent. But the former position, *any* version of *creatio ex nihilo,* has this most serious flaw:

To the doctors of Theology, the things and their Potentialities are something new (i.e. temporal events, produced) and *they* move (from their original place) and are created in a fashion somewhat similar to (the act of) a carpenter wishing to build a house. He plans according to the potentialities of the things known to him (in His Knowledge). He then builds a house. The house is a thing, created, the form of the house in his mind is also a thing created; both of them are something new. . . .

Al-Attas 1970: 373

Houses go wrong. (As I was writing this, a water tank in my house overflowed.) Hamzah considers any such creative and temporal relation between God and the creatures one that would render God inadequate:

if He does not already have within Him (i.e. as Potentialities in His Knowledge) the hypocrite and the unbeliever, and He causes one to become an unbeliever, and having

---

[4] This is the expression of Marshall Hodgson (1974).

caused one to become an unbeliever He then casts him into Hell, then He is unjust.
God the Glorious and Most Exalted is not like that. If such qualities are present in
Him, then His nature is deficient.

Al-Attas 1970: 373

Affirming Divine Power, Hamzah argues that the whole drama must from
the start be already in the Divine Essence. Whatever is, whatever happens,
must be somehow connected up with the perfection of God. At this point, we
could expect a cry of gratitude — 'I am, thank God, one of the elect; pity the
sinner.' Hamzah does not make this move. For the damned as well are from
God.

The logical problem, if I dare put it so, is that we are presented with a
conditional: if God does not knowingly make the sinners, then He is imperfect.
Sinners exist, but it is a *petitio principii* to say that God is, of course, perfect.
To meet this problem Hamzah again resists a separation, this time between
knowledge and being; he moves to a view of knowledge as not mere
acquaintance or even 'meeting' where knower and known are already separate,
but as the first relation between one and the other where these are in reality
the same. God does not 'know' that which is 'created': 'creation' is God
knowing himself.

Hamzah puts the problem that he resists thus:

Should He cause the whole world to be created believing without causing some to be
created unbelieving, then He is lacking (in Wisdom); should He create all to be
unbelieving without creating also believing, then He is lacking (in Wisdom); should
He create Heaven without also creating Hell then He is lacking (in Wisdom and
Power); and should He create Hell without also creating Heaven (then He is lacking in
Wisdom).

Al-Attas 1970: 374—5

Is Hamzah another structuralist? He moves from the contingent, 'it is so', to
the celebration of a radical necessity — 'You cannot have this ever without
that.' No pleasure without pain, no good without evil (and vice versa, of
course); no universe without God. Once this perception of necessity, of
essential fit, takes hold, *anything* can happen and be understood to have its
place in the cosmic whole. But it is not just a matter of the cosmos as a whole
giving us the expalnatory context for a particular event. Maybe I can explain
why some human beings are so transgressively violent, just as one can
perhaps explain why dinosaurs became extinct or why a natural disaster had
long-term beneficial consequences. Yet the explanation, tight as it may be,
offers no comfort — to the victims or to the guilty perpetrators, let alone to

the hapless dinosaur. At the end of the day, what is missing is a sense of goodness to that whole. Instead, a neatly ordered universe presents us with formidable absurdity.[5]

The story so far needs something else. At this stage on the path we must return to the idea of the Unity of Being.

Having rejected both a doctrine of creation and an argument for the co-eternality of God and the universe, the Sufis of this tradition articulate their vision of cosmic unity in terms of a 'process' whereby the Divine Essence articulates itself to itself. They make it clear, however, that this 'process' is not temporal — occurring in time — but rather that it is constitutive of time and that the historical process language is metaphor alluding to a constant coming-to-be of the universe we inhabit. This universe is the phenomenal surface of the Divine Essence. The 'process', of which there are different versions in the teachings, involves the infinite particularization, the outward manifestation, of an Absolute Unity, the 'Inwardly Hidden'.

The account begins with the unknowable, utterly transcendent Essence, beyond even the Name Allah, often referred to obliquely as *Huwa* (*He*) and characterized as a state of indeterminacy (*la ta ayyun*) or pure unqualified unity (*ahadiyyah*) (see Al-Attas (1970: 360) for Hamzah's discussion). At this stage there is no distinction of any kind. A favourite metaphor of Hamzah is that of the ocean, upon which waves appear when the ocean moves. The force of the metaphor lies in the idea that the waves are in no way separable from nor have any existence independent of the ocean.

When the ocean heaves, the first determination (*pertama ta ayyun*) 'occurs'. Hamzah characterizes it as the emergence of the Seven Primary Attributes distinguishing Allah:[6] life, knowledge, will, power, speech, hearing and sight. (I will not discuss the logic of the Seven here: elsewhere Hamzah characterizes the first determination as a fourfold emergence.) Correlative with these Attributes, the 'Primordial Potentialities' of the Essence are known to God. Within a Unity of Self-consciousness, all that is possible is at once and already known. It is God knowing and seeing himself. Hamzah emphasizes this by asserting that knowledge precedes the known, knowledge at this level being active not passive, and 'in reality' one with the other attributes that are one with the Essence.

The second determination results immediately: the forms, the 'Fixed Prototypes' of everything that can be, the particularizations are moved into

---

[5] For a further discussion of radical necessity versus radical contingency and a more detailed account of the 'appearance' of the universe, see Bousfield (1983).

[6] Once distinction is conceptualized thus, it is appropriate to refer to Allah as His First Name.

place at the Creative Command 'Be!' (*Kun!*). We are still at the level of Unity, but it is a unity-in-diversity. After this, a progressive materialization results in the exteriorization of the Essence, from spirit through ideas to the animal, vegetable and mineral worlds. The series ends in the human being who, containing the whole, is potentially the Perfect Man (*al-insan al-Kamil*), the microcosm.

Everything that is exemplifies one or more of the names of Allah, and these names are best thought of as the logical forms of the Attributes. Two points are crucial: first, the Attributes of Allah are numberless; but second, they are progressive particularizations of the Primary Attributes, and these in turn are ultimately one. So each particular is nevertheless a particularization of the Essence, the Real. We can now confront evil and the evildoer.

'The Essence', writes Hamzah, 'is all-pervasive' (Al-Attas 1970: 441). In this mystical interpretation, the name that conveys this pervasiveness is al-Rahman, the Compassionate One; for, according to this teaching, it is the Sigh of Compassion, of a metaphysical Mercy, that heaves the ocean and brings forth the world. The Essence is in everything, but particularized. The first particularization, the first determination, brings forth the Primordial Potentialities of suffering and of the evildoer under the attribute of majesty (*al-Jalal*), which is a specification of Power. The crucial link is between evil and power. Majesty is manifest in the power to give and to take away, the might to change and destroy. Ageing, I was told, manifests the force of Majesty. And Majesty is particularized further in other names, the Irresistable and the One Who Subdues. All that is *particularly* good comes from the specification of Divine Beauty (*al-Jamal*) — the Gracious One, One who gives Strength, and so on:

Since the Potentialities of all believers come from (His Attributes of) Divine Beauty, the Potentialities of all unbelievers come from (the Attributes of) Divine Majesty — for Beauty represents the Gracious One and Majesty the Irresistible One — hence God the Glorious and Exalted brings forth by His Acts from the Gracious One, the strengthened (in faith); from the Irresistible One, the submissive (*to deviation from what is right*). Since His Names are One who gives Strength and One who Subdues, He causes them to enter (Heaven and) Hell according to the Law of their Potentialities. . . .

Al-Attas 1970: 442

The translator's interpretation (italicized) characterizes the drama in terms of an exemplary temptation or weakness — or even a terrible manipulation. This still looks as if the sinners are made to deviate not because they are deviators in essence. Hamzah also says:

As for those unbelievers, He grants them the power to commit sins, to oppose belief: and he puts hatred in their hearts so that they do not have faith. Since He sees that their Potentialities are from the Names Irresistible One and One who Subdues He commands them to commit acts of sin, and He then causes them to enter Hell.

Al-Attas 1970: 442

Hamzah adds that *this* is justice! Can we penetrate still further?

What if we say that the sinner, the rebel, is *per se* an exemplar of Majesty, the power to resist, the power of transgression? So that the command 'Be!' brings forth that form of power and the whole ensuing logic of submission and redemptive suffering? It involves a change of grammar, as follows. If I am made, then made to sin and then punished, there is injustice. If I am *in essence* a sinner, and that means being part of this drama, then the circle is complete. But what of all this suffering that is said to be just? Who is suffering? Only when the secret of the self is understood can this be answered: 'Whosoever knows himself knows his Lord.'[7] The discovery of the 'process' described involves a movement inwards to one's own essence. In the end, it is realized in gnosis that there is no self, that nothing exists other than God. The evildoer and the sufferer are God. Hamzah writes:

Question: 'If you say that the Essence of God pervades all creatures, who experiences the tortures of Hell and who experiences the delights of Paradise?'
Answer: 'Just as in the case of gold and the Ashrafi coin; if the coin is burnt, the coin alone is burnt away, not the gold. Even though gold and coin are not separate from one another, no matter; if they are refashioned a hundred or a thousand times, yet when they are burnt the coin alone is burnt (and annihilated), the gold remains subsistent. . . . the coin is like the creatures, gold is the Creator; only the creatures are burnt and annihilated.'

Al-Attas 1970: 433—4

God suffers both as agent and as patient of evil, and in that is made manifest to him his own Power, his own Majesty. The secret, closing the circle, is that the eye that sees God is the eye of man who sees the universe, and the agent of God is man who enacts and watches this drama unfold.

Finally, though the Command brings forth *all*, once the particularization occurs, God, *particularized to us* as He who Wills and Approves, wills only that which is good (beautiful). Hence *that* contradiction is removed. We are enjoined to follow the Law and are strengthened in that, even though

---

[7] This is attributed in the Tradition to the Prophet himself and is often quoted by Sufis in its esoteric sense.

ultimately the transgression of that Law originates in Him too. One might say that God as the revealed supporter of religion, Islam, enjoins fidelity and righteousness, but the Ultimate Reality *includes* this divine—human relationship and is not constituted by it.

Two related questions arise. Does the Sufi cosmology not obliterate any sense of ultimate goodness to the universe which in the face of good-with-evil could generate a positive sense of life? And, coming down to earth with a bump, does it at all relate to the experience of ordinary Muslims? Does it offer anything?

I have tried to show how the Sufi vision, rather than avoiding or escaping certain religious contradictions, totalizes them, distils them into an experience of the radical necessity of all that is, and opens on to an encounter with the Real. Sufis talk of opening (*kashf*) and of being opened. In extinction, the traveller reaches that state of unity where, in the words of the great shaikh Muyid'Din Ibnal-Arabi, 'I was you within *It* and we were all you, and you were He.'[8] It is a return to the level of the Predispositions and is described as a state of sublime intimacy. It is only in this state that the unorthodox and heretical utterances, 'I am God', 'I am the Real' (the famous utterance of the Sufi martyr Al-Hallaj) are appropriate, because at that level one cannot say that it is this particular person who is speaking. It is the utterly ambiguous cosmic 'I'. The Sufis 'get there' with the grace of God, through devotional exercises which include fasting and asceticism in general, intense rigour in carrying out the duties of Islam, and centrally recitation, remembrance (*dhikr*) of Allah. In terms of the cosmological scheme, we could say that it ceases to be the individual who recites the names of Allah or the *tahlil* — *la illahah illallah* ('There is no God but Allah') — and it is the names of Allah and the Real itself reciting through the individual. Some Sufis do actually talk of a state of 'attraction' (*majdhub*), like possession; when 'drawn' into the presence of God the individual is as if crazy, drunk, out of control. Others think more in terms of a meditational intuition of the meaning of the words recited.

The experience is characterized as intense and often ecstatic. On 'coming down' the Sufis talk of a sweet taste, a pervasive sense of goodness represented by the taste in the mouth. In answer to our question, Is there an ultimate sense of goodness? we are referred to this experience. If we ask for a characterization we in turn are asked, 'Can you describe the sweetness of sugar?'

So, for the individual who has tasted, the knowledge that all comes from God leaves a comforting assurance that ultimately all *is* well. Elsewhere

[8] (See Al-Affas (1970: 371—4) for Hamzah's discussion of this influential saying. See Affifi (1936), Ibn Al-Arabi (1980) and Schimmel (1975) for Ibn Al-Arabi's thought.

(Bousfield 1983) I have discussed how Sufis deal in levels of consciousness, and the situation that arises is that it is possible both to affirm God's Omnipotence — indeed, to live it — *at one level* and to inhabit the world as a human being *at another level,* striving to be righteous before the Law. The follower of the Sufi path can be liberated and heartened by this vision, not devastated and crushed. So, within the drama, the sinner may be redeemed through Islam; at one level, the sinner initiates the change, and at another, in a conjunction of personal and cosmic time, he sees that the change itself is 'from God'. The individual redemption is amplified through the cosmic redemption. The orders (*tariqah*) have always had a considerable hold in the Malay world, and it seems that now their popularity is increasing again (Awang 1983). One can suggest reasons why such a movement should be gaining membership, both in the urban centres and in the countryside, in the face of rapid social change. What I have tried to present here is the appeal to Muslims inherent in the ideas and practices themselves. But, given the concurrent assertion of orthodoxy in Pan-Islamic movements, the position of these teachings is questionable. How does the Sufi mediate the two dimensions of the Islamic experience?

Strengthened, energized by their experience, Sufis are able, it is claimed, to fulfil their duties as Muslims with ease, and their relation to the Law is twofold. First, they assert that only within the boundaries of *shariah,* as the road, can *tariqah* as the path be followed. Only within the ritual purity of the Law will the experience and the power it brings be contained. Without that constraint, their power becomes dangerous. Hamzah warns against the power of magic and miracles and he refers to the latter as the menstruation of males! The power of the vision, if diverted through such display — the usurpation of that which is for God only — becomes polluting. The idea is captured for Hamzah in a powerful image drawn from social relations. Once again, the connection between power and evil is drawn; the miraculous is evil and we might say the exercise of such power initiates the whole drama of Divine Majesty in the person of the unleashed Sufi.

Second, conversely, they do not regard the Law as a matter of external constraint but encounter it as essential, their natural predisposition. We might say that, just to the extent that mystical power is contained, the legitimate, social power of the *shaikh* (the head of the order) increases. The power of the Sufi that comes from the endurance of the experience of Unity is like that of the Piaroah wizard or the Giriama Vaya, necessary but dangerous (see chapters 13 and 14 below). It is the energy that gives power to the good, but also the power that destroys. Majesty is both. It can be contained by the Sufi who keeps it at the right level, but will turn to evil if it is unbound. It is as if the redemption is reversed and the very same gnosis that gives strength will, when appropriated by the selfish and arrogant individual, turn that person into an essential sinner. Yet always the totalizing vision of the Sufi can in turn see this too as the inevitable and constant recurrence of the drama. One both inhabits the world and struggles with evil, or seeks redemption and learns to see the struggle as essential.

We can now return to the notion of sin which motivates the cosmic drama enunciated. It seems odd, at first, that infidelity should be the supreme sin when so much else is directly and overtly evil, disruptive and violent. But that is because, for those inhabiting a secular world, fidelity and infidelity no longer constitute a fundamental moral axis. For a community defined by adherence to the Injunction of the Law, the paradigm sinner — that transgressor whom I have characterized as evil in some radical sense — is the infidel, both within and without the community. For that infidelity, construed as refusal and treachery, is the source of all serious transgressions and so in turn the explanation of such transgression. We can begin to locate the position of evil in this monotheistic tradition.

In the discussion so far, there has at times been a suggestion that the problem of evil is introduced by monotheism — and, when we are thinking of a contextual and relative sense of good and evil, the tone is almost accusatory (see chapter 8 above). Yet at the same time, we have shown ourselves reluctant to give up the category of absolute, irredeemable evil where the offence is perceived as so transgressive as to be inexcusable. The inexcusability leads on to the failure to explain, and we are faced with the paradox of the 'inhuman human' whom we find difficult to blame precisely because we cannot locate the intention that leads to the act (see chapter 3 above). It is as if we were caught between different traditions and did not know which way to turn. We are uneasy with the resort to *evil* as the explanation. That constitutes one possibility. Evil as a cosmic force invades and causes suffering and so explains it. The closed circle is like this: someone does evil because they are Evil (or in some relation to Evil); and they are Evil because they do evil. The destructive intentions both initiate Evil and are initiated by it. A further explanatory resource is to personify or individualize Evil just as we may individualize and hypostatize death — what causes death if not Death?

The moves we make seem to ensnare us hopelessly in the absolute category of evil. At some point we cannot explain it without invoking it, unless we lose our hold on the moral altogether. We are caught between explaining evil as the effect of non-moral factors, external to or beyond the individual, e.g. the pathological; or, refusing to give up cherished moral categories, we are left asking why someone could have intended to do what they did. It is easy again to suggest a transgressively destructive will. We are, I suggest, the inheritors of monotheism without the recourse to Divinity.

The Sufis have that recourse. In the theological context from which they work, evil demands an explanation, given the institution of justice as a Law guaranteed by an Omnipotent and Benevolent God. The explanation of evil lies in sin, the category of the willful rejection of the Law. That explanation in turn, however, generates the problem of the place of sin in the cosmic scene initiated by God. Hamzah takes the last resort and has it both ways.

I want to conclude by suggesting how to locate this 'branch' of the Sufi tradition, in one direction in relation to European and in the other to South-East Asian thought. The issue of translation is at the forefront. The great Sumatran shaikhs such as Hamzah Fansuri themselves translated the Sufi tradition into the Malay language and culture. They used texts, teachings and idioms from the Arab and Persian heartlands and succeeded in relocating this great cosmology in the South-East Asian context. That cosmology itself draws upon and elaborates the Quranic experience in idioms drawn from hellenic philosophy and also pre-Islamic Persian cosmology. They use terms and think in ways that become part of the European heritage through their appropriation by medieval scholasticism. Not long after Hamzah Fansuri must have written his texts, Spinoza in a different world elaborated another version of the Unity of Being transformed differently through the idiom of geometry and mechanics. Completing the circle, we find ourselves translating Malay Sufism into terms that we have inherited, and which themselves form part of the same tradition out of which Hamzah comes. The context for translation is thus more global than local.

In the South-East Asian context, some further remarks apply. The often made suggestion that the first stages of Islamization in South-East Asia involved a pantheistic and essentially 'impure' Islam is not adequate: the Sufism of Hamzah Fansuri presents itself powerfully as orthodox, and the controversy over the teachings pervaded the whole Islamic world, not just South-East Asia. It is more plausibly suggested, nevertheless, that the mysticism of the orders that became established throughout the area appealed to the populace directly, whereas '*shariah*-minded' Islam did not. One is led to imagine the Hindu ritual specialists and village shamans perceiving their own world view mirrored in the teachings and practices of the Sufis. Extinction would have appeared to the Buddhist as *nirvana* and the 'pantheistic' God of Sufism as Brahma. The spiritual hierarchy of saints, visible and invisible, invoked by the Sufis or the institution of initiation directly by the Prophet in dreams could have been taken as parallel idioms. But then one might equally imagine the response, 'So what's new?' We can put it better like this. The 'feel' of Sufism (I am playing here with the Javanese idea of *rasa,* intuitive sense but also the 'feel' of reality) is different; its tonality is not that of other mystical ways. The sense of Unity is mediated by the redemptive drama of the

Quranic vision, with its harshness as well as its offer of relief. There is a violent quality to the 'liberation' offered by the path. Yet, as I have argued, the liberation consists in being able to have it both ways. Rather than presenting either divine determination or personal responsibility as a hopeless choice, the Sufi way claims to offer a path to action as well as wisdom.

The sweet taste in the mouth has lasting effects.

REFERENCES

Affifi, A. (1936). *The Mystical Philosophy of Muhyid'Din Ibnul-Arabi.* Cambridge: The University Press
Al-Attas, S.N. (1970). *The Mysticism of Hamzah Fansuri.* Kuala Lumpur: University of Malaya Press
Al-Attas, S.N. (1966). *Raniri and the Wujudiyyah of 17th Century Aceh.* Singapore: Malaysian Branch of the Royal Asiatic Society, Monograph III
Awang, P.B.H. (1983). 'Ahmadiyya Tariqah in Kelantan'. Unpublished M. Phil. dissertation. University of Kent
Bousfield, J. (1983). 'Islamic Philosophy in South-East Asia'. In Hooker, M.B. (ed.) *Islam in South-East Asia.* Leiden: E. J. Brill
Hodgson, M.G.S. (1974). *The Venture of Islam* (3 vols) Chicago and London: The University of Chicago Press
Ibn Al-Arabi (1980). *The Bezels of Wisdom* (trans. R. W. J. Austin). London: SPCK
Schimmel, A. (1975). *Mystical Dimensions of Islam.* Chapel Hill: University of North Carolina Press

12

Do the Fipa have a word for it?

Roy Willis

However unfamiliar the dualistic pattern of mythological thought as revealed by Lévi-Strauss may have seemed to his Western readership, binary conceptual systems are apparently as commonplace in the great civilizations of the East as they are in the small-scale, non-literate cultures of Africa, or as they were to our Celtic, Greek or Hebrew ancestors (cf. Granet 1933; Green 1983; Lloyd 1966; Leach 1969). What evidently needs explaining is the decline of conceptual binarism in our own culture, coupled with the emergence of a dominating monism. As Ellul has described it, the single role of the Technological Imperative is 'to bring everything into light, and by rational use to transform everything into means' (1965: 142). Recent history has shown how easily traditional ideas of 'good' and 'evil' can be submerged by the non-human rationality of the bureaucratic state, the political embodiment of modern technology. So Hannah Arendt (1963) could speak of 'the banality of evil' with reference to the Nazi mass murderer Adolf Eichmann.

Convincing as Ellul's argument is as analysis of current Western and world ideology, it does nothing to explain how this somewhat bizarre state of affairs came about. For that we need to understand our own ideological history, to recognize with Ricoeur that 'we were born to philosophy by Greece and that as philosophers we have encountered the Jews before encountering the Hindus and the Chinese' (1969: 23) — or, for that matter, the Africans or the Amerindians. Ricoeur sees the 'hermeneutic circle' of modern theological learning as grounded, through the language of symbolism, in experience of the sacred:

The hermeneutics of modern men is continuous with the spontaneous interpretations that have never been lacking to symbols. . . . The dissolution of the myth as explanation is the necessary way to the restoration of the myth as symbol.

Ricoeur 1969: 350

In this chapter I consider the symbolism of evil on the other side of the great epistemological divide where myth is still explanation and where the hermeneutic circle of Western scholarship has its informal equivalent in the dialogical consensus of village society, with its 'spontaneous interpretations'.

The Fipa of south-west Tanzania are Bantu cultivators who live in semi-permanent, concentrated settlements and whose ethical code enjoins sociability and non-violence (Willis). Strange to say, not only do the Fipa lack a word for 'evil' in Southwold's 'strong' sense of radical evil, but they do not have a word or expression that could properly be rendered as 'good' in the 'strong', moral English sense. A person may be 'beautiful' (*-siipa*) in appearance; but this 'beauty' (*usiifu*) may be rather less than skin-deep and may owe much to skilful impression management: 'The beauty of a person is his clothes', as a seemingly cynical aphorism has it (Willis 1978: 120).[1] The adjectival participle *-siipa* can also be applied to any man-made thing to convey approval of its aesthetic value: a finely turned wooden stool, a millet beer of pleasantly creamy texture. A related term is *-fukusu*, 'pleasing', 'well done'. Used of persons, *-fukusu* denotes pleasingly courteous behaviour; used of artefacts, it means 'serviceable', 'proper', 'clean'. As with *usiifu*, 'beauty', the substantive *ufukusu* (and the related verbal form, *-fukuka*) is used only of human beings and conveys the idea of a construct — in this case, a way of behaving rather than a physical appearance — which conforms to the elaborate and subtle code of Fipa courtesy and is experienced by others as pleasurable.

There is an asymmetry about Fipa notions of 'badness' or 'evil' (in the 'weak' sense), in that the participle - *saamsu*, 'bad' is used of persons only, never of things. I think this feature is related to a basic distinction in Fipa ideology and social experience that sees what is 'good' in human beings as openly on display, and what is 'bad' as concealed. It follows that there is an inherent uncertainty about identification of 'evil' in persons. *Asaamsu,* 'bad people', are thieves, adulterers and sorcerers. But since their nefarious activities are characteristically carried on in secret, it is not easy to know who they are; indeed, the term *-saamsu* itself is rarely heard. In contrast, material objects and social situations, like the behaviour of persons, can be evaluated immediately. Accordingly, the participle *-ųpa*[2] is used both of 'bad' things and events and of putatively lying or deceitful people whose behaviour may none the less appear impeccable. The term may thus be applied (in one sense) to sour-tasting millet beer, rotten eggs, a poorly constructed implement or a

---

[1] A similar thought is apparent in the proverbs 'The greatness of a tree is its bark' and 'The greatness of a fowl is its feathers' (Willis 1978: 120).

[2] Fipa is a seven-vowel language and I indicate sounds intermediate between the sounds *i* and *e* and *o* and *u* by the respective signs ļ and ų (cf. Willis 1978: ix).

bereavement, as when mourners are conventionally greeted '*Caaŋpa!*' ('It is bad!'), and in another sense to human beings whose 'badness' is merely inferred. Thus '*Yaŋpa!*' means both 'They are deceivers!' and 'They are bad people!' and '*Mwaŋpa!*' means both 'You are lying!' and 'You are wicked!', though the latter expression is most often heard in a jocular context, and the meaning is 'weaker' and less perjorative than *-saamsu.* This subtle modulation in the sense of the Fipa term that most nearly corresponds to the commonly used 'weak' sense (cf. chapter 8) of the English word 'evil' would seem to derive from a culturally pervasive contrast between the 'overt' and the 'covert' that I shall return to later in this chapter.

Duality is a well attested phenomenon in conceptual systems, and may be grounded in the structure of the human brain: the connection, if it exists, would appear to be with the large-scale organization of the brain, notably the lateral division of the cortex into left and right hemispheres, as Hertz (1909) had already implied, rather than with the micro-level of neuronal structure.[3] Since Hertz first drew attention to the generality of bilateral symbolism, much has been published on conceptual and symbolic dualism; a representative recent collection, apart from the curious absence of Lévi-Strauss, is Needham (1973). The form of these systems has often been misrepresented and distorted, usually through the unwarranted imposition on the ethnographic material of categories derived from Western, literate thought (Goody 1977; Beattie 1978). Nevertheless, it is now evident that the two logical principles identified by G. E. R. Lloyd in the pre-classical thought of ancient Greece — polarity and analogy (or opposition and association) — occur universally in human conceptual systems (Lloyd 1966). What has yet to be extensively studied are the various ways in which different peoples have used the basic cognitive bricks of dualism to construct edifices of symbolic meaning. Many cultures have been and are aware of dualism as a cognitive fact and see it as a problem to be transcended through various techniques and practices. Such doctrines are to be found not only in the sophisticated philosophies of the East or in the esoteric traditions of European mysticism and magic, but also in many a small-scale, non-literate society. Victor Turner has richly described Ndembu ritual aimed at resolving clusters of perceived oppositions in a moment of spiritual wholeness (Turner 1969), and Overing writes in chapter 14 below of Piaroa concern with achieving a proper balance between cosmological dualities.

In the vast east—central African culture region we have ethnographic data on relatively few dualistic systems, notably Needham (1960) on the Meru,

[3] The results of recent experimental work in psychology bearing on this problem are summarized in Trevarthen (1983).

Beidelman on the Kaguru (1961) and the Swazi (1966), Rigby (1966) on the Gogo, Willis (1967) on the Fipa, Feierman (1974) on the Shambaa and Needham (1967) and Beattie (1976) on the Nyoro. There appear to be fundamental differences, none the less, in the way these different cultures organize their social experience, in what conceptual oppositions are invested with symbolic significance and what are not. For example, in the dualistic symbolic system of the Fipa there is no trace of the opposition between 'cool' and 'hot' that dominates the ideology of the Bemba, to whom the Fipa are closely related linguistically, and which is prominent in many other cultures of east—central and southern Africa (de Heusch 1980). But apart from differences of cultural content, what is largely lacking from our understanding of symbolic dualism is a sense of how the 'givens' of dualism are experienced and manipulated by actors in different cultures. For instance, the Nuer of the southern Sudan are aware of a basic duality opposing Spirit and Creation, but they are also aware, perhaps in moments of heightened understanding, that Creation is part of Spirit in unitary wholeness (Evans-Pritchard 1956). This seeming contradiction, this assertion that one equals two, may be connected with Nuer social experience of being both autonomous and submerged in higher and more inclusive orders of structure (cf. Evans-Pritchard 1940).

The Fipa possess a dualistic cosmological system, ordered by the two principles of polarity and analogy, which is both elaborate and internally consistent (Willis 1967, 1981). Two dominant and analogical symbolic polarities, Settler/Stranger and Head/Loins, define a cognitive and semantic space that includes the lesser polarities of male and female, sky and earth, village and wilderness, senior and junior, centre and periphery, intellect and energy, etc. Whereas the opposition between culture and wild nature is salient in the symbolism of the Ndembu (Turner 1969) and in many other African cultures (cf. de Heusch 1972; Cosentino 1982), Fipa cosmology privileges the social and the personal. Moreover, and to paraphrase Bergson, the emphasis in Fipa culture is not on the ideas of duality and division, but on the unitary process by which Stranger becomes Settler, by which the energies of the lower body, the 'Loins', are converted into socially valuable action by the directing higher faculties, or 'Head'. Instead of the periodic ritual project of the Ndembu to transcend duality and achieve a momentary wholeness, Fipa appear devoted to a continual endeavour in the mundane arena of village society to achieve unity and harmony. To an extent that has surprised a succession of European visitors from the later nineteenth century onwards, the Fipa would seem to have succeeded in attaining these objectives (cf. Willis 1981: 95—7). Or at least, they have succeeded as far as surface appearances go. 'We knew there was no more peaceable race in Central Africa' according to the late nineteenth-century Scots explorer Joseph Thomson (1881, II:

201), and the Fipa of the 1960s still appeared remarkably non-violent to this anthropologist. I saw no physical fighting during the 19 months I was in Ufipa, even among children. In reality, conflict, as one might expect, is not absent from Fipa society: but it is certainly well concealed, for most of the time. I associate this appearance of social unity with an ideology that emphasizes unitary process rather than distinction between opposed categories. In general, Fipa culture is fuzzy about categorical boundaries (Willis 1974: 45—51). For instance, it seems consistent with this easygoing attitude that the Fipa, unlike many societies, are noticeably 'cool' about menstruation.[4]

The Fipa have a number of stories about the origin of the world and human society, but they are few and brief (Willis 1978: 1; 1981: 10). The missionary and amateur ethnographer J. M. Robert, who includes several in his informative account about Fipa religion, notes that 'les Wafipa eux-mêmes ne semblent pas considérer ces légendes comme le fondement principal de leurs croyances' (1949: 41). The few tales and fragments of tales of this kind that I collected referred cryptically to a cosmogonic event when the Earth separated from the Sky, falling to its present position. There was no indication of what caused this cosmic schism, nor did I notice any curiosity about it. Along with the Earth there fell the first man in the world, Ntaatakwa ('The Unnamed One'), and the aboriginal royal village of Milansi ('The Eternal Village'). But for the Fipa the most interesting and meaningful story is the traditional text which purports to describe the origin of their social order.

This text has a special status in Fipa ideology, analogous to that enjoyed by the Adamic myth in the Judaeo-Christian tradition. As Ricoeur informs us, 'The pre-eminence of the Adamic myth does not imply that the other myths are purely and simply abolished; rather, life, or new life, is given them by the privileged myth' (1969: 309). The special status of the corresponding Fipa myth, which both validates a present social order *à la* Malinowski and describes, in symbolic language, a historical transformation by which that order came into being, led me to call this text the 'key myth' of Fipa society and culture (Willis 1981). Replete with cosmological dualities, it tells the story of how the king of Ufipa, living descendant and representative of the skyborn Ntaatakwa, had his kingship usurped by the leader of three strange women, all associated symbolically with Earth, during his temporary absence in the wilderness on a hunting expedition. But in a further episode the two parties reach an agreement: in return for legitimizing the female strangers'

---

[4] I was told of no prohibitions related to menstruation. Menstrual blood occurs as an ingredient in 'medicine' used to enable a person to 'see' otherwise invisible sorcerers. It may be significant that the primary meaning of the Fipa verb 'to menstruate', —*fulala*, is 'cleanse oneself'.

rule over the bulk of Fipa territory, the king retains his ancient office with its title to ultimate authority, even though his effective power is restricted to a tiny enclave in the heart of Ufipa, the mountain site of the 'Eternal Village' of Milansi. The 'key myth' of the Fipa thus describes a transaction between two protagonists who at once represent the significant dualities in the Fipa universe and, through their primal transaction, transform the static principle of polarity into the structured process that is Fipa history, and Fipa society.

Like Ricoeur's privileged Adamic myth, the central myth of the Fipa describes an event that inaugurates history and invests it with a special meaning that also illuminates the present. As a social paradigm, the Fipa myth helps to explain why there is so little emphasis on classificatory distinctions in Fipa society, including the anthropologically classic symbolic oppositions of 'right' (*iluunji* or *ililyo*) and 'left' (*imaasu* or *kamaani*); why males and females, contrary to the segregationist norm prevailing over most of Africa (Goody 1982), sit down together to eat meals (cf. Willis); why people were so courteous and welcoming to strangers, including this anthropologist; and why evil is so hard to find.

A typical Fipa village consists of a collection of cognatic kindreds, most of which will have branches and members in a number of other and neighbouring villages. The wealthier householders in each kindred, including the elected head, are bound to their poorer fellow-members by norms of reciprocity and mutual aid and by economic ties involving the asymmetrical exchange of labour for food, particularly millet beer, resulting in a situation in which less than one-fifth (18 per cent) of the total number of householders in four representative village communities held more than half of the cultivated land (Willis 1981: 124). There is fierce and unrelenting competition between kindreds to attract members, bearers of labour power and reproductive potential. I had my first insight into how fierce this competition was shortly after arriving in Ufipa when my female patron, kindred head Magdalena Ngalawa, gave me to understand that I risked an early and painful death from poisoning by associating with people she clearly regarded as rivals and enemies. Shortly thereafter I was introduced to a companion and guide in the person of my patron's thirty-five-year-old classificatory grandson Ivor Ntile, who endeavoured, not always with success, to see that I mixed only with the better class of person.

Fipa village communities are thus arenas of clandestine conflict, where kindred heads resembling the 'big men' of Melanesian anthropology strive to retain the loyalty of their followers and to increase their numbers at their rivals' expense, and where there is substantial economic inequality (Willis 1981: 123–8). Yet Fipa norms emphasize the unitary character of the village community and the equality of the constituent householders: under the indigenous polity, according to a custom continued into the late 1960s and only formally superseded, the collectivity of householders elects the village headmen, *aeene nnsi.*[5] Since the 1920s the inherent contradiction between overt norm and clandestine reality has been periodically resolved by anti-sorcery cults in which the wealthy minority of householders in Fipa village society have been prime targets for the cultists' public denunciations, ritual branding and forcible administration of anti-sorcery 'medicine'.[6] The accused householders commonly 'confess' to causing the deaths of fellow villagers, killing livestock and damaging crops — all by occult means. The accused are probably persuaded that their 'confessions' are required by the norm of communal integrity. The 'medicine' is held to ensure the immediate death of any sorcerer who attempts to return to his wicked practices, while providing protection against sorcery to the innocent. Typically, the accused persons thereafter remain in their village communities, resuming their social roles of senior householder and patron (Willis 1968).

To be part of a village community is to be part of a benign network of caring, generosity and mutual respect that relegates the malign force of sorcery to the secret 'underlife' (Karp 1980) of village society. The anti-sorcery cults' public identification of culprits reflects no more than a momentary consensus in the continuing informal dialogue through which community members define an always-provisional collective definition of significant events. Probably because of the hidden nature of the malign 'underlife' they evoke, Fipa concepts about that life seem particularly dependent on consensual definition: the sorcerer is a shadowy figure associated with night until his ephemeral emergence into the public light of day in the exceptional situation of cultic activity. The relevance and denotation of such concepts appears inherently negotiable.

Another example connected with the clandestine is the concept of *incila*, a mysterious and potentially fatal affliction which has no visible symptoms but connotes a subjective sense of being pressed downwards as if by a great weight (Willis 1972). *Incila* has an associated verbal form *-cila*, meaning 'to cause a third party to be afflicted with sickness, or cause an existing sickness to

---

[5] Those so elected were invariably from the less influential kindreds in each village community, according to my observations.

[6] The regularity with which these cults arise every ten years has still to be explained. The latest outbreak in Ufipa occurred in 1974, a decade after the last reported upsurge in 1963–4 (Willis 1968, and personal communication from Mr Joseph Mullen). I suspect a connection with cyclical changes in rainfall, linked in turn to the solar cycle of 11.2 years, which is about the period between the appearance of one cult in Ufipa and the appearance of the next.

worsen, by contact with that third party, after entering into an adulterous relationship'. A woman in labour can be so afflicted by her husband's adultery, or a nursing infant may similarly suffer from the adultery of either parent, who may also afflict one another. An unfaithful spouse who approaches the bedside of a sick partner will make his or her sickness worse. Death will ensue unless appropriate magico-medical remedies are taken.

The *-cila* concept belongs to the clandestine 'underlife', being associated with illicit sexuality and akin to sorcery in its association with the secret infliction of injury.[7] It is inherently ambiguous and indefinitely negotiable. The lack of any visible and objective symptoms signals its clandestine essence. Secrecy is also inherent in adulterous liaisons. The negotiations that decide whether or not the *-cila* concept is relevant to a particular case of affliction may well include the partners to a marriage, the kinsfolk of the afflicted person and the local indigenous doctor (*sing'aanga*) whose diagnosis will typically be framed, as numerous studies of African systems of divination have demonstrated, in accordance with his skilled perception of local consensus (cf. Turner 1975: 237).

There is a built-in tautology in a conceptual and moral system like that of the Fipa in which evil is consigned to a covert domain of which one may not speak but can merely insinuate, to borrow Wittgenstein's well-known aphorism on the limits of language. A person's polished and agreeable exterior may conceal unimaginable depths of depravity. Fipa folk tales often feature horrendous beings called *ifituumbu* who appear and behave like ordinary human beings but in reality are cannibalistic monsters. Their real nature is apparent only on close acquaintance with these monsters, who love to fatten up and then devour their guests (Willis 1978). Such behaviour is inconceivable in human beings (cf. Pocock's 'inexplicable evil' in chapter 3 above); hence a standard phrase in these Fipa tales: 'they were not people, they were cannibalistic monsters' ('yataal' aantu, yaal' ifituumbu').

Yet the covert domain is not entirely evil. This becomes apparent when we examine the full range of concepts cognate with the Fipa notion of the covert, hidden, obscure. The key term is *ufiisu,* the primary meaning of which is 'black' or 'dark', but which also has the extended meaning of 'hidden', 'secret', 'private', as well as 'pollution' or 'defilement'. Related terms are the nouns *akafiiso,* a private or hidden place, *amafii,* excrement, *ufii,* lies, and the verbs *-fiisa,* to hide or conceal, the reversive form *-fiisula,* to explain the meaning of a cryptic saying, such as a proverb, and *-fiina,* to bewitch or ensorcell.[8] The

---

[7] This concept, and the root *-cila* (or *-kira*), appear to be widely distributed in East Africa (see Parkin 1978).

[8] The verb *-fiina* patently has a distinct etymology from the Fipa noun *uloosi,* sorcery, and *aloosi* (s. *unndoosi*), sorcerers.

verbal form of *ufiisu,* 'black', which is *-fiita,* to blacken or darken, is used not only with the sense of dirt and pollution, as in

(1) big cloths keep on getting dirty
    imyeenda imikulu ikulu*fiita*

but also in the distinctly different senses of

(2) to give someone a return gift
    fiita um'minwe (lit., 'to blacken the fingers')

and

(3) to become pregnant
    fiita uku'mwiili (literally, 'to blacken the body')

The meanings of the somewhat puzzling metaphors in (2) and (3) can be elucidated by considering the significance of black in ritual contexts. In the traditional Fipa wedding ceremony both bride and groom wear black cloths around their lower body and loins.[9] After the marriage ceremony the bride continues to wear this cloth until she has born a child for her husband. Another example of the ritual use of black occurs during ironsmelting, when the newly built kiln, *iluungu,* is painted black and represented as a pregnant woman. In magical operations concerned with the germination and growth of crops, black is the prescribed colour for sacrificial animals.

These various examples from linguistic usage and ritual suggest that the symbolic meaning of the colour black in Fipa cosmology has a polar structure. At one pole are the negative attributes, which cover a wide range, from its association with shit to metaphorical associations with lies, with the unknown perils of the night, with the hearts of sorcerers and all those with grudges against their fellows (cf. Willis 1972), with malign ancestral spirits, called *ifiiswa* (s. *iciiswa*), the ghosts of sorcerers, suicides, creditors and women who die in childbirth, and with sorcery, *uloosi,* itself. But there is also a complementary, positive semantic pole, where 'black' symbolizes the mysterious creation of new life, or of new wealth as in the ore invisibly formed by the ironsmelting kiln.[10] The expression 'to blacken the fingers'

---

[9] The cloth worn by the groom is called *ikafiifii,* a word apparently related to the 'black' root, *-fii*. The bride's cloth is called *inkuwaalo.*

[10] Fipa appear to make a sharp contrast between the *creation* of wealth, natural or artificial, and the *invention* of novel artefacts. The latter activity belongs to the realm of 'inexplicable evil' since it is associated with the monstrous *ifituumbu.* This word itself is based on the root *-tuumbuka,* which has the dual senses of 'invent' and 'burst out' (as the contents of a squashed tomato).

used of gift exchange shows the Fipa to be Maussian *avant la lettre.* 'Black' here symbolizes the yet-unrealized good that gift-giving can produce, the incalculable ways in which generosity bears fruit.

Black, *ufiisu,* the symbolic index of the underlife, is thus a duality that opposes a cluster of ideas concerned with pollution, defilement and occult danger, with another cluster concerned with ideas of creation and generation. But to understand the full significance of the symbol black we need to consider it in relation to two other symbolic colours in Fipa cosmology: red and white.

It seems likely that physiological factors underlying visual perception in all human beings have produced the high incidence in non-literate cultures of symbol systems that exploit the chromatic differences of white, black and red (see also Inden, chapter 9 above). V. W. Turner has suggested that the white—black—red triad is 'a primordial classification of reality' that is common to all human beings because rooted in physiological experience (1966: 81). Since Turner's now classic paper, Berlin and Kay (1969) have produced evidence for the existence of universal 'focal colours' in human perception and suggested an evolutionary schema in which white/black, and then red, are the first colours to be nominally distinguished in all cultures. Subsequent experiments designed to test the Berlin—Kay thesis on focal colours have pointed to a pre-linguistic structuration of colour perception in human cognitive development (Heider 1972: 20). What has still not been adequately explained, or, given the physiologically based universality of the three symbolic hues, is the reason why the triadic form is so widespread in non-literate cultures. Before suggesting an answer to this question, however, I must complete the analysis of the system of meanings embodied in the Fipa colour triad.

In that triad, red (*ukasuke*) is both analogous to black and distinct from it. Structurally, red is a mirror image of black, since it is also polarized into positive and negative clusters of concepts. At the positive pole red includes the concepts of energy, movement, labour, sexual and reproductive powers; the negative pole includes warfare, killing and all other expressions of physical violence, including the pain and bloodshed of childbirth (cf. Willis 1967, 1981). Like black, red connotes action and change. But where the action and change symbolized by black occurs in a domain of occult obscurity, the domain of symbolic red is overt and public.[11]

---

[11] Childbirth is an event that concerns the whole community, and particularly the female community, whose representatives in the village, the senior women called *amaloombwe,* assume authority in the mother's hut during the birth period. The husband is treated by these women as a servant, ordered to bring foodstuffs, cut firewood, etc.

White (*utiswe*) is the remaining member of the triad and, as will be seen, in a sense its primary member. *Utiswe* connotes ideas of clarity (from the verb *-swefya*, to become white or clear) and forgiveness (the verb *-tisya* to forgive, and *itisyo*, forgiveness). Opposed to the negative associations of black with pollution, defilement, sorcery, malign spiritual powers and death, white in Fipa symbology is associated with purity, beneficent intentions, such as are normally attributed to indigenous doctors, sometimes called 'doctors of life' (*asing'aanga ya uumi*), with benign spiritual powers, and with life itself. In opposition to red, a different set of concepts is associated with white. These include most importantly the ideas of kingship, social seniority and intellect (Willis 1967, 1981). It is apparent that there is a qualitative difference between the two kinds of ideas evoked by the 'white' symbol when opposed to each of the other two members of the triad. Yet these ideas are not polarized into positive and negative concepts in the way that 'red' and 'black' ideas are polarized. In contrast to the dualistic structure informing the concepts associated with both red and black, white is a unitary category. It simply manifests differently in the opposed domains of the hidden or covert, symbolized by black, and in the overt or public red domain. The white—black opposition is evoked in ritual contexts, which is to say that its evocation is discontinuous; the white—red opposition is inherent in Fipa social ideology and is therefore continuously, if implicitly, present; as mentioned earlier, Fipa culture gives prominence to the interactive process between the structural categories of the public domain, rather than their duality. The complex of ideas organized by the colour triad is represented in figure 1.

This diagram shows white with a privileged position in the symbolic triad. It presides over and brings together the separated domains of the overt and the covert, the red and the black. This separation is so absolute that Fipa never pair red and black symbols, making symbolic oppositions only between red/white and black/white. This conceptual hiatus corresponds to the repressed status of the subterranean 'underlife' of village society, the 'negative black' area of deception and occult injury. Turner describes a broadly similar configuration of ideas when he says of the Ndembu colour triad:

white seems to be dominant and unitary, red ambivalent, for it is both fecund and 'dangerous', while black is, as it were, the silent partner, the 'shadowy third', in a sense opposed to both white and red, since it represents 'death', 'sterility', and 'impurity'. Yet . . . in its full significance black shares certain senses with both white and red, and it is not felt to be wholly malignant.

Turner 1966:57

Ages before Newton discovered experimentally that white light subsumes all

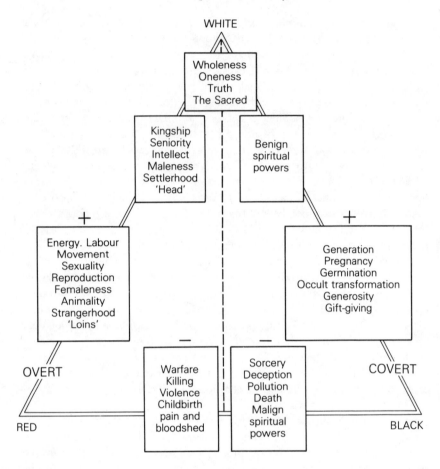

FIGURE 1   The Fipa colour triad

spectral colours, white has symbolized oneness and wholeness for the generality of humankind, as Turner has already implied (1966: 81—3). The 'white' symbol in non-literate societies would be cognitively equivalent to Buddhistic concepts of the Void, wherein all distinctions and dualities disappear (cf. Watts 1957) or the 'Cloud of Unknowing' of Christian mysticism. The experience evoked in these literate traditions and represented by the white symbol is one that obliterates all distinctions and hence can never be described in words. Attempts to do so inevitably issue in contradiction and paradox, as when Ndembu tried to render a picture of the white spirit Kavula:

He is an ambiguous and self-contradictory being who both conceals and reveals himself, who is a god and not a god, a man and not a man, an ancestor spirit and not an ancestor spirit. He brings misfortune on the Ndembu and brings benefits to them. He reviles his adepts and promises to help them. He is likened to a great chief but is slain like a slave. . . .

Turner 1975: 179

The symbolic triad is the structure that most parsimoniously accommodates the conceptual principles of both dualism and monism, hierarchy and opposition. If the widespread occurrence in unrelated cultures of the colours white, black and red is evidence of humankind's evolutionary heritage, the generally privileged position of the 'white' symbol is, on this hypothesis, evidence of a universal religious quest for wholeness. This is an experience that dissolves the moral antinomy of 'good' and 'evil' along with all other cognitive dualities; conversely, as Pocock makes clear in chapter 3 above, awareness of this ideal state also, and inevitably, compels recognition of defect, failure, 'evil'. Evidently the religious quest takes various and divergent forms in different cultures. In modern Western civilization it appears to have been largely secularized and collectivized under the sign of the Technological Imperative. The Fipa attempt to make of sociality a religious experience; yet the shadow of evil remains, ineluctably part of the scheme of things, only just beyond the limits of polite society.

REFERENCES

Arendt, H. (1963). *Eichmann in Jerusalem: A Report on the Banality of Evil.* London: Faber and Faber

Beattie, J.H.M. (1976). 'Right, Left and the Banyoro'. *Africa,* 46: 217—35

Beattie, J.H.M. (1978). 'Nyoro Symbolism and Nyoro Ethnography: A Rejoinder'. *Africa,* 48(3): 278—95

Beidelman, T.O. (1961). 'Right and Left Hand among the Kaguru: A Note on Symbolic Classification'. *Africa,* 31: 250—7

Beidelman, T.O. (1966). 'Swazi Royal Ritual'. *Africa,* 36: 373—405

Berlin, B. and Kay, P. (1969). *Basic Color Terms.* Berkeley: University of California Press

Cosentino, D. (1982). *Defiant Maids and Stubborn Farmers: Tradition and Invention in Mende Story Performance.* Cambridge: Cambridge University Press

Ellul, J. (1965). *The Technological Society.* London: Jonathan Cape

Evans-Pritchard, E.E. (1940). *The Nuer.* Oxford: Clarendon Press

Evans-Pritchard, E.E. (1956). *Nuer Religion.* Oxford: Clarendon Press

Feierman, S. (1974). *The Shambaa Kingdom.* Madison: University of Wisconsin Press

Goody, J. (1977). *The Domestication of the Savage Mind.* Cambridge: Cambridge University Press

Goody, J. (1982). *Cooking, Cuisine and Class.* Cambridge: Cambridge University Press

Granet, M. (1933). 'La Droite et la Gauche en Chine'. Communication to the Institut Français de la Sociologie, 9 June; reprinted in M. Granet, *Etudes sociologiques sur la Chine.* Paris: Presses Universitaires de France, 1953: 261–78

Green, D. (1983). 'Passages to the Otherworld'. *The Hermetic Journal,* 22: 24–30

Heider, E.R. (1972). 'Probabilities, Sampling and Ethnographic Method; the Case of Dani Colour Names', *Man,* n.s., 7, 3: 448–66

Hertz, R. (1909). 'La Pré-éminence de la main droite: étude sur la polarité religieuse', *Revue philosophique,* 68: 553–80

de Heusch, L. (1972). *Le roi ivre.* Paris: Gallimard

de Heusch, L. (1980). '"Hot" and "Cool" in Thonga Thought', in I. Karp and C. S. Bird (eds), *Explorations in African Systems of Thought.* Bloomington: Indiana University Press

de Heusch, L. (1982). *Rois nés d'un coeur de vache.* Paris: Gallimard

Karp, I. (1980). 'Beer Drinking and Social Experience in an African Society', in I. Karp and C. S. Bird (eds), *Explorations in African Systems of Thought,* Bloomington: Indiana University Press

Leach, E.R. (1969). *Genesis as Myth and Other Essays.* London: Jonathan Cape

Lloyd, G.E.R. (1966). *Polarity and Analogy.* Cambridge: University Press

Needham, R. (1960). 'The Left Hand of the Mugwe: An Analytical Note on the Structure of Meru Symbolism', *Africa,* 30: 28–33

Needham, R. (1967). 'Right and Left in Nyoro Symbolic Classification', *Africa,* xxxvii: 425–51

Needham, R. (ed.)(1973). *Right and Left: Essays in Symbolic Classification.* Chicago: University of Chicago Press

Parkin, D. (1978). *The Cultural Definition of Political Response: lineal destiny among the Luo.* London: Academic Press

Ricoeur, P. (1969). *The Symbolism of Evil.* Boston: Beacon Press

Rigby, P. (1966). 'Dual Symbolic Classification among the Gogo of Central Tanzania'. *Africa,* 36: 1–16

Robert, J.M. (1949). *Croyances et coutumes magico-religieuses des Wafipa païens.* Tabora: Tanganyika Mission Press

Thomson, J. (1881). *To the Central African Lakes and Back* (2 vols). London: Cass

Trevarthen, C. (1983). 'Development of the Cerebral Mechanisms for Language'. In U. Kirk (ed.), *Neuropsychology of Language Reading and Spelling.* New York: Academic Press

Turner, V.W. (1966). 'Colour Classification in Ndembu Ritual'. In M. Banton (ed.), *Anthropological Approaches to the Study of Religion.* London: Tavistock

Turner, V.W. (1969). *The Ritual Process.* London: Routledge & Kegan Paul.

Turner, V.W. (1975). *Revelation and Divination in Ndembu Ritual.* Ithaca: Cornell University Press

Watts, A.W. (1957). *The Way of Zen.* London: Thames and Hudson

Willis, R.G. (1967). 'The Head and the Loins: Lévi-Strauss and Beyond'. *Man,* n.s., 2(4): 519—34

Willis, R.G. (1968). 'Kamcape: An Anti-sorcery Movement in Southwest Tanzania'. *Africa,* 38(1): 1—15

Willis, R.G. (1972). 'Pollution and Paradigms'. *Man,* 7(3): 369—78

Willis, R.G. (1974). *Man and Beast.* London: Basic Books

Willis, R.G. (1978). *There was a Certain Man.* London: Oxford University Press

Willis, R.G. (1981). *A State in the Making: Myth, History, and Social Transformation in Pre-colonial Ufipa.* Bloomington: Indiana University Press

Willis, R.G. 'Power Begins at Home: The Politics of Male—Female Commensality in Ufipa'. In W. Arens and I. Karp (eds), *The Symbolism of Power Relations.* Bloomington: Indiana University Press

13

Entitling evil: Muslims and
non-Muslims in coastal Kenya

*David Parkin**

Many of the chapters in this volume note the difficulties in ethnocentrically imposing on other cultures the senses of the English word 'evil'. Let me begin the other way round and assume, for the moment, some common awareness of evil acts, thereafter raising the question of how and to what extent certain kinds of behaviour and phenomena come to be identified by this or a comparable term.

In his study of the personification of evil, J. B. Russell provides vivid examples of human acts that few readers of this volume would hesitate to call evil. He takes Dostoevsky's description of a terrified mother with babe in arms. She is surrounded by invading marauders who play with the baby, make it laugh, let it reach out happily for a pistol held in front of it, and then blow its brains out. A modern news story from the United States is of a drug-distressed sixteen-year-old girl who had slashed her wrists and arms and, rushing to the steps of a church, held a razor to her throat. A large crowd gathered and, delighted at the spectacle, cheered her on to finish the job, cheering still further when the girl collapsed from loss of blood. An example taken from Solzhenitsyn is of an eight-year-old girl who, before her father's execution, had been a normal, happy, healthy child, but thereafter never smiled again, and died a year later of inflammation of the brain, calling for her papa as she died (Russell 1977: 17–19).

Within as well as between cultures, people may have strongly differing views as to whether a particular act is morally evil. We also witness cases of human suffering that may hint at, yet cannot easily be called, evil. I met a troubling instance during my fieldwork among the Giriama and Swahili in

* Like others, I have benefited from the general contribution of colleagues and especially thank Lionel Caplan, Brian Moeran and Joanna Overing for their written comments.

Kenya, and I introduce it here in order to show that it is often our uncertainty as to whether an act is evil or not that disturbs us as much as the clear realization that evil has been committed. When there is no doubt among us that evil has been done, we can at least join forces against it, perhaps resolving, if we can, never to let it happen again. But when our experience of the act leaves us with nagging uncertainty, nothing gets done: the horrible act may have been justified, but why, then, should it disturb us for years afterwards? And even if the uncertainty is resolved in favour of a firm decision that the act *was* evil, does not this then present the more general moral problem: why was there hesitancy in the first place? And how just can a decision be that was preceded by so much uncertainty?

In the compound next to the village in which I and my family lived was a young Giriama mother with two children. One was a suckling baby, and the other a two-and-half-year-old girl. This little girl was sick with what was, I could easily tell, the protein-deficiency disease called kwashiorkor. But the parents and other relatives were not aware of diseases caused by malnutrition. 'People may die of hunger, but how can they die when they receive at least some food?' Advanced kwashiorkor in young children has a secondary effect of progressively limiting the amount of food that can be taken in. The child was clearly dying. But what kind of affliction did the Giriama themselves think had gripped the child?

Here begins the puzzle. My family offered the parents eggs to mix up in watered-down maize porridge: it had done the trick before. We offered also to take the child to a distant mission hospital. The father seemed genuinely concerned, and accepted our interference. But he seemed unwilling to intervene between his wife and the sick child. He stood on the periphery, so to speak, clearly anxious for the child, and giving it great care and affection, but always as if constrained. It was obvious that the mother did not give the eggs to the child. Eggs are not, it is true, customarily eaten, being left to hatch normally. But there is otherwise no prohibition on their use as food. So why did the mother not take up the suggestions of her husband and others around her?

The mother gave the firm impression that she had given up on the child, that she was literally leaving it to die. She would wave it away dismissively when it came to her, withdrawing all show of affection. More than this, she would laugh at the child's whimpering cries of distress as the child groped towards her. There was a sad air of confusion among the Giriama who were around as the child got worse, but the matter was not talked about. People would only say that the child was sick, but would not elaborate beyond that. Within a few weeks the child died. The mother carried on as if the child had not existed, and the child was never mentioned again in ordinary conversation.

I, however, did ask for an explanation of the mother's behaviour. The Giriama themselves could not agree on one. Some vaguely suggested that the mother had acted as she did to contain a contagious affliction which would affect the second child. *Mavingane* and *kirwa* are the names of two such afflictions, each caused, though in different ways, by adultery or incest on the part of a parent or by some breach of an avoidance taboo between senior and junior relatives. *Kirwa* is like *ncila* among the Fipa described in chapter 12, and both are instances of an Africa-wide spread of etymologically linked concepts (see Parkin 1978: 142–64; 327–30). Other Giriama countered that, had such afflictions been diagnosed, the mother could have sought therapy to reverse their effects, secretly if necessary; but she did not.

Was, then, the child herself in some way evil? For instance, a child who is born feet first, or one whose first two top teeth grow before his or her bottom ones, is believed to bring misfortune or to become a deviant, being considered in much the same way as twins in a number of societies. Traditionally, and still often today, the child will be killed. This is done not by the mother but by an old (probably unrelated) woman. The child is taken to a tree-shaded area (*muhi wa peho*, literally, cold, damp or shady tree) and there drowned by immersion of the head. The body is not buried but is thrown into the surrounding bush, the place being called *katsaka ka ana ai*, literally, the copse of bad/evil children. A child is about six months old when it cuts its first teeth, and mothers desperately try to prevent the child's slaughter. Elders, notably the Vaya (see below), will insist that it be carried out, and the government chief or sub-chief can do little more than advise the parents to move to another area. The parents would thereafter be obliged to move on to other areas every two years or so as news of the 'bad child' catches up with them. There is no evidence that parents acquiesce in the elimination of breech birth children or those who cut their top teeth first. Indeed, the Giriama understand the conflict between parental love and the danger to the community that such children bring. Again, in the case I am considering the mother's behaviour did not fit this pattern.

Some Giriama opined that the mother ridiculed the child in an attempt to mock capricious and destructive forces that might have possessed her. But it was unclear why the mother should do this and why she did not agree to rituals being carried out which might appease any possessing spirit. An outside observer might speculate that the mother was trying to distance herself emotionally from the child, being convinced that the child would die. But other mothers do not do this, and other Giriama did not venture this as an explanation of her behaviour. Nor was it suggested that the mother was intrinsically evil, mad or possessed by a spirit. The business remained a puzzle.

Nevertheless, witnessing the event was for the Giriama and myself a horrifying experience, in which, from my perspective at least, something approaching a sense of evil was very strongly present. Yet we could *not* say with assurance that either the mother or some spirit or force was the evil agent. If evil was present, its agency was indeterminate.

My own response alone may suggest a paradox in Western thinking about evil. On the one hand, this indeterminacy, uncertainty and hesitancy in defining particular acts as evil may be profoundly disturbing, perhaps by its moral incompleteness. On the other hand, there is sometimes comfort in suspending moral judgement in this way, the corollary being the indignation often felt towards those indivdiuals or regimes that claim to know without further question what is and is not evil.

Uncertainty here acts as a buffer between people's indignation at having evil defined for them in an authoritarian manner and that which they claim 'naturally' to feel with regard to the kinds of behaviour with which I began this chapter, which they may unambiguously hold to be evil. Uncertainty protects people from either of these two possibilities. It is part of the existential experience of evil before it is socially and even politically defined as such by rules, norms and language.

A consequence of this shift in the direction of defining experiences unambiguously as evil is the tendency to subdivide evil: people may speak of evil in the strong as against weak sense, of inexplicable and explicable evil, and of unforgivable and forgivable evil (see chapters 3 and 8 above). The metaphorical implications of this kind of subdivision are that evil is a quantifiable commodity and that its status can be negotiated. The further ontological implication is that evil can therefore be transacted (since it is both a commodity and negotiable) and redirected to different 'owners' or 'producers'. In other words, the blame for any evil act can be shifted, or its severity reduced, to the extent even of excusing the original perpetrator.

In short, then, naming experiences as evil sets up a tension as to whether people continue to regard them as absolutely so, or whether, by distinguishing types of evil, they effectively excuse some of them. Another moral dilemma arises from this tension. To refuse to reconsider whether and how much acts and agencies are evil is uncharitable by the prevailing standards of modern Western liberalism. Yet to be charitable in this way is, in the eyes of some other fellow members of society, to condone unacceptable behaviour and situations.

In this chapter I wish to see how far this moral dilemma arises among other peoples. I discuss how far the consciousness of evil as a concept helps us understand the limits of human charity. I find that, in societies in which evil is not verbalized in any clear manner, human frailties are more tolerantly accepted; that is to say, they are regarded as shared by everyone. By contrast, where the idea of evil is especially marked, people seem less likely to take the view that the evil in others is potentially that which exists in all of us. Evil is here more likely to be the work and ultimate responsibility of other persons or peoples, and even of a God.

The argument is woven into the ethnography of two neighbouring peoples of Kenya, the Swahili, who are Muslim, and the Mijikenda, who are not. (The Giriama, whom I have already mentioned, are the largest sub-group of the Mijikenda, but I shall henceforth speak only of the latter.) As is often the case with neighbouring peoples, the non-Muslim Mijikenda and the Muslim Swahili claim to be culturally the obverse of each other in many respects, while at the same time sharing some important customary practices and beliefs. One difference concerns the relative value they each place on hierarchy and egalitarianism. While the Mijikenda expect people to resemble each other and as much as possible to be equal, the Swahili emphasize personal differences of worth and status.[1] Among both peoples, terms of personal evaluation highlight this difference: people are 'good' or 'bad' according to the respective moral precepts.

The Swahili appear to have a larger vocabulary of words denoting destructive and malicious behaviour than the Mijikenda, but some of these terms are of Arabic origin and often refer to offences against Islam. As among the Mijikenda, the everyday words are commonly Bantu. In neither of the (closely related) languages of the two peoples are there words that correspond to the English ones proportionally distinguishing 'evil' (as 'very bad') and 'bad'. On the other hand, contextual uses indicate different strengths of feeling towards an inauspicious, unwanted or harmful event or perpetrator, and in both languages there are a number of descriptive terms denoting personal characteristics of wickedness, lust, cruelty, malice, envy, jealousy and greed. An important feature of the most common terms, to which I shall refer in more detail towards the end of this chapter, is that they presuppose the idea of 'good' and 'bad' being visible.

Both peoples personify malicious and destructive behaviour and situations — what I am translating as evil — in varying ways and degrees. Neither really has an idea of absolute evil, though the Swahili concept of Satan and their clerics' views on alcohol and the animistic practices of the non-Muslim Mijikenda are almost that. Among the Mijikenda themselves, witches in general are evil. More ambivalently a potentially very evil agency, who may in

---

[1] Ethnographically, it is proper to refer to the Muslims as Intermediary Swahili, for they are mostly of Mijikenda descent and can rarely demonstrate membership of any of the 'aristocratic' (*waungwana*) Swahili 'tribes'.

other contexts actually be called a witch, is a member of the much-feared human secret society called the Vaya. The Vaya, it will be remembered, are prime among those who insist that 'bad children' be killed in order to avert misfortune befalling a community.

The old men who make up the Vaya are traditional figures who long preceded colonial times and who, from time to time, were regarded by colonial district officers as legitimate authorities. But this recognition was at best ambivalent and often withdrawn, and has become virtually non-existent in independent Kenya. The Vaya make up the most exclusive Mijikenda secret society: only the most aged elders are eligible, but they are approached by existing Vaya elders and do not themselves apply. They are seen as representatives of each significant section of clans. As with all the societies, there is among the Vaya an internal division between novices and experts, the latter making up the inner circle who possess awesomely powerful medicinal, magical and ritual secrets. This inner circle, sometimes called 'the elders of the hyaena' (*azhere a fisi*), live or are based in the traditional capital, called the Kaya, which is enclosed by a forest and, still today, is not normally entered by other persons.

Even though their methods are often condemned by government, the Vaya elders exercise much of their influence and authority through their control of the hyaena oath (*kiraho cha fisi*). Oath-taking inspires awe and terror in a number of African societies (e.g. the Kikuyu during the Mau Mau movement and in much later post-independence years), and Giriama society is no exception. Yet, while the Vaya are feared for their role as oath-givers, and are seen as inevitably hard-hearted, sinister and, through occasional capriciousness, evil, they are also regarded as necessary.

Admittedly, they are evil only in the weak sense, for it is only through occasional abuse of their powers that the Vaya may be evil. To a lesser extent, the same can be said of herbalists and diviners who, after falling from grace, may be accused of being witches or sorcerors. The Vaya, however, most closely personify the proposition that evil is necessary.

In the case of the Swahili, evil is never necessary. Satan fell from grace but no one needs him. It is not that, by allowing Satan to continue his maleficence, God is impotent. Rather, it is that God has relinquished concern in the affair; man is responsible for Satan, and so it is up to man to drive out the evil that Satan represents.

This contrast between necessary and unnecessary evil among the Mijikenda and Swahili respectively has implications for their ontologies. Among the Mijikenda everyone in some respects resembles everyone else, and should often strive to do so. Therefore the Vaya are merely what other Mijikenda are but to a greater degree. At the lower end of the ladder of capriciousness, possessionary spirits are also rather mischievious, sometimes very bad, but again mirror people's own lusts and frailties. The spirits, however, unlike the Vaya (and herbalists and diviners), are not at all necessary. They are nuisances and do people no good at all.

As part of an ontological complementarity, the Vaya and spirits present a puzzle. Vaya are evil, but resemble ordinary people in this respect. They represent the necessity in all Mijikenda for evil. The spirits are bad rather than evil, but also resemble people. They do not, however, represent any need for people to be contrary. Phrased as a general Mijikende proposition, it can be said that humans sometimes need to be evil, like the Vaya, but they don't need to be contrary and capricious, like the spirits. Phrased differently again, being a nuisance is not a necessary human trait; being evil is.

As human traits, whether necessary or not, both contrariness and evil are excesses of behaviour. But the contrariness of spirits is the more easily avoidable, for few spirits are that clever. They may, for instance, demand a white horse in sacrifice, but you can fool them with a white goat or even a chicken, by simply calling it a white horse. The spirits are not regarded as likely to have seen a horse, though they will have heard that it has rarity value, and are assumed to be asking for one only out of an inflated sense of self-importance.

The threats of the Vaya elder and the effects of his hyaena oath are, however, irreversible. You *must* speak the truth in the confession accompanying the oath-taking, and you must have good intentions thereafter. Failure to comply with these requirements will cause the oath-taker's death, and there are many vivid cases given to illustrate this. When this legitimate oracular power is abused by the Vaya elders who possess it, then this is an excess of behaviour that becomes an irremovable evil. It is a kind of sorcery or witchcraft motivated by the Vaya's own human weakness of anger, greed, revenge and malice. The Vaya can act as a court of appeal against other witches. But when Vaya themselves become malevolent, there is no recourse to a higher appeal. No confession will help. Here, the Mijikenda implicitly recognize that absolute authorities inevitably combine the powers of both good and evil in their persona (see Southall 1979).

The difference for the Swahili is that no human agency is regarded in this light. Humans may certainly have different amounts of good and evil in them, but their malevolence is not a necessary condition of their status and being. While the (non-Christian) Mijikenda have an extraordinarily feeble notion of a High God, the Swahili couple God and Satan together as making up the inevitable and absolute forces of good and evil in the world. In other words, the Swahili transpose to a level of divinity what the Mijikenda keep among humans. For the Mijikenda, it is humans who necessarily embody the worst of evil; for the Swahili it is a fallen god, Satan himself, who never was human.

This actually fits the different ontological emphases of the two peoples. The Mijikenda are supposed to be like each other, and so it is consistent that humans and not gods or demons should be capable of the worst and best acts against fellow-humans. Morality is, so to speak, kept within the human family: it is, indeed, a matter of family resemblances. Among the Swahili, morality is very much more a matter of triangular negotiation between humans, God and Satan and his demonic manifestations.

Among the Mijikenda, then, evil is both a necessary part of the human condition and yet also a form of excessive behaviour: it consists of acts and intentions that simply go too far, cause damage, yet stem from a power that people need in other contexts. There are here similarities with the Piaroa Amerindians described by Overing in the next chapter. Among the Swahili, evil is also excessive behaviour, but is quite unnecessary for humans, having been foisted on mankind by the negative forces of divinity. For the Swahili the problem of what to do with evil is relatively clear: control excesses of behaviour and you eliminate it. Hence the highly moralistic sermons and teachings of the Muslim clerics. This is not to say that the Swahili see themselves as on the point of clearing away all evil. But at least this expurgation becomes a theoretical possibility. Unlike the Pancaratra Vaishnavas discussed in chapter 9 by Inden, the Swahili theory of morality is based on this assumption, however much of an ideal it appears to us in practice. The Mijikenda also try to contain the excesses of behaviour, through attempts to control sorcery and by keeping a respectful distance from the Vaya elders. But, because they see evil as a necessary condition of humanity, and as not residing in any more ultimate source than that of man's own intentions, its elimination is for them not even a theoretical possibility. To eradicate evil completely would be to alter the way people naturally are, and that is impossible. The problem of how to deal with evil is, then, for the Mijikenda a complex one: contain the excesses of which evil behaviour is made up, yet recognize that this same excessive behaviour is part of the humanity of the Vaya elders whom ordinary folk need and whom they resemble by virtue of also being human. Pushed further, we would have to say that, for the Mijikenda, evil behaviour, being necessary, must therefore be good. That is to say, if the Vaya elders are needed, then they must be good for society: and, if the occasionally capricious and evil acts of the Vaya elders are part of what makes people fear and obey them, then those evil acts themselves must also be good for society. This is, indeed, how Mijikenda have argued when discussing the Vaya.

As an outside Western observer, how do I react to these two views of evil among the Swahili and Mijikenda? I think that it is fair to say that the Swahili view more closely corresponds with my own, whether or not I believe in God. Thus, most Western social and political systems are premised on the assumption, however Utopian or hypocritical, that the lot of humanity should progressively be improved and that wanton malevolence, like poverty, should eventually be eliminated. By contrast, few Westerners would concur with the Mijikenda view, which I am abstracting, that evil is (1) necessary for effective authority, and (2) an ineradicable feature of being human. Even fewer would wish to go further and say that, in some degree, evil is actually good for them, and that all they hope to do is to try to limit the necessary dosage. (Fortunately, at least, the Mijikenda do not push the proposition to the extent of arguing that, if evil is good, then the more of it the better.)

This non-Utopian view, then, is that a little evil keeps people in order through the fear that it instils in them, but that they can at least try to contain its excesses. Is it a pessimistic or optimistic viewpoint? On the one hand, it places ultimate responsibility for man's destiny in his own actions and intentions rather than in those of a divinity or divinities. Morality is to that extent recognized as man-made. This can be seen as a kind of optimistic clear-thinking that precludes any need for de-mystification. At the same time, however, the view precludes the promise of a significant improvement in men's relations with each other. People need the Vaya's oracular power to take away controllable evils like sorcery, and the price for such services is to suffer the Vaya's own bad tempers and occasional injustices. This can be seen as a rather pessimistic view of a constantly recyclable evil. Thus, the hatred and envy of others cause sorcery and the death and the sickness of a person's loved ones and the loss of his material achievements: these evils can be contained only by the power and potentially greater evil of the hyaena and other oaths; but the oracle points out the evil-doers and brings malice to the victim's own heart, resulting in his own sorcery against them. He is therefore himself likely to be forced to take an oath, and so on.

Except that the notion of recyclable evil is repetitive, it is a remarkably static view of morality. It promises no way out to a world in which evil is absent or at least substantially reduced, or can progressively be transcended and perhaps wholly conquered.

Is this view of a recycled and static morality typical of all religions we conventionally call animistic? Much, of course, depends on notions of an afterworld and on the extent to which ancestors are believed to live a better life. Nevertheless, though there are some variations in this respect, it is remarkable how frequently the lot of ancestors in animistic religions continues to be dogged by human-like emotions. Ancestors experience envy, anger and greed, but can also reciprocate human generosity and, sometimes on impulse, can bless their descendants, though usually only after special supplications. It would seem that the Vaya elder in death is not much different from the Vaya alive. Like other men, he never transcends but perpetuates his human frailties.

This static morality assumes a cyclical form in another context, namely the periodic anti-sorcery or witch-finding movements. These spring up every so often among the Mijikenda and among other peoples throughout Black Africa and have themselves been called cyclical or repetitive (Willis 1968). It is important here to recognize how this static, self-producing morality actually conforms to the Mijikenda stress on resemblance and equivalence among themselves. That is to say, just as people should differ from each other as little as possible — or, at least, their differences should be reducible to a common level — so repetitive witch-hunting movements occur which reproduce common themes, while being cast in a novel idiom contemporary with the times.

What are the themes that are reproduced in these movements? First, let me briefly describe one of these witch-finding activities which I happened to witness while in the field in 1966. The movement was certainly frightening. I shared some of the fear felt by people around me. It was headed by a young witch-finder believed to have miraculous powers of detection. He had a powerful personality, easily capable of drawing a crowd with his rhetorical denunciations and his demonstrations of magical devices. He would sweep through one village after another, accompanied somewhat wearily by a few elders appointed to restrain him from too many excesses. Eventually, they could not keep up and were replaced by younger men. The vehemence of his and their accusations against discovered witches was considerable. They attacked Muslims as well as non-Muslims. One old man suffered a heart attack, and the leader, called Kajiwe, was for a time apprehended on a charge of manslaughter, before being released. Kajiwe saw himself as a saviour delivering the community from the bondage of witchcraft and superstition, and, though hardly educated himself, proposed the virtues of literacy, modern medicine and even Christianity. For him, traditional methods of cure, divination and dispute settlement, including the administration of oaths, were all evil. Yet he himself on a number of occasions summoned the help of the Vaya elders to administer oaths to witches who had been arrested by him and brought together for a communal confession. On one occasion witnessed by myself, 111 old men were assembled and, huddled together, had to take the oaths.

The Vaya elders were later denounced by the young witch leader who claimed that they were nothing more than witches themselves, using their evil powers to control others. To speak in this way against the Vaya was at the time a remarkably courageous act and, not surprisingly, he was not supported by other Mijikenda, at least not in public. The Vaya elders shortly thereafter liaised with the district officer and, claiming that the movement had got out of hand (which was indeed arguable), had Kajiwe gaoled and the movement temporarily halted.

Though the movement's leader failed, he can be seen as a revolutionary. For, in wishing to subvert the power of the Vaya elders and to replace the power of witchcraft with that of literacy, modern medicine and Christianity, he was trying to transpose the creation and control of evil on to a level that exists outside indigenous Mijikenda society. That is to say, he was arguing that evil should be taken care of not by the Mijikenda themselves, but by such institutions as schools, hospitals, modern doctors and worship of a foreign God, who had been brought to the threshold of Mijikenda from outside. Yet, given that these institutions involve a hierarchy of specialization which only a few can ever attain, he was also in effect proposing to destroy the Mijikenda theory of existence that people should as much as possible resemble and be equal to each other. He was indeed proposing to replace the static, recyclable morality with one based on gradations of piety and worthiness ultimately located in a Christian High God and in the achievements of Western knowledge.

Now, it would be churlish to deny that Western knowledge has brought medical benefits, and education some enlightenment. But, as is also well known, the extent of these benefits is still confined to a few. At the same time, people have come to regard more and more favourably the hierarchization of knowledge and of personal status and achievements that accompany so-called 'westernization'. One result is that the indigenous ontology of resemblance is being severely countered, at least among the young, by one of difference. In this general respect, the Mijikenda are moving in the direction of the Swahili.

We can characterize the Mijikenda as moving from an existential theory of resemblance to one of difference based on Western values of individual achievement, and at the same time as redefining evil as ultimately regulated by agencies other than themselves.

One might think that, in this general sense, the Mijikenda and the Swahili might end up having comparable theories. The religions might be different, but they would both have notions of complementary positive and negative divinities, that is God and Satan.

While this may indeed be so, the dynamics of Swahili morality threaten to move in the opposite direction. That is to say, while the Mijikenda seem about to externalize the projection of evil by giving a Western god and Western knowledge the ultimate say in deciding who and what is evil, the Swahili see themselves as facing the problem of how to combat the forces of African animism which threaten their religious hierarchy of morality. This is a problem for the Swahili because, whether or not they are always willing openly to admit it, their culture operates at two levels: the Islamic and the animistic. There are numerous ways by which this can be shown, and it is a theme that constantly recurs in sermons by Muslim clerics. Witchcraft, herbal and magical medicine, spirit possession, oath-taking — all conveniently summarized in the term *ushirikina* (broadly, 'superstition' and deriving from an Arabic term, *shirk,* meaning to share other gods with God and so polytheism) as well as by more specific terms — are denounced as anti-Islamic. Yet they are the normal explanatory recourse for most people at some time. They are certainly living activities. The same term *ushirikina* has the added connotation of hopeless addiction to such superstition and mirrors the ambivalence expressed by Swahili when they talk about these animistic modes of explanation. On the one hand, Swahili wish to be as devout Muslims as possible, and to demonstrate to each other their piety, increasing as far as possible their religious status and even, through the marriages of daughters to high-born Swahili or Arabs, improving the religious pedigree of their grandchildren. On the other hand, they see animism as providing immediately understandable and seemingly effective explanations and cures of misfortune as well as the predictions and good luck needed for future events. Because animism is seen to consist of forces amenable to and ultimately controlled by such ritual experts as doctors and diviners, its cures and prognoses are to that extent more easily controlled by ordinary people themselves. A person can negotiate with a man or woman ritual expert in a way that is not possible with a remote High God. The expert, like his client, has his human frailties as well as his virtues, and can bend his will in sympathy with his client's predicament. You hate that witch, for he killed your child; the witch-doctor understands your feelings and, for a fee, will do something about it. The difficulty with a Muslim High God is that, as well as being so remote, he is also extremely virtuous. He leaves the work of evil intentions to Satan, with whom there is no apparent direct means of communication. In short, then, retaining animism as an explicable morality is preferable to abandoning it in the way that Islamic clerics wish.

Nevertheless, those Swahili who retain *ushirikina* and yet also try to be good Muslims are blamed by their fellows and may admit to feeling guilty. The blame that Swahili put upon each other for such equivocation prevents evil behaviour from ever becoming regarded as necessary. That is to say, the evil power that underlies sorcery can never be viewed as the inevitable accompaniment of beneficial power. Those who have authority over the Swahili are the *maalims* and other clerics, and they are supposed to be wholly virtuous. Ritual experts who reverse sorcery are also important and may themselves sometimes practise sorcery, but it is held that they exist only because mortals have not come up to God's moral expectations. If mortals could meet God's standards by curbing their greed, envy, drinking and dissolute ways, and by attending mosque and praying regularly, and also fasting properly, then the evil intentions of humans would cease. Malevolent spirits alone would remain, whose effects, unlike those of witchcraft, are rarely fatal and are more easily contained.

The contrast between the traditional Mijikenda quest for resemblance and equality and the Swahili one for individual distinctiveness is thus curiously at odds with their respective views of who ultimately defines what is evil behaviour. For the Mijikenda, as I have explained, it is men and not a God who measure what passes for evil. Among the Swahili it is God, as expressed in the Koran and as interpreted by clerics, who defines evil. The Mijikenda, being the creators of their own evil, are thus closer to understanding it. Ethnocentrically, we might say that their comprehension is sophisticated, for they know only too well that evil can not be eradicated but only contained, preferably periodically. The Swahili, by contrast, may be responsible for their own practice of evil, but, since it is defined by God, they can hardly be said to have created it. Because its dissolution is ultimately a matter for God to judge, the Swahili can do no more than hope to aspire to these high standards set by divinity. The individuality that Swahili prize before God is thus negated by the impotence of all individuals before the fact that it is God who determines what is or is not worthy. The Mijikenda need to make no compromises before a High God: their quest for resemblance and equality may lead to a static morality, which often stifles individual innovativeness, but it does not deflect them from recognizing that evil is both defined and controlled by man and is an inevitable counter-balance to any notion of human virtue.

We may characterize the Mijikenda as traditionally having an agnostic view of evil, and the Swahili as having a deistic one. It is therefore curious that each people is currently encountering the force of explanations that would reverse these views. More Mijikenda seem to be becoming more dependant on Western knowledge and Christianity for explanations of evil, while the Swahili continue to resort to African animistic beliefs. The Swahili accommodate spiritual beings in a manner not dissimilar to that of Catholicism and south Indian Pentecostalism discussed in chapters 2 and 7, respectively. The Swahili do not forsake a divine explanation of evil; for, in turning to animism, they merely supplement their ways of dealing practically with evil. As more Mijikenda become Christian, and as Swahili continue to be devout Muslims, both peoples will share a common assumption that the mysterious whys and hows of evil behaviour can be answered fully only by God.

An agnostic view would simply be that, for all their other differences, the

Mijikenda are joining the Swahili in allowing themselves to be mystified by the causes of and responses to evil, by deifying its definition. But there is in fact a paradox here. In both Christianity and Islam as practised by these two peoples, evil is actually spoken about a great deal. It is a recurrent and dominant theme of sermons and interpersonal recrimination among the Swahili and among Christian Mijikenda. It is, therefore, not simply talked about but also reflected on. Words to describe evil take on new connotations, and new semantic associations are formed. Among the Christians, Bible translators had to find Mijikenda words that would serve to convey the ideas associated with evil. Among the Swahili, Arabic loan words have for a long time had this function. In both cases a huge semantic field comprising ideas about evil enables people to reify it as an overwhelmingly powerful force with which only a supra-human agency can ultimately cope.

The paradox is that, in spite of this increased capacity by individuals to talk about evil as a phenomenon in both Christianity and Islam, the ways of dealing with evil are taken out of the hands of individuals and placed in those of priests and clerics and, through them, a High God. On the one hand, then, people acquire the semantic means to identify evil as an isolable concept and so can discuss it. On the other hand, it is specialists and their respective divinity who control the terms of discussion.

One not surprising result is that the new terms of discussion increasingly characterize evil as a sin. That is to say, evil becomes codified as disobeying a set of commandments or as the breach of prohibitions. The idea of evil as wanton, malicious and humanly destructive thoughts and actions gets lost. The avoidance of evil becomes instead the avoidance of sin and therefore conformity to the dictates of a High God and his human intermediaries.

Evil thus becomes marked in this way. Yet it is in its unmarked, animistic expression that evil better describes the reality that it is man who both creates and controls his own inevitable destructiveness. This implicit recognition that evil is none other than human wanton destructiveness comes out in the institution of the confession, whether in the oath-taking conducted by the Vaya for two people or in that conducted for a large assembly of captured witches. In this respect, Catholicism is closer to the Mijikenda traditional view than it is either to non-confessional Christianity or Islam. For both the Vaya and the Catholic priest exact a full acknowledgement that it is the human who is responsible for his evil. Thereafter, the similarity ends, for, as I have explained, Catholic evil becomes sin while the traditional Mijikenda view of wrongdoing remains a relatively unmarked and uncodified idea.

To understand what evil is, then, we need to strip off the codified forms in which it is presented. We have to go back to the point at which evil is pre-verbal, that is to say, not semantically identified and yet implicitly recognized as human destructiveness. The traditional relationship of Mijikenda to the Vaya and the handling by the Vaya of oath-taking and witchcraft are among the most important areas of social life in which this pre-linguistic view of evil is presented. One is asked not to confess to having committed a sin, but to having, say, bewitched someone or stolen his property. Nor is the perpetrator accused of being an evil person: rather, he is accused of having committed the wrongdoing, which may or may not have had what we would translate as injurious mystical consequences.

Of course, the Mijikenda have their terms for what we might translate as 'good' and 'bad'. But the terms themselves point to a wide range of states, conditions, acts, intentions and consequences, none of which carries the sense of evil as an especially marked feature of human or extra-human behaviour.

I think that a clue to what I may dare to call a primordial sense of evil and virtue is found in the dominant sense of the main terms for 'good' and 'bad'. This applies to the Bantu terms in Swahili as well as to the closely related terms in Mijikenda.

If you want to call someone 'bad' or 'good', you have in each case a number of terms at your disposal. The most commonly used, however, refer to the observability of the quality that is being described. The 'good' or 'bad' thing or person is visibly so. This means, as in many languages, that the one term can denote both a person's moral virtue and his or her physical beauty, while the other can refer to his moral unworthiness and physical ugliness or deformity. When applied to things rather than persons, the distinction comes out as whole or wholesome, and as rotten or decayed. Good fruit is sound not rotten; good persons are sound and not rotten. States of decay are bad in both.

Thus, in Swahili, *-baya* (adj.) = very bad, materially, morally, intellectually and aesthetically, and also ugly; *-ovu* (adj.) = wicked, corrupt, unjust; and is linked to *-bovu* = rotten, physically having gone too far, of fruit and persons. In Mijikenda (Giriama), *muwi* = a bad/evil person, or an ugly person (cf. archaic Swahili *mui*); and *-olovu* = soft, rotten fruit, and something or someone who has 'gone bad'; *ukolo* = physical or moral impurity. Some Swahili terms for morally good, physically beautiful and wholesome are *-ema*, *-zuri* and *-zima,* while some Mijikenda ones are *-dzo, -baha, -tana* and *-tsululu.*

There are many such words, and the total repertoire of terms of personal evaluation is very wide. Sometimes a person's physical and moral states are seen as one, as in the case of 'bad children' (for example, breech births) or of adults who die of 'bad deaths' (for example, falling from a palm tree or drowning at sea) and whose polluting bodies must be buried outside the homestead. The primacy of even the few terms just given reveal a dominant Bantu view. This is that evil is first evidenced as a material condition. It is only by extension that the perpetrator's intentions (if any) are also regarded as evil. As non-Muslim, and therefore 'pure' Bantu (to use their own characterization), the Mijikenda most obviously display this viewpoint. The Swahili, while they may be regarded as 'basically' Bantu, have through Islam come to place more weight on evil as an inner state of intentions separable from its observable consequences.

The Mijikenda perspective differs from that of peoples, including some in Western society, who place considerable emphasis on certain thoughts and intentions as being evil even when there is no evidence of harmful, physical results. Intense suspicion of one's fellows, such as Rheubottom records in chapter 5 above among Yugoslavian villagers, is not necessarily accompanied by an equal stress on personal guilt. But many Western ideas presuppose its centrality in reflection and motivation, and persons may be expected to feel guilty about acts that they have only ever thought about and will almost certainly never commit. No doubt the Mijikenda also feel such guilt. But, among them, such unconsummated thoughts rarely if ever become the focus of public attention, judgement and confession. Guilt is more likely to remain private. Regret, remorse or bad thoughts, which are some ways in which we might translate private guilt among the Mijikenda, are only bad when the acts that precipitated them have been *seen* by others to have been bad. Indeed, the term most easily translatable as guilt is the word *kilatso* (literally, 'bloodily' and from the term 'blood'), which traditionally had specific reference to the thoughts of a man who had killed another in battle. The blood on his hands was the visible evidence of his feelings and fears. The perpetrator of another's 'bad death' is himself, like his victim, polluting.

The association of evil with physical decay, deformity or ugliness, in Mijikenda language and thought (and perhaps Bantu generally), prompts consideration of a suggestion by Ricoeur (1967: 25–46). This is that a notion of defilement, as in the concepts of 'bad death', 'bad birth' and childhood deformities, is seen by people as a staining or disfigurement of what is or should be pure, clean, whole and beautiful: and that this notion of defilement precedes public and institutionalized ideas of guilt and sin. I would rather see such institutionalization as the development of ways of talking about defilement, that is to say, of a semantically marked concept of evil. In other words, the idea of 'defilement' becomes the word 'evil' or some equivalent.

How does this occur? Coupled with the idea of defilement is that of disorder or chaos: if something is spoiled it becomes not only dirty and ugly but also confusing or less understandable, for its comprehensibility had rested in its inviolate state. An irredeemably desecrated work of art or religion sets puzzles as to its meaning. A 'bad death' does the same. Answering such puzzles is intermediary between the act of defilement itself and calling the act evil. Let me show what I mean by treating the two themes of defilement and disorder separately as ways in which a pre-linguistic sense of evil is conveyed and converted into words.

On the one hand we have the notion of defilement or dirt. Hence the cleansing operations for which African witchcraft eradication movements are famous, and which also characterize many rituals of expurgation of both individuals and communities. Terms used to describe virtuous persons often also have the meanings of cleansed and pure. On the other hand, we have the idea that things have become crossed, tangled, or have gone too far. They are in disarray or disorder. I have elsewhere suggested that a Bantu root term for being crossed (over) or made crooked has echoes in other languages of the world and points to a semantic archetype denoting mystical disorder which must be straightened out (Parkin 1982). This same condition of chaos can be used to create new social and cosmological possibilities.

The two ideas of defilement and of entanglement are dealt with in two broadly contrasting ways. Defilement is eliminated in so-called rituals of purification, in which the culpability of perpetrators, where they are known, is often not a major issue. However, the procedure of straightening out a wrong that has been seen to have been committed is most effectively done through confession, often coupled with a demand to pay compensation, and with the perpetrator left in no doubt as to his culpability.

It is perhaps clear from this distinction that Mary Douglas's characterization of dirt as matter out of place, and therefore as the origin of ideas of classificatory anomaly (1970), conflates two separate issues. Dirt by itself simply requires eradication. In the rituals of purification that I have observed, the cleansing is rarely accompanied by words. People use brushes to sweep an afflicted compound, or water to wash away the evil in a place or on a person, usually with the minimum of words. Indeed, the act is most effectively carried out through actions and not words. Symbolic cleansing is a most poignant piece of silent drama.

By contrast, to make relationships straight normally needs more than silent drama. For a start, formal relationships of kinship, affinity, neighbourhood and others have to be identified as, say, between accuser and accused, or between these and witnesses. Second, the content of relationships between adversaries and others with regard to the issue at hand needs to be described. Since the purpose of the event, for example an oath-taking, is didactic and restorative, the complexity of the formal and informal details of the particular relationships would be hard to convey to an audience by mime alone. Hence the need for confession of the motives and intentions of the disputants who are obliged to take the oath.

Thus, that dimension of evil that we call defilement leads to purification rituals that require limited verbal explanation. The entangling or disordered dimension of evil needs verbal confessions.

It is therefore the idea of the confession that provides the link between pre-linguistic ideas of evil and the semantically marked notions familiar to Western agnostics and to those who follow Christianity, Islam and Judaism. Though it is preserved in Catholicism, the confession has otherwise been taken up into judicial and ecclesiastical laws which are of variable secular and religious significance. We confess in a secular Western court when we say we are guilty, and are often induced into doing so by the promise of at least partial absolution. Mijikenda witches, many of whom are assuredly unaware that they have committed evil, may assent to a confession for the same reason. The confessions before the Inquisition sometimes brought death, but in many other cases were tantamount to protestations of innocence: if I have committed the evil then I was unaware of it, or at least did not really mean it, and am prepared to repent.

The counterpart to confessing evil is to be accused of it. In a modern court of law this may lead to counter-accusations, as is the case also in the Mijikenda disputes which thereafter require judgement by oath. Accusation, counter-accusation and eventual confession become more than simply the verbal means of disentangling classificatory confusion. They become a whole field of discourse, as is the case in modern Western law. But at this point evil becomes almost talked out of existence. Excuses are found, the reasonableness of both sides is considered, ambivalence is found in their motives. The result is that, as in secular Western society today, evil is a term reserved for particularly heinous acts, and more in written than in spoken language, as for example newspaper headlines referring to IRA bombers as 'despicably evil'. The term 'evil' is thus used to refer to the unthinkable that nevertheless happens. Discourse then takes a new turn: first it is soldiers, then civilians, and next perhaps children in schools who are killed.

Just as the traditional Mijikenda regard evil as a regrettable necessity in their view of the Vaya's authority and of social order, so Westerners may have to face the unpleasant possibility that, for them, the little used concept of radical evil is the only way they can recognize the existence of the unacceptable. It is perhaps small wonder that, in between the Mijikenda animistic view and the Western secular one, peoples turn to monotheistic religion. It is a hard job for history always to place judgements about man's destructiveness towards fellow-humans in the hands of man himself and his agents. It is good from time to time to have a God to take on that responsibility. I suspect that the recurrent nature of religious enthusiasm and puritanical moralities derives from this more than any other fact. They play on the possibilities of ending evil, whose very end, being located ultimately in the intentions of individual humans, is to redefine those same moralities. Evil is morality reflecting on itself.

I can perhaps go back to the case of the Giriama mother for some key to understanding how the characterization of evil may bring about this contemplation on the inadequacy of our existing moralities. The key to it all may be, to return to the theme, an existentialist one. I may feel absolute horror at the evil I have perpetrated. As Ricoeur would put it, I must then seek natural death (suicide) as the only escape and punishment from the unnatural, living death of irremovable guilt. But the passage of time and the counsel of others, or, more commonly, of oneself, does funny things. I find myself compromising the evil but calling it not compromise but *entitlement.* Perhaps (to parody Raskolnikov in *Crime and Punishment*) I was, after all, entitled to kill the old woman for her money — after all she did not need it, and I, an impoverished student, did. The interest in 1983 in what proved to be the bogus Hitler Diaries may at one level have been no more than an attempt to understand what kind of a person could have perpetrated the horrors of Nazism; but at another level, does the investigation push us dangerously close to blaming it all on his distorted psyche and, in effect, claiming that it is in the nature of distorted psyches to commit such evils, and therefore that they, in their own terms, are entitled to do so? The Giriama mother may (we do not know) have genuinely believed that her afflicted child was irredeemably contaminated, not through her own or the child's fault, but to such an extent that the suckling baby was endangered by the sick child's proximity. To spurn the sick child, and eventually to allow it to be eliminated by withdrawing nutritional and medical aid and affection, may have been for this mother her own hapless final solution to a dilemma not of her own creation. If this was the case (and it seemed to other Giriama the most plausible of the explanations), then the mother and many other Giriama believers around her might say that she was *entitled* to take this action.

I do not in the least wish to draw a parallel between Raskolnikov, Hitler and the Giriama mother. Rather, it is the difference that is critical: Hitler and Raskolnikov articulated their own entitlement to their actions; the Giriama mother, and those of us around her, remained inarticulate. Evil may have been in the air on that sad occasion, but we had no words for it, and there was no discussion of alternative possible courses of action. Moral judgements as to what is good or evil may inscribe dogma, but, provided they are open to contention, they presuppose the possibility of other judgements and discourses.

REFERENCES

Douglas, Mary (1970). *Natural Symbols.* London: Barrie and Rockcliffe
Parkin, D. (1978). *The Cultural Definition of Political Response.* London: Academic Press
Parkin, D. (1982). 'Straightening the Paths from Wilderness: Simultaneity and sequencing in divinatory speech. In *Paideuma,* 28, 71—83 (earlier version in *Journal of Anthropological Society of Oxford* 1979. *10:* pp 147—60)
Ricoeur, P. (1967). *The Symbolism of Evil.* Boston: Beacon Press
Russell, J.B. (1977). *The Devil.* Ithaca and London: Cornell University Press
Southall, A. W. (undated). Paper on evil, power, and political legitimacy. Presented to a seminar of the Department of Anthropology and Sociology, of the School of Oriental and African Studies, during December 1979.
Willis, R. (1968). Kamcape: An Anti-Sorcery Movement. *Africa,* 38, 1—15

14

There is no end of evil: the guilty innocents and their fallible god

*Joanna Overing**

In Piaroa mythology the creator and original owner of most culture, Kuemoi, was the god of night and a mad, diabolical buffoon. He was a tyrannical madman whose power was wild, dangerous. He was also ridiculous, a figure for high comedy, not tragedy. Kuemoi shrieked in outrage and stamped his feet; when overtaken by total madness, he ran endlessly around in circles. He acted without reason and had no dignity. In short, he never managed mastery over his own emotions.[1] Even his appearance, although monstrous and evidence of his danger, was absurd: he was a two-headed cannibal with one head to eat meat raw and the other to eat meat cooked. Poisoned by the forces of culture that he himself created, Kuemoi was during mythic time evil

* The fieldwork upon which this paper is based was carried out in 1968 and 1977 with M. R. Kaplan, to whom I am deeply indebted in general for data collected jointly. The research in 1977, upon which much of the presentation is based, was financed by the SSRC Grant HR 5028, Central Research Funds of the University of London, London School of Economics Research Funds, and the Institute of Latin American Studies Travel Funds. The SSRC also later gave me a Research Grant (HRP 6753) which allowed me the time to analyse data acquired in 1977. I am also most grateful to Peter Rivière, Peter Metcalf, Mark Hobart, Ron Inden, David Parkin, Michael Saltman and Sybil Wolfram for their kind interest in and insightful discussion of the more general issues raised in the paper.

[1] I have combed the literature for similar representations of evil as buffoonery. The only example that I have found where the devil is portrayed as both a dangerous and a ridiculous figure is Robert Nye's depiction of him in *Merlin:* 'He grins like a fox eating shit out of a wire brush'; the Devil is 'snoring as loud as a pig'; 'he giggles and he writhes' (Nye 1979). The Piaroa would appreciate Nye's humour and his understanding of the hilarious, absurd and mockable side of wickedness.

incarnate, and as such serves today as vivid exemplar of the darker side of human nature — as the Piaroa perceive it — and of the potentiality of man for odious and wicked behaviour.

It is immediately obvious that evil and wickedness have intriguing associations in the thought of the Piaroa, Amerindians of the Venezuelan rain forest, and it is upon these associations that I shall dwell throughout this essay. The Piaroa identify evil with madness and buffoonery, which as a triadic set are further identified with knowledge and the poisonous wildness of its force. In due course I shall show the Piaroa mad and foolish god of knowledge to be but one logical (and imaginative) aspect of a highly sophisticated general theory of ethical behaviour.

Girard has noted (1978: 42—3) that structuralism, along with Marxism and Freudianism, is always looking for hidden significations, reducing, in so doing, literal or manifest meanings to other hidden meanings; and it is for this reason that structuralism is insensible to the formidable simplicity of the greatest literary effects, the comic and the tragic. He observes (p. 178) that the dramatic elements of mythology as such do not interest Lévi-Strauss, and states further (p. 170), perhaps not so justly, that this lack of interest is no more than a part of the more general purging of anthropology by Lévi-Strauss of a large number of interesting questions having to do with religion, belief and morality. We might phrase the problem less harshly. Lévi-Strauss has ineludibly transformed our own vision of the social and the relationship of thought to it; yet, there are also issues that structuralism cannot handle, which lie outside its method.[2] In structuralism we do not find the means to unfold the ontologies or the moral systems of particular cultures, or the method by which to relate the ontological and the moral. Structuralism gives short shrift to beliefs and emotions, deceits and desires. Nevertheless, the very fact that we can return once again to the examination of such aspects of human experiences — that lie perhaps beyond the purely rational — with some feeling of confidence is because we have structuralism as a base, and not as a method to overcome.

As I discuss the tragic and the comic events of Piaroa mythology, I will not be treating the reader to a structural analysis of mythic cycles, but rather to its

---

[2] Needham also speaks of the limitations of structuralism. He says that, along with other 'isms', structuralism becomes increasingly 'detached and abstract, and it is this detachment that leads to the neglect of concerns of any moral and metaphysical interest (Needham 1978: 6). Also see Lévi-Strauss (1969a: 10—12), where he describes his own endeavour as an attempt to arrive at a syntax of South American mythology and his ambition to discover the conditions in which systems of truth become mutually convertible, taking on 'the character of an autonomous object, independent of any subject', and to show 'how myths operate in men's minds without their being aware of the fact'.

drama, to the overt story told in them of the origin of the world, of the character of the actors in this dramatic history and of the moral and the immoral nature of their relationships. Structural analysis did precede this particular exposition, for Piaroa cosmic history abounds in oppositions — the subterranean and the celestial, earth and water, night and day, the raw and the cooked — and their (attempted) resolution. However, to relate the specific manner in which structural understanding directed and indeed allowed for the present discussion would be a difficult task beyond the one at hand. What is clearly the case is that structuralism cannot incorporate as grist for its mill the myth as dramatic performance. Although a myth, or even a section of it, may be treated as an isolated text, as if it is a written word or a musical score, the myth in its telling is a unique event that is created by a performer for a particular audience.[3] The story is known by all — or, more correctly, the dramatic events of the entire mythic cycle are more or less known by all; but the exact combination of event with event and the stress upon one event over another, or upon one character over another, are rarely repeated.[4] Because the performer creates and recreates the surface narrative, the narration itself is not preordained by structural demands.[5] The narrator performs for his audience: he makes them laugh at the slapstick antics of his characters; he makes them gasp at horrid doings. He entertains; but he also makes use of dramatic effect for didactic gain. The particular moral lessons and the reception of the audience to them can be known only by participating in the

[3] Lévi-Strauss recognizes this point (1969a: 12; 1968: 365—6) and suggests that we view 'the total body of myth belonging to a given community' as 'comparable to its speech'. He explicitly states that his interest is not with the structure of the surface level of expression, but with the unconscious laws underlying it (1969a: 10). In Hawkes's words (1977: 39), Lévi-Strauss stalks *langue* 'through the particular varieties of its *parole*'.

[4] The literary historian, Viktor Shklovsky, in speaking of the nature of narrative, makes the important distinction between 'story', the basic succession of events, and 'plot', which represents the distinctive way in which the 'story' is made strange, creatively deformed and defamiliarized (Hawkes 1977: 65—6). Also see Culler (1981: 169—70) on the distinction in narratology between story and discourse: the sequence of events as opposed to the discourse that orders and presents events.

[5] Contrast with Greimas and Propp, whose theories of narrative assume that a competence of narrative generates the performance (Hawkes 1977: 95). Also see Culler's discussion (1975: 232ff.) of the superficiality of the structuralist treatment of character. For Todorov, for instance, 'characters are not heroes, villains or helpers; they are simply subjects of a group of predicates which the reader adds up as he goes along' (p. 235). Culler argues that on the contrary, to understand the narrative force of, say, tragedy and the tragic hero two alternative logics are at work, that of story (a sequence of events) and that of discourse, where event is not a cause but an effect of theme. The interplay of these two irreconcilable logics, an interplay that is necessary to narrative force, put into question the possibility of a complete grammar of narrative (Culler 1981: 175—6).

drama, by being a member of the audience. As collector's tale on written page, the didactic aspects that are such an obvious and powerful part of the myth as performed become lost: structures can be found, but not the narrative force of the comic and the tragic, or the moral messages that are played out in differing manner through each.

Just as we cannot with honesty discard our heritage of Lévi-Strauss, nor can we strip ourselves of our everyday knowledge of Freud — when a crucial aspect of the discussion centres around human emotions. It was Freud who said that:

The principal thing is the intention which humour fulfills, whether it concerns the subject's self or other people. Its meaning is: 'Look here! This is all that this seemingly dangerous world amounts to. Child's play — the very thing to jest about!'

Freud 1963: 268

What better way can there be to deal with a devil god or a devil neighbour than to treat them as buffoons?

Nevertheless, in this discussion my interest is not so very much in hidden meanings or hidden structures, but in the evaluative discourse of the Piaroa on honourable and dishonourable behaviour, on goodness and wickedness, on their *stated* understanding of events and gods of the mythic past and their judgements both of them and of social behaviour in the world of present-day time. My concern is not so much with human nature, as with Piaroa theories of human nature. My attention is not upon human rationality, but upon Piaroa theories of rationality: their understanding — and not ours — of the relation between emotions and reason, between knowledge and reason, between consciousness, reason and (a)social behaviour. These are not investigator-imposed themes, but issues that play an integral part in daily Piaroa talk and concern that deals with everyday decisions involving principles of action, choice and responsibility.

As in our own Western moral philosophy, Piaroa reasoning about such matters as the relation between the passions and rationality or between consciousness and motivation link with the even grander themes of the true character of man and the nature of the good society, i.e., how people must interact socially so as best to cope with the needs of human welfare. Notions about the nature of the good society, the character of man — his capacity for good and evil — and human well-being are, of course, beliefs that are culturally relative. Thus, the strong value placed by the Piaroa upon the freedom of the person, their aversion to political tyranny, their concern with the ambiguous relationship between personal freedom and social or political right or constraint, may surprise the reader, as too may the presupposition of metaphysical dualism (see below) through which they reason about such values. The idea that the good society should allow for both personal freedom *and* the attainment of harmonious relationships with one's fellowmen did not have its sole origin in Enlightenment thought.

J. S. Mill, the nineteenth-century moralist on social and political tyranny, argued that the good society is one in which governmental constraint would be limited to making its citizens answerable for doing evil to one another (1972: 74). Only then could society allow for individual differences in the development of desires and impulses and thereby for individual genius and creativity (p. 118). However, Mill also maintained that it was only the nineteenth-century mind and culture that was ready for such privilege: despotism, he believed, was the legitimate form of government for 'barbarians' and simpler societies where strong desires were not yet matched with strong consciences (pp. 73, 119).

These beliefs on the part of a nineteenth-century liberal philosopher in the progressive change of human nature for the better sound remarkable to us, who are today of a more sceptical age with regard to ideas on human progress, human perfectibility and the rationality upon which such perfectibility would be based. Yet, despite the efforts of anthropological theory, and of structuralism in particular, to demonstrate the unity of the human mind, anthropology has not dispelled the notions of the 'primitive' and the credulous character of pre-literate moral philosophy. In fact, we have no comparative anthropology of systems of morality.[6] This is especially unfortunate in that the area of personal relationships, as Horton (1979)[7] has so forcefully argued for African theory, is precisely the one where we should expect in pre-state systems of thought a sophistication that far exceeds that forthcoming from modern Western society,[8] where sophistication in theory-building is with the non-personal. For the most part, we have not in our investigations directed our questioning in such a way that would allow us to attain knowledge, except superficially, about particular systems of morality.

Worse still, our own anthropological jargon might well do subtle injustice to the theories we are describing, the sophistication of which is often obscured through labelling that designates 'primitiveness', i.e., egalitarian pre-state society. We are caught in a bind: we wish to capture 'the other', his difference

---

[6] See Wolfram (1982), where she persuasively argues for greater sophistication on the part of anthropologists in their approach to systems of morality. She notes that anthropologists tend to conflate sanction, rule and morality. Moreover, anthropologists, she says, rarely include what is thought to constitute a bad and odious moral character.

[7] Also see Lévi-Strauss (1968: 365—6), where he stresses the emphasis placed on personal relationships in pre-literate societies.

[8] I argued this point in a paper on South American Indian theory; see Overing (1985).

from ourselves; yet in so doing, perhaps for cultural and political reasons that lie outside our own analyses, we denigrate 'the other' to 'the lesser'. For this reason, I have self-consciously not used certain labels normally associated with discussions of tropical forest Amerindians. By changing the name for something, we also transform its impact, both emotionally and intellectually. Thus, rather than 'shaman', 'culture hero' or 'demiurge', I have used instead the equally appropriate — and more 'uplifting' — labels of 'wizard' and 'god'. Except for convention, there is no reason in this case why these labels should not be interchangeable.

Also, in my analysis I have felt no qualms about translating Piaroa moral notions with such Western labels as 'sin', 'fault', 'guilt' and 'salvation'. As the reader will see, the Piaroa make a very interesting distinction between what I shall label as 'fault' and 'sin'. Piaroa thought about the universe is sufficiently alien to our own that such small efforts in translation are warranted, especially where Western words fit as well as do those usually expected by anthropological convention. On the other hand, much of Piaroa reasoning about moral behaviour will be familiar to those who have read, as ethnographies of ourselves, Western moral philosophy, where the puzzling problem of the relationship between reason, the emotions and social behaviour is always of central moral concern. The Piaroa answers are idiosyncratic to themselves, but the Western reader should be well acquainted with the issues.

In the Piaroa view, the logic of which I shall detail below, man commits evil acts because of foolishness. The evil deed entails a set of preconditions, a particular sequencing, which is explained in their ethical system through (1) a theory of motivation, (2) a theory of cultural capability and (3) a theory of fallibility or bad judgement. These are theories that revolve around what are for the Piaroa the problematics of innocence and knowledge, madness and disease, desires and reason, personal responsibility and freedom, and the question of how to achieve a 'good life'. Before turning to the myths of creation, where the origin of evil, its nature and its place in the world are explained, I shall discuss the Piaroa ethical predicates of good and evil, a discussion that is based upon their own evaluative discourse that centres about the value of moderation.

THE 'LIFE OF THE SENSES' AND THE 'LIFE OF THOUGHT'

The Piaroa understand human beings to have both a 'life of the senses' (*kákwà*) and a 'life of thought' (*ta'kwarü*), a distinction akin to the Platonic one between the 'pleasures of the senses' and the 'pleasures of the mind'. The dualism of mind and body distinguishes humans from animals, who normally have only a 'life of the senses', and also from present-day celestial gods,[9] who have no 'life of the senses' but do have a 'life of thought'. Humans are fallible (and I shall elaborate their fallibility in later sections), as animals and celestial gods cannot be, because they have conjoined within them both a life of desires and a life of knowledge. For the Piaroa there is a connection between virtue and the mastery of both passions and thought: the good life (*adíunà*) is the tranquil one (*adiupàwí*), where moderation is achieved in both the 'life of the senses' and the 'life of the mind'. The very good man has what is said to be the imagination to live tranquilly (*màriyà adiunàku*), or, literally, 'the wizardry to live tranquilly'. Personal wealth is equated with both virtue and wisdom, and thus it is only a wizard who can live a wealthy life, a state to be attained where through tranquillity one allows one's thoughts to be awakened (*ta'kwa poiàchi*) and thereby one's 'life of the mind' (*ta'kwarü*) to be well developed. Although high value is placed upon the life of the mind, there must nevertheless be a balance in the wizard between his 'life of senses' and 'life of thought': they must be *equally* mastered and developed.[10]

Such mastery is achieved through *ta'kwakomenà*, one's will, consciousness and sense of responsibility. I shall dwell for a moment on the three related concepts — the 'life of thought', knowledge and capabilities, and responsibility or will — which together form a theory of mind. To have *ta'kwarü*, a 'life of thought', entails the acquisition of both culture (*ta'kwànya*) and responsibility — or consciousness (*ta'kwakomenà*). *Ta'kwànya* can best be translated as the knowledge of the customs of one's people, including its language, its social rules, its processing of food, its ritual, *and* the capabilities for carrying it out; thus, white people have the *ta'kwànya* for making machines, while the Piaroa have the *ta'kwànya* for making blowguns or curare. *Ta'kwàkomenà*, on the other hand, refers to one's own responsibility for such capabilities, and is one of the very commonly used words in everyday Piaroa speech. It is an abstract concept the meaning of which varies in critical fashion depending upon the context of its use. When one asks a Piaroa why he is doing something, he is most likely to reply 'cha'kwakomenà',[11] a first-person-possessive form which can be variously translated as 'I do it because it is *my* will' or 'because *I* want

---

[9] It is important to distinguish between the earthly creator gods of mythic time and the celestial gods of post-mythic times. Mythic time gods had both a 'life of thought' and a 'life of the senses'.

[10] Compare with Aristotle on the doctrine of the mean, where he defines moral virtues as the mean between the extremes of either emotion or tendencies to action. On emotions themselves, he argues that, if we feel them too much or too little, we are wrong (*Nichomachean Ethics,* bk 2, ch. 6). Also see J. S. Mill in his essay 'On Liberty' (1972: 118), where he argues for the proper balancing between desires and conscience and, given this balance, for the right of individual difference in the development of their strength.

to' or 'because it is *my* custom' or 'of *my* people'. The last two phrases, 'it is *my* custom' and 'it is of *my* people', are two different answers: the stress in the first case is upon one's own idiosyncratic manner of doing something, while in the second it is on one's society's idiosyncratic ways. The expression *ta'kwakomená* can equally well refer to one's responsibility, guilt or fault. A calamity occurs, and one says 'a'kwakomená': 'it was *his* fault'; a woman menstruates, and she says 'cha'kwakomená': 'it is my guilt', being a danger to others. The expression further refers to comprehension: the sentence, 'tü ahúkusa cha'kwakomená', can be translated depending upon circumstance as 'I listen to whom I wish' or as 'I am able to understand.' *Ta'kwakomená* also refers to one's mastery over wizardry, but not to its possession, which as cultural capability would be included within *ta'kwánya*.

While *ta'kwánya* refers in rather Tylorian fashion to culture and the capability for it, which — in the Piaroa case — includes fertility as a cultural ability,[12] *ta'kwákomená* refers to one's motivation or intentionality in using custom, one's comprehension or consciousness of it, one's responsibility for its use. The term overlaps with, or includes, concepts that we tend to distinguish: 'will', 'consciousness', 'rationality' and 'conscience'. Thus, it is through

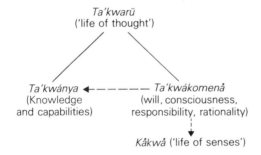

FIGURE 1   The relationship between the 'life of thought' and the 'life of senses'

---

[11] As with most Piaroa nouns, *ta'kwákomená* is a possessed noun:

tü cha'kwakomená	— my responsibility
uku kwa'kwakomená	— your responsibility
chu a'kwakomená	— his responsibility
yahu kwa'kwakomená	— her responsibility
uhutu ta'kwakomená	— our responsibility
ukutu kwa'kwakomená	— your responsibility
hitu ta'kwakomená	— their responsibility

[12] One's child is one's *a'kwa* (thought). Also, the Piaroa equate women's fertility and men's wizardry.

ta 'kwakomenà that one is able to master both one's emotions (*kàkwà*) and the knowledge of and capabilities for one's culture (*ta 'kwánya*).[13] As an ontological scheme, the relationships between *ta 'kwarü* ('life of thought'), *ta 'kwánya* (knowledge and capabilities), *ta 'kwakomenà* (rationality, will and so on) and *kàkwà* ('life of senses') are shown in figure 1. In short, the 'life of thought' includes knowledge and capabilities and the consciousness to master both them and the passions.

Ta 'kwakomenà (will, rationality and consciousness) is as much a learning process as is the acquisition of *ta 'kwánya* (knowledge and capabilities), and, indeed, the former precedes the latter in formal learning procedure.[14] Learning *ta 'kwakomenà* is the first step toward acquiring *ta 'kwarü* (a 'life of thought'). The first lessons of children when they are six or seven years of age are on morality. A wizard teaches them the art of living, the wisdom of leading a tranquil life and how to go about achieving it.[15] Basically, they are taught what in our own moral philosophy are called 'the other-regarding virtues', those that are useful to others rather than to the self, those that enable one to take responsibility for one's actions towards others. The virtue of living tranquilly with others is favoured in general by the Piaroa over the more self-regarding virtues such as personal courage, ambition, talent and industry.[16]

The Piaroa consider the children's lessons as part of a 'domestication'

---

[13] Socrates also sees the constitution of the human soul or personhood as an integration of three different elements: impulses, thought or reason, and between these two an element capable of curbing impulses and also capable of taking orders from thought or reason (Ryle 1967: 329). His scheme is not identical to that of the Piaroa one, but he nevertheless is attempting to deal in a rather similar manner with the integration within the person of will, reason and desire. He conflates thought, reason and perhaps knowledge, while the Piaroa conflate reason and the third element suggested by Socrates, which might be translated as 'will'. The Piaroa scheme is the more sophisticated in that it specifically separates knowledge and rationality.

[14] Compare with Aristotelian thought: the will for Aristotle is rationally guided desire, formed by moral education and training (Abelson and Nielsen 1967: 85).

[15] Compare Rousseau in *Emile* (1762), where he states that the first lessons of a child should be on 'the art of living', which includes the teaching of both sensibility and reason, but sensibility should be taught first. The purpose of such lessons is to teach the ability to live harmoniously with one's fellowmen, to live without the clash of personal wills. A truly positive education begins only when the child becomes aware of his relationships with other people. With the growth of sensibility, reason and imagination, the child leaves the self-sufficiency of the undomesticated stage for a life involving relations with the physical realm of nature and the world of human beings. All education must be carefully timed to allow for orderly and harmonious development (Grimsley 1967: 221).

[16] See the distinction made by J. S. Mill in his essay 'On Liberty' (1972) and the discussion by Taylor and Wolfram on the distinction between the self-regarding and the other-regarding virtues (1968a,b).

process, one through which the child must take more and more personal responsibility for his actions. Young children before they have had their first lessons on restraint are called *'u'ur'o,* 'the newborn of animals', an expression that quite literally describes their undomesticated state, one of a pure 'life of the senses', and thereby one that is unfit for *social* living. This first set of lessons teaches the child sociality — to have respect for others and not to quarrel. The wizard teaches them to recognize social deficiencies, especially those of ill-nature, cruelty, malice, arrogance, jealousy, envy, dishonesty and vanity.[17] The character traits most odious to the Piaroa are those of ill-nature, arrogance and malice, for it is these that are considered the most disruptive to peaceful living. The wizard teaches the child, as well, such social rules as the proper use of kinship terms and proper behaviour towards types of kinsmen. In brief, he is giving the children the means through which they can behave socially with others, which will then enable them to lead a tranquil life, one in harmony with those around them.

The Piaroa emphasize in these lessons mastery over the emotions, a step that on the whole is required of a person before he/she acquires most cultural capabilities.[18] Desires or emotions *per se* are neither good nor bad: they are merely wild (see below) until a person's will determines their form, *tames* them. As mastery over *sociality* is developed, *ta'kwakomenà* (will, responsibility, etc.) can then be further matured to care for other knowledge and capabilities that one learns as one grows older, such as hunting, gardening, the making of artefacts, child-bearing and ritual.

Ta'kwakomenà, it must be remembered, refers to the freedom of the will, and not only to responsibility. The wizard teaches about 'the good life'; he does not order it. Free will comes only with consciousness, and first of all with the consciousness of self with respect to others. The Piaroa obviously consider that responsibility to others to be but one aspect of the development of personal responsibility. Which virtues the child in fact develops is upon its own decision, as too is a personal decision later about what other aspects of knowledge and capabilities to develop — over which one must take personal responsibility, just as one must also do over one's own social relationships.

[17] The Piaroa gave me descriptive examples of virtues and deficiencies. Our terms are fairly good glosses of these examples.

[18] The Piaroa were highly puzzled over the abilities of one small child who at the age of four or five assisted his father in the preparation of game and fish.

THE LIGHT OF THE MOON AND THE LIGHT OF THE SUN

Piaroa ethical standards conjoin moral good with the clean, the beautiful, the restrained; while wickedness is evidenced by dirt, ugliness, madness and excess. The imagery of cleanliness runs throughout their discourse on both the possession of virtue and its acting out. A man is handsome (*a'kwakwa*) and a woman beautiful (*a'kwakwahu*) when freshly bathed and painted in body designs. As indicated by the root *a'kwa* (thought), the outer state of beauty and cleanliness is but pictorial, outward manifestation of the inner state of one's 'life of thoughts' (*ta'kwarü*). However, the Piaroa recognize that outer appearance may well deceive: the designs on the handsome perfumed hunter may be merely a product of vanity and deceit, rather than a statement of inner tranquillity and order. His inner thoughts may be in disarray, a state that may well lead him to a life of promiscuous wandering and arrogant display.[19]

Good powers of wizardry are described as 'beautiful', 'clean' and 'fresh', and it is the clear but moderate light of the moon that is designated as 'the precious light of wizardry'. The light of the moon, its clear, fresh light without colour, is the light of the words of the wizard's life-giving and life-protecting chants. The moon-lit water within the crystal boxes of song and wizardry owned by the gods is clean, clear and fresh, and it is with this water that the wizard each night cleanses and beautifies the words of his chants. The land of the gods, which lies behind the clean, fresh spray of waterfalls, is one of ethereal bliss where its inhabitants live in immortality a pure 'life of thoughts' (*ta'kwarü*).

Evil powers come from the immoderate heat or light of the sun: circles or rains of rust stained by the sun's force fall from the sky and are filled with madness. Powerful hunting poisons or charms can be taken from vulture down, sky rust, centre-of-the-sky down, all of which are filled with the dangerous force of sun down. The hunter who makes use of such powers will be poisoned by the bright force of the sun into a state of paranoia (see below). More generally, the social side of the signs of dirt, ugliness, the monstrous and fierce sunlight are the negative qualities of excess, madness, quarrelsomeness and arrogance.

The image of the morally good life that emerges from the above discussion should appear familiar to anthropological readers as one in which dirt and excess are associated with disorder, and cleanliness and restraint are linked with order. It is an image that even the most superficial of structural analysis

---

[19] The promiscuous, ill-natured, but handsome hunter is a frequent motif in Piaroa myths.

would unfold, and it does seem reasonable to view Piaroa ethics as a code forthcoming from a particular world ordering where one acts correctly to keep chaos at bay, to maintain the harmony necessary to happy social living. Such a gloss of utilitarianism is not wrong; but what at first glance appears to be a highly idealistic moral code in fact speaks of the horror of the human predicament, of the human condition, and the danger of it.[20]

KNOWLEDGE AND MADNESS

I noted above the association of one's clean and beautiful outer appearance with one's inner moral state of *ta'kwarü* ('life of thought'), which includes both *ta'kwánya* (knowledge and capabilities) and *ta'kwakomená* (responsibility, will). One might assume that the Piaroa are saying that knowledge and capabilities (*ta'kwánya*) are beautiful, clean and fresh, as indeed the benevolent powers of the wizard are described. However, many of the powers (as a part of *ta'kwánya*) within the wizard are not so reconcilable with the notions of freshness, beauty and cleanliness: the 'spirit of songs' (*autuisa*) within him is also the 'spirit of hunger' and the 'spirit of jaguar's breath'; the spirit of the hallucinogen, *yopo*, within him is the 'spirit of battle' (*tekwá*).

The point is that the clean and the beautiful refer not to the actual content within one of *ta'kwánya*, but to one's mastery of *ta'kwánya*, which includes one's development of *ta'kwakomená* (will, responsibility), and indicates the state within one of one's knowledge (*ta'kwánya*). As I shall explain in the next section, much of knowledge is poisoned by madness. The celestial gods give to each Piaroa most of his knowledge and his capabilities for it, which are contained within the body enclosed in 'beads of life', and which are also sent by the gods. Men's painted face designs are referred to as 'the path of beads' or as 'the path of the words of the chant', and are said to be identical to the design of beads contained within the body.[21] Men's face designs, which indicate the forces of knowledge within them, are called '*k'erau pàratàmï*'. *K'eràu* is the name of the red dye that is used for these stamped designs, and it is also the name of the disease of madness, a form of paranoia caused by the poison of the sun and unmastered knowledge within one. The handsome hunter may have within him the *takwarü* to hunt, but not the mastery over it sufficient to dispel its poison. The Piaroa, in labelling the designs of knowledge on one's face as *k'eràu* (madness), are equating them with the designs of poisonous

---

[20] See Ricoeur (1967: 217) for a similar discussion on Greek theology.
[21] Women's face designs and beads are said likewise to be the outer marks of their powers, 'the path of their menstruation'.

knowledge within them. The gods give the Piaroa the moderate and the safe cleansing power of the moon to enable the individual to rid the forces of knowledge within him of their poison, especially that of the sun. Thus, when the wizard each night cleanses and beautifies the words of his chants, he is ridding them of their poisonous madness.

The beads within one that contain the forces of knowledge are called 'the beads of life', *kàkwàwà reu,* and are, as the label *kàkwàwà* designates, the force for the 'life of the senses' (*kàkwà*), which enables one to breathe, to have hunger and lust, to need sleep and water — in short, to have desires and impulses. The beads of the 'life of the senses' are also in need of cleansing: they are made from a special granite that the Piaroa say is the outcroppings of faeces of the most powerful and dangerous force of the universe, the tapir/anaconda, the supreme deity who lives beneath the earth. A man's 'spirit of thought' (*t'akwa ruwang*), an homunculus that dwells within the eye, cleans the beads of their dirt and wildness.

This is man's predicament: he has conjoined within him the wild 'life of the senses' and the poisonous 'forces of knowledge'. I shall now turn to the Piaroa myths of creation, wherein we can find an explanation for the equation of knowledge and capabilities with madness and evil: in Piaroa cosmogony the origin of most knowledge on earth entailed the receiving of madness and thereby the potentiality for evil. As the reader will see in the following sections, the Piaroa mythic cycle defies classification within Ricoeur's (1967) typology of creation myths about the beginning and end of evil where he distinguishes between, (1) the creation-drama type of myth, an 'epic' mode of ontogenesis according to which order comes at the end and not the beginning of the drama: through violence the divine is promoted at the expense of primordial brutality; (2) the Adamic myth, which details the Fall of man which supervened upon a perfect original creation; and (3) the intermediate type, a tragic theology such as that of the Greeks, whereby man is not the origin of evil, but finds evil in the world and continues it. The Piaroa myths of creation have within them elements of all three types.

THE BUFFOON DEVIL AND THE ORIGIN OF
POISONOUS KNOWLEDGE AND EVIL

In Piaroa cosmogony, before the terrestrial and celestial worlds were created, all of the forces of the universe were contained beneath the earth's surface, its face yet unconstructed. As these subterranean powers became slowly unleashed on earth, it was their force that was responsible for the creation of all elements and beings of the surface level and for the knowledge and capabilities that allowed for existence there. Most of the powers responsible for the form and the life of the earth's surface came from the underworld home of the tapir/anaconda deity: it was through the means of two great wizards, Kuemoi and Wahari, whose births were the tapir/anaconda god's deed and whose powers he gave them, that most of the features of the terrestrial world of the Piaroa were created. Wahari, the master of the jungle, created the topography of the earth, its mountains, its rocks, its river systems, its rapids and its sky. He gave light to the world by dragging the sun and the moon from beneath the earth and, by leaping, placed them in their celestial position. He also created the Piaroa. Kuemoi, the master of water, created plant food, artefacts and the capabilities for using them, e.g., hunting, gardening and the processing of food. It is upon Kuemoi's character and antics that I am focusing in this section, the narration of which in Piaroa myth-telling always combines the wicked with the comic.

The original forces that the tapir/anaconda deity gave to the creator gods for these two sets of creation on earth — that of natural elements and that of the capabilities to use the earth's resources — were distinctly different in quality. Kuemoi's forces of knowledge and capabilities were venomous in their wildness, while the powerful forces given to Wahari for his acts of creation were tame. The Piaroa, contrary to structuralist thinking on the dichotomy of nature and culture, associate what we normally would classify as 'culture' with the wild and the poisonous, while what we label as 'natural' they perceive as a stable force which is neutral and tame in origin. It is 'culture' that man must domesticate, not nature. As a footnote, the Piaroa consider much of their material resources to be poisonous, as in fact much of them are. Their garden staple, bitter manioc, is highly poisonous, and must be properly processed to rid it of its toxin, as too must many jungle fruits. They fish with poisons that they manufacture, and also with them. They grow special poisons for revenge magic, and the hallucinogens they take daily may also be poisonous. In short, much of 'culture' must literally be tamed for it to be of use.

Kuemoi, the creator god of poisonous culture, was not conceived by natural means: he grew from the roughage of a powerful and poisonous hallucinogen that his tapir/anaconda father placed through wizardry within the womb of Isisiri, the goddess of the lake. This poisonous drug was his only nourishment as a child. As an adult he took drugs as poisonous as those he received as a child by withdrawing their ingredients from the heart of the light of the sun and from the heart of the large armadillo. His strength to create cultural resources was given to him by the poisonous drugs that he took prenatally and continued to take throughout his life; thus, the primordial source of the knowledge that he created was poisoned by the powers of the sun and by other venomous ingredients. Through his wizardry he was creator and 'master' of all edible fruits and vegetables in the world and the father of the garden plants, maize, squash, yuca and guamo. He was the creator of hunting and of curare, and of the charms for hunting success. He was the first owner of fire used for processing both plant and animal food; fire had its origin in the lake of his birth. In brief, Kuemoi was the creator of most of the means through which one could acquire and process food. It is this aspect of Piaroa culture — including food itself — that is poisoned by the force of the sun.[22]

Kuemoi is always depicted in the narration of myth as a terrible madman; for the poisonous powers sufficiently strong to create the knowledge for the acquisition and the processing of food poisoned Kuemoi from the time he was in the womb.[23] Moreover, as first owner of *all* this knowledge, he had the power to satisfy all his (culinary) desires, and having the total force of poisonous knowledge within him made his desires go wild. His mastery over self is so lacking that he is portrayed not only as evil, but — as my introduction states — as a diabolical buffoon. As eater, he is the hunter cannibal. Through the desire for and the malice towards jungle beings, he created all the poisonous snakes and insects of the world; he created poisonous toads; he poisoned all large rock formations and streams. As evil as he might be portrayed and as dangerous, the dramatic details of both his creations and his plottings are staged through slapstick comedy, and the listener to the narrative knows that Kuemoi's entrance on the scene will be met with his own glee at Kuemoi's inevitably hilarious excesses and mishaps.

Kuemoi's plotting often misfires upon himself. When Kuemoi wanted a beast for the hunt, he foolishly created all types of jungle cats, including jaguars, as house pets of his 'House of Night'. After their creation the cats went out into the jungle to hunt all forms of jungle animals, which they ate, bones, fur and all.[24] They returned to Kuemoi's plaza where, after sunning themselves, they vomited and then defecated their meal upon Kuemoi's doorstep. Kuemoi created poisonous hallucinogens to kill his enemies, but since it was he who took them first he went berserk on their strength — which he himself gave them. His biting insects took their first turn on him.

---

[22] Before he acquired and thieved culture, Wahari ate hallucinogens for food; although he was fisherman, in contrast to Kuemoi the hunter, he could not eat his catch until he stole fire from Kuemoi.

[23] Compare Kuemoi with the demiurge in gnostic thought. As the evil lord of the lower powers and creator of the material world, he was the source of evil in the world, to be opposed to the transcendent god of salvation who had nothing to do with bringing the world into existence (Blumenberg 1983: 128).

[24] This is an example of mythic licence: jungle beings by other myths did not assume animal form until the end of mythic time. See below.

Even when his malice succeeded, his plots were ridiculous: to trap young male inhabitants of the jungle for his meals, he tempted them with his daughter, within whose womb he planted piranha and other biting or poisonous fish. Each introduction of Kuemoi into the scene of the narrative is structured through highly standardized comic effects: Kuemoi lurks, he does not hide; he laughs raucously over his own scheming; he runs round in circles; he stamps his feet; he never walks with dignity.

Girard, in a discussion on comedy, suggests (1978: 124ff.) that all forms of comedy are associated with a loss of autonomy and self-possession. The comic technique, he says, being based as it is upon structured patterns, focuses the attention of the audience upon these patterns and away from the individual actor, with whom therefore there is little identification and who is thereby transformed into 'other'. Laughter has a two-fold effect: it gives the one who laughs the illusion of superiority, a feeling of heightened control,[25] which is aided in this process by laughter itself, which strips its object of both its sovereignty and its individuality.

Girard's insights into comedy are highly relevant to an understanding of the role of the character of Kuemoi as the arch-typical villain of mythic time and of the Piaroa reaction both to him and to evil-doers in their own society. For the Piaroa, evil is caused by excess, by lack of mastery over the powers and the knowledge within one.[26] Such lack of mastery is mockable, and a Piaroa knows that his own show of excess will be met by disdain. In a society where high value is placed upon one's freedom of will, the threat of the loss of personal autonomy is a sharp check on such display. The most extreme punishment (or cure, see below) given by the Piaroa in real life for excessive behaviour is indeed quite literally the destruction of one's autonomy over self, as one case-study illustrates. A wizard in Piaroa land during my first visit there lived alone, and though he was portrayed as a comic and rather pitiful man, he was also gently cared for by his close relatives and allowed to perform the occasional curing rite. That he was allowed to perform such rites was merely to assuage his pride, for he was said to be without power, and his performance was therefore viewed with amusement. The story of his plight is that a few years before, when relatives had left him to live with another wizard who they viewed as more powerful, he had lost his temper and dramatically cursed his relatives in public. Soon thereafter several children of his family died. Although the result of his cursing was seen as murder, the

---

[25] See Girard's discussion (1978: 125) of the comic and the tragic.

[26] One must have equal mastery over his 'life of senses' and his 'life of thought'. As one develops one's 'life of thought', one must at the same time increase one's mastery over one's 'life of senses'.

cursing event, caused by the disease *keràu*, was described to me as hilarious, as similar in tone to one of Kuemoi's antics. Obviously, the lack of dignity of the occasion did not negate its power. Other wizards gathered together and decided to take away the mad wizard's 'thoughts', i.e., all of his powers of wizardry, and he was thereafter never allowed to learn them afresh. His autonomy was destroyed. The tale of Kuemoi, the evil buffoon, becomes the means through which wickedness in Piaroa society can be handled as part of the absurd, its terror thereby somewhat warded off — through laughter.[27]

Wickedness, a madness, is caused by the poison of unmastered knowledge within one. Wahari, the creator of the natural elements of the world, arrived on earth without the knowledge for the acquisition and processing of food, and without the power for its creation. He spent most of mythic time stealing as much of this knowledge as he could from Kuemoi, attempting to transform his spoils into tamer, more efficacious, forces for both his own use and for that of other jungle beings, among whom were the Piaroa. Mythic time was one of violent disorder, a world of reciprocal violence, where the two creator gods fought continual battles with one another for the control of resources over which each was respectively master: Kuemoi stalked beings of the jungle for food; Wahari stole cultural artefacts from Kuemoi.[28] The Piaroa apply the concepts of 'control' and 'ownership' in their mythic narratives, and it was because of the privatization of resources in mythic history that thievery was possible and reciprocity impossible (Overing Kaplan 1981, Overing 1982). One lesson from mythic history, in the Piaroa view, is that private ownership of scarce resources — and greed — entails violence, thievery, disorder. The poison of unmastered knowledge fed — and, indeed, was the cause of — the disorder of mythic time.

Wahari periodically went mad from the traps of poisonous knowledge Kuemoi set for him, and in his madness he committed violent acts, including murder. In the end, both creator gods were killed for their evil deeds, and mythic time finishes with the guardianship of the knowledge and the capabilities created by Kuemoi being given to celestial gods.[29] Thus, in

---

[27] The Piaroa are consistent in their response. One day I was told about a powerful wizard from another territory who had accidentally killed two of his apprentices with an overdose of drugs. The young men in telling the story were mocking the wizard for his foolishness in attempting something he could not do.

[28] As was the case with another 'guilty innocent', Prometheus, one of Wahari's most important thefts and benefactions was fire (see Ricoeur on this aspect of the myth of Prometheus (1967: 224—5)).

[29] This sequence of events fits precisely with Ricoeur's creation—drama type epic, where mythic gods are vanquished at the end of mythic time and order is achieved through the victory and the establishment of a new divinity (Ricoeur 1967: 178—81).

present-day time the powers mighty enough for the original creation of the capabilities for the use of the resources of the earth are housed safely *outside* of the world in which social life is played out, as too are the forces to tame it. These immortal gods who live within their celestial temple, Nyuema, possess crystal boxes within which are housed and thereby enclosed their specific powers — their light, their quartz stones, their crowns, their beads, their hunting powders, the words of their songs. All are powers — the knowledge of and the capabilities necessary for human existence on earth — that they now give to the Piaroa to fill up their 'beads of life'. Unlike the god of Rousseau (1947: 33) or of Descartes (see Williams 1967), who is the source of all that is good in man, a goodness that flows from the greatest of god's gifts to humanity — rationality — Piaroa gods give the gifts of the 'life of the senses' and poisonous knowledge. It is up to mankind to develop the rationality (*t'akwakomenà*) to use both wisely.

As in Ricoeur's example of the Sumero-Akkadian theogonic myths (1967), Piaroa myths recount the origin and the vanquishing of evil on earth, the appearance of the present world order and of man as he now exists. No orderly social life was possible when the wild and poisonous forces of knowledge remained free for the taking or thieving. Their continued unleashed existence would, as it did in mythic time, encourage acts of cannibalism, incest, madness, stealing and murder,[30] all asocial compulsions mocking the morality and social rules upon which, in the Piaroa view, society is dependent for its continuity and tranquillity. It is the responsibility of the wizard to order the relations between the forces of knowledge that lie outside society with society itself: his chore is to bring them back into society, upon an individual's request, safely contained within beads as first protection against their poison (see Overing 1982).

Although the celestial gods captured poisonous knowledge within their crystal boxes, the Piaroa still suffer from evil, and they commit evil deeds today. For an explanation of their predicament one must look more closely at the Wahari aspect of the epic. Wahari was a fallible god, but not an evil one: as benefactor and creator of the Piaroa, he was the tragic hero of the epic whose suffering was that of the guilty innocent, and it was this role — that of the guilty innocent — that he bequeathed to the Piaroa.[31]

---

[30] See Overing (1982) for a fuller description of mythic events.

[31] See the discussion by Ricoeur (1967: 222−5) and that by Girard (1978, 1979) on the theme of the guilty innocent.

THE TRAGIC HERO AND THE LOSS OF INNOCENCE

As creator and benefactor of the Piaroa, Wahari laid down their social rules and gave them culture, but they were rules that he himself broke and culture that he had stolen. Social rules and the knowledge of food acquisition are both a part of *ta'kwánya* (custom), or *ta'kwarü* ('the life of thought'), but their acquisition by the Piaroa in mythic time, as in present-day learning procedures, was a sequential process. First came the receiving of social responsibility or social consciousness, and then came the capabilities for food acquisition and the responsibility that the knowledge of it requires.

Because the themes contained within the Judaeo-Christian story of the Fall and the Piaroa myths about their own loss of innocence are highly similar, as too are the details about the consequences of this loss, I shall summarize briefly certain key episodes of the Adamic story towards the end of highlighting those of the Piaroa myths. One main difference in the Adamic and Piaroa myths about humanity's loss of innocence is that in the Piaroa case mankind experienced a set of losses, which are conflated into a single event in the Adamic myth.

In Genesis 2:15–17, the Lord God commanded of Adam when he placed him in Eden that 'You may freely eat of every tree of the garden; but of the tree of knowledge of good and evil you shall not eat, for in the day that you eat of it you shall die.' Then, in Genesis 3:1–6, the serpent told Eve about the knowledge of good and evil; he gave her the *desire* to make herself wise. Eve herself, after eating of the tree of the knowledge of good and evil, tells (Genesis 3:13) the Lord God that 'the serpent beguiled me, and I ate.' God then expels Adam and Eve out from Eden, and he tells (Genesis 3:16–19) the couple of the hardships and mortality that they would thereafter experience. After the expulsion, God placed cherubim to the east of the garden of Eden, and a flaming sword which turned every way to guard the tree of life from man who, because he had eaten of the tree of the knowledge of good and evil, would live for ever if he then ate of the tree of life (Genesis 3:24). It was after this event that Eve conceived and bore Cain (Genesis 4:1).

Note the following features of the Fall: (1) the tree of knowledge was of good *and* evil; (2) Adam and Eve's sin was the *desire* to be wise; (3) Eve was *tempted* by this desire; (4) the tempter, the one who beguiled, was the serpent; (5) with the acquisition of the knowledge of good and evil, mankind thereafter suffered hardship and mortality; (6) desires became controlled by knowledge, as is suggested by the phrase, 'Now Adam *knew* Eve, his wife, and she conceived' (my italics). With the acquisition of knowledge also came fertility, an idea parallel to that of the Piaroa one, where fertility is explicitly included as part of cultural knowledge and capability. The basic structure of the Adam and Eve story is highly comparable to the following series of Piaroa myths, with the exception of the Judaeo-Christian notion of a perfect original creation, which has no place in Piaroa myth. Nevertheless, we find unfolded in both the Judaeo-Christian and the Piaroa myths on the loss of mankind's innocence stories about the tempter serpent, the tree of the knowledge of good and evil, the tree of life and, finally, the connection between the loss of innocence and the origin of social consciousness with the origin of mortality and hardship.

Myth 1: The loss of innocence and the acquisition of social knowledge

The myth tells of the time the Piaora lost their hard, shiny blue anuses (and genitals).

Paruna married the sister of the creator god, Wahari. Paruna one day found he had no ingredients for *yopo*, an hallucinogen, growing near his home. He therefore set out to visit elsewhere to acquire the drug he desired. Shortly after his brother-in-law's departure, Wahari visited Paruna's house where he copulated with his sister and then from her vagina withdrew *yopo*. Meanwhile, Paruna had visions of his brother-in-law taking *yopo* at his house and of his wife lying naked in her hammock. The irate husband hurried home to confront his brother-in-law over the circumstance of the *yopo*. Wahari lied, and told Paruna that he had found the drug's ingredients near Paruna's house. The brothers-in-law began quarrelling, and in this version of the myth Wahari was damned to eternity to quarrel with Paruna at the edge of the world. At the moment the quarrel began, the Piaroa lost their hard, shiny blue anuses. The question is, why?

We find in other myths, the details of which I do not here have the space to present (but see Overing Kaplan and Kaplan 1980), the following set of equivalences:

$$
\begin{aligned}
\text{mirror (hard, reflecting)} &= \text{eye} \\
\text{eye} &= \text{anus} \\
\text{buttocks} &= \text{head} \\
\text{blue eyes} &= \text{ignorance}
\end{aligned}
$$

The Piaroa associate blue eyes with the red deer, a reincarnation of the elder brother of Wahari and his twin sister, and with the absence of knowledge. To create his siblings, the elder brother withdrew them from his eyes.[32] In so doing, he withdrew his own thoughts, leaving his eyes blue and empty and himself in ignorance.

In this myth we are dealing with a set of symbols that contrast an asocial primordial state with a social state of being. In the 'upside-down' world of presociety people lived in ignorance, symbolized by man having a blue eye situated on his bottom. Standing up, man would look down towards the 'land of the animals' beneath the earth and not up towards the 'land of the gods', the source of knowledge. Or an equally good interpretation would be that man walked backwards in ignorance. The transformation came with the social recognition of the rule, the recognition of the rule of sexual exchange and the rule against incest. Simultaneous to the recognition of the rule came the loss of innocence (hard, shiny blue anuses), the acquisition of social knowledge and the hardship of quarrelling. Piaroa theory has much akin to that of Lévi-Strauss in *The Elementary Structures of Kinship* (1969b): concomitant with the advent of society is the advent of both the intellect and the rule. With the loss of shiny, blue anuses, mankind received social consciousness, the form and content of which are taught to the child, as described above, in his first lessons on morality. When such lessons are not well followed, mankind must suffer the quarrel.

The Piaroa associate the loss of *cultural* rather than social innocence with the receiving of the knowledge for food acquisition and processing forthcoming from the creations of Kuemoi. The myths about the loss of cultural innocence are also about Wahari, but the implications of this loss are very different from those of the loss of social innocence with regard to the evil that man suffers. Wahari desires Kuemoi's knowledge, and it is this *desire* that is the cause of his worst misfortunes, and also those of mankind who receives his stolen bequest of knowledge and who therefore suffers both Wahari's fate and his guilt.

Myth 2: Wahari cuts down the Tree of Life and receives cultivation

On the Tree of Life were all of the edible plants in the world. Wahari, to get the fruit, felled it with the help of his sister's sons. As they were chopping it down, Wahari became arrogant with one of his nephews, who in retaliation connived with relatives to entrap Wahari through a head filled with madness. Wahari then became lost while trying to find water to quench the thirst this madness gave him.[33] He wandered lost for years, out of control, having affairs

---

[32] To make sense of the Wahari creation myths, it must be realized that his birth was a sequential one. The tapir/anaconda deity gave Wahari's brother the force to visualize his siblings: this was the first stage of their creation.

[33] The force of *k'eráu* comes from the poisons of the sun, thus would cause extreme thirst.

with women of other tribes and fighting with their men.[34] Finally, he found his way back to his Tree of Life, only to find left for himself one lone pineapple — containing within it the disease of *k'eràu* in all forms of its sun-filled madness. The receiving of the knowledge of cultivation entailed for Wahari the gift of the poison of madness.[35] The tree is of knowledge and madness, or, equally well, as in the Adamic myth, of the knowledge of good and evil.[36] Also, as in the myth of Adam and Eve, in which a flaming sword guards the Tree of Life and withholds its gift of immortality from mankind, so, among the Piaroa, human immortality was lost at the end of mythic time when the felled Tree of Life was transformed into the celestial temple of the Nyuema gods, where today they live with their crystal boxes of knowledge.

A set of myths 3: The tempter serpent and wisdom's poison

As discussed above, most of Wahari's cultural acquisitions were thefts from Kuemoi, the mad wizard and the creator of cultural artefacts. Kuemoi tempted Wahari to make him desire his capabilities: he left his poisoned artefacts unguarded as deadly lures. Kuemoi was also the tempter serpent: he often transformed himself into anaconda, and after his death he was reincarnated as anaconda. Although Wahari was frequently able to tame his thefts, he was nevertheless often made mad from handling them. Throughout Wahari's quest for knowledge he was always tinged with madness, and therefore not in total mastery of himself. In courting his bride, one of his capers was to lasso her with a vine of thorns; when he wrapped himself within his wizard canoe to fly to distant places beneath and above the earth's surface, he usually missed his target. One time, after handling poisoned hunting charms from Kuemoi's house, Wahari in a fit of paranoic madness killed his old grandmother: he was under the delusion that she had handled his sacred ceremonial flutes, their sight being forbidden to women. Kuemoi also at times wilfully zapped Wahari with pure forces of madness: he once constructed conductors of the madness, *k'eràu*, from three mountains in such a way that narrow translucent streams of *k'eràu* flowed from the mountains to meet on earth where they captured Wahari in the centre of this force field of madness. Wahari went into a mad coma, and was finally cured of it by relatives.

---

[34] See Ricoeur (1967: 73—4) on missing the mark and on going astray, both of which he views as symbols of alienation and dereliction.

[35] Wahari also received the gift of cultivation and food processing through his marriage with the daughter of Kuemoi, whose name was *Kwawa Nyamu* (Corn Food).

[36] In Piaroa myth the Tree of Life is also the Tree of Knowledge; whereas in Adamic myth they are two distinct trees (see Genesis 3: 22).

Wahari's last great theft was of ritual, a form of knowledge that had neither belonged to Kuemoi nor been created by him: its original owners were the primordial fathers of jungle beings whose homes were beneath the earth.

Myth 4: The theft of ceremony, the origin of animal food and disease

The theft of the cultural capability to acquire and process food brought not only mortality, but also disease. Disease appeared at the end of mythic time and became a part of man's condition as a cultural being. The story goes as follows.

Early in Wahari's career he visited, beneath the earth, all of the fathers of land beings and saw at their homes their beautiful ceremonies where they played flutes in glorious song. Upon his return, he told his sister about the music he had heard. She mocked her brother, telling him that if he were really great he would perform at their home ceremonies identical to those he had seen beneath the earth. Towards the end of mythic time, Wahari, maddened by the poisonous hallucinogens of Kuemoi, had visions of jungle beings, *his own house-mates*, in animal, edible form. Thereafter Wahari plotted: he planned a feast to which he invited all inhabitants of the jungle. At the finish of the feasting, he transformed his guests into animals and stole all of their ceremonial knowledge which had been owned by their fathers who dwelt beneath the earth.

Thus, while Kuemoi was the creator of all plant food on earth, Wahari created, or rather made edible for man (as against for Kuemoi, who ate human beings), all animal food on earth. He was able to do so by taking the poisonous drugs of Kuemoi which contained within them the sun-filled force for creating food and the knowledge of its acquisition. Animals *as food* are therefore just as much a part of man's cultural heritage as are edible plants, both cultivated and wild. Animal food is the most poisonous element of this heritage. When Wahari stole ceremonial knowledge from the fathers of the animals, he gave the animals in its stead all forms of disease, which he himself had received from the tapir/anaconda deity when Wahari was within his crystal womb box of birth.[37] The animals themselves do not suffer disease; they give disease to the Piaroa.[38] However, it is not on the animal's own volition that it sends disease; for with the loss of its knowledge it lost the *ta'kwarü* ('life of thought') through which it could be so motivated. Rather,

[37] Wahari, after being created by the visions of his brother, was placed in the crystal womb box for his first period of growth.

[38] A full account of the Piaroa disease complex, its classificatory logic, is given in Overing and Kaplan (1985) and in Overing 1982.

the 'grandfathers of disease', the thunder gods and the gods of the sun, order the animal to send disease to the Piaroa. As the Piaroa received ceremony from Wahari, the animals lost ritual, and the Piaroa in exchange for this aspect of their own humanity received disease from the animals.

The most elaborate ceremony performed by the Piaroa is the great annual *sari/warime* (maize beer/masked dancers) feast, a replication of the great feast presented by Wahari at the end of mythic time. Since its sacred flutes originally belonged to the fathers of the animals, and since its masked dancers (wild peccary and monkey) were an imitation of them, the means through which the Piaroa today celebrate their own humanity and culture is the very ceremony they stole through Wahari from the animals. The parallel with the last feast of Wahari goes much further: through the *sari/warime* ceremony the jungle becomes replenished with edible animal life, especially with wild peccary. In bringing the animals up to earth from their primordial homes beneath it where they live in human form, the Piaroa are performing a mimetic re-enactment of Wahari's treacherous act when he transformed his jungle neighbours into animal food. The Piaroa express their communal guilt and communal expiation of their own treachery at the end of the ceremony when its sponsor beats all adult participants to make each forget the events of the ritual. Communal guilt so experienced is externalized and driven out of the community in the beating ritual.

The Piaroa continue to suffer disease as punishment for eating animal meat, but it was the fate of Wahari to suffer death for this last bequest of culture to the Piaroa. Wahari as the tragic figure of mythic time was the original victim, much in accord with Girard's victim as he describes him (1978, 1979) in his theory of the spontaneous scapegoat symbol. Shortly after Wahari gave his feast, his relatives (Piaroa or transformed animals?) avenged themselves of his deed: with the aid of hunting dogs, they hunted him down as if he were an animal and lynched him. Wahari was then reincarnated on earth as tapir.

It must be remembered that Wahari is the wondrous and good creator god of the Piaroa,[39] and it is precisely such a divine figure — the 'good' tragic hero

[39] I do not classify Wahari's wondrous feats as 'fantastic' ones, nor would I label Piaroa myth as a genre of the fantastic. Todorov in his analysis of the genre of the fantastic argues (1970: 76—92) that the role of the fantastic has always been to set the 'real' (i.e., capable of natural explanation) against that which is imaginary or supernatural. As such, the genre is a product of the nineteenth century, and hence it can exist only as a genre in a society that articulates its own experience in terms of that dichotomy. Also see Hawkes (1977: 102ff.) and Culler (1975: 136—7) on the cultural relativity of genres. In brief, the argument is that any particular genre can exist only when the society's presuppositions have a place for it. Culler's argument, in particular, for the cultural boundedness of 'possibilities of meaning' makes weaker the structuralist dogma that meaning is an unconscious process.

— that Girard argues is required for the original sacrificial victim, an incarnation of supreme violence who, after being killed, is transformed for the community into the eternal source of peace, strength and fecundity (see Girard 1979: 274ff.). For instance, Piaroa stress that present-day civic order was made possible by Wahari's gift to them of morality and social rules. His own death ensured the 'purging' of violence from the community and served as the community's protection from the truth of its own dark and dangerous origins, the intolerable truth here being that cannibalism — the eating of human/animal meat — is the cultural condition of mankind.

The 'tragic flaw' of Wahari's character which led him into violent rivalry with Kuemoi and to violent actions against his own relatives was his desire for wisdom. Although his motives were good ones and it was through wisdom acquired that he could give to and benefit others, his fallibility was the desire itself. Kuemoi, the serpent, beguiled him, and Wahari ate of wisdom's poison; but he fell prey to Kuemoi because he desired ever more knowledge, and his guilt in the end was foolishness, made manifest in his desire to acquire knowledge which he was incapable of mastering. His desire for more begat immoderation, an immoderation that led him to misfortune and to the 'sins' of greed and pride.[40] Thus, Wahari periodically went mad with wisdom's poison, and in this state committed the 'sins' of pride and arrogance, announcing to the world that he was the greatest wizard of them all. His slogan became: 'I am the master of the land, of the mountains, of the sky, of the rapids, of the lakes.' He suffered sexual excess, and in the state of suspicion and paranoia he murdered.

The narration of the creation myths makes clear the tragedy of Wahari, a sharp contrast to the slapstick comedy through which Kuemoi's evil is told. Wahari suffered, as Kuemoi never did, remorse for his own evil deeds; he took responsibility for them as Kuemoi, the god with infinite knowledge unlimited by any internal law, could never do. Although the content of some of Wahari's unmastered behaviour amuses, his lack of self-possession provokes not hilarity in the listener, but rather concern over his immorality and acceptance of the inevitable. As Ricoeur notes (1967: 219), ethical denunciation is not the business of tragedy, but of comedy: the tragic hero is shielded from moral condemnation and offered as an object of pity to the spectators as one who is destined to suffer. The actions of Kuemoi and those of Wahari are therefore decoded in a very different manner, which places the one character firmly within the genre of the comic and the other within the genre of the tragic,[41] a differentiation which in the end can be interpreted as a

[40] See the discussion by Ricoeur (1967: 222) on the 'tragic figure'.
[41] See Culler's discussion (1975: 136—7) on comedy and tragedy where he says that each of these genres demand different decodings (or re-codings) on the part of the reader (or listener).

distinction between the 'outsider' and the 'insider'. Even the death of Kuemoi (the archtypical, dangerous 'outsider') is a ludicrous one, in striking contrast to the sombre deliberate horror of the lynching of Wahari. Wahari, transformed as eagle hawk, killed Kuemoi: he pounced on Kuemoi who was sunning himself on his plaza, grabbed his nose with his beak and flew with Kuemoi shrieking all around the world until he died. The audience can with glee condemn Kuemoi and enjoy his derisible death.

Wahari as a guilty innocent was a tragic figure caught within the dialectics of fate and freedom which, according to Ricoeur (1967: 220—1), are but the twin sides of tragedy, whereas Kuemoi was never innocent — within his mother's womb he was fed with the poisonous force for wisdom. It is the same paradigm as held for Wahari, the evil-doer, that is transferred upon the evil-doer in Piaroa land where there, too, the road to madness is filled with the best intentions.

It is clear from the myths that man, like Wahari, lost his innocence, but was not the origin of evil. Evil, with the birth of Kuemoi, became both the past and the future of human existence in the world: the Fall is not the fall of man; rather, it falls on him (again, see Ricoeur on tragedy, 1967: 210). It is the fate of man to be a guilty innocent, which is but one aspect of his cultural being. Innocence is a relative state: one loses innocence with knowledge acquired and remains innocent of knowledge untouched. As happens to Wahari in Piaroa myth, man experiences a multiple loss of innocence, a process for ever lasting, something to be lost time and time again. Humanity *finds* evil in the world, takes it within itself, and continues it in guilty innocence. The Piaroa do not equate innocence with perfectibility or 'the good'; nor do they associate knowledge *per se* with evil deeds or a fall. Badness, evil deeds and death are all a result of the fallibility of man, his *foolishness*. Man is not innately evil: he is not born evil;[42] no man *is* evil, although he may commit evil deeds. In the following section on the Piaroa understanding of the bad and the evil actions of which man is capable, I shall show that they do not believe that all humans can do evil to others. Everyone past the age of six can act badly, but only a wizard can do evil; it is only he, as a man of knowledge, who has the capabilities of doing so.

FAULT AND SIN: TWO DISEASES OF MADNESS

The Piaroa label all formal learning, whether early lessons on morality and social rules or later ones when one acquires the capabilities for food acquisition,

---

[42] It is not so much that the Piaroa carry the guilt of Wahari's evil deed when *he* transformed jungle beings into animals, but rather that each year they themselves *re-enact* the event.

food processing, ritual and sorcery, as *maripa teau*, the learning of wizardry; and the content of all such learning forms a person's *ta'kwarü* ('life of thought'). The extent of one's learning determines the degree to which one can do damage to others. Piaroa society is one that totally disallows physical violence (see Overing Kaplan 1975); violence against others is possible only through *maripa*, or wizardry. While a great wizard continues his knowledge intake throughout his life (Overing 1982), many men go no further in their learning process than their lessons at age 12 or 13 when a wizard incorporates for them into their 'beads of life' the basic capabilities for hunting, fishing and ritual (see Overing 1982). The equivalent acquisition of knowledge for women is at the onset of her menses, when the wizard incorporates fertility into her 'beads of life'. At this stage of learning, one can commit what I wish to label a 'fault', but not a 'sin'; or in Piaroa terms, one may suffer the children's disease of *k'iràu*, but not the disease of madness, *k'eràu*.[43]

In the myths on disease, *k'iràu* is classified as a children's disease. If a young child is suffering a bout of bad diarrhoea, it is said to have the disease *k'iràu*. Older children and both men and women may also suffer *k'iràu*; however, its symptom for them is not excessive defecation, but rather excessive (unmastered) social behaviour. By the age of six all Piaroa have learned responsibility (*t'akwakomenà*), or the domestication of one's desires, which in turn allows one to master all knowledge and capabilities acquired thereafter. *K'iràu* is the disease one suffers when one illustrates a lack of mastery over the first capability (*t'akwánya*) learned — that of *sociality*. If one loses restraint over oneself and indulges in incest, thieving or wild laughter, or in other ways ignores social obligations through excessive behaviour, as would also be the case with promiscuity, one is committing a *social fault*, and therefore said to be suffering from the disease *k'iràu* and to be *uniwa* (crazy, but not mad). The offending person is judged guilty (*a'kwákomenà*) of not restraining his passions. Incest is given the label 'he did not think'. It is unmastered knowledge within him that has affected his will and led him to act in a foolish manner. He must therefore be cured of *k'iràu* by a wizard, who will enable the patient to master the undomesticated knowledge that affected his ability to act responsibly. The question of fault is not without its ambiguity, and the Piaroa see it as ambiguous. A wizard wishing to do damage might have sent knowledge into his victim knowing it to be beyond his victim's

---

[43] Technically, a man with little knowledge can suffer from *k'eràu* when the forces of the sun strike him directly. Nevertheless, he is not able to act evilly towards others; rather, he goes berserk and runs wildly into the jungle. The danger is for himself, and not for others. For him it is a physical disease much in the same way *k'iràu* in its form of diarrhoea is for the child.

ability to tame, or it might be the case that the capabilities for hunting and ritual were not fully mastered by the patient, and it was they that poisoned his will and therefore his desires. Wherever the chain of fault began, asocial behaviour is viewed as an illness:[44] emotions and knowledge must be brought back into balance, and the patient must learn once more how to take responsibility for this balance. Each person must realize his own limitations: after the first lessons on sociality, and the next which give other basic elements of culture, each man decides if and how much he both wishes and is capable of learning further (see Overing 1982).[45]

Piaroa society is one with no civil law, no supra-familial means of judging, controlling and punishing ordinary misdemeanours. There are no courts, no formal council of elders. The Piaroa see custom and law to reside within the person and not without. Logically, then, there is no rational need for an authority system to impose itself formally upon the members of the community. Therefore, instead of civil or criminal law that punishes, it is therapy that cures which is the means through which Piaroa citizens keep themselves personally in line. Whenever one fails to master one's passions and the knowledge within one, one must go to a wizard and be cured, i.e. gain mastery over both the 'life of thought' and the 'life of the senses' within one.

The Piaroa do not view the disease, *k'iràu*, to be a serious one; and it is for this reason that I have labelled it a 'fault' instead of a 'sin'. The misdemeanours symptomatic of the disease, if not trifling, do not cause serious harm to others or to the community. Like a small child, the patient acts in an 'undomesticated' manner; and also like a small child, his knowledge unmastered is not sufficient for him to have the power to commit an evil deed. Children, women and unknowledgeable men cannot commit evil deeds, i.e., considerable harm to others. They can be bad, commit a social fault and be a nuisance, but they do not have the capabilities for dangerous action.

The adult disease of excessive behaviour, *k'eràu*,[46] is another matter; for the one who suffers this disease of madness can seriously violate human rights and in so doing cause grievous harm to others. A wizard who has taken a large amount of poisonous capabilities and knowledge from the safety of the crystal boxes of the gods is by definition always vulnerable to this disease, and he must take great pains to protect himself, and thereby society, from it. The Piaroa state that all death is caused by the actions of powerful wizards who are

---

[44] The comparison with the legal system of Butler's *Erewhon* is too obvious not to be mentioned.

[45] The Piaroa make one exception to such freedom of choice. The child who throws many temper tantrums is not allowed in his adult life to learn wizardry (sorcery).

[46] See n. 38 above.

suffering from *k'eràu*. It is not infrequent for a wizard, made mad by unmastered knowledge within him, to kill through wizardry some of his own close kinsmen, as the case history given in an above section is an example.

It is important to note that a wizard's kinsmen do not speak of such deeds with anger, although they are quick to say the damage was the wizard's responsibility. The model the Piaroa repeatedly use for interpreting a wizard's wicked behaviour is that presented to them by the example of Wahari. In positing a particular sequence of preconditions for evil-doing (see figure 2),

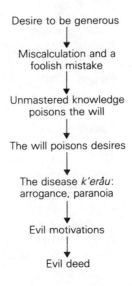

FIGURE 2   *The sequence of the evil deed*

they stress the wizard's role both as guilty innocent and as one made wicked through enticement. The initial fault is that of misjudgement: like Wahari, the wizard in desiring further capabilities to benefit his community — such as the dangerous cure for snake bite or the ritual for the feat of *sari* — takes knowledge beyond that which he can manage; his motives are excellent, but he makes a foolish mistake. The unmastered knowledge within him, which he took from the gods, then poisons his will and he becomes ill with *k'eràu*, the temporary madness of arrogance and paranoia. In this state his *motives* for action become malicious, his emotions go wild, and he murders, becomes guilty of a 'sin'. Upon his cure, when poisonous knowledge within him is restrained, he feels remorse and recognizes his guilt. This is the paradigm of explanation for the evil deeds of a kinsman, while for the foreign wizard the sequencing of preconditions may well be ignored: a model approaching that of Kuemoi's behaviour is used where the stress is only upon the evil deed itself as forthcoming from a mad and wild source. The mad behaviour of the wizard affine is also treated as equivalent to the evil buffoonery of Kuemoi: through a quick twist of social logic, the affine is re-classified from the status of 'insider' and kinsman to 'outsider' and anaconda.[47] When he has sufficiently demonstrated his restraint, the model of the guilty innocent is then belatedly applied to him. One could not live in close proximity to one permanently categorized as Kuemoi, the wicked buffoon.

In Piaroa theory it is man's fate to have conjoined within him a life of desires, a life of knowledge and capabilities, and a life of will or rationality. As in the ethical philosophy of Aquinas (see Abelson and Nielsen 1967), each person is held responsible for his own actions because he has within him the conditions of desire, knowledge and deliberation. The critical faculty for the Piaroa in the preconditions of *evil* action is that of knowledge, or the powers of capability: deliberation formulates desire; capabilities can poison deliberation, which in turn then poisons desires (see figure 3). The greater

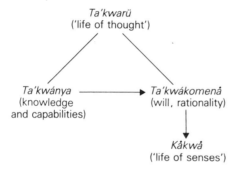

FIGURE 3   K'erau *and the evil deed. Unmastered knowledge poisons one's will, which in turn poisons one's passions. One's* ta'kwákomenâ *loses its mastery over knowledge and desires*

one's achievement on the level of knowledge and capability, the greater must be one's mastery over desires and deliberation; for if this mastery lapses, one becomes — at least temporarily — a mad and evil buffoon.

In distinguishing between *k'iráu* and *k'eráu*, or 'fault' and 'sin', the Piaroa

[47] See Overing Kaplan (1975, 1984) for the significance of such re-classification for Piaroa political organization.

are delivering a theory of knowledge that posits a radical difference between two states of attainment and the respective responsibilities attached to each. *Social* responsibility requires the knowledge of morality and social rules; while wizardly responsibility, extensive mastery over cultural knowledge, entails far more than the knowledge and the playing out of sociality. To take within oneself a large number of capabilities gives one a greater awareness of the nature of the cosmos, a knowledge of what the world is. At this level of achievement, reflexivity is of a much higher order than that required to behave correctly socially. To do the latter requires knowledge of only the minimum conditions — including that of acquiring food — necessary to leading an ordinary social life; there is no need to know of what the world is comprised. Man, however, is capable of far more than mere correct social action: he can know about the nature, the whys and the what-fors, of these rules, a much broader level of knowledge. The predicament is that with such knowledge a mistake has dangerous consequences: if one does not tame the mad capabilities that make one wise, they can overwhelm both one's will and desires and lead to insanity. This is why learning must always be a gradual process; to know too much is to become insane, absurd and madly foolish, a state in which one can do evil.

'GUILT', 'SIN' AND 'SALVATION'

In *The Symbolism of Evil*, Ricoeur (1967) begins his discussion by positing an evolutionary scheme of ethical orders which progressively moves away from the symbolism of defilement to a symbolism of sin (pp. 11–27). He distinguishes, on the one hand, the 'archaic' ethical system where doing or suffering evil is not (yet) differentiated from a 'cosmobiological' order of experiencing evil, which is given evidence by the richness of its imagery of defilement, and, on the other, the development of the more symbolically impoverished ethical systems which are no longer tied to their cosmic roots. In the latter, a more abstract symbolism revolving around the twin notions of sin and guilt develops, reflecting an advanced point of a radically individualized and interiorized experiencing of evil — one suffers evil as a religious experience rather than as a disruption of a cosmic ordering. In the 'archaic' system, man is 'burdened' with 'fault' and 'defilement' when ritually unclean (p. 101), while in the more advanced system, he suffers 'guilt' as the author of a 'sinful' deed (pp. 101ff.). As Ricoeur also argues (p. 105), the change is one from the experiencing of 'communal sin' to that of experiencing 'individual guilt'.

It is without question that the Piaroa system of ethics cannot be separated from the Amerindian, tropical forest cosmology within which it is based: the Piaroa symbolism of evil is replete with symbols of defilement, those of stain, rust, the brightness of the sun, the monstrous, the excessive — diarrhoea and madness; evil, misfortune and disease are not dissociated (see Ricoeur, 1967: 27). Yet, to say that for the Piaroa man suffers evil because he is ritually unclean would be a highly facile description of what, on the contrary, turns out to be a much more complex theory of the experiencing of evil, which is but one aspect of a sophisticated theory of human nature. I shall argue that, even within the framework of Ricoeur's own discussion of defilement, fault, guilt and sin, it is legitimate to label some Piaroa actions as sinful and the experiencing of them by the actor as guilt, while other actions are best labelled by such terms as communal guilt and communal expiation. In brief, Ricoeur has not presented us with what we should take on face value as an evolutionary typology of evil but he has rather distinguished for us various ways in which evil can be experienced, symbolized and judged — many of which can be incorporated within one and the same system of ethics.

The principle theological problem in claiming that the Piaroa recognize what we label as 'sin' and 'guilt' is the crucial phrase, 'before god': sinning is the religious experience of violating a personal bond with a god and the recognition that such violation is the real situation of all men before god (see Ricoeur 1967: 52). Ricoeur, in order to extend the concept of 'sinning' to earlier and non-Judaeo-Christian religions, suggests that the 'religious consciousness of god' is possible both before the development of theology and in polytheistic representations where the 'concerned god' is but one of many (p. 51), as opposed to the one *and* the many. The Piaroa have in Wahari an 'anthrotropic' god, before whom — even in his reincarnation as tapir — they do claim the feeling of guilt. It was he who laid down their social laws and, indeed, he who died for them and from whom they inherited their human plight. According to the schema of sin, evil is a situation in which mankind is caught as a single collectivity, and it is precisely this, the analysis of what the Piaroa see to be the human predicament, that this paper has explored. The phrase that troubles me in Ricoeur's analysis is that of the 'religious consciousness of evil', which raises the old question of how we are to identify institutions in different cultures as 'the same' and therefore as 'interestingly different' (see MacIntyre 1972). Why, for instance, should Ricoeur deny, as he seems to do, a religious consciousness of evil for the person experiencing or doing ill in a society where its ethics are still tied to a particular cosmological order? Why, in other words, distinguish religion from cosmology?

However, the force of Ricoeur's argument in distinguishing the archaic experience of fault[48] from the later experiencing of sin and guilt is his stress on the latter as entailing a judgement of personal imputation of evil (Ricoeur 1967: 105): it is this aspect of his argument on the experiencing of guilt and sin that is much easier to handle on a cross-cultural level of analysis. If guilt, as Ricoeur argues, is defined as the situation in which one must answer for the consequences of one's action, of being its cause, its agent, and the author of the motives for one's act (pp. 102—3), then it is clear that the Piaroa experience guilt and sin (the feeling of sin is a feeling of guilt — p. 103) in precisely this manner: they are taught to take responsibility for their actions and feelings — for their motivations — from the age of six. Mill's assumption that strong consciences are a prerogative of the nineteenth century is without base (1972: 73, 119). If, as Ricoeur argues (1967: 102), guilt over the bad or evil use of liberty, an individualization of fault, is a revolution for man in the experiencing of evil, then such a revolution can occur in any society at any time — and the occurrence does not need to *replace* other modes of experiencing guilt. As a collectivity, the Piaroa also expiate in highly ritualized form their guilt over the eating of human/animal meat. 'Before animals', then, fault, in Ricoeur's terms, is recognized communally; while 'before god' (Wahari) and — as I would add — 'before men', the Piaroa place the burden of sin and bad deeds on the person.

Ricoeur suggests further (1967: 105) that, in those cases where sin is personalized, so too might be 'salvation'. In accord with this insight, there is in Piaroa theology a notion of 'salvation': the spirit of a great and good wizard after his death joins the celestial gods in their ethereal mountain top home.[49] The wizard, unlike normal men, is able to see other worlds, including the celestial abode of gods, in his flights to them in nightly ritual. When he dies, he sheds his 'life of the senses', as the gods also have done, and there, with them, he lives in immortality a pure 'life of thought'.[50]

Finally, and in summation, for the Piaroa it is human nature to have conjoined within the person wild desires and poisonous knowledge, both of which must be mastered by personal will. Forthcoming from this view of human nature is a moral philosophy that insists upon the necessity of learning personal restraint; for it is only through each person's domestication of self that the happy life can be achieved, the tranquil one that is so highly valued by the Piaroa. Their theory of the nature of man and society is almost the

[48] My use of 'fault' in the previous section differs from that of Ricoeur, who is positing a difference in the suffering of evil within the framework of an evolutionary scheme.

[49] There are variations from region to region in Piaroa theology on the specifics of the residential destiny of the great wizard after death.

[50] See Overing (1982) for a discussion on the Piaroa afterlife. Also see Overing and Kaplan (1985).

obverse of that of Hobbes (*Leviathan*), who says that it is man's natural state (before the social contract) to be aggressive, and that to restrain this aggressiveness man enters into the social state. In Piaroa theory, man is not naturally aggressive, or good, or bad: rather, aggression is the danger of the social and cultural state of mankind, a state that, once acquired, allows for the possibility of knowledge to act poisonously upon the will and hence upon the passions. Again, man is not evil, but fallible, because he has within him both a 'life of desires' and a 'life of thought'.

REFERENCES

Aristotle (1941). The Nichomachean Ethics. In *The Basic Works of Aristotle* ed. R. M. Mckeon. New York
Abelson, R. and Nielsen, K. (1967). 'History of Ethics'. In *The Encyclopedia of Philosophy*. New York: Macmillan
Blumenberg, Hans (1983). *The Legitimacy of the Modern Age.* Boston: MIT Press
Butler, S. (1908). *Erewhon.* Edinburgh: Ballantyne Press
Culler, J. (1975). *Structuralist Poetics.* London: Routledge and Kegan Paul
—— (1981). *The Pursuit of Signs.* London: Routledge and Kegan Paul
Freud, S. (1963). 'Humour'. In his *Character and Culture.* New York: Collier Books (first edn 1928)
Girard, R. (1978). *'To double business bound': Essays on Literature, Mimesis and Anthropology.* Baltimore: The Johns Hopkins University Press
Girard, R. (1979). *Violence and the Sacred.* Baltimore: The Johns Hopkins Press
Grimsley, R. (1967). 'Jean-Jacques Rousseau'. In *The Encyclopedia of Philosophy.* New York: Macmillan
Hawkes, T. (1977). *Structuralism and Semiotics.* London: Methuen and Co.
Hobbes, T. (1968). *Leviathan,* ed. C. B. Macpherson, Pelican Books.
Horton, R. (1979). 'Material-Object Language and Theoretical Language: Towards a Strawsonian Sociology of Thought'. In S. C. Brown (ed.), *Philosophical Disputes in the Social Sciences.* Brighton: The Harvester Press
Lévi-Strauss (1968). *Structural Anthropology* (trans. Claire Jacobson and Brooke Grundfest Schoepf). London: Allen Lane
—— (1969a). *The Raw and the Cooked* (trans. John and Doreen Weightman). London: Cape
—— (1969b). *The Elementary Structures of Kinship.* Boston: Beacon Press
MacIntyre, A. (1972). 'Is a Science of Comparative Politics Possible?' In *Philosophy, Politics and Society,* Fourth Series, ed. by P. Laslett, W. G. Runciman and Q. Skinner. Oxford: Basil Blackwell
Mill, J. S. (1972). 'On Liberty'. In J. S. Mill, *Utilitarianism, Liberty, Representative Government* (ed. by H. B. Acton). London: Everyman's Library

Needham, R. (1978). *Primordial Characters*. Charlottesville: The University Press of Virginia
Nye, R. (1979). *Merlin*. Harmondsworth: Penguin Books
Overing Kaplan, J. (1975). *The Piaroa*. Oxford: Clarendon Press
Overing Kaplan, J. (1981). 'Review Article: Amazonian Anthropology'. *J. Lat. Amer. Stud.* *13*, 1, 151–64
Overing, J. (1982). 'The Paths of Sacred Words: Shamanism and the Domestication of the Asocial in Piaroa Society'. Presented in symposium on 'Shamanism in Lowland South American Societies'. (J. Overing organizer) 44th International congress of Americanists, Manchester
Overing Kaplan, J. (1984). 'Dualisms as an Expression of Difference and Danger: Marriage Exchange and Reciprocity among the Piaroa of Venezuela'. In *Marriage Practices in Lowland South American Societies* (ed. K. Kensinger). Urbana: University of Illinois Press
Overing, J. (1985). 'Today I Shall call him Mummy: Disorder in Piaroa Systems of Classification'. In J. Overing (ed.) *Rationality and Rationales* A.S.A. Monograph No. 23. London: Tavistock Publications
Overing Kaplan and Kaplan, M. R. (1980). 'Mythology of tropical South America'. In R. Cavendish (ed.) *Mythology*. London: Orbis Publishing Ltd.
Overing, J. and Kaplan, M. R. (1985). 'Los Dea Ruwa', in *Los Aborigenes de Venezuela,* vol. 3. Caracas: Fundacion La Salle
Taylor, G. and Wolfram, S. (1968a). 'The self-regarding and other-regarding virtues', *Philosophical Quarterly,* vol. 18, no. 72.
Taylor, G. and Wolfram, S. (1968b). 'Mill, Punishment and the self-regarding failings'. *Analysis,* vol. 28, no. 5
Todorov, T. (1970). 'The Fantastic in Fiction', trans. Vivienne Mylne, in *Twentieth Century Studies,* Issue No. 3.
Wolfram, S. (1982). 'Anthropology and Morality', *Journal of the Anthropological Society of Oxford,* vol. XIII, no. 3
Ricoeur, P. (1969). *The Symbolism of Evil.* Boston: Beacon Paperback
Rousseau, J. J. (1762). *Emile.* Geneva.
Rousseau, J. J. (1947). *The Social Contract.* New York: Hafner Publishing Co. (first published 1762)
Ryle, G. (1967). 'Plato'. In *The Encyclopedia of Philosophy.* New York: Macmillan
Williams, B. (1967). 'René Descartes'. In *The Encyclopedia of Philosophy.* New York: Macmillan

Notes on Contributors

John Bousfield is Lecturer in Philosophy and South-East Asian Studies at the University of Kent. From 1976-83 he was Lecturer in Philosophy at the University of Kent and has been a member of the Centre for South-East Asian Studies there since 1979.

Lionel Caplan is Reader in Anthropology with reference to South Asia at the School of Oriental and African Studies in the University of London. He is the author of *Land and Social Change in East Nepal* (1970) and *Administration and Politics in a Nepalese Town* (1975), and has published a number of papers on his recent research among South Indian Christians.

Mark Hobart is Lecturer in Anthropology with reference to South-East Asia at the School of Oriental and African Studies in the University of London. He is the co-editor (with R. Taylor) of *Context and Meaning in South-East Asia* (1985) and has written numerous articles on politics and symbolism and on philosophical anthropology.

Ronald Inden is Associate Professor of South Asian History and Associate Member of the Department of Anthropology at the University of Chicago. His books include *Marriage and Rank in Bengali Culture: A History of Caste and Clan in Middle Period Bengal* (1975) and (with R. W. Nicholas) *Kinship in Bengali Culture* (1977). He is currently working on a 'critical history' of Hinduism and kingship, the first in a series of monographs.

Alan Macfarlane is Reader in the Department of Social Anthropology at the University of Cambridge and Fellow of King's College. He is the author of *Witchcraft in Tudor and Stuart England* (1970), *The Origins of English Individualism* (1978) and *A Guide to English Historical Records* (1983) and a number of other works.

Brian Moeran is Lecturer in Asian Anthropology at the School of Oriental and African Studies in the University of London. His books are *Lost Innocence: Folk Craft Potters of Onta, Japan* (1984) and the forthcoming *A Country Diary*. He is currently preparing one monograph on Japanese social institutions and another on the production, marketing and evaluation of art in Japan, and has published numerous articles on the vocabulary and social effects of advertising and aesthetics.

Joanna Overing is Lecturer in Anthropology at the London School of Economics and Political Science. She is the author of *The Piaroa* (1975) and the editor of *Social Time and Social Space in Lowland South American Societies* (volume 2 of *Act. XLII Congrès International des Americanistes*, 1976, together with an introduction and a conclusion) and *Rationality and Rationales* (1985). She has also written numerous articles on Amazonian anthropology, marriage alliance and kinship, and on indigenous metaphysical systems.

David Parkin is Professor of African Anthropology at the School of Oriental and African Studies in the University of London. His books include *Palms, Wine and Witnesses* (1972), *The Cultural Definition of Political Response* (1978) and *Semantic Anthropology* (1982), as well as others specifically on Africa. He is interested in politics, cross-cultural semantics and indigenous philosophies.

David Pocock is Professor of Social Anthropology in the School of Oriental and Asian Studies at the University of Sussex. His books include *Understanding Social Anthropology* (1975).

David Rheubottom is Lecturer in Social Anthropology at the University of Manchester. He is the author of several essays on Macedonian kinship, marriage and symbolism including 'Dowry and wedding celebrations in Yugoslav Macedonia' (1980) and 'The Saint's Feast and Skopska Crna Goran social structure' (1976), and has conducted research and published on the political economy of a fifteenth-century Dalmatian city state.

Martin Southwold is Senior Lecturer in Social Anthropology at the University of Manchester. He is the author of *Buddhism in Life* (1983).

Donald Taylor is Senior Lecturer in Religious Studies at the Middlesex Polytechnic in London. He is currently completing a thesis in the social anthropology of religion at the School of Oriental and African Studies, London.

Roy Willis is Fellow in Social Anthropology and African Studies at the University of Edinburgh. Since 1965 he has held academic teaching posts at University College London, the Universities of Edinburgh and Virginia, and the University of California at Santa Cruz.

Index